MATTHEW'S TRILOGY OF PARABLES

Wesley Olmstead examines the parables of The Two Sons, The Tenants and The Wedding Feast against the backdrop of the wider Matthean narrative. He explores Matthew's characterisation of the Jewish leaders, the people and the nations and assesses the respective roles of Israel and the nations in the plot of Matthew's Gospel. Against the current of contemporary Matthean scholarship, Olmstead argues both that the judgement this trilogy announces falls upon Israel (and not only her leaders) and that these parables point to the future inclusion of *the nations* in *the nation* that God had promised to raise up from Abraham. Bringing both literary-critical and redaction-critical tools to bear on the texts at hand, Olmstead not only elucidates the intended meanings of this parabolic trilogy but also attempts to determine the responses the evangelist hoped to elicit from his first readers. Transcending Matthean scholarship, this book has implications for all Gospel studies.

WESLEY G. OLMSTEAD is Associate Professor of New Testament and Academic Dean at Briercrest Bible College in Saskatchewan.

SOCIETY FOR NEW TESTAMENT STUDIES

MONOGRAPH SERIES

General Editor: Richard Bauckham

127

MATTHEW'S TRILOGY OF PARABLES

Matthew's Trilogy of Parables

The Nation, the Nations and the Reader in
Matthew 21.28–22.14

WESLEY G. OLMSTEAD

Briercrest Bible College, Saskatchewan

CAMBRIDGE
UNIVERSITY PRESS

PUBLISHED BY THE PRESS SYNDICATE OF THE UNIVERSITY OF CAMBRIDGE
The Pitt Building, Trumpington Street, Cambridge, United Kingdom

CAMBRIDGE UNIVERSITY PRESS
The Edinburgh Building, Cambridge, CB2 2RU, UK
40 West 20th Street, New York, NY 10011–4211, USA
477 Williamstown Road, Port Melbourne, VIC 3207, Australia
Ruiz de Alarcón 13, 28014 Madrid, Spain
Dock House, The Waterfront, Cape Town 8001, South Africa

http://www.cambridge.org

First published 2003

Printed in the United Kingdom at the University Press, Cambridge

Typeface Times 10/12 pt.   *System* LaTeX 2_ε [TB]

A catalogue record for this book is available from the British Library

ISBN 0 521 83154 7 hardback

CONTENTS

ACKNOWLEDGEMENTS

As I prepare to 'sign off' on this manuscript, I am delighted to acknowledge at least some who have helped me bring this study to completion.

In its 'former life', this monograph was a Ph.D. dissertation, submitted to King's College London in 1999. Professor Graham Stanton supervised my research; his gentle correction and his encouragement from the first day until now have been a consistent source of motivation for me. (Years earlier, my first Gospels teachers – Carl Hinderager and Scot McKnight – inspired me by their passion for Jesus' teaching and profoundly influenced the course of my life.) Professor John Riches and Dr Ivor Jones examined the thesis, and their penetrating questions helped to clarify my thinking at several points. I am also grateful to Professor Richard Bauckham for his interest in this study and for recommending its inclusion in this series.

My research was supported by the generous assistance of Briercrest Bible College in Canada and by the industry of dozens of Canadian college students who planted trees under my direction in the wilds of Northern British Columbia and Alberta.

Tyndale House in Cambridge was both my primary place of study and a home for my family while we were in the UK. I cannot begin to list the many whose friendships filled those years with memories to cherish, but to several fellow students I owe a more tangible debt. Steve Bryan in particular listened to many of my ideas before they ever made it onto paper. Larry Lahey, David Miller and Colin Nicholl kindly read and critiqued portions of this work. My friend and colleague Calum Macfarlane read the thesis in its entirety. Without exception, I have benefited from the feedback they offered.

As they have throughout our lives, our families supported us in every way. Our parents joyfully accepted the role of 'long-distance' grandparents and we record our thanks to God for them.

My wife, Faith, and our children, Bryn and Brooke, made many sacrifices on this journey, but never begrudgingly. They adopted this project as their own and made our years in England a great delight. Their love lends perspective to everything I do. To them I dedicate this work.

ix

PART ONE

Prolegomena

1

INTRODUCTION: OF AUTHORS, READERS AND APPROACHES TO THE PARABLES

1.1   On reading the Gospel narratives

The landscape of Gospels scholarship has shifted dramatically in the last three decades. Redaction criticism has yielded pride of place as the primary method in Gospels studies but there has been no single obvious successor. Instead, Gospels critics offer readings from a bewildering variety of interpretive stances[1] and, increasingly, refer to the methodological pluralism that undergirds their work.[2]

Nevertheless, narrative criticism, in its various forms, posed some of the earliest and most persistent challenges to a redaction-critical approach.[3] The early exponents of a more 'literary' approach commonly set themselves over against more traditional historical critics, mourning the poverty of a redactional approach and proclaiming the end of an era. Similar sentiments – or at least interpretations that reflect these sentiments – continue to punctuate the discourse of Gospels scholarship.

But it has also become more common for scholars on both sides of the methodological divide to call for a more cooperative, interdisciplinary approach. To date, the most significant of these have tended to operate under the assumption that literary and historically oriented methods complement one another by casting light in rather different directions. Where narrative critics focus on the *unity* of the final text, redaction critics turn their attention to the evangelists' reworking of their *diverse sources* that gave rise to the text in its 'final' form. Where narrative critics devote attention to the *narrative world* that emerges from the Gospel *stories*, redaction critics are concerned instead with the *historical world of the evangelist* out of which and for which he writes. Finally, where narrative critics embrace the *reader* and are especially sensitive to the *affective* impact of the Gospel texts, redaction criticism remains an *author*-oriented discipline whose concerns have typically been *cognitive* ones. In short, narrative critics and redaction critics proceed from different presuppositions, aim at different goals, and employ different reading strategies.

3

As such, it is maintained, if narrative- and redaction-critical approaches to the Gospels are to work in partnership, it must be by asking rather different questions of the narrative.[4]

In what follows, however, I argue that if we carefully define our aims in reading,[5] these very different reading strategies can form an alliance of a rather different – and perhaps more fundamental – nature. More specifically, I argue that narrative and redactional approaches to the Gospels can function as allies by addressing the same issue from their distinct vantage points. Throughout this study I return repeatedly to one historical question: 'What response[s] did the evangelist intend to elicit from his readers?' In an attempt to answer this question, I bring both literary-critical and redaction-critical tools to bear on the texts at hand. This introductory chapter offers justification for such an approach.

Obstacles to a cooperative venture

Integrity vs. fragmentation

Petri Merenlahti and Raimo Hakola suggest that 'a strong emphasis on the inherent unity of the gospel narratives must be considered the most salient feature of narrative criticism'.[6] Not surprisingly, then, narrative critics read *holistically* – they find the significance of the parts in relation to this wider unity.[7] Redaction critics, by contrast, read *comparatively* – they find the significance of the parts at least as much in comparison with the traditions that underlie the current narrative as in relation to the wider whole.[8] Indeed, from the vantage point of the narrative critic, this preoccupation with sources almost inevitably leads to the fragmentation of the Gospel narratives.[9] Either the redaction critic fails to take seriously the narrative integrity of the Gospels or, having paid lip-service to this wider unity, loses sight of it amidst the exhaustive spadework of detailed source analysis. Where redaction criticism does devote attention to the wider Gospel, typically its interests are in structure and theological motifs rather than in concerns such as plot and characterisation that are central to narratives in general.

For their part, redaction critics object that the nature of the unity that narrative critics presuppose is not consonant with the data. An artistic unity may well have been crafted, but it is a unity that is rather more like a patchwork quilt than a seamless garment. The narrative has not been created from whole cloth but has been sewn together from various sources that previously had independent existences. For the redaction critic, a careful study of the Gospel texts will hardly be able to ignore the shaping of this prior tradition.

Both the redaction critics and the narrative critics offer important insights about the unity of the Gospel narratives. Redaction critics correctly challenge the *nature* of the unity assumed by narrative critics.[10] Narrative critics are hardly unaware of the prior history of the Gospel traditions but, in practice, they may as well be. M. A. Powell admits as much:

> Literary criticism does not deny these observations regarding the development of the text, but it does ignore them. Ultimately, it makes no difference for a literary interpretation whether certain portions of the text once existed elsewhere in some other form. The goal of literary criticism is to interpret the current text, in its finished form.[11]

But, if our aim in interpretation centres upon explaining the text's intended meaning and function,[12] then it becomes difficult to understand why we should bracket out one potentially fruitful line of investigation – the author's treatment of his sources. The secondary nature of the unity of the Gospel narratives would seem to justify redaction-critical examination of the formation of this new 'unity'.

However, unless the evangelists expected their readers and hearers to have access to their sources and engage in critical comparison,[13] we must conclude that they expected their narratives to be read and heard on their own terms. In practice, this justifies a holistic approach to the story they tell. Here, too, and perhaps especially, we should expect to find evidence of the purposes for which these narratives were composed.

As such, while the presuppositions that underlie typical narrative- and redaction-critical approaches obviously differ, their reading strategies may be mutually corrective. Narrative criticism's persistent focus on the unity of the Gospel narratives can protect against the fragmentation that, if not inherent in a redaction-critical approach, is nevertheless too often its accompaniment.[14] By the same token, redaction criticism's careful analysis of the sources of the Gospels may offer a correction to potentially ahistorical and subjective narrative-critical readings.

History vs. Fiction[15]

Closely related to the presupposition of the integrity of the Gospel narratives is the conviction held by some narrative critics that each of these narratives gives rise to an autonomous and fictional story world. On this model, the Gospels are to be read more as powerful stories than as historical dramas. Often, what counts here is not so much what happens *in* the narrative as what happens *to* the reader when she encounters the narrative world. For Fowler, for example: 'The Gospel is designed not to say something about the disciples or even to say something about Jesus, but to do something to the reader.'[16] Or again:

> Lest we become nervous about what Mark may be thereby asserting about the twelve apostles, the historical pillars of the early Christian church, let us recall that this narrative does not claim to be history. It is not even referentially oriented. Rather, it is pragmatically or rhetorically oriented. It is not 'about' its characters; it is 'about' its reader. The Gospel writer's chief concern is not the fate of either Jesus or the Twelve in the story but the fate of the reader outside the story.[17]

More cautious narrative critics would demur at Fowler's casual denial of an historical orientation in the Gospel narratives, but are none the less careful to avoid the 'referential fallacy', which consists of 'construing the signifier alone as the sign and as referring directly to the real world, without regard to the signified as the conceptual aspect of the sign'.[18] For Howell, this caution is essential because of the impossibility of creating a narrative world that corresponds exactly to the real world.[19]

If narrative critics typically presuppose a *fictional* story world and focus on its impact upon the reader, then redaction critics commonly presuppose a specific *historical Sitz im Leben* out of which (and for which) the narrative arose, and focus on the recovery of that setting. Emphasis on the fictional world of the story gives way to emphasis on the historical world of the evangelist. Redaction-criticism's orientation has been historical, but has largely focused on the setting out of which the evangelists wrote rather than upon the events that their narratives report. In quite different ways, then, narrative and redaction critics have both distanced themselves from the historiographic nature of these narratives.[20]

Once more, we can learn from both narrative and redaction critics. Narrative critics have demonstrated the fruitfulness of the study of the Gospels as story. For many redaction critics, a preoccupation with the historical setting from which the evangelists wrote and with their 'communities' has deflected attention from the narratives they composed.[21] But probably we ought not subordinate history to fiction as a corrective. F. Watson has recently offered a cogent defence for viewing the Gospels as narrated history.[22] The implied readers of these documents find in the events of these narratives not only powerful and imaginative religious visions but also the creative *re*-tellings of events now past. Nevertheless, because these events are taken up and emplotted in a narrative format, they are susceptible of the kinds of narrative analysis profitably employed by narrative critics.[23]

In my view, then, the disjunctions Fowler poses are unnecessary. The Gospels *are* designed to say something about the disciples and, supremely, Jesus, *and also* to do something to the reader. Nevertheless, Howell is correct to note the lack of exact correspondence between the narrative world of the evangelists and the historical world of the events they narrate (or, as he rightly notes, between any narrative and the events upon which it is based). But equally, this concession hardly justifies the dismissal of what seems, prima facie, to be the clear historiographic intention of these narratives. Otherwise, since a 'one-to-one correspondence' between the narrative world and the real world is impossible, *any* writing about *any* historical event would only succeed in generating its own fictional narrative world. But, whatever their similarities, and however complex it may be to distinguish between them at times, there remains a difference between history and fiction – historical narratives are constrained by prior historical events in a way that fictional narratives obviously are not.

More precisely, the difference between historical and fictional narratives centres upon generic rules and conventions. We have already noted that historical and fictional works cannot necessarily be distinguished by unique rhetorical devices or format. Nor is the critical distinction simply whether or not the events narrated actually happened. Fictional narratives can incorporate historical events and historical narratives can present as historical fictive incidents – they can make false claims. Instead, it is the nature of these claims that stands at the heart of the distinction between history and fiction. Meir Sternberg's comments are instructive: '[H]istory-writing is not a record of fact – of what "really happened" – but a discourse that *claims* to be a record of fact. Nor is fiction-writing a tissue of free inventions but a discourse that *claims* freedom of invention. The antithesis lies not in the presence or absence of truth value but of the commitment to truth value.'[24] Or again: 'Whatever its faults, real or imagined, bad historiography does not yet make fiction. For if fiction contrasts with fact, it contrasts even more sharply with fallacy and falsity, which are value judgments passable on factual reporting alone. Falling between fallacy and falsity, therefore, *bad* historiography is bad *historiography*: no more, no less.'[25] The author of a fictional narrative may or may not make important truth claims; he may or may not include historical components; but the story he invites his readers to share in is finally an imaginary one *with no claim to historicity*. It is precisely this *claim*, however – that the people introduced are historical figures and that the events portrayed actually happened – that separates history from fiction. The fundamental difference, then, is the nature of the agreement that an author enters into with his (envisioned) readers.

To be fair, it is not clear to me that Howell wishes to deny the historiographic intent of the Gospel narratives. Instead, I think, he urges caution and cedes priority to the narrative world. Powell, on the other hand, seems to approach such a denial when he defines the *referential fallacy* as the interpretation of 'literary elements in terms of their supposed antecedents in the real world'. These 'literary elements', such as characters in the narrative, are constructs of the implied author who have poetic but not referential function.[26] This study, by contrast, aims to avoid the problems associated with the referential fallacy not by denying historiographic intent, nor even by ceding priority to the narrative world, but rather by explicitly acknowledging that a narrative depiction of reality always represents a particular perception of that reality and can never provide an exact representation of the complex people and events it describes. Here I am not advocating the naïve acceptance of anything that expresses an historiographic intention. Instead, my point is only that, if a narrative – implicitly or explicitly – makes such a claim, it will hardly do to dismiss that claim if we are concerned to explain the intended function of that narrative.[27]

Yet again, redaction- and narrative-critical approaches can be mutually corrective. Put positively, in studies that aim to explain the intended meaning and function of the narrative, Gospel critics would do well to incorporate both the tools for narrative analysis from the narrative critics and the historical orientation of the redaction critic. Put negatively, the critic's focus should rest neither upon the *fictional* world of the story, nor, primarily, upon the historical world of the *evangelist*.[28] In this study, we aim to take up the narrative critic's tools and employ them in the study of a narrative that is fundamentally historiographic in nature.

Author vs. reader

Perhaps the most significant hermeneutical development that we have witnessed in recent decades has been the shift in focus from author to text to reader.[29] Not surprisingly, this shift is reflected in the move from redaction criticism's focus on the author and his intention, to narrative criticism's emphasis on the text and its impact on the reader. As a narrative critic, M. A. Powell distances himself from historical critics by aiming to uncover the intent of the *text* rather than the intent of its *author*.[30] D. Howell, while not wishing to make the reader the exclusive arbiter of the meaning of a text, none the less insists that the reader 'has a role in the production of textual meaning'.[31] R. Fowler is less cautious. Numbering himself among the reader-response critics he describes, Fowler declares that, 'whatever meaning is and wherever it is found the reader is ultimately responsible for determining meaning'.[32] From one vantage point, these moves are dramatic; from another, they are, at least potentially, deceptive.

On the one hand, the move from an author-oriented study of the manipulation of traditional sources designed to isolate the evangelist's theology and *Sitz im Leben* to the analysis of the rhetorical strategies employed in the final form of the text and the way that these strategies influence the reader is nothing less than dramatic. Redaction criticism's focus on the author's construction of the text has given way, for some narrative critics, to an analysis of the text's construction of its reader. Moreover the preoccupation with ideas that often marked redaction criticism has been subordinated to the effect achieved by the text – the cognitive domain has yielded to the affective, and what a text says may well be less important than what it does. These are momentous shifts, changing the nature of interpretation itself.

On the other hand, momentous as these shifts are, they remain potentially deceptive because careful attention to the author and to the reader are not mutually exclusive.[33] In spite of rhetoric to the contrary, there is no necessary incompatibility between a method that devotes attention to the author's treatment of his sources and one that examines the consequent rhetorical strategies embodied in the final form of the narrative. Nor, as we shall see, is there any necessary incompatibility between focus on the author and his intent and reflection on the impact of the narrative upon the reader. Indeed, I shall argue that a study of the Gospels that incorporates concerns along both of these lines will offer not merely a more comprehensive, but also – at least potentially – a more persuasive and satisfying reading.

Narrative-critical treatments of the author are particularly instructive at this point. In a 1997 thesis R. G. Mills demonstrates that many narrative approaches to the Gospels (including some that purport to avoid questions about the real author) remain, in fact, author-oriented in their interpretive agenda.[34] While the scope of their interest has been broadened to include investigation of the rhetorical strategies employed in the text and their impact on the implied reader, their fundamental questions remain author-centred questions. For many narrative critics, as the examples to which we now turn illustrate, interest in the text and the reader has not eclipsed interest in the author, even when this interest is not explicitly in the foreground.

The author as architect. For many narrative critics an author's influence, like an architect's, is pervasive. The author, for example, determines the *point of view*,[35] the perspectives – ideological, phraseological, spatio-temporal and psychological – from which the story is told,[36] and, in establishing the perspectives from which the story is told, the author also determines the perspectives from which the story is heard and experienced.[37] Since the reader sees what the author wishes him to see and from the vantage point he determines, point of view becomes, in the hand of the skilful author, a powerful tool by means of which he may influence the reader's response to his narrative. In the words of Rhoads and Michie: 'The narrator speaks from an ideological point of view . . . So the narrator is always there at the reader's elbow shaping responses to the story – even, and perhaps especially, when the reader is least aware of it.'[38]

Similar things might also be said of the narrative's plot. W. Booth, for example, argues that:

> the author's single most important creative act is to invent what Aristotle calls the 'synthesis of incidents', the 'plot' in the sense of the plotted narrative line (which sometimes includes, but is never reducible to, the kind of surface intrigue we refer to when we say 'The plot thickens'). It is always to some degree a doctoring of the raw chronology of events with a quite different chronology of telling. And it is always – in fiction that works well enough to earn our respect – ordered towards some powerful effect inherent in our picture of *these events happening to these characters, as perceived in the transforming vision of this storyteller.*[39]

Narrative critics of the Gospels have not failed to underline this point. Petersen can speak of the 'self-conscious' manner in which Mark plots his narrative with his reader directly in view, and Kingsbury insists that Matthew creates a plot in order to elicit from his reader the desired response.[40]

Moreover the author, who stands like an architect behind both the plot and the point of view of the narrative, is also responsible for the moulding of the story's characters,[41] and thus once more for shaping the way his readers experience the story. By controlling the distance between the reader and the various characters in the narrative, the author invites the reader to sympathise or to condemn, to rejoice or to mourn, to emulate or to despise, to worship or to scorn.[42]

aims and reading strategies of narrative and redaction critics respectively have curtailed the cooperative pursuit of the intended function of the narrative by representatives of the two disciplines, but, when we recognise that both disciplines can, and often do, pursue an author-oriented agenda, the methodological gulf no longer seems unbridgeable. Sober redaction-critical analysis can only strengthen the best narrative-critical analysis, and vice versa. The suggestion that any given rhetorical strategy seems designed to elicit a particular response will be strengthened by recognition of the evidence that points in a similar direction in an evangelist's manipulation of his tradition. Of course, this same evidence may call into question other readings. Equally, conclusions that arise from the analysis of Gospel sources may rightly be regarded with suspicion if they are not corroborated by the rhetorical strategies employed in the final form of the wider narrative. It is not only narrative-critical readings that are susceptible to the subjectivity of their interpreters. This, then, is the agenda I have set for this study: to explicate the response that this trilogy suggests the author intends to elicit from his readers. In so doing, I employ the tools of both redaction and narrative criticism.

If methodological upheaval has accompanied the critical study of the Gospel narratives, this is hardly less true of the parables. The remainder of this chapter turns to examine briefly questions of method in reading the Synoptic parables, focusing upon two issues confronting a critical reading of the parables that have particular relevance for this project – issues that are in one sense subsets of the problems addressed above.[57]

1.2   On reading the Synoptic parables

Integrity vs. fragmentation: *whose* parables shall we study?

As components of the wider narrative, the Synoptic parables are susceptible to the tension between integrity and fragmentation highlighted in our earlier discussion: should they be read *comparatively* or *holistically*? In the case of the parables, however, this tension is exacerbated by a century of research conducted in the shadow of A. Jülicher.

The legacy of Jülicher, Dodd and Jeremias

In 1886 Jülicher published the first of a two-volume treatment of the parables that would irreversibly alter the interpretation of the Synoptic parables.[58] He argued that Jesus' parables were clear, concrete, powerful stories designed to instruct simple Palestinian peasants. The evangelists, however, (mis)understood Jesus' parables to be mysterious allegories and were themselves responsible for sending the church into a blind alley from which it would take nearly two millennia to escape. If we are to hear the literal speech of Jesus once more, we must excise those allegorical elements that the later tradition added. C. H. Dodd[59] and J. Jeremias[60] accepted and extended Jülicher's conclusions with such effect that in 1976 N. Perrin could pay the following tribute to the extraordinary influence of Jeremias's work:

> it is to Jeremias above all others that we owe our present ability to reconstruct the parables very much in the form in which Jesus told them. Indeed, when we talk of interpreting the parables of Jesus today we mean interpreting the parables as Jeremias has reconstructed them, either personally or through his influence on others who have followed the method he developed.[61]

Today, in spite of criticisms – in some cases trenchant ones – that have been levelled against Jeremias's approach,[62] it is not uncommon for contemporary scholars simply to *assume* Jeremias's reconstructions as the *starting point* for their own reflection.[63]

For our purposes, the obvious significance of all of this is that for much of this past century most parables scholarship has focused on the *reconstructed parables of Jesus* rather than on the parables in their present form in the Synoptic Gospels. The problem of the fragmentation of the Gospels that narrative critics have lamented is, in one sense at least, compounded when we come to the study of the parables.[64]

Redaction criticism and the parables

The influence of the Jülicher tradition thus meant that redaction criticism never exercised the same kind of methodological sway in the study of the Synoptic parables that it did elsewhere in Gospels studies.[65] Very few monographs treated the parables from a distinctively redactional vantage point.[66] Nevertheless, journal articles and the standard commentaries provide ample evidence that redaction critics did not neglect the parables. Their work, with its characteristic focus on the contributions of the evangelists, represented a step away from the fragmentation of the Synoptic parables that had become part and parcel of the Jülicher tradition. But, of course, their treatment of the parables was marked by the strengths and weaknesses that marked the method as a whole.

Narrative criticism and the parables

If redaction critics have offered comparatively few full-length treatments of the parables, they have nevertheless thus far eclipsed the contributions of narrative critics.[67] In part, we may attribute this to the relative newness of the latter discipline. More importantly, perhaps, the holistic nature of the narrative-critical enterprise means that narrative critics have been more apt to devote their attention to blocks of the narrative than to the treatment of particular forms. If, however, the Synoptic parables are worthy of investigation in their own right, then it would seem that narrative criticism has a role to play in the rehabilitation of the evangelists' parables. *Gospels parables help shape both the characterisation of the story's leading players and its developing plot. Conversely, the impact of the wider story leaves its mark upon the reader's reception of these parables.* The tools of narrative criticism are especially well suited for consideration of issues like these, and chapters 3 and 4 of this study seek to employ these tools in the study of the three parables at Matthew 21.28–22.14.

Here, however, we turn to examine the problem for which the most vigorous modern debate has been reserved – the question of the parable's function.

Author vs. reader: how does a parable function?

The Jülicher tradition

Jülicher is, of course, most famous for his emphatic rejection of the allegorical readings that had long dominated the church's interpretation of Jesus' parables.[68] Nor may Jülicher's verdict be dismissed as a mere historical relic. Even among scholars who disagree fundamentally with Jülicher about what Jesus' parables are and how they function positively, widespread agreement remains that they are not allegories and Jülicher still stands as the champion of this position.[69] For good reasons, however, the sharp distinction he drew between parable and allegory has not gone unchallenged.

In two important works, P. Fiebig underlined several parallels between the rabbinic *meshalim* and Jesus' parables and noted, in the *meshalim*, the presence of stock metaphors that pointed the reader to historical actors and events outside of the story.[70] To be sure, the extant rabbinic literature post-dates the NT period,[71] but it does demonstrate that these rabbis drew no sharp distinction between parable and allegory. Nor, apparently, did Israel's Scriptures. Scott insists that there are no parables – short narrative fictions – in the Hebrew Scriptures,[72] but more than once David pronounces judgement on characters in fictional narratives only to be 'caught' by his own verdict (cf. 2 Sam. 12.1–7; 14.4–13). Elsewhere the prophets tell fictional stories that depict Yahweh's dealings with Israel (Isa. 5.1–7; Ezek. 17.3–10).

In the LXX παραβολή, which translates משל, can designate a wide variety of figurative sayings – proverbs (1 Kgs. 5.12 (4.32 EVV); Ezek. 18.2–3), riddles (Sir. 39.3; 47.15), bywords (Deut. 28.37; 2 Chron. 7.20), laments (Ezek. 19.14) and allegorical narratives (Ezek. 17.2) – in addition to prophetic oracles (Num. 23.7, 18). The evangelists' use of παραβολή, falls well within this range of LXX uses, if not achieving the same breadth.[73] Matthew, for example, prefers to use the term to describe (allegorical) narrative fictions (e.g., 13.3, 24), but also employs the term of proverbial utterances (15.15; 24.32). What is noteworthy in all of this is that the evangelists' use of παραβολή to denote enigmatic utterances – utterances that demand special attention and wise interpretation – is far from novel.[74] We can hardly discount the possibility that Jesus, as heir to this biblical tradition, employed both enigmatic and allusive references linking his stories to that tradition and to the world of his hearers.[75]

The discussion is important, but in one sense the point becomes moot when we turn to the interpretation of the Synoptic parables. The evangelists plainly label as 'parables' fictional narratives that have allegorical components, and invite their readers to pay close attention to their allusive references to the Scriptures and to the world outside the story.

It was not, however, Jülicher's banishment of allegory but his assumption that the parables were essentially *instructional* in nature that would face the most radical challenges in the decades to come.

Ernst Fuchs and the 'New Hermeneutic'

Ernst Fuchs and the New Hermeneutic offered the first serious challenge to this notion that the parables of Jesus were basically didactic in function.[76] For Fuchs and his students,[77] Jesus' parables function as *language events* (*Sprachereignisse*) for those with ears to hear. The hearer is drawn into the world of Jesus' parables not as an observer but as a participant and, as a participant, does not so much interpret the parables as be interpreted by them: 'The text is therefore not just the servant that transmits kerygmatic formulations, but rather a master that directs us into the language-context of our existence, in which we exist "before God".'[78] We cannot, therefore, separate the form of the text from its intent.[79] It is rather in confrontation with the text itself that we encounter Jesus' faith, his vision of the kingdom, and are ourselves interpreted. Instead of propositional truth to be interpreted, these texts offer confrontation at the deepest levels of our existence and enact an event that opens up to us new possibilities for a more genuine existence.

This image of the parable as a language event is a particularly fruitful one. The insight that Jesus' parables offer more than didactic illustrations of abstract moral and theological concepts, as they tended to be regarded by Jülicher and his heirs,[80] is certainly to be welcomed. The parables execute a performative and not merely an informative function. Similarly welcome is the contention that the form of the parable constitutes no mere husk to be discarded once the kernel – the *message* of the parable – becomes apparent. Once we acknowledge the capacity that these stories have *to grasp* their readers, we can hardly dismiss the form of the story as merely ornamental.

On the other hand, the sharp distinction that Fuchs drew between propositional and performative communication cannot be sustained. Following J. L. Austin, Thiselton argues that, in some instances at least, informative assertions and truth-claiming propositions 'constitute a condition of effective performative force'.[81] The story that Nathan told David (2 Sam. 12) aptly illustrates this point. It elicits from the king a verdict – in this case (as often in parables) a self-indictment (2 Sam. 12.5–6) – and ultimately provokes his repentance (2 Sam. 12.13). But finally this performative utterance depends, for its effectiveness, precisely on David's acknowledgement of the truth claim that stands behind the parable (2 Sam. 12.7–13). Surely something similar happens with Jesus' parables. The hearer must embrace the portraits Jesus' stories offer of God and his reign if the stories are to wield the desired performative force. Therefore Jesus' parables are more, but not less, than propositional.[82] It is not so much that his parables bear no message that can be translated into discursive speech as that they forfeit their rhetorical *impact* in the process of premature translation.[83]

Certainly the evangelists saw no necessary disjunction between propositional and performative functions in Jesus' parables. For Matthew, appropriate hearing of Jesus' parables cannot be restricted to things cognitive and cerebral. The one who hears the parable rightly is the one who '*hears the word and understands, who bears fruit and yields . . .*' (13.23). Hearing must give way to obedience, but it is equally obvious – both in The Sower and elsewhere where Matthew takes pains to *explain* Jesus' parables (e.g., 13.36–43; 13.49–50; 13.51; 15.15–20; 18.35) – that the evangelist regards understanding as a necessary condition for the obedience for which the parables call. And, since my main concern in this study is with hearing the parables that Matthew records, I intend to inquire after both the performative function that Jesus' parables seem designed to execute (now for *Matthew's* hearers and readers) and their underlying truth claims.

B. B. Scott and the American discussion

On the other side of the Atlantic, a group of American scholars echoed many of Fuchs's contentions, but moved beyond him in their distinctive understanding of metaphor, and the consequent open-endedness of the parables. B. B. Scott's *Hear Then The Parable* represents the culmination of a generation of this particular branch of American scholarship that gave rise to both the SBL Parables Seminar and the Jesus Seminar.[84]

For Scott, as for D. Via[85] before him, the parables are aesthetic objects. He places the parables in a first-century Jewish context but suggests that the aesthetic nature of the parables grants them independence over this context: 'As narrative fictions they have priority over their context. To put it another way, they interpret the context, not the other way around.'[86]

Not surprisingly then, parables are open-ended and polyvalent.[87] If the parables are aesthetic objects that have priority over their contexts, they are capable of eliciting a variety of readings: 'Words and, even more, connotative narratives naturally move towards polyvalency. It is a manipulation of reality to select only one out of a number of possibilities suggested by a narrative. A methodology that seizes on the one point of likeness as a parable's meaning destroys the parable.'[88] Scott insists that the parable can have external referents – Jesus' parables regularly 'reference' a symbol, the kingdom of God – but no one reading exhausts the number of legitimate readings that arise from these stories.[89]

The centrality of the metaphorical process to language remains crucial for Scott, as it was for Wilder, Funk and Crossan before him.[90] But here he tempers the earlier enthusiasm of his colleagues, acknowledging that the Romantic view of metaphor upon which they drew was naïve, especially in its insistence that metaphor yielded a direct apprehension of reality and in the sharp distinction posited between metaphor and allegory.[91]

In my view, the American discussion is most fruitful when it echoes the concerns of the New Hermeneutic. Funk's work is a case in point. He insists that the parable remains open until the listener is drawn in as a participant. Having been caught up in the story, the hearer must then render a judgement.[92] Both of these observations strike me as helpful reformulations of Fuchs's most important concerns.

Too often, however, a-priori considerations determine the course of the discussion, and too often Scott and his predecessors build uncritically upon the results of earlier parables scholarship.[93] When Scott insists, for example, that parables have priority over their contexts, the only defence he offers (aside from noting the appearance of both rabbinic and Synoptic parables in more than one context) is that, as narrative fictions, the parables are aesthetic objects and therefore must be independent of and have priority over their context.[94] But surely this amounts to little more than an assertion of his position, and fundamentally important conclusions about the nature of parables – not least their polyvalence – arise from this assertion.[95]

Reader-response criticism

If Scott and his predecessors have stressed the aesthetic nature of Jesus' parables and their consequent polyvalence, then reader-response critics have emphasised the participation of the reader in determining the meaning of *any* text.[96] The earlier work of Fuchs, Funk, Via and Crossan has probably meant that the application of a reader-oriented criticism to the parables has been less innovative than its application to the broader Gospel narratives. Like the New Hermeneutic, reader-response criticism stresses the self-involving nature of the text, both in the sense of drawing the reader into the world of the text and of eliciting response. For the reader-response critic, however, this happens not because the words of the text create a 'language-event' but because of the capacity of the reader to engage and be engaged by the text. Over against the New Hermeneutic, it is not so much that the meaning of a parable cannot be expressed propositionally as that the meaning (propositional or otherwise) found in the text is inexhaustible and limited only by the perception of its readers. Here reader-response critics align themselves more closely with deconstructionists[97] than with the proponents of the New Hermeneutic, and, whereas Fuchs and his students, situated as they were in the midst of the new quest for the historical Jesus, sought to hear the parables as Jesus' original audience would have,[98] reader-response critics have focused their attention on the text of the Gospels. Without divorcing the reader from the author, chapter 5 of this study takes up this question of the response to the written text emphasised by reader-response critics.

With their distinctive emphasis on a temporal reading, reader-response critics rightly treat the parables as important components of the larger Gospel stories. In other respects, I suggest, although they build upon quite different philosophical foundations, as a critical tool for the study of the parables, the strengths and weaknesses of reader-response criticism closely parallel those of the New Hermeneutic.[99] Both rightly stress the self-involving nature of the parables, but both rather overstate the radical open-endedness that such participation entails.

Conclusion

Two conclusions have emerged from our brief discussion. First, the task of reconstructing Jesus' parables has too often led to the neglect of the parables in their current forms in the Gospel tradition. Nevertheless, this quest has reminded us once more that the Synoptic parables are texts with a prior history. This study makes no attempt to reconstruct the 'original' parables of Jesus, but does aim to make judicious use of redaction criticism in tracing the evangelist's adaptation of his tradition. Alongside this redactional investigation I shall employ narrative-critical tools, attending to the contribution of the parables at Matthew 21.28–22.14 to the wider Gospel narrative, and to the shaping influence of that wider story on the reception of these parables. This approach seeks to underline the integrity of the parables both as stories in their own right and as components of the evangelist's larger communicative action.

Second, the disjunction between performative and propositional language that may be traced back to Fuchs is a false and unnecessary one. But Fuchs's insight was tremendously important – for those with ears to hear, the parable becomes a self-involving language event capable of grasping the hearer at the deepest level.

In the chapters that follow, this study returns to both of these concerns, seeking to demonstrate the fruitfulness of the type of alliance between redaction- and narrative-critical approaches proposed above. Chapter 2 consists of a *Forschungsgeschichte* of earlier twentieth-century studies of the trilogy of parables at Matthew 21.28–22.14 and, in response to recent challenges by S. Van Tilborg and I. H. Jones, a vigorous defence of its Matthean composition. The evangelist himself is responsible for the formation of the trilogy and, as we shall see, its careful design reflects distinct interest in the reader and her response.

Chapters 3 and 4 broaden the focus from the trilogy itself to the wider Gospel and explore the impact that this wider narrative makes upon the implied reader. The exercise is of fundamental importance. Each of the parables in this trilogy indicts the Jewish establishment, announces their exclusion from the kingdom of God and makes reference to those who would replace them as the subjects of God's reign. However, throughout the church's history exegetes have found in these parables an indictment not merely of the Jewish establishment, but also of the *nation*, and, if the nation was excluded, then – not surprisingly – it was the *Gentile nations* that were included. While there are Matthean specialists who still defend this interpretation, in recent years it has become increasingly common to find readings of these parables that insist that the indictment in view here must be restricted to the Jewish authorities, and that there is no obvious reference to Gentiles anywhere in the trilogy. In these chapters I seek to bring the evidence of the wider narrative to bear on these questions and, if my conclusions more nearly approach the former of the two readings noted above, I nevertheless shall argue that the wider narrative prepares the reader for a more nuanced reception of these stories than either of these alternatives would suggest. Chapter 3, which examines Matthew's portrait of the nation of Israel and devotes special attention to the contrasting characterisation of the Jewish leaders and the people, concludes that the judgement that this trilogy announces falls upon Israel and not only upon her leaders, though they remain chiefly responsible for the nation's catastrophic fall. Chapter 4 turns from the nation to the nations and argues that these parables point to the future inclusion of τὰ ἔθνη in τὸ ἔθνος that God had promised to raise up from Abraham.

Against the backdrop that this study of the wider narrative provides, chapters 5 and 6 turn once more to concentrate upon the trilogy of parables itself. The two chapters both approach the problem of envisioned response, but from distinct vantage points. Chapter 5 focuses upon the reader,[100] offering a narrative-critical reading of the parables that pays special attention both to their setting in this trilogy and to the rhetorical strategies employed in the trilogy that seem designed to entangle the reader in the concerns of these stories and to shape his response to the parables. Chapter 6 focuses upon the author, employing a more traditional redaction-critical approach that highlights the distinctive Matthean features of the trilogy, but once more bringing the results to bear on the question of anticipated response. Both chapters conclude that as important as salvation–historical matters are in this trilogy, they by no means exhaust its concerns. Instead the trilogy builds towards the paraenetic climax achieved at 22.11–14.

Chapter 7 presents the conclusions of this study and is followed by an appendix, which offers a fresh analysis of the parable of The Two Sons' complex text–critical problem. I shall argue there that one of the implications of seeing the evangelist's careful design in the trilogy is that the reading of the parable supported by B, Θ, et al., is to be preferred over the reading accepted by NA[27].

2

MATTHEW'S TRILOGY OF PARABLES: 21.28–22.14

The later chapters of this study argue that reading the parables of The Two Sons (21.28–32), The Tenants (21.33–46) and The Wedding Feast (22.1–14) as a trilogy offers important insight with respect to the responses the evangelist wished to elicit from his readers. In this chapter we survey previous twentieth-century studies of the trilogy before turning to defend the conclusion that Matthew himself was responsible for its formation.

2.1 *Forschungsgeschichte*: the trilogy in twentieth-century Matthean studies

Commentators have long recognised the presence of both formal and conceptual parallels that bind these parables together. These conceptual parallels were already important for Chrysostom, who drew attention to the strategic arrangement of the parables that underscored the failure of the Jewish leaders: 'Therefore He putteth [The Tenants] after the former parable, that He may show even hereby the charge to be greater, and highly unpardonable. How, and in what way? That although they met with so much care, they were worse than harlots and publicans, and by so much.'[1]

In the modern era, Matthean scholars have drawn attention with increasing precision to the striking formal links that unite the three parables. B. Weiss's nineteenth-century commentary noted in The Wedding Feast the clear repetition of entire phrases from The Two Sons and, especially, The Tenants:[2]

21.29	22.3
οὐ θέλω	οὐκ ἤθελον
21.34	22.3
ἀπέστειλεν τοὺς δούλους αὐτοῦ	ἀπέστειλεν τοὺς δούλους αὐτοῦ
21.36	22.4
πάλιν ἀπέστειλεν ἄλλους δούλους	πάλιν ἀπέστειλεν ἄλλους δούλους

For Weiss, 21.28–22.14 functions as a great parable trilogy that confronts the Jewish hierarchy with its guilt and its judgement with increasing intensity.[3]

Early twentieth-century approaches to the trilogy

Many twentieth-century commentators have echoed these observations and conclusions. In the early part of the century, for example, W. Allen (like Weiss) noted the twofold sending of the servants that links The Wedding Feast to The Tenants, but also added that by the insertion of 22.6–7:

> the editor has adapted this, and brought it into line with Mk.'s parable of the Husbandmen, and the preceding parable of the Two Sons. The Jewish nation in the person of its rulers had re-fused to listen to God's call to repentance (21[32]), had rejected the Messiah (v.[39]), and had neglected the summons to the marriage feast (22[5]). Consequently, judgement upon them was at hand.[4]

For Allen, then, it was the evangelist himself who had formed this triad of 'prophetic parables,' which together foretell 'the divine judge-ment impending over the Jewish nation'.[5] A. Plummer likewise credited the evangelist with the arrangement of the parables: 'Mt., as so often, gives us a triplet.'[6] And, once more, this alignment underscores the com-ing judgement. The parables tend 'to enforce the moral of the withered fig-tree, that the empty profession of the Jews, and especially of the hierarchy at Jerusalem, will provoke severe judgments'.[7] In similar fash-ion, E. Klostermann drew attention to the trilogy's threefold exposition of the failure of 'the representatives of Judaism' and their consequent judgement.[8] He also, however, discussed the interpretive significance of the echo of 21.36 at 22.4. In the end he concluded that it is not clear whether 22.4, like 21.36, points to an invitation that was offered 'be-fore the time of the Son', or subsequently, on the lips of the apostles.[9] Klostermann's answer was uncertain, but the question he addressed – the function of the echoes that link these parables – is an important one to which this study shall return. Finally, of the many comparable treatments of the three parables that could be reviewed, we note that for McNeile also the trilogy was the construction of the evangelist and that each of the parables conveyed the same message: 'the leaders of the nation being unworthy, those whom they despise will take their place (v. 31, 43, xxii. 10)'.[10] Here, however, a slight shift in emphasis is perhaps discernible: *judgement* gives way to *replacement*.

Subsequent twentieth-century research would adopt and extend many of the formal observations noted above. Surprisingly few scholars, however, would devote more than passing attention to the hermeneutical function of the trilogy in the First Gospel. W. Trilling, one of the early German redaction critics, was perhaps the first notable exception.

Redaction-critical approaches to the trilogy

Wolfgang Trilling

Trilling once more drew attention to the dual missions of the servants and their repeated rejection that linked The Wedding Feast to The Tenants, but also noted that the two Matthean parables depart both verbally and materially from their Synoptic counterparts at precisely these points. The Marcan parable of The Tenants reports three sendings of individual servants that give way, finally, to many others (πολλοὺς ἄλλους; Mark 12.5), all of whom are mistreated, some killed. In the Lucan parable of the Great Supper[11] one servant is sent once to call the invited guests to the banquet (Luke 14.17–20). For Trilling, it is Matthew himself who is responsible for the obvious alignment of these parables and for the formation of the trilogy more generally.[12]

The burden of Trilling's 1960 essay is actually to explain the tradition history of The Wedding Feast (22.1–14). He argues that, since elsewhere a single overriding purpose marks Matthew's parables, the presence of two dominant motifs here – paraenesis on the one hand and polemics on the other – betrays pre-Matthean redaction. It was, moreover, the Matthean community that developed the paraenetic thrust of the parable; the evangelist himself was responsible for the polemical rewriting. In part, this polemical emphasis was determined by the context into which the parable was placed – both within the immediate context, following The Tenants and, more broadly, within the escalating controversy that runs from 21.12 through 23.39. More fundamentally, however, a polemical purpose lay behind the entire final stage of redaction.[13]

Trilling suggests that this polemical rewriting may have been executed in an ad hoc fashion. Indeed, the evangelist's rather rough editing of his Marcan *Vorlage* suggests to Trilling that Matthew probably had originally planned no parable trilogy here.[14] The Jewish leaders' recognition that Jesus spoke his parables about them (21.45), for example, becomes redundant after the important redactional insertion at 21.43. None the less, with the new introduction to the third parable (22.1), the three parables are linked together and form another cycle of parables – a compositional feature of which the evangelist is fond.[15]

As we have noted, for Trilling the function of this new cycle of parables is chiefly polemical – they underscore Israel's guilt. If The Two
Sons is included by the evangelist to assist in the development of the
polemical motif already present in the Marcan parable of The Tenants,[16]
the entire first half of The Wedding Feast is edited anew for the same
purpose.[17] But the hermeneutical function of the trilogy is not merely
an emphatic one. The Wedding Feast has not only been aligned to The
Tenants; instead, in a sense, it also *continues* the story that The Tenants
begins.[18] In fact, Trilling suggests, the trilogy is marked by an inner gradient (*ein inneres Gefälle*) that reaches its low point (*Tiefpunkt*) at 22.7.[19]
What is announced at 21.43 as a punishment ('the kingdom of God will
be taken from you') has now been accomplished and found its external
expression in the destruction of the city and the annihilation of the murderers (22.7).[20] As such, the parables in this new cycle provide mutual
clarification.[21] This also means, for example, that neither of the first two
groups of servants in the Wedding Feast (22.3, 4) may be identified with
the apostles or Christian missionaries. On the contrary, since these servants parallel the servants in The Tenants, who point indisputably to the
OT prophets (21.34, 36), they must be identified as OT prophets here as
well.[22]

We noted above that Chrysostom found a polemical emphasis in the
arrangement of these parables. Interestingly, he also seems to anticipate
Trilling in reading them as a continuing story:

> He had planted a vineyard; He had done all things, and finished;
> when His servants had been put to death, He sent other servants;
> when those had been slain, He sent the son; and when He was put
> to death, He bids them to the marriage. They would not come.
> After this He sends other servants, and they slew these also.
> Then upon this He slays them, as being incurably diseased.[23]

Chrysostom, however, seems to envision a more thoroughgoing continuation than Trilling. Trilling speaks of a continuation, but his *continuation*
might more aptly be described as *clarification*. Unlike Trilling, Chrysostom thought the third story picked up where the second left off. The
servants in The Wedding Feast are replacements; the others (from The
Tenants) are dead.

Sjef Van Tilborg

S. Van Tilborg's *The Jewish Leaders in Matthew* devotes a chapter to
21.28–22.14 and 23.29–39. In underlining the repetition of words and
phrases that unites the three parables – 'the clearest indication that an

editor has been at work here'[24] – Van Tilborg extends earlier work. At the conceptual level, Van Tilborg points first to the contrast between the son who first refuses his father's appeal but subsequently repents (21.28–31) and those twice invited who nevertheless reject the king's invitation to the wedding feast (22.3–5). But second, noting the dual mission of the servants (21.34, 36, cf. 22.3, 4), their mistreatment and murder (21.35, cf. 22.6), and the subsequent retaliation by their master (21.41, cf. 22.7) that feature prominently in The Tenants and The Wedding Feast, Van Tilborg follows O. Steck[25] in locating these parables within the tradition of Jewish writings that traces the judgement of Yahweh against Israel to Israel's rebellion against her God generally, and, more specifically, to her murder of Yahweh's prophets.[26]

If, however, these parables are linked both verbally and conceptually, for Van Tilborg it was not the evangelist who was responsible for forging this unity. Analysis of the relevant seams in the trilogy leads him to argue that the parables were linked in prior tradition. Nevertheless, the evangelist has strengthened the traditional links between the parables, and so enhanced this unity.[27]

Van Tilborg pays little explicit attention to the hermeneutical function of the trilogy, but his argument seems to imply that the alignment of the traditional parables has a salvation–historical function: this 'pericope', together with 23.29–39, 'expounds . . . the cause and effect of the definitive rejection of Israel'.[28]

Eduard Schweizer

In a fascinating essay on Matthew 21–25 published the year after Van Tilborg's work, E. Schweizer draws attention to the common vineyard setting and also to the surprising presence of βασιλεία τοῦ θεοῦ that the first two parables share[29] and, once more, highlights the verbatim repetition of the dual mission of the servants in the second and third parables of the trilogy (22.3–4, cf. 21.34–36), but he also notes the important link that unites all three parables to the preceding pericope with its focus on the authority of Jesus.[30] For Schweizer, the four pericopes from 21.23 to 22.14 comprise a carefully crafted unity that should be attributed to the evangelist himself.[31]

More importantly, this carefully constructed sequence has an important hermeneutical function. The parables portray a series of progressions: the first revolves around a man, the second a landowner, the third a king; the first concerns Israel's response to the Baptist, the second to Jesus, the third to his disciples. But 21.23–22.14 also depicts a more fundamental

Table 1

Word/Phrase	The Two Sons	The Tenants	The Wedding Feast
ἄνθρωπος	21.28	21.33	22.2; ἄνθρωπος βασιλεύς
πρωτος	21.28, 31	21.36	
ἀμπελών	21.28	21.33, 39, 40, 41	
οὐ θέλω	21.29		22.3
ὕστερον	21.29, 32	21.37	
μεταμέλω	21.29, 32		22.5; ἀμελέω
ἀπέρχομαι	21.29, 30		22.5; εἰς τὸν ἀγρόν
ἀπέρχομαι	21.29, 30		22.5; ἐπὶ . . . ἐμπορίαν
ὡσαύτως	21.30	21.36	
κύριος	21.30	21.40, 42	
τίς . . . ἐποίησεν	21.31	21.40; τί ποιήσει	
ποιέω τὸ θέλημα τοῦ πατρός	21.31	21.43; ἔθνει ποιοῦντι τοὺς καρποὺς αὐτῆς	
λέγουσιν	21.31	21.41	
λέγει αὐτοῖς ὁ Ἰησοῦς·	21.31	21.42	
βασιλεία τοῦ θεοῦ	21.31	21.43	22.2; τῶν οὐρανῶν
λέγω ὑμῖν	21.31	21.43	
ἦλθον	21.32	21.40	22.3
πρός + acc.	21.32	21.34, 37	
ὁδός	21.32		22.9–10
ἰδόντες	21.32	21.38	
παραβολή		21.33	22.1
ἀποστέλλω		21.34, 36, 37	22.3, 4
δοῦλοι αὐτοῦ		21.34, 35	22.3, 6, 8, 10 (δοῦλοι ἐκεῖνοι)
δοῦλοι ἄλλοι		21.36	22.4
ἀποκτείνω		21.35, 38, 39	22.6
πάλιν		21.36	22.1, 4
υἱός		21.37	22.2
ἀπόλλυμι		21.41	22.7

progression. At 21.23–27 the chief priests and elders of the people seek to put Jesus on trial, challenging his authority. In fact, his counter-question turns the tables and puts them on trial. Their evasive answer may forestall a verdict, but only temporarily. The trilogy of parables proceeds from this trial (*Verhör*; 21.23–27) to pronouncements of a verdict (*Schuldigsprechung*; 21.28–32; esp. v. 31), sentence (*Strafzumessung*; 21.33–46; esp. vv. 41, 43), and execution of this sentence (*Urteilsvollstreckung*; 22.1–10; esp. v. 7). In all of this Israel's terrible guilt is underscored. But none of this brings the trilogy to its conclusion or accomplishes its most important function. Instead, the trilogy reaches its climax at 22.11–14, where Matthew turns to address the community of Jesus' disciples. The trial, verdict, sentence, and execution of judgement against Israel do not exist merely to dramatise her guilt. On the contrary, their more important function is to issue a sharp warning to the church – what had happened to Israel could surely happen to her.[32]

Schweizer's treatment of the trilogy is distinctive not only in treating it as the progressive stages of Israel's trial and in stressing that the entire trilogy builds towards the paraenetic climax of 22.11–14, but also in defending his reading by an appeal to the wider structure of Matthew 21–25. The drama staged in 21.23–22.14 is repeated in 22.15–25.46. Matthew 22.15–46 rehearses again the trial of Israel, 23.1–32 issues the verdict, 23.33–36 declares the sentence and 23.37–24.2 outlines the execution of this frightful sentence, but, once more, all of this is preparatory. Matthew 24.3–25.46 again shifts the focus to the church and, like 22.11–14, warns her of the perils of walking the path that Israel had chosen. For her unfaithful servants, as for Israel's, there will be weeping and gnashing of teeth (24.51, cf. 25.30).[33]

Akira Ogawa

In the course of his 1979 essay devoted to these parables,[34] A. Ogawa notes both the manner in which the introductions to the parables unite the members of the trilogy and the assimilation of The Wedding Feast to The Tenants.[35] Explicitly building upon R. Walker's analysis (but also echoing the conclusion of some earlier exegetes), Ogawa sees a chronological progression in the trilogy: the three parables focus upon the missions of John, Jesus and the apostles respectively.[36] But, while he thinks that the evangelist's redactional hand may be observed throughout the trilogy, Ogawa follows Van Tilborg in attributing 22.1 to pre-Matthean tradition. He finds in the plural παραβολαῖς (22.1), together with the similarity in form and content that mark the parables at 13.24–30, 18.23–35 and 25.1–13, evidence of a pre-Matthean grouping of parables.[37]

Ogawa's central purpose, however, is to argue that the trilogy does *not* depict the replacement of Israel by the church.[38] Matthew 21.43 (as well as 22.6–7 and 22.11–14), which is often thought to express this replacement most explicitly, does come from the evangelist's own hand, but the function of his redaction here, as throughout the trilogy, is polemical and paraenetic – not salvation–historical.[39] He does not deny that the parables allude to a salvation–historical loss for Israel, but insists that Matthew is concerned not with the transfer of the kingdom per se, but with explaining *why* it was transferred.[40]

Jan Lambrecht

J. Lambrecht's recent study of Matthean parables devotes three chapters to these parables.[41] The Two Sons and The Tenants, he notes, are linked by common settings,[42] terminology[43] and stylistic features – both conclude with dialogue and become juridical parables.[44] More importantly, however, both parables address the failure of Israel, and especially her leaders, to yield to the prophetic authority of John and Jesus.[45] The parable of The Wedding Feast has been assimilated to The Tenants: both depict the severe punishment that is meted out to Israel because of her violent rejection of Yahweh's prophets, and her replacement by a new, more obedient, people.[46]

He concludes that '[t]he parable trilogy . . . clearly is a Matthean composition'.[47] Whatever other factors may have been involved,[48] the chief reason for this Matthean arrangement of the parables was their content: 'Matthew feels compelled to comment on the lack of belief in the Baptist manifested by the Jewish authorities in 21:25.'[49] The trilogy becomes an occasion for the evangelist to meditate upon Israel and the church and God's dealings with them both.[50]

For Lambrecht, the placement of the parables in the trilogy has an important hermeneutical function. Since the three parables must be considered together, in one sense, at least, The Two Sons is merely preparatory: *the tax gatherers and prostitutes prefigure the Christian community* that will make an appearance in the two subsequent parables.[51]

Ivor H. Jones

I. H. Jones's learned study of Matthean parables devotes careful attention both to the parables in their current narrative setting and to features that may betray pre-Matthean tradition. When he turns to examine these parables, he refers to Van Tilborg's demonstration of the verbal links between the three parables of the trilogy, but especially emphasises the ties between The Two Sons and The Tenants. In its Matthean form, The Tenants has been assimilated to The Two Sons. Both parables link John and Jesus together and both portray the failure of the Jewish leaders to acknowledge their prophetic authority. Both parables, moreover, point to this failure in explaining the surprising replacement of the Jewish elite with an equally surprising cast of alternates.[52] The themes of the violent rejection of the prophets and the subsequent replacement of the Jewish leadership also mark The Wedding Feast and link it to the preceding parables.[53]

What makes Jones's study especially significant for our purposes, however, is not his treatment of the trilogy, but rather his argument that the grouping of these parables belongs to an earlier stage in the development of the tradition. Jones offers a detailed defence of this proposal, based on a careful analysis of both lexical and syntactical features.[54] I shall take up several of his arguments later in this chapter as I defend the Matthean composition of the trilogy.

Ulrich Luz

In a brief discussion, U. Luz offers five reasons to conclude that these three parables together form one unit (21.23[55]–22.14) in Matthew's Gospel.[56] First, as parables, The Two Sons, The Tenants and The Wedding Feast are linked formally. In the case of the first two, the formal parallel becomes even more pronounced. At the completion of his story, Jesus poses a question to his hostile hearers and, in a *paradigmatischen Rechtentscheid*, they pronounce their own condemnation (21.31, cf. 40–41). Second, an analysis of sources reveals that only the middle parable in the trilogy, The Tenants, stands here in the Marcan narrative – the first and third have been inserted. Third, the introductions to the second (ἄλλην παραβολήν; 21.33a) and third parables (πάλιν; 22.1) bind the three stories together. Fourth, the parables are linked by their common content. All three are directed to the Jewish leaders and pronounce judgement upon them. If the first depicts only their 'No' to John the Baptist, the second and third augment it, broadening the purview to include salvation-history in its entirety. Finally, the presence of common *Stichworte* underscores their impressive unity. For Luz, as for most redaction critics, the evangelist himself is the architect of this trilogy.

Narrative-critical approaches to the trilogy

Early narrative-critical treatments

The early narrative-critical treatments of Matthew devote scant attention to this trilogy. R. Edwards passes over this portion of Matthew's story almost without comment on any relationship between the parables. He does note that both The Two Sons and The Tenants address the question of authority raised by the Jewish authorities at 21.23, but discussion of the relationship of The Wedding Feast to the two earlier parables is restricted to a reference to the presence of violence in the preceding parable. In fact, he treats The Wedding Feast under a separate heading (The Controversy Intensifies (22.1–46)).[57] J. Kingsbury notes only that the parables pronounce judgement on Israel for her repudiation of John (21.28–32), Jesus (21.33–46) and Jesus' messengers (22.1–14), preferring to focus rather on the contribution of The Tenants to the unfolding plot of the story.[58] D. Howell's discussion of the trilogy is also brief, but he does suggest that this series of parables that underline Israel's failure to respond to the rule of God builds towards the climax that the Wedding Feast, with its 'thinly disguised allegory of the destruction of Jerusalem',[59] provides. But Howell also notes that the addition of 22.11–14 testifies to the evangelist's paraenetic interests. This second judgement scene (22.11–14, cf. 22.7) lends a hortatory accent to the entire trilogy: like Israel, Matthew's community must act (21.28–32), bear fruit (21.33–46) and accept the invitation of the Kingdom (22.1–14).[60]

Warren Carter

The most extensive – and also the most recent – narrative-critical treatment of the parables at Matthew 21.28–22.14 as a trilogy comes from the pen of W. Carter.[61] Following the lead of earlier scholars, he notes the structural features that unite these parables and highlights the role of the trilogy in elaborating 'the action of the first part of Matthew 21, especially the conflict scene of 21:23–27'.[62] The three parables grow out of the same conflict, confront the same recipients, and address the same issue, broadly speaking – the nature of Jesus' authority. Surprisingly, given the nature of his project,[63] Carter pays little attention either to the contribution of the trilogy to the developing plot of the Gospel or to the impact of the wider narrative on the reader's reception of the trilogy, largely restricting his observations to the role of the parables in their immediate context.

Because, in this study, Carter has bracketed redactional questions, the problem of the trilogy's origin is not raised. However he does address – albeit indirectly – the problem of the trilogy's hermeneutical function. As the audience progresses through the parables, both the narrative context and the audience's encounter with the earlier portions of the trilogy help to shape its reception of subsequent portions. Thus: 'The immediate following of the first parable with a second, and Jesus' opening comment, "hear another parable",' create for the audience the expectation that this second parable will reinforce and develop the insights of the previous parable in several ways'.[64] Near the end of his essay, Carter acknowledges that his reading of The Tenants helps shape his conclusion about The Wedding Feast's presentation of mission to Israel and to the nations.[65] As for the pragmatic function of the parables more generally, he concludes 'that the parables function primarily to provide affirmation and insight for the audience in its way of life faithful to God's purposes'.[66]

Conclusion

If we step back to review the preceding survey, two important conclusions emerge. First, earlier discussions have clearly demonstrated that these three parables currently stand together as a tightly connected triad within Matthew's narrative. The narrative links that bind the parables both to each other (21.28a, cf. 21.31b–32, 33a, 45–46; 22.1) and to one distinct setting (cf. 21.23–27), together with the remarkable string of echoes – both verbal and conceptual – that run through these parables, firmly establish this conclusion. Second, verdicts about the original composition and the hermeneutical function[s] of the trilogy are much less clear. Here, no comparable consensus exists. Who should be credited with the formation of the trilogy? Most redaction critics have assumed that Matthew himself brought these parables together in their current setting, but the two most detailed examinations of the problem – by Van Tilborg and Jones respectively – have challenged this assumption, arguing that the parables already stood together in pre-Matthean tradition. With respect to the hermeneutical function of the trilogy, the waters are murkier still. How might placement in this trilogy have influenced the reception of the individual parables? How have the parables been reshaped by their inclusion in this trilogy? How does the string of echoes that confront the reader as she moves through the trilogy influence her understanding of the parables? Have the parables been placed together chiefly to underline Israel's (or her leaders') dramatic failure? What role has been assigned to the trilogy in the story that the wider narrative tells?

The remainder of this chapter addresses directly the first of these problems – the composition of the trilogy. The more fundamental question of the hermeneutical function of the trilogy is reserved, largely, for the subsequent chapters of this study.[67]

2.2   The composition of the trilogy

In our defence of the Matthean composition of the trilogy, we turn first to a discussion of the triad as a distinctive structural feature of this Gospel.

Triads in Matthew

The reader of Matthew's Gospel need wait no longer than the first verse to meet Matthew's first triad: Jesus is Messiah,[68] son of David, son of Abraham. The genealogy, structured around these three figures, is explicitly divided into three groups of fourteen (1.2–17). Three stories follow in the 'birth narratives' that guide the reader from Jesus' supernatural conception to his settling, with Joseph and Mary, in Nazareth (1.18–25; 2.1–12; 2.13–23). Chapter 3 comprises another triplet of stories, in each of which John the Baptist features prominently (3.1–6; 3.7–12; 3.13–17). Moreover, it is tempting to find one more triad at 4.1–22 (4.1–11; 4.12–17; 4.18–22)[69] that gives way to Jesus' inaugural sermon. Among the numerous triads that one might detect in the sermon, 6.2–18 with its threefold illustration of 6.1 ('Beware of practicing your piety before others in order to be seen by them') is immediately obvious. Further examples could be multiplied.[70]

Indeed, recently D. Allison – both in a 1987 article and in the commentary he co-authored with W. D. Davies – has argued that the use of triads is one of the dominant features of Matthew's literary style.[71] The triad has not featured prominently in discussions of Matthean style, but some scholars have drawn attention to Matthew's penchant for arranging his material in groups of three. Table 2 records texts that appear in at least two of the lists of Matthean triads prepared, respectively, by W. Allen, J. Moffat, U. Luz[72] and Davies and Allison.

If, however, previous scholars had noted Matthew's preference for groups of three, Davies and Allison's discussion nevertheless remains distinctive in its attempt to find triadic groupings at the macro-structural level of the Gospel. Indeed, for them the pervasiveness of triads in Matthew becomes one of three 'foundation stones' (together with the five major discourses and the alternation in Matthew between narrative and discourse) upon which future analysis of the structure of this Gospel must build.[73]

Table 2

		Triads in Matthew: Previous Research			
Text	Triad	Allen (1907) 1922	Moffat (1911) 1918	Luz (1985) 1989	Davies/Allison 1988
1.2–17	Genealogy: 3 × 14	* (1.17)	*		*
1.18–2.23	3 stories	*		*	*
1.18–2.23	3 Angelic appearances		*		*
4.1–11	3 Temptations	*	*		*
5.17–7.12	3 Divisions of the Sermon (5.17–48; 6.1–18; 6.19–7.12)			* (5.21–7.11)	*
5.21–32	The antitheses: First triad			*	*
5.33–48	The antitheses: Second triad			*	*
6.1–18	Cult instructions	*	*	*	* (6.2–18)
6.9c–10	Lord's Prayer: 3 'Thou' petitions	*a		*	*
6.11–13	Lord's Prayer: 3 'We' petitions	*		*	*
6.19–24	True treasure			*	*
8.1–15	3 Miracle stories	*	*	*	*
8.23–9.8	3 Miracle stories	*	*	*	*
9.1–17	3 Complaints of the Pharisees	*		*	
9.18–34	3 Miracle stories	*	*		*
11.7–9	3 Questions about John		*		*

Reference	Description		
12.1–24	3 Incidents that anger the Pharisees	*	*[b]
13.1–32	3 Parables of sowing	*	*
18.1–14	3 Sayings about the 'Little Ones'	*	*
19.12	3 Classes of eunuchs	*	*
20.19	3 Punishments	*	*
21.9	3 Cries	*	*
21.28–22.14	3 Parables	*	
22.15–40	3 Questions for Jesus	*	*
23.8–10	3 Warnings	*	*
23.20–22	3 Oaths	*	*
23.23	3 Spices and vegetables	*	*
23.23	3 Weightier matters – justice, mercy, and faith	*	*
26.36–46	3 Prayers	* (26.39–44)	* (26.36–45)
26.67–27.44	3 Scenes of mockery	*	* (27.39–44)
26.69–75	3 Denials of Peter	*	*
27.17–23	3 Questions from Pilate	*	* (27.17–22)
27.56	3 Women		*

[a] For Allen three 'aspirations' (6.10) give way to three 'petitions' (6.11–13).
[b] Moffat refers to 'the threefold attack on the Pharisees'; 12.2f., 10f., 24f.

Not surprisingly, then, Davies and Allison propose that large portions of Matthew's Gospel are organised in triadic sections. The Sermon on the Mount, for example, is structured in triads from beginning to end. Three sets of three beatitudes introduce the sermon (5.3–12) and correspond to the three warnings with which the sermon concludes (7.13–27). The body of the sermon itself consists of three sections that address, respectively, Torah (5.17–48), Cult (6.1–18) and Social Issues (6.19–7.12). Each of these units, in turn, is comprised of additional triads. 5.17–48, for instance, divides naturally into two groups of three so-called antitheses (5.21–32; 5.33–48). Moreover, the syntactical markers to which Allison draws attention demonstrate that this division does not exist only in the mind of a creative critic. With the exception of the third antithesis, which begins simply with ἐρρέθη δέ (5.31), ἠκούσατε ὅτι ἐρρέθη introduces each of the six antitheses.[74] The fourth in this sequence, which in Allison's scheme stands at the head of the second triad, prefaces the formula with πάλιν. The conclusion he draws is secure:

> Why the adverb? (It occurs nowhere else in the Sermon on the Mount.) The word's presence, which in no way affects the content of the surrounding material but which does break the rhythm of chap. 5, becomes explicable only if Matthew wished to indicate that with v 33 he was in some sense making Jesus start over or begin a new series. That is, πάλιν marks an editorial dividing line . . . So the evangelist is thinking in terms of triads. Rather than there being six so-called antitheses, there are actually two sets of three: 5:21–32 and 5:33–48.[75]

Allison offers three additional observations that confirm this analysis. First, in 5.31–42 the threefold ἐγὼ δὲ λέγω ὑμῖν is, in each case, followed by ὅτι. In 5.33–48 it is not. Second, the full phrase ἠκούσατε ὅτι ἐρρέθη τοῖς ἀρχαίοις appears only in the first verse of each triad (5.21, cf. 5.33). Third, '[w]hereas in 5:21–32 "But I say to you" prefaces a legal ordinance that employs ὅτι, in 5:33–48 the expression prefaces straightforward imperatives'.[76] Similar, if not always equally compelling, analysis marks the remainder of his discussion of the Matthean sermon.[77]

Davies and Allison also find evidence of the evangelist's proclivity for triadic structure in Matthew's subsequent discourses. In the Matthean parables discourse of chapter 13, the evangelist largely follows Mark through verse 23, but Matthew's introduction of new material at 13.24 also signals a return to the familiar Matthean triads. Two groups of three consecutive parables follow immediately and, once more, the clear syntactical markers present link the parables in the respective triads to each other and distinguish them formally from the other group of three. Each of the first three parables receives a formulaic introduction: ἄλλην παραβολήν + αὐτοῖς[78] + ὡμοιώθη/ὁμοία ἐστίν ἡ βασιλεία τῶν οὐρανῶν + dative. The similar, but distinct, ὁμοία ἐστίν ἡ βασιλεία τῶν οὐρανῶν + dative (or πάλιν ὁμοία . . . in the second and third parables) introduces each of the parables in the second triad (13.44, 45, 47): 'Matthew is counting as clearly as possible: ὁμοία ἐστίν, πάλιν ὁμοία ἐστίν, πάλιν ὁμοία ἐστίν: one, two, three.'[79]

Each of the parables in the second triad is, in the Synoptic tradition,[80] uniquely Matthean. For our study, however, the first of these triads is especially significant because its composition is remarkably similar to that of the triad of parables at 21.28–22.14. In both triads the first parable is unique to Matthew (13.24–30, cf. 21.28–32). Again, in both triads the second parable already stood at the corresponding place in the Marcan narrative (13.31–32, cf. 21.33–46); both Matthew and Luke include it.[81] Again, in both triads, the third parable is absent from Mark, but Luke includes a parallel in a different context (13.33, cf. 22.1–14). Probably, then, the same hand is responsible for the formation of both triads.

For Davies and Allison, the structure of the final discourse is entirely reminiscent of the parables discourse. By and large, Matthew follows his Marcan source from the beginning of chapter 24 through verse 36. Like 13.24, 24.37 signals both the end of the Marcan material and the beginning of Matthean triads. Three short hortatory parables that urge preparation for the Lord's return (24.37–51) give way to the three long eschatological parables that conclude the discourse (25.1–46).[82] When they turn to chapters 10 and 18, Davies and Allison find a triadic structure that runs right through both discourses.

Davies and Allison also detect evidence of Matthew's preference for groups of three outside of the discourses. Chapters 8 and 9, for example, are composed of nine miracle stories arranged in three groups of three (8.1–15; 8.23–9.8; 9.18–34). A summary report (8.16–17) and Jesus' encounters with two men inquiring about discipleship (8.18–22) separate the first unit from the second (8.16–22); the call of Matthew (9.9–13) and Jesus' encounter with John's disciples (9.14–17) signal the transition between the second and third triads. More dramatically, they propose that the first twelve chapters of the Gospel are organised according to a carefully planned triadic structure. Matters, however, are quite different in the rest of the Gospel: 'try as we might, we have not been able to unearth significant triads in the narrative material after chapter 13'.[83] They attribute this rather striking structural distinction to the fact that Matthew has now used up almost the entire reservoir of the Q tradition;

he reserves most of what is left for the discourses at chapters 18 and 24–25.

How should we evaluate Davies and Allison's defence of the Matthean preference for triads and the resulting structural analysis that emerges from their study? First, they have clearly demonstrated that triadic arrangement is an important structural feature of Matthew's Gospel. In several instances, as we have seen (cf. Matt. 5.21–48; 13.24–33, 44–50), they have highlighted syntactical patterns that point decisively to a deliberate organisation in triads. Second, the recognition of these (and other) obvious triads naturally prompts the reader to look for similar structural arrangements elsewhere in the Gospel. Davies and Allison, of course, do just this. Along the way, several of their proposals – for example, their analysis of the miracle stories that punctuate chapters 8 and 9 – seem quite plausible.

Nevertheless, some of their proposals do seem improbable. Where, for example, are the syntactical or conceptual markers that suggest we should find three groups of three beatitudes that stand in antithetical correspondence to the warnings that conclude the sermon (5.3–12, cf. 7.13–27)? And does the sermon conclude with three warnings or four? But perhaps this is mere quibbling. While remaining sceptical of some of the triads they propose and of the 'perfect symmetry' of their outline of chapters 1–12, I think Davies and Allison have demonstrated that the triad is a common structural feature in the First Gospel.

If, however, we grant that the evangelist was fond of triadic groupings, we must still ask, 'Of what significance is this for understanding Matthew's Gospel?' U. Luz addresses this question directly: 'The number *three* is frequent in Jewish texts. One has to beware of interpreting it as to content, for example, as a number of perfection. It is only a literary systematizing principle, one which is frequent in oral instruction.'[84] Of course, one need not assign symbolic value to the number to find Matthew's triadic grouping significant exegetically. The distinctive functions of the parable of The Sound Eye in Matthew (6.22–23) and in Luke (11.34–36) illustrate this point clearly. In the First Gospel, as part of a Matthean triad, the saying underlines the need for generosity in place of greed. In Luke the saying seems to point in a rather different direction. As Luke Johnson explains: 'Jesus as prophet is like the lamp that is lit and stood on a stand. Whether they see the light or stay in darkness depends on their choice, and whether their eye is "simple" or "evil".'[85] Chapter 5 returns to this question of the hermeneutical function of the trilogy.

Structural divisions are notoriously slippery but, even on the basis of a very conservative estimate, we must acknowledge Matthew's inclination

to arrange his material in groups of threes. The formation of the trilogy
at 21.28–22.14 certainly corresponds to this tendency, and, if Matthew's
fondness for triads establishes the plausibility that *he* designed this trilogy,
then a careful examination of the evangelist's editorial activity confirms
that this conclusion is not only plausible but also probable. Here we confront the most telling evidence that the evangelist himself is responsible
for the composition of the trilogy.

The case for Matthean redaction

Van Tilborg introduces his discussion of the formation of the trilogy in
the following sentences:

> Who has established the mutual coherence? We will have to
> go carefully here step by step. Even if it has been shown that
> the framework of the pericope Mt 21, 28–22, 14 is from Mt,
> one cannot infer from it that the unity is due to Mt. Not until
> it has been shown that the introductory verses of the parables
> have been written by Mt himself, has one found an argument
> for attributing the composition to the gospel-writer. Even this
> would only mean that Mt has placed the three parables one after
> the other. Not until it has been demonstrated that the stresses
> that have been laid here correspond to what we know about Mt
> from elsewhere, is the proof conclusive. Only then can Mt be
> the author of this pericope in its totality.[86]

Van Tilborg chooses the framework of the pericope as his point of departure; we begin here as well.

The narrative framework

In fact, Van Tilborg acknowledges that Matthew's careful redaction of
21.23–27 and 22.15–22 does provide a distinctive framework for these
parables.[87] According to Van Tilborg, although Matthew takes over traditional Marcan material in both of these pericopes, the evangelist's redaction – especially of their introductions – grants to them distinctive shape,
and modifies their function in the narrative. At 21.23 Van Tilborg attributes to the evangelist's redactional hand προσέρχομαι, οἱ ἀρχιερεῖς
καὶ οἱ πρεσβύτεροι τοῦ λαοῦ, and διδάσκοντι, the last of which he judges
especially important: 'The pericope Mt 21, 23–25, 46 is seen through the
eyes of Mt as the exercise of the teaching-activity of Jesus.'[88] Nor is
Matthew's editorial shaping of 22.15 insignificant. The evangelist takes

over the traditional Marcan notion of the testing of Jesus (Mark 12.13b) but rewrites it in anticipation of the distinctive features of 22.15–46. The Pharisees who *take counsel*,

> are the subject in the verses that follow until Jesus silences them (22, 46). As far as Mt is concerned 22, 15–46 forms a unit. The Pharisees of 22, 15 are structurally connected with those of 22, 34 and 22, 41. This is the reason why Mt 22, 15 can be said to have been transformed by Mt to fit his pattern.[89]

Van Tilborg concludes that since the evangelist himself has carefully edited the traditional framework into which these parables are set, '[i]f the linking verses between the parables could now be attributed to Mt, one could say that Mt has placed the parables one after another'. Nevertheless, he continues: 'the conclusive arguments proving this cannot be found'.[90] On the contrary, however, I think that there is strong evidence of Matthean redaction in these linking verses.

The relevant seams

Matthew 21.28. With τί δὲ ὑμῖν δοκεῖ Jesus poses the question that links the first of the parables to its narrative context. δοκέω itself is not especially Matthean (Matt. 10x; Mark 2x; Luke 10x). The introductory question, however, is another matter: it occurs six times in the Synoptic tradition, but nowhere outside of Matthew.[91] Twice the question occurs in material that is unique to Matthew (17.25; 21.28). Elsewhere the question introduces material that Matthew shares with either Luke (18.12) or Mark (22.17, 42; 26.66), but each time the question stands only in the First Gospel. Moreover, in the LXX[92] and NT outside of the Synoptics, the formula occurs only at John 11.56 and there with different word order (τί δοκεῖ ὑμῖν;). There is little reason, then, to attribute the question in its current form to pre-Matthean tradition, but every reason to think that the evangelist himself is responsible for this introduction.[93]

Matthew 21.31b–32. If Van Tilborg has demonstrated that the evangelist has been active in editing the framework into which these parables have been set, perhaps he has failed to note the importance of the links to this narrative framework *from within the trilogy*. The most obvious, and perhaps the most important, of these links stands at 21.32. There Jesus grounds the exclusion of the Jewish leaders from the kingdom (21.31c) in their rejection of the Father's ambassador, the Baptist: ἦλθεν γὰρ Ἰωάννης πρὸς ὑμᾶς ἐν ὁδῷ δικαιοσύνης, καὶ οὐκ ἐπιστεύσατε αὐτῷ.

But οὐκ ἐπιστεύσατε αὐτῷ clearly echoes the words of the chief priests and elders from the preceding pericope (21.25, cf. Mark 12.31) and turns their musings into a powerful self-indictment. As 21.32 unfolds, the phrase is repeated twice in slightly modified form as the evangelist sets out the stark contrast between the Jewish leaders and the tax gatherers and prostitutes they despise. Even if we were to grant that these parables already circulated as a unit in pre-Matthean tradition, it seems clear that this accommodation to the preceding context that dominates verse 32 is one that takes place when the parable[s] is inserted into the *Marcan* framework and so, most naturally, by the evangelist himself.[94] This point is only strengthened when it is coupled with the demonstration that at the other relevant 'seams' we find further evidence of Matthean redaction.

Matthew 21.33.   Matthew's introduction to The Tenants differs from Mark's in three ways and, in each case, there is every reason to think that the evangelist himself is responsible for the alteration. Most obviously, Mark's καὶ ἤρξατο αὐτοῖς . . . λαλεῖν has fallen by the wayside since, in Matthew, this is *not* the beginning of Jesus' parabolic response to the challenge of his authority (21.23, cf. 21.28–32). A second redactional change is closely related – Mark's ἐν παραβολαῖς becomes ἄλλην παραβολήν. Both Matthew and Luke have modified Mark's plural ἐν παραβολαῖς, perhaps finding ἤρξατο αὐτοῖς ἐν παραβολαῖς λαλεῖν a curious introduction to the single parable that Mark records.[95] But, whereas Luke simply replaces the plural παραβολαῖς with the singular παραβολήν, Matthew imports two other parables into this context with the result that the Matthean Jesus does speak *in parables* to his adversaries (21.28–22.14).

Comparison with Matthew's treatment of Mark 4 lends further support to this suggestion. There Mark reports that Jesus taught the crowd in many parables (ἐν παραβολαῖς πολλά; 4.2). Again, at the conclusion of the Marcan discourse, we read: καὶ τοιαύταις παραβολαῖς πολλαῖς ἐλάλει αὐτοῖς τὸν λόγον . . . (4.33). In his parallel account, Matthew reworks the Marcan summary so that it now reads: Ταῦτα πάντα ἐλάλησεν ὁ Ἰησοῦς ἐν παραβολαῖς τοῖς ὄχλοις. But, although Matthew has eliminated Mark's reference to the many other parables that Jesus taught, he seems to have taken his cue from it and imported at least five other parables into this context. Here Matthew appears to have responded to the plural ἐν παραβολαῖς in similar fashion. ἄλλην παραβολήν, then, both introduces this parable and links it to the first in the trilogy – The Two Sons. Finally, the modification of the Marcan introduction is completed with the insertion of ἀκούσατε.

Moreover, the introduction as it now stands bears clear traces of Matthean style. While neither ἄλλος nor παραβολή is distinctively Matthean, ἄλλην παραβολήν, which never occurs in Mark or Luke,[96] introduces each of the three parables in another Matthean triad (13.24–33) with important compositional parallels to the triad at 21.28–22.14.[97] Although these parables in chapter 13 appear to arise from distinct sources, in each case ἄλλην παραβολήν comprises part of the uniquely Matthean introduction. The most economical explanation is that the phrase comes from Matthew's pen.[98] As there (13.24, 31, 33), so also here (21.33).

The insertion of ἀκούσατε points towards the same conclusion.[99] ἀκούω features prominently in the vocabulary of each of the evangelists, especially in parabolic contexts, but in the Synoptic tradition only here and at Matthew 13.18 does παραβολήν stand as the object of ἀκούω. Both here (21.33) and at 13.18, the most plausible explanation for the presence of ἀκούω is that Matthew has inserted it into the traditional account he has taken over from Mark. As I shall argue in later discussion of 21.33, this fits well with Matthew's distinctive use of ἀκούω in these two contexts. Besides 13.18 and 21.33, one other text is noteworthy. At 15.10, following Mark, Matthew's Jesus calls for hearing and understanding of his parable about the nature of defilement. By eliminating the μου that follows ἀκούσατε in Mark, Matthew shifts the focus subtly from hearing *Jesus*, as in Mark, to hearing the *parable*. Like τί δὲ ὑμῖν δοκεῖ; which introduced The Two Sons, ἄλλην παραβολὴν ἀκούσατε should be attributed to the evangelist himself.

Van Tilborg acknowledges that there is some reason to speak of Matthean redaction in 21.33, but remains sceptical and insists that '[t]he main point of the argument has to be sought in Mt 21,45–46; 22, 1',[100] which he concludes are largely traditional. One might wonder why 22.1 and 21.45–46 should be given preference over 21.(28, 31-)33 in this evaluation of sources. But, in any case, the evidence for Matthean redaction at 21.45–46 and 22.1 seems more compelling than he allows.

Matthew 21.45–46.   Matthew 21.45–46 looks like a typically Matthean modification of his Marcan source. ἀκούσαντες recalls the distinctive ἀκούσατε (21.33), with which Matthew introduces the parable, and is itself probably redactional. ἀκούσας frequently provides a narrative link in Matthew.[101] Furthermore if, as I shall argue below,[102] ἄλλην παραβολὴν ἀκούσατε (21.33) recalls Matthew's parables discourse and, especially the parable of The Sower, then Matthew's use of ἀκούσαντες (21.45) is laden with irony, underlining the failure of the Jewish leaders *genuinely to hear* the parable.

This is not the first time that Matthew has highlighted the failure of the Jewish leaders to hear Jesus' teaching with his ironic use of ἀκούω. We have already noted Matthew's redaction of the Marcan parable of The Things that Defile (15.10–12, cf. Mark 7.14–15) where, by eliminating Mark's μοῦ (along with πάντες), Matthew subtly changes the object of Jesus' charge to listen from Jesus himself to the parable he is about to speak (15.10). As in The Tenants, this modification of the Marcan introduction recalls The Sower (cf. 13.18). The elimination of μοῦ πάντες also has the effect of tightening the link between ἀκούετε καὶ συνίετε which, in turn, clearly recalls Matthew's distinctive employment of συνίημι with ἀκούω in 13.12–23.[103] More importantly for our purposes here, following the brief parable Matthew adds in verse 12 – which apart from reference to the disciples is entirely without parallel in Mark – Τότε προσελθόντες οἱ μαθηταὶ λέγουσιν αὐτῷ· οἶδας ὅτι οἱ Φαρισαῖοι ἀκούσαντες τὸν λόγον ἐσκανδαλίσθησαν; as in the Matthean parable of The Tenants, then, Jesus introduces the parable with the charge to hear. And as in The Tenants, the Jewish leaders in Matthew 15 do indeed hear, but ἀκούοντες οὐκ ἀκούουσιν οὐδὲ συνίουσιν (13.13). Most probably, then, ἀκούσαντες in both 15.12 and 21.45 comes from the hand of the evangelist himself. Nor is this the only clear signal of Matthean redaction.

Mark's singular τὴν παραβολήν becomes τὰς παραβολὰς αὐτοῦ to accommodate the prior insertion of The Two Sons. Similarly, because for Matthew Jesus' parabolic response to the Jewish leadership will also include The Wedding Feast, Mark's καὶ ἀφέντες αὐτὸν ἀπῆλθον can no longer stand here – Matthew postpones it until 22.22. Again, in accord with Matthean preference, τοὺς ὄχλους now replaces Mark's τὸν ὄχλον.[104] More importantly, Matthew's careful reworking of Mark 12.12 enables him to underline the important parallelism between Jesus and John the Baptist. Mark 12.12 reads: καὶ ἐζήτουν αὐτὸν κρατῆσαι, καὶ ἐφοβήθησαν τὸν ὄχλον, ἔγνωσαν γὰρ ὅτι πρὸς αὐτοὺς τὴν παραβολὴν εἶπεν. The final clause introduced by γάρ seems to explain why the Jewish leaders wanted to arrest Jesus.[105] Matthew substitutes for this final clause, the substance of which he records earlier (21.45), his own unique conclusion with the result that his text now reads: καὶ ζητοῦντες αὐτὸν κρατῆσαι ἐφοβήθησαν τοὺς ὄχλους, ἐπεὶ εἰς προφήτην αὐτὸν εἶχον (21.46). In Matthew's version this last clause now explains not why they wanted to arrest Jesus, but why they feared the crowds: because the crowds held Jesus to be a prophet. And this plainly recalls Matthew's redaction of the Marcan report of the Baptist's execution. There, against Mark, Matthew asserts that, although Herod wanted to kill John: ἐφοβήθη τὸν ὄχλον, ὅτι ὡς προφήτην αὐτὸν εἶχον (14.5, cf. 21.11, 26).

Finally, Mark's indefinite reference to the Jewish leaders (ἐζήτουν; 12.12) gives way to οἱ ἀρχιερεῖς καὶ οἱ Φαρισαῖοι in Matthew (21.45). Van Tilborg insists that this addition supports his case:

> An important argument in favour of the traditional character of the verse is the subject οἱ ἀρχιερεῖς καὶ οἱ Φαρισαῖοι. Not only is this combination not found anywhere else in Mt except in Mt 27, 62, but there is also the element that it does not fit in with Mt 21, 23. If Mt edited 21, 23, it would have been much easier for him to edit 21, 45, because Mk 12, 12, left the subject undetermined.[106]

Once more, however, I find Van Tilborg's argument unconvincing. It is surprising to find sudden reference to the Pharisees when Jesus has clearly been engaged in dispute with the chief priests and elders of the people (21.23). But, in this narrative, redactional references to the Pharisees in polemical contexts are certainly not uncommon. More importantly, the insertion here clearly anticipates 22.15 – the redactional bridge between the trilogy and the subsequent series of disputes – which, as Van Tilborg himself acknowledges, looks forward to the redactional references to the Pharisees at 22.34, 41. 22.15–46, in turn, prepares for and gives way to Jesus' final denunciation of the scribes and Pharisees that extends throughout chapter 23. In this context, then, it is hardly necessary to appeal to prior tradition to explain the reference to the Pharisees at 21.45.[107] Once more, the links from within the trilogy to the Matthean framework in which it is set bear witness to the evangelist's deliberate editorial activity.

Matthew 22.1. For Jones, Matthew 22.1 points emphatically to pre-Matthean tradition: 'The Matthean parable of the Feast (22:1) provides evidence that there was a grouping of several parables at a pre-Matthean stage: every item in the verse, including its curious word order, points to tradition rather than to Matthean editorial activity.'[108] He notes that the position of αὐτοῖς is unusual (finding a parallel in Matthew only at 13.13), and that nowhere else in the Synoptic tradition do we find either the formula ἀποκριθεὶς . . . εἶπεν punctuated by πάλιν or a modifying phrase between εἶπεν and αὐτοῖς. Furthermore, he adds that, unlike here, elsewhere in Matthew the plural παραβολαῖς is explicable in terms of context. Finally, he observes that there is nothing, contextually, to which ἀποκριθεὶς . . . εἶπεν responds.[109] Van Tilborg raises still another objection: if 22.1 were Matthean, we should expect δέ to take its normal place in the formula but instead we find καί.[110]

Nevertheless, I think that 22.1 should also be attributed to the First Evangelist rather than to prior tradition. The position of αὐτοῖς is indeed unusual, but 13.13 offers a more important parallel than Jones allows since there the construction is uniquely Matthean (diff Mark) and since there, as here, αὐτοῖς is preceded by ἐν παραβολαῖς. Moreover, 13.34 is remarkably similar: Ταῦτα πάντα ἐλάλησεν ὁ Ἰησοῦς ἐν παραβολαῖς τοῖς ὄχλοις . . . Once more the construction is unique to Matthew (diff Mark) and, once more, ἐν παραβολαῖς precedes the indirect object. In fact, of the six times that we meet ἐν παραβολαῖς in Matthew's Gospel, only once (13.3; par Mark) does the indirect object precede this prepositional phrase.[111] As part of this construction, then, it is difficult to dismiss the position of αὐτοῖς as 'un-Matthean'. These same observations remove the sting from the objection that nowhere else do we find a modifying phrase between εἶπεν and αὐτοῖς since nowhere else does Matthew use εἶπεν . . . αὐτοῖς in conjunction with ἐν παραβολαῖς. And, while πάλιν occurs with this formula only here, elsewhere in Matthew it does function, as here, to link a Matthean triad of parables (cf. 13.45, 47). These supposed departures from Matthean style, then, must be balanced by a consideration of other distinctively Matthean features and the unique requirements of each context.

With respect to the *inexplicable* use of the plural παραβολαῖς here, the fact that Matthew has altered Mark's παραβολαῖς in his introduction to the previous parable makes it unlikely that he has adopted a traditional reading uncritically here. More probably the evangelist chooses the plural form deliberately, perhaps in part under the influence of Mark 12.1, but probably also, and more importantly, with a conscious glance backward towards chapter 13. The phrase appears six times in Matthew's Gospel; its five other occurrences are all found in chapter 13 where it describes Jesus' chosen method of communication to those who, although they look and hear, refuse to see and understand.[112] As I noted briefly above, by framing the introduction and conclusion to the parable of The Tenants as he has, Matthew has portrayed the Jewish leaders as classic examples of those whose spiritual senses are failing – hear as they might, they fail to understand. Once more, then, at the outset of the third parable in his trilogy, Matthew returns to this theme with this distinctive echo of ἐν παραβολαῖς from chapter 13. The Matthean Jesus speaks ἐν παραβολαῖς because of his hearers. Far from being inexplicable, the use of ἐν παραβολαῖς binds this parable to the preceding one by pointing back to 13.10–17.[113]

As to Matthew's use of the formula here ('To what does 22.1 reply?'), two brief observations may be made. First, it is just possible that Matthew intends to remind his readers that this parable continues (πάλιν) Jesus' response to the challenge of his authority (cf. 21.23–27). Alternatively, the use is formulaic as, on occasion, it seems to be elsewhere in Matthew.[114] In either case, its presence offers little support for the conclusion that 22.1 is pre-Matthean.

Finally, while it is more common in Matthew to find the conjunction δέ introducing the formula (ἀποκριθεὶς . . . εἶπεν), seven times in Matthew καί introduces the formula. Of these, 11.4 (par Luke 7.22) and 21.27 (par Mark 11.33) are certainly traditional, but the remainder are unique to Matthew. Matthew 8.8 (diff Luke) reads: καὶ ἀποκριθεὶς ὁ ἑκατόνταρχος ἔφη. At 24.4, Mark's ὁ δὲ Ἰησοῦς ἤρξατο λέγειν αὐτοῖς (13.5) gives way to Matthew's καὶ ἀποκριθεὶς ὁ Ἰησοῦς ειπεν αὐτοῖς. In the uniquely Matthean portrait of the last judgement, καί once more introduces the formula, now with the finite verb in the future tense: καὶ ἀποκριθεὶς ὁ βασιλεὺς ἐρεῖ αὐτοῖς (25.40). Finally at 27.25 in the distinctively Matthean insertion into the Marcan trial narrative we read: καὶ ἀποκριθεὶς πᾶς ὁ λαὸς εἶπεν. Matthew prefers ὁ δὲ ἀποκριθεὶς εἶπεν, but there is surely enough variation in his use of this formula to account for the presence of καί here without appealing to an earlier tradition.

On closer inspection, then, the supposed irregularities in Matthean style at 22.1 are all explicable and, in some instances, actually provide positive evidence for Matthean redaction. As at 21.28, 31–32, 33, 45–46, here at 22.1 there seems to be little reason to appeal to pre-Matthean tradition. On the contrary, the positive evidence of Matthean redaction is striking; but that is precisely what one would expect if the evangelist himself was responsible for insertion of The Two Sons and The Wedding Feast on either side of The Tenants and, thus, for the formation of still another triad.

Conclusion

Both Matthew's demonstrable preference for triads, and, especially, the evidence of his editorial activity suggests that the evangelist himself has constructed this trilogy. As we shall see, the convergence of several distinctively Matthean theological motifs in this trilogy offers confirmation of this conclusion. We must, however, reserve our discussion of these for chapters 5 and 6. Before that, we turn our attention in chapters 3 and 4 to an examination of the wider Matthean narrative and the manner in which it helps shape the reader's reception of this trilogy. Chapter 3 focuses in particular upon Matthew's characterisation of the nation of Israel, her leaders and their people, and chapter 4 upon Matthew's portrait of the nations.

PART TWO

The trilogy in narrative-critical perspective

3

JESUS' ENCOUNTER WITH ISRAEL:
THE NATION, ITS LEADERS AND
THEIR PEOPLE

I suggested in chapter 1 that narrative criticism has a role to play in the re-habilitation of the Synoptic parables both as stories worth examination in their own right (not merely as the necessary starting points for reconstruct-ing Jesus' parables) and as part of the evangelists' wider communicative actions. Part two of this study aims to contribute to this rehabilitation. Chapters 3 and 4 consider the relationship of the parables to the wider narrative, asking both what impact they make upon the developing story-line and, especially, how this wider story influences the reader's reception of the trilogy. Chapter 5 attends to the parables themselves, exploring the ways in which this trilogy addresses its readers.

In this third chapter, we turn our attention to the narrative's portrait of Israel for the following reasons. First, the trilogy is set in the midst of Jesus' escalating conflict with the Jewish establishment. Second, Jesus addresses each of these parables to the Jewish leaders. Third, The Tenants rehearses the story of Jesus' reception in Israel. Fourth, following both The Two Sons and The Tenants, the Jewish people are distinguished from their leaders. Fifth, from the earliest scenes, Jesus' encounter with Israel is seldom far from centre stage in the dramatic story that Matthew tells. Indeed, at one level, Matthew's narrative *is* the story of Jesus' encounter with Israel. Sixth, this story is already well advanced before the reader meets this trilogy of parables. Finally, throughout the church's history exegetes have found in this trilogy the declaration of Israel's salvation–historical loss and her replacement, by the church, as the people of God. This chapter, then, aims to elucidate the manner in which the larger story that this Gospel tells of Jesus' encounter with Israel might have been expected to shape the reception of these parables.

Because of the prominent role granted to comparison and contrast in ancient narratives[1] – not least this Gospel – and because of the explicit juxtaposition of the Jewish leaders and the people in 21.31b–32, 45–46, special attention is given to the narrative's portrait of the leaders vis-à-vis the people in assessing Israel's role in the plot of Matthew's story. I treat, first, in the same order as they appear in the story, those texts in which both the leaders and the people appear, before turning, secondly, to a brief summary of Matthew's portrayal of these groups elsewhere in the Gospel.

Primarily, then, I intend to ask what sort of responses a careful reading of the wider narrative evokes from the *reader*. Occasionally I summon redaction criticism as an ally: where there is evidence of the process of design that offers assistance in isolating the responses for which the *evangelist* hoped, I attempt to draw out its significance.[2]

My conclusion is simple: the wider story of Jesus' encounter with Israel that this narrative relates invites the reader to conclude that the judgement pronounced in this trilogy cannot be restricted to Israel's leadership. Nevertheless, while Matthew's polemic against the Jewish leadership is bitter and unrelenting, he has crafted his narrative in a manner that seems designed to elicit sympathy for the people. This sharp distinction that Matthew draws between the leaders and the people serves chiefly to distinguish levels of culpability and secondarily, perhaps, to suggest that, far from abandoning hope for the people of Israel, the evangelist envisions and engages in a continued mission to them.

3.1   Characterisation by analogy: the Jewish leaders and the people

Looking back: Israel in the preceding narrative (1.1–21.27)

Matthew 2.1–23

The Jewish leaders make their first appearance in Matthew's story with the arrival of the Magi in chapter 2, in a narrative segment laden with irony.[3] Summoned and questioned by the king, the response of the chief priests and scribes[4] to Herod's question marks them as experts in the Scriptures, but, while *they* know where Messiah is to be born, only *the Gentile Magi* proceed to Bethlehem to pay homage. That Herod summons the Jewish leaders seems significant, since the narrative will subsequently reveal them to be allies of the Herods.[5] The narrative's presentation of Herod underscores the seriousness of this alliance. In this series of episodes, he is marked chiefly by his ruthless and persistent opposition to the child–king. His deceitful design thwarted by the Magi, or rather by God himself (2.12), Herod erupts in rage and issues a command that exposes both his real purpose and the desperate, violent, measures he is willing to take to achieve that goal (2.16). Repeated references to the divine intervention necessary to protect the child reinforce this characterisation of Herod as the would-be murderer of the young Messiah (2.12, 13, 20, 22–23).

The people make only a fleeting appearance in these scenes. From the lips of the Magi, we learn that a king has been born (2.2) who will, as the Scriptures say, shepherd his people Israel (2.6).[6] Not surprisingly, King Herod's interest is piqued, and he is troubled. Curiously 'all[7] Jerusalem' echoes his response. Will Jerusalem also join hands with Herod? The evangelist has crafted his narrative, preparing the reader for an encounter between this city and her king many years hence. For now, the mixed portrait of the people that emerges here leaves the question open.

Matthew 3.1–10

Like the arrival of the Magi, the appearance of the Baptist also evokes response from Israel. But, whereas 'all Jerusalem' had been troubled by the claims of the Magi, now 'Jerusalem, and all Judea, and all the region about the Jordan' flock to the Baptist, confessing their sins (3.5–6). And, if the people are especially responsive to John's preaching, then this positive characterisation becomes more pronounced in contrast to the portrait of their leaders painted in 3.7–10.

Like the people, the leaders – here the Pharisees and Sadducees – are drawn to John's baptism. But John greets them with stinging words that question their sincerity (3.7b), underline their need for 'fruit worthy of repentance' (3.8), challenge dependence on their privileged ancestry (3.9) and threaten destruction and judgement (3.10).[8]

Matthew 7.28–29

At the conclusion of the Sermon on the Mount, Matthew records the crowds'[9] response to Jesus' teaching. They were astonished 'for he taught them as one having authority, and not as their scribes'. The nature of this distinctive authority is a crucial issue to which the narrative will return. Here, in the minds of the crowds, it separates Jesus from their teachers. This perception seems to depict Jesus and the religious authorities as rival leaders, to whom the masses may grant allegiance. Openness to Jesus' teaching distances the people from their leaders.[10]

Matthew 9.2–8

In 9.2–8, a group of scribes is characterised by their own thoughts (or, perhaps, private speech: εἶπαν ἐν ἑαυτοῖς [9.3]), by Jesus' rebuke and, once more, by comparison with the crowds. A controversy erupts when Jesus declares the sins of a paralysed man forgiven. Not surprisingly, a group of scribes is indignant. The reader is granted access, with Jesus, to their thoughts: οὗτος βλασφημεῖ (9.3).[11] Knowing exactly what the scribes think, the reader immediately learns what Jesus thinks. His response shapes the reader's perception of the scribes' objection: to challenge the authority of the Son of Man to forgive sins is not merely to defend the divine prerogative to forgive,[12] but to think evil![13] Only at the conclusion of the pericope, after Jesus heals the man and thus vindicates his authority to forgive, are the crowds introduced. In stark contrast to the scribes who, accusing Jesus of blasphemy, 'think evil in their hearts', the crowds are afraid[14] and praise God. No mention is made of the scribes' response: they are conspicuous by their absence.[15]

Matthew 9.9–13

At 9.9–13, the Jewish leaders (but now the Pharisees) are again characterised by their objection to Jesus' action – here his table fellowship with tax collectors and sinners – and by the rebuke he issues in response. But, in this response, Jesus also invokes the prophet Hosea[16] with the result that the Pharisees are portrayed as failing to understand their own Scriptures and, thus, failing to understand (and so obey) the central place that God has assigned to mercy. In essence, the Pharisees are depicted as religious leaders whose misguided religious concerns have prevented them from serving their people and thus from penetrating to the heart of faithful allegiance to their God. While the Pharisees despise the tax gatherers and sinners, Jesus sits at table with them (9.10) and invites them to a life of discipleship (9.9, 13).

Matthew 9.32–34

As at 9.1–8, but perhaps more poignantly, in 9.32–34 the crowds and the leaders are characterised by their response to Jesus – here, to his deliverance of a dumb demoniac. In contrast to the crowds who marvel and say, 'Never was anything like this seen in Israel', and also in contrast to the blind men who in the preceding pericope address Jesus as the Son of David, the Pharisees counter:[17] 'By the prince of demons he casts out demons.'[18] The evangelist presents not merely two different responses to Jesus' mission, but a second response intent on subverting the first: 'the crowds grope towards recognition of Jesus but are cut off by the Pharisees, who themselves cannot hear or speak the truth'.[19] Again the reader is left with the impression that the Jewish leaders care little for the plight of their people. The release of the demoniac is of little consequence to the Pharisees.[20]

Matthew 9.36–38

Matthew 9.36–38 depicts not the people's response to Jesus but rather his response to them. Granted an 'inside view'[21] of Jesus' perception of the crowds, the reader sees them through his eyes: they are 'harassed and helpless like sheep without a shepherd' (cf. Num. 27.17). Their condition elicits compassion from Jesus, and from the sympathetic reader who, knowing Jesus' identity (1.1–25, cf. 3.13–17), naturally adopts his perspective. The harvest that 9.37–38 envisages is surely to be reaped among these abandoned sheep. This pericope is not, then, in the first instance at least, about the Jewish leaders, but the plight of the sheep is also an indictment of the shepherds (cf. especially Ezek. 34). In this case, if Matthew's wider narrative is to guide us, not only have the shepherds left the sheep to the ravages of the wild animals, but they themselves have harassed their flock.[22]

Matthew 11.16–19

Matthew 11.16–19 is representative of a series of texts in which Jesus indicts 'this generation'.[23] Since 11.7, with the departure of John's disciples, Jesus has been addressing the crowds. As such, when he turns in these verses to bring his charge against 'this generation', the reader naturally thinks quite broadly of Jesus' contemporaries, of whom the crowds are representative. But, while this conclusion would not quite be wrong, closer analysis casts a rather different light on the matter. The responses of 'this generation' to John and Jesus here delineated are noteworthy (11.18–19). Thus far in the story the only ones set in opposition to John are the Jewish authorities (3.7–10).[24] Nor will this change as the narrative develops. From beginning to end, the people embrace John as a prophet (3.1–6, cf. 14.5; 21.23–27, 28–32) while, like Herod who takes his life (14.1–12), the religious leaders reject both the Baptist's authority and his call for repentance (21.23–27, 28–32). Similarly, the only opposition to Jesus' association with the tax gatherers and sinners has come from the Pharisees (9.10–13). Moreover, the reference to Jesus' association with these marginalised characters reminds us that the rejection of the generation was not absolute. All of this encourages the reader to think *first* of the Jewish leaders when Jesus arraigns 'this generation'.

The special prominence of the Pharisees in the remaining 'this generation' texts perhaps confirms this reading.[25] Nevertheless, that the cities
of Chorazin, Bethsaida, and Capernaum are condemned in the following
pericope (11.20–24) suggests that Jesus' indictment of 'this generation'
cannot be limited to its leadership.

Matthew 11.28–30

Matthew does not identify the audience that receives Jesus' invitation at
11.28–30. On the one hand, Jesus' invitation may beckon 'hard-pressed'
disciples since 11.25–27 contrasts the disciples ('babes') with the wise
and learned and since, after the mission discourse of chapter 10, Jesus'
followers might appropriately be described as those 'who labour and are
heavy laden'.[26] On the other hand, 11.7–24 is explicitly addressed to
the crowds; πάντες (11.28) is an inclusive term; 12.1–14, which follows
immediately, suggests that the phrase may at least equally well describe
those who suffer under the excessive load placed on them by the Jewish
leaders; and 23.4, with its similar terminology and clear reference to the
oppression of the people by the scribes and Pharisees, may suggest that
here, too, the crowds are in view.[27] If we should think of the audience
as the crowds, then the resulting portrait bears striking resemblance to
that offered in 9.36–38. The crowds become the recipients of the onerous
demands of their leaders on the one hand and of Jesus' gentle invitation
on the other.

Matthew 12.22–32

Matthew 12.22–24 deliberately points the reader back to 9.32–34.[28] As
there, so also here Jesus delivers a dumb demoniac – here blind as well.
The demon having been cast out, once more the crowds marvel. Their
speech, however, seems to suggest an advance in understanding of Jesus'
person and mission: the hesitant 'Can this be the Son of David?' replaces the now inappropriate 'Never was anything like this seen in Israel'
(9.33).[29] Are they at the point of perception? But if the crowds' position has progressed, the Pharisees' has not. Resolute in their opposition
to Jesus, the Pharisees quickly repeat their earlier accusation (9.34, cf.
10.25): far from being the Son of David, he is in league with Satan![30] Is
it incidental that this demoniac is blind as well as dumb? Immediately
before the first of the Matthean doublets (9.32–34), Jesus had healed two
blind men who had proclaimed him Son of David (9.27–31). Even before
their sight was restored, they saw more clearly than either the crowds or

the leaders. Here, while the demoniac receives his sight, the crowds hover at the point of perception, and the Pharisees stubbornly refuse to see.[31] Once more, the line between the crowds and their leaders is drawn starkly. The crowds are to be pitied; their queries about Jesus' true identity are crushed by their leaders.

Matthew 15.1–20

At 15.1–11, 15–20, the Pharisees and scribes are characterised once more by their encounter with Jesus.[32] After the series of incidents in which the Jewish leaders have objected to the behaviour of Jesus or his disciples and against the backdrop of Jesus' ministry of healing among the people (14.34–36, cf. 14.13–14), the reader is prepared to see in their complaint (15.2) another instance of their focus on things trivial. Jesus' answer confirms this expectation (15.3). The tradition that the Pharisees guard so zealously is merely a collection of man-made rules that avails for nothing in establishing and maintaining purity (15.11, 15–20). As Jesus portrays them, they are teachers without understanding. Worse, they are hypocrites whose allegiance to God is only verbal. Their elevation of human tradition has made them enemies of God's word.[33]

At 15.12–14 the polemic continues. Hearing Jesus' response to their complaints, the Pharisees have been scandalised. Jesus has just called the crowd to hear and understand (cf. 13.18–23); the Pharisees have heard his pronouncement, but once more their senses have been dulled (cf. 13.15). They have become paradigmatic of those whose hard hearts prevent perception. Nor does the irony end here. Though they may perceive themselves as God's own plant and as guides for the blind,[34] Jesus insists they are blind guides[35] who, not having been planted by God (cf. 13.38?), will be uprooted.

The crowd has only a minor role to play in this pericope. As in the parables discourse, they are given instruction but not interpretation (15.10–11, cf. 15.15–20), but, if they remain outside, they are as much to be pitied as blamed. Blind guides are leading them into a pit (15.14).

Matthew 19.1–9

As Jesus leaves Galilee and moves towards Jerusalem, great crowds continue to follow him[36] and he continues to heal them.[37] But, while the crowds continue to be the beneficiaries of Jesus' mission, the Jewish leaders continue to challenge him. Following the lead of the tempter (4.3, cf. 4.1), in 19.3–9 the Pharisees put Jesus to the test, engaging him in a debate about divorce.[38] As in earlier legal disputes, Jesus wins the day. On his lips οὐκ ἀνέγνωτε[39] again (cf. 12.3, 5) underlines the failure of the Jewish leaders to understand the significance of their own Scriptures.

Matthew 21.1–17

The passage at 21.1–11 marks the pinnacle of the popular allegiance to Jesus. Spreading both garments and branches on the road ahead of him (21.8, cf. 2 Kgs. 9.13), the crowds[40] hail Jesus as the Son of David who comes in the name of the Lord (21.9, cf. Ps. 118.25). This is the only time they declare him to be Son of David, here echoing the cry of the blind men they had only recently rebuked (20.29–34) and anticipating the confession of the children in the temple (21.15). As the procession that has proclaimed Jesus their Davidic king enters the city, 'the whole city of Jerusalem' is shaken (21.10, cf. 2.3!), asking 'who is this?' It is possible to regard the crowds' response – 'This is the prophet Jesus from Nazareth of Galilee' (21.11) – as a regression that reveals that they have spoken the truth unwittingly in hailing Jesus as the Son of David.[41] More probably, however, these verses[42] underline a motif that this narrative elsewhere highlights. It is as a *prophet*[43] (cf. 21.33–46; 23.29–39) that Jesus enters the city of his destiny (cf. 16.21–23; 17.12–13, 22–23; 20.18–19). Inside the city, Jesus briefly occupies the temple where he heals the blind and the lame (21.12–14). But, angered by the wonders he performs[44] and by the cries of the children ('Hosanna to the Son of David'), the Jewish leaders, embroiled in conflict with Jesus, are unable to rejoice at the display of God's mercy.[45] And yet again, in contrast to the blind (20.30–31) – here joined by the crowds (21.8–9) and the children (21.15) – they cannot see Jesus' identity as the Son of David.

Matthew 21.23–27

In the aftermath of Jesus' royal entry into the city and his demonstrations in the temple, the chief priests and elders of the people confront Jesus upon his return to the temple, challenging him with an issue that has been live at least since their first open confrontation (9.1–8) and, for the reader, since the conclusion of the Sermon (7.28–29): 'By what authority are you doing these things, and who gave you this authority?' The leaders present themselves as defenders of orthodoxy. But, when Jesus responds in kind with a question about John's authority, they retreat into private discussion, which paints quite another picture: they are those who reject God's appointed messenger (cf. 3.1–6) but are compelled to be silent, paralysed by their fear of the crowd.[46] The crowd indirectly comes to

Jesus' defence because the people had embraced the prophet whom their leaders had dismissed.

The impact of the preceding narrative on the reception of the trilogy

The frequent juxtaposition of the Jewish authorities and the people and the sharp distinction between the two character groups that emerges in the preceding narrative (including the immediately preceding 21.23–27) have prepared the reader to expect similar disparity here. This expectation will not be disappointed. Jesus' application of The Two Sons contrasts the chief priests and elders of the people not merely with the people but with the notoriously impious among the people: while the tax gatherers and prostitutes have heard the voice of God on the lips of his prophet the Baptist and repented, the authorities have persistently refused to repent and have thus failed to do the will of the Father (cf. 3.7–10). The people they despise enter God's kingdom before them (21.31b–32, cf. 21.23, 26).

Similar observations can be made of The Tenants. Together, Jesus' story of the vineyard and the chief priests and Pharisees' response depicts them as the last in a long line of Jewish leaders who have rejected, abused and murdered God's servants. Their opposition to Jesus is all too predictable, but, if the parable presents the Jewish leaders as Jesus' mortal enemies, then it also depicts the crowds as his defender. As their estimate of John had earlier immobilised this same group of leaders (cf. 21.25),[47] so now the crowds' similar regard for Jesus keeps their leaders at bay (21.46). Each of the three parables is not only addressed to the Jewish leaders, but also marked by a stinging indictment of the Jewish establishment. Prima facie, there is no comparable condemnation of the people.

Not surprisingly, then, a growing number of scholars have abandoned the more traditional interpretation that finds in these parables an indictment of the nation.[48] On the contrary, the judgement that Jesus declares is reserved for the Jewish leadership alone. J. A. Overman's comments are representative:

> In no way does this passage . . . denote the rejection of Israel, or Jews. And it does not denote that Matthew understands his community as somehow separate from other Jews and from Israel. The people under scrutiny here, and those being judged by Jesus' words, are the leaders with whom he is contending. Matthew makes this perfectly clear in the following verse (21:45) when he records, 'When the chief priests and the Pharisees heard his parables, they perceived that he was speaking about them.'[49]

In an essay published a year earlier, Overman proposed that one way forward in interpreting the difficult *crux interpretum* at 21.43 might be a thorough discussion of Matthew's portrait of Israel.[50] Unfortunately, neither this essay nor his subsequent commentary develops this suggestion.

If, however, thus far in Matthew's narrative the diverging portraits of the Jewish leaders and the crowds have given the reader ample reason to find in these parables reference to a judgement that is restricted to the Jewish establishment, a dramatically different picture awaits as the narrative moves towards its conclusion. As we shall see, the careful distinction between the Jewish authorities and the people is maintained, but in the end the leaders successfully entangle the people in their evil plot to destroy Jesus and, in so doing, elicit a divine judgement whose scope cannot be limited to the leadership alone.

Looking forward: Israel in the succeeding narrative (22.15–28.20)

Matthew 22.23–33

Indicted by Jesus, the Jewish leaders respond by confronting him with a series of probing questions (22.15–40). The sequence opens with the Pharisees plotting to trap Jesus in debate (22.15). Their potentially volatile question about the legitimacy of paying taxes to Caesar is couched in flattery, but Jesus recognises their evil design and astonishes them with his answer (22.16–22). At 22.23–33 the Sadducees approach Jesus to challenge his understanding of the resurrection, but they err, knowing neither the Scriptures nor the power of God. The failure of Israel's experts in the Scriptures to understand their significance has become a recurring theme in the Matthean narrative. The silence of the Sadducees, together with the amazement of the crowds,[51] once more signals the Jewish leaders' defeat, and, as in the preceding narrative, it aligns the crowds with Jesus, against their leaders.

Matthew 23.1–7

At 23.1–7, Jesus launches his massive indictment of the scribes and Pharisees that culminates in the condemnation of 'this generation' (23.34–36) and his lament over Jerusalem (23.37–39). He warns the crowds and his disciples of a group of leaders whose religious performance contravenes their instruction,[52] who bind heavy burdens on men but stand unwilling to offer assistance, and who do all their deeds to be seen by men. The crowds are again distanced from their leaders when they join the disciples as the explicit recipients of Jesus' denunciation of the scribes and Pharisees. And, at 23.4–5, the people (ἄνθρωποι) are portrayed both as those who are oppressed by the Jewish leadership (cf., e.g., 11.28–30; 12.1–8; 15.1–10) but also, ironically, as those from whom the leadership aims to win approval as they parade their piety (cf. 6.1–6, 16–18).

Matthew 23.13, 15[53]

After the paraenesis of 23.8–12, Jesus resumes his arraignment against the scribes and Pharisees. 23.13, 15 constitute the first two of the seven woes that the Matthean Jesus issues against the Jewish leaders, and both focus on the devastating consequences their false teaching has had for the people. Not only do the scribes and Pharisees fail to enter the kingdom, they also prevent others from entering. Their converts,[54] like them, become *sons of Gehenna*. And, if the Jewish leaders are portrayed as false teachers, then the people are characterised, incidentally, as those whose entrance to the kingdom has been blocked by their leaders.

Matthew 23.23–24

Matthew 23.23–24 presents the fourth in the Matthean series of woes. Although maintaining exacting tithing standards, by neglecting justice, mercy and faith, the Jewish leaders have strained out a gnat while swallowing a camel. As Jesus denounces the Jewish leaders, the reader recalls the several times throughout the narrative that the authorities have maintained a preoccupation for legal exactness at the expense of justice and mercy – at the expense of the people (e.g., 9.1–8, 32–34; 12.1–8, 9–14, 22–30; 15.1–20).

Matthew 23.29–39

Matthew 23.29 introduces the last in the series of seven woes as Jesus' indictment of the Jewish leaders reaches its climax. In spite of attempts to distance themselves from their forebears who put the prophets to death, they are, Jesus insists, the very 'sons of those who murdered the prophets' (23.29–31). For the reader this declaration holds no surprise. At least since the first of the passion predictions (16.21) the reader has known that Jesus himself will suffer and die at the hands of the Jewish leaders who now protest their innocence. The parable of The Tenants has dramatically underlined this point. Here Jesus charges them to bring their fathers' sin to full measure and, like John, addresses them as a *brood of vipers* who will not be able to flee the judgement of Gehenna.

διὰ τοῦτο links 23.34–36 to 23.29–36. Having ironically[55] urged them to fill up the measure of their fathers' sins in the previous pericope, Jesus now promises to provide the opportunity by sending his servants; and he predicts that the Jewish leaders will oblige. The Jewish leaders *will* kill, crucify and scourge the prophets, wise men and scribes Jesus sends to them and so bring upon themselves reprisal for all the righteous blood shed on the earth (23.34–35). They are indeed 'sons of those who murdered the prophets'. But, perhaps curiously, the scope of this retaliation is immediately broadened: ἀμὴν λέγω ὑμῖν, ἥξει ταῦτα πάντα ἐπὶ τὴν γενεὰν ταύτην (23.36). Once more the Jewish leaders stand at the front of *this generation*, but once more, if our previous analysis was correct,[56] they do not exhaust it.

At 23.37–39 the tone of the passage shifts dramatically as Jesus turns to mourn over Jerusalem. The city of the great king (cf. 5.36) has become the murderer of the prophets (23.37). Since Jerusalem has persistently resisted Jesus' attempts to gather her children, her house has become desolate (23.38). Nevertheless, even this – while eliciting a terrible judgement – apparently does not put her beyond the pale of her God's forgiveness. Should she even now recognise Jesus as the one who comes in the name of the Lord, she will once again see her Messiah.[57]

Matthew 26.3–5

At 26.3–5, the Jewish leaders contrive a plan (συνεβουλεύσαντο) to seize Jesus by treachery and to put him to death.[58] The setting for the plot spun by the chief priests and elders of the people (cf. 21.23) is a meeting in the court of the high priest, Caiaphas.[59] It is an official action. Once more the people are carefully distanced from their leaders, who feel compelled to seize Jesus by stealth and after the feast[60] to prevent a riot among the people (26.5). The use of λαός both to qualify οἱ πρεσβύτεροι (26.3) and to describe the crowds (26.5) underlines the developing conflict between the two groups.[61] The leaders' admission testifies both to the people's unflagging regard for Jesus and to their own continuing fear of the crowds (cf. 21.23–27, 46; but here λαῷ).

Matthew 26.47–56

The plan of the Jewish leaders moves towards fulfilment in 26.47–56. With the aid of Judas and the crowd that they have commissioned, the chief priests and elders of the people[62] seize Jesus in the garden. The arrival of the great crowd with swords and clubs is particularly ironic, since Jesus forbids the use of force in his defence (26.51–54, cf. 5.38–39). In contrast to the Jewish leaders who have plotted, and employed both treachery and coercion to accomplish their purposes, Jesus, whose single utterance can alter his destiny (26.53), renounces violence and marches obediently towards the accomplishment of his father's purposes (26.36–46, 51–56). The Jewish leaders are characterised here by the pointed contrast between them and the criminal they arrest. Who is the *robber* (26.55, cf. 21.13)?[63]

Twice in this pericope Matthew refers to the crowd that was sent to arrest Jesus (26.47, 55). Whether we are to think here of 'a mere hired rabble',[64] or the temple police,[65] or the temple guard augmented by others including, perhaps, a contingent of Roman soldiers,[66] is less than certain. Probably, however, we should reject Kingsbury's suggestion: 'Despite all of this, however, at Jesus' arrest the same crowds whom he had daily been teaching in the temple, armed with swords and clubs and acting on orders from the chief priests and the elders, suddenly appear with Judas in order to take Jesus by force (26:47, 55).'[67] The narrative has offered no hint that the crowds, whose regard for Jesus had, as recently as 26.5 (cf. 21.46), paralysed the Jewish leaders and prevented his arrest as he taught openly in the temple, have suddenly altered their allegiance. Instead, at least in part, the point of 26.55 seems to be that what Jesus' opponents were afraid to do in public (where the crowds protected him!) and during the day, they have accomplished in secret and at night. More probably, the evangelist employs ὄχλος πολύς and ὄχλοις to emphasise the size of the delegation, ironically underlining the fear of the Jewish leaders and Jesus' control of the entire situation (cf. 26.52–54, 56). Perhaps, however, this terminology[68] also foreshadows events now only a few hours hence.

Matthew 27.20–26

In these two paragraphs several of the narrative strands that Matthew has been tracing throughout his Gospel reach their climax, but they also mark a striking reversal in the people's relationship with Jesus. In 27.20–23 the crowds are characterised by their united appeal for Jesus' crucifixion. Granted power over Jesus' destiny, they clamour for his death, but are also portrayed as the pawns of their leaders. Against the backdrop of 27.19, where the pagan governor's wife pleads Jesus' innocence, the chief priests and elders are successful in persuading the crowds, previously

Jesus' defenders, to ask for Barabbas's release and Jesus' destruction. The crowds *all*[69] take up the chant, 'Let him be crucified.' The blind leaders have led their people into a pit (cf. 15.14). As we shall see, the consequences are enormous.

At 27.24–26, while the Gentile ruler attempts to wash his hands of the guilt for Jesus' blood in the face of the developing riot,[70] *all the people* invoke upon themselves and their children responsibility for his innocent blood. 'All the people' recalls both 'the whole city' (21.10) and 'all Jerusalem' (2.3):[71] 'In chapter 2 Herod sought to kill Jesus, but in chapter 27 Jerusalem succeeds.'[72] Like their leaders, the people have joined hands with the Herods, but also with generations of their fathers before them. As their fathers had murdered the prophets (21.33–46; 23.29–31), so now they have claimed responsibility for the execution of Jesus, the prophet from Nazareth (21.11). It is not the Jewish leaders alone who have taken the life of the vineyard owner's son (21.33–46).

Matthew's narrative devotes special attention to this 'innocent blood' motif that appears here. At 23.35 δίκαιος occurs twice, modifying αἷμα and Ἄβελ:[73] 'so that upon you may come all the *righteous* blood shed on earth, from the blood of *righteous* Abel to the blood of Zechariah.' In 27.3–10 Judas confesses: 'I have sinned by betraying innocent blood' (αἷμα ἀθῷον; 27.4). At 27.19 Pilate's wife bids him: 'Have nothing to do with that innocent (δικαίῳ) man.' Here, at 27.24, the governor declares himself innocent of the blood of this righteous man (ἀθῷός εἰμι ἀπὸ τοῦ αἵματος τοῦ δικαίου τούτου).[74] Like their fathers, the people have spilled innocent blood.[75]

The story of Susanna offers striking parallels at this point. Like Jesus, the innocent Susanna is falsely accused by the elders of the people and sentenced to death (Sus. 1–41, cf. Matt. 26.57–27.2). And, as in the Matthean narrative, so in Susanna a lone voice raises protest, and in words that find an echo in Matthew (καθαρὸς[76] ἐγὼ ἀπὸ τοῦ αἵματος ταύτης; Sus. 46, cf. Matt. 27.24: ἀθῷός εἰμι ἀπὸ τοῦ αἵματος τοῦ δικαίου τούτου). Again, in both stories 'all the people' (πᾶς ὁ λαός; Sus. 47,[77] cf. Matt. 27.25) answer the objection, but, whereas Daniel rises to the defence of the innocent in the earlier story,[78] here the pagan governor plays the role of defender. And, more importantly for our purposes here, whereas *the people* heed Daniel's protest, here they turn a deaf ear to Pilate's objections (27.23). Whereas Susanna is vindicated and delivered (καὶ ἐσώθη αἷμα ἀναίτιον ἐν τῇ ἡμέρᾳ ἐκείνῃ; Sus. 62), Jesus is crucified.

There is a most tragic irony in all of this. As the evangelist now describes this mob that accepts responsibility for Jesus' death – previously οἱ ὄχλοι (27.20) – as ὁ λαός, the reader recalls 1.21. There the angel of the Lord explains the name to be given to the son Mary carries in terms of his mission: 'you are to name him Jesus, for he will save his people (τὸν λαὸν αὐτοῦ) from their sins'. Although he came to deliver his people, his people now call for his execution. Nor does the irony end here. In spilling his innocent blood (cf. 23.35: αἷμα δίκαιον ἐκχυννόμενον) and so evoking divine judgement, the people have none the less taken the life of the one who, according to the will of his father (26.39, 42, 44), would spill his blood for many for the forgiveness of sins (26.28; τοῦτο γάρ ἐστιν τὸ αἷμά μου τῆς διαθήκης τὸ περὶ πολλῶν ἐκχυννόμενον εἰς ἄφεσιν ἁμαρτιῶν). In the very act of rejecting the forgiveness Jesus came to provide, his people bring his mission to completion and so make possible for the many that same forgiveness.[79]

Moreover, it is not merely the people (ὁ λαός) but *all* the people (πᾶς ὁ λαός) who accept responsibility for Jesus' death and they do so not only on their own behalf, but also on behalf of their children. Both of these features offer important clues to the significance with which Matthew invests this part of his narrative. 'All the people' no more condemns all Jews than 'the people of Jerusalem and all Judea . . . and all the region along the Jordan' (3.5) exonerates each inhabitant of Judea (et al.) in the days of the Baptist (3.6). But neither will it do to restrict the reference to 'the bulk of Jews in Jerusalem, both the inhabitants and those there for the festival, who support Jesus' execution.'[80] The parables of The Tenants and The Wedding Feast, and the massive indictment of chapter 23 that gives way to the 'stone saying' of 24.1–2, have prepared the ground too well. Having shared in the responsibility for the murder of the vineyard owner's son, *all the people* share in the judgement it has summoned: the suspension of national privilege.[81] 'The kingdom of God will be taken from [them] and given to a nation producing its fruits' (21.43). For Matthew, this judgement is given visible expression in the siege and destruction of Jerusalem (21.41; 22.7; 23.34–36; 24.1–2). Surely, this is how we should understand the last phrase of 27.25: 'His blood be on us *and on our children!*' The solemn formula that the people employ of course has biblical antecedents.[82] I Kings 2.33 is notable because of the contrast it affords with the Matthean expression of this formula. Solomon, eager to clear himself and his father's house of the guilt of the innocent blood that Joab had shed, orders Joab's execution (1 Kgs. 2.31) and exclaims: καὶ ἐπεστράφη τὰ αἵματα αὐτῶν εἰς κεφαλὴν αὐτοῦ καὶ εἰς κεφαλὴν τοῦ σπέρματος αὐτοῦ εἰς τὸν αἰῶνα . . . In contrast to its occurrence on the lips of Solomon, in Matthew the formula places responsibility on the children (τὰ τέκνα) rather than the descendants (τὸ σπέρμα) and, more importantly, does not include 'forever' (εἰς τὸν αἰῶνα). It was the children, with their fathers, who suffered the horrors of the Roman siege. That the evangelist, who has earlier drawn a tight connection between the rejection of Messiah and his messengers on the one hand and the punishment of 'this generation' on the other, should return to this motif here at the moment of destiny is not surprising.[83]

In Matthew's portrait, then, the people of Israel have rejected their Messiah. They have called for his death. They have accepted responsibility for his execution. Even so, following 27.20–23, the crowds' action can only be understood in light of the 'inspiration' of their leaders. Above all, *they* are responsible for the murder of Jesus Messiah, Son of God.

The failure of the people has been devastating; but the ground has been carefully prepared, both in terms of hints of this final rejection and, more obviously, in the distinctly different portraits the evangelist has painted of the people and their leaders. In the end, the people are pawns of their leaders. As such they are, for the reader of Matthew's gospel as for Jesus himself, the objects of compassion and sorrow. There is no hint here that the mission to these people has been abandoned. Moreover, if the national privilege they have enjoyed has been suspended, then the boundary lines of the new nation are emphatically *not* drawn along ethnic lines. No ethnic group is excluded – the kingdom is given to the one who returns to the God of Israel the fruit that is rightfully his (21.41, 43).

Matthew 28.11–15

Matthew 28.11–15 answers to 27.62–66.[84] Upon learning of Jesus' resurrection from the soldiers guarding the tomb, the Jewish leaders, in their final appearance, extend their perversity to final measure. Confronted with the *divine vindication* of Jesus' claims, the Jewish leaders not only fail to repent; they also persist in multiplying their sin by extending their deceit.[85] After 'taking counsel',[86] the chief priests and elders bribe the soldiers to say that Jesus' disciples stole his body by night. As in 26.14–16, silver becomes an instrument of evil in their hands. That this report still persists among 'the Jews' (but Ἰουδαίοις lacks a definite article) once more suggests a picture of a people who continue to be manipulated for evil at the hands of their own religious leaders (cf. 23.13, 15, 23–24). But if this final 'snapshot' again distances the people from their leaders, it also clearly distinguishes them from Jesus' followers.

These are the texts in this Gospel in which the reader meets both Israel's people and leaders. Our survey of Matthew's characterisation of the people and their leaders concludes with a brief sketch of their depiction in the many texts where one, but not the other, character group makes an appearance.

3.2   The Jewish leaders

The conflict between Jesus and the Jewish leaders is, of course, one of the dominant narrative threads that Matthew weaves through his entire Gospel. As we shall see, the portrait of the Jewish leadership that emerges from the texts in which they appear together with the people is consistent with what may be observed elsewhere in the Gospel. In the wider Gospel story, the Jewish leaders appear as blind guides and oppressive shepherds, as the mortal enemies of Jesus over whom he nevertheless finally triumphs.

Blind guides

The blindness of the Jewish leadership that Matthew is so careful to highlight[87] manifests itself in at least three ways. First, this blindness means that they are unable to perceive their own devastating failures and inconsistencies. Matthew calls this hypocrisy and reserves the designation *hypocrite* almost exclusively[88] for the religious authorities and, especially, the Pharisees: 'Woe to you, scribes and Pharisees, hypocrites! For you clean the outside of the cup and of the plate, but inside they are full of greed and self-indulgence. You blind Pharisee! First clean the inside of the cup, so that the outside also may become clean' (23.25–26). Similar examples could be multiplied.[89]

Second, as *experts* in the Scriptures, the Jewish leaders none the less remain blind to their true significance. Time after time, having challenged Jesus, they are defeated in interpretive debate.[90] After a series of fruitless attempts to ensnare Jesus in word, 22.46 places an exclamation point over Jesus' defeat of the Jewish leaders: 'No one was able to give him an answer, nor from that day did anyone dare to ask him any more questions.' Even so, evidence of the Jewish leaders' ignorance of the Scriptures extends into the passion narrative where they inadvertently effect their fulfilment.[91]

Third, the blind Jewish leaders are false teachers:[92] 'Woe to you, blind guides, who say, "Whoever swears by the sanctuary is bound by nothing, but whoever swears by the gold of the sanctuary is bound by the oath."

You blind fools! For which is greater, the gold or the sanctuary that has made the gold sacred?'[93] As we have seen, their teaching has disastrous consequences for the people (23.13, 15, cf. 28.11–15), but this introduces the second main strand of our summary. If the Jewish leaders are blind guides, then they are also oppressive shepherds.

Oppressive shepherds

Jesus' conflict with the religious authorities often focuses on matters of mercy and justice. 9.9–13 is illustrative.[94] Failing to understand the central place that God gives to mercy, the Pharisees object to Jesus' table fellowship with tax collectors and sinners.[95] Misguided religious concerns prevent them from penetrating to the heart of faithful allegiance to God, thus rendering them ill-equipped to care for his people. At the end of this chapter, Jesus' compassion for the crowds is stirred because they are 'harassed and helpless, like sheep without a shepherd' (9.36). In this narrative, as we noted above, the shepherds themselves harass the sheep.

Mortal enemies

From the earliest stages in Matthew's story the Jewish leaders appear as Jesus' hostile opponents. By 12.14 this hostility has evolved into a resolve to destroy him that, at one level, dominates the plot of the remainder of Matthew's story.[96] And if, on the one hand, the religious authorities play the role of Jesus' persistent adversaries, then, on the other hand, they act as allies of the Herods and of Satan himself. Like Herod the Great, they both seek his life (2.13, 16, 20, cf. 12.14) and provoke his withdrawal (2.14–15, cf. 12.15).[97] Like Antipas, while initially stymied by the crowds (14.5, cf. 21.23–27, 46), they none the less eventually succeed in claiming the life of their victim; in the one case of the forerunner and in the other of the Messiah himself (14.1–12, cf. 17.9–13; 27.20–26). Not unlike John's Gospel (cf. John 8.34–44), this narrative highlights the ties between Jesus' Jewish opponents and Satan. Like the evil one, they are evil (6.13, cf. 12.34, 38; 16.4). Like the tempter, they persist in putting Jesus to the test (4.1–11, cf. 16.1; 19.3; 22.18, 35).[98] Although they accuse *Jesus* of allegiance to Beelzebul (9.34; 12.24), *they* are a brood of vipers (3.7; 23.33), sons of Gehenna (23.15), the planting of the enemy (13.24–30, 36–43, cf. 15.13). They will not escape the sentence of hell (3.7; 23.33). Moreover, as the Jewish leaders establish themselves as Jesus' deadly foes, so, too, they are portrayed as the adversaries – at times the mortal enemies – of Jesus' followers.[99]

Defeated foes

Finally, the Jewish leaders in Matthew's story are Jesus' defeated foes. Time and again they must surrender to Jesus in debate. Tragically, their loss does not end here. In rejecting the Messiah, Son of God, they seal their eternal destiny.[100] While many will come from east and west and sit at table with Abraham and Isaac and Jacob in the kingdom, they themselves will be cast out. Matthew's portrait of the leadership is consistently dark, but the same cannot be said of the people.

3.3   The people

The lost sheep of the house of Israel

If one image could capture Matthew's portrait of the people, then it would surely be that of the 'lost sheep'. On the one hand, these sheep, harassed and helpless, are the objects of manipulation and oppression at the hands of their shepherds.[101] On the other hand, as 'lost sheep of the house of Israel', they are the recipients both of Jesus' teaching and healing[102] and of the mission of his followers.[103] Moved with compassion, Jesus twice miraculously feeds the people (14.14; 15.32) and a third time commissions his disciples to pray that the Lord of the harvest would raise up workers for Israel (9.36). The crowds, however, are depicted not only as the passive recipients of Jesus' ministry but also as active and responsive followers.[104] The two can hardly be separated, of course. Great crowds follow Jesus[105] and he heals them.[106] In fact, as we have seen, the esteem with which they regard John and Jesus sets them up as guardians of the prophets.[107]

'But from the one who has not . . .'

As we have also seen, however, Matthew makes no attempt to conceal the people's failure. They do remain receptive to Jesus until almost the last hours of his life. But as early as the arrival of the Magi when, with Herod, 'all Jerusalem' is troubled (2.3), the evangelist begins to prepare the reader for the people's final rejection of Jesus.[108] The parables discourse (especially 13.1–2, 10–17, 34–35) makes this rejection explicit. At 13.1–2 great crowds are present once more and Jesus now speaks to them in parables. After the first of these parables (13.3–9), in response to the query of his disciples, Jesus describes the crowds as those to whom the mysteries of the kingdom have not been given. 13.13–15 proceed to explain this not so much in predestinarian terms as in terms of the tenacious and culpable spiritual dullness that marks 'this people'.[109] If the crowds are often favourably contrasted with the Jewish leaders, here they are measured against the disciples and fall tragically short. They are portrayed as persistently dull, as those who see and hear without perception or understanding.[110] Even what they have will be taken from them (13.12).[111] 13.34 and 36 reinforce this portrait of the crowds – Jesus speaks in parables and only in parables to them (13.34) but, having left the crowds (13.36), he offers interpretation and further parabolic teaching to his disciples (13.37–52). 13.35 however, with its citation of Psalm 77.2 (LXX), perhaps ameliorates this harsh picture by reminding the reader that Jesus' parables reveal even as they conceal. Still, 'this people', having rejected Jesus Messiah, will not escape the divine judgement.[112]

The portrait Matthew paints is a clear one. From the outset, and consistently throughout the narrative, the Jewish leaders confront Jesus as his bitter adversaries. The people, by contrast, follow Jesus in great numbers, and marvel at his teaching and the wonders he performs; but in the end they succumb and follow their blind leaders into a pit. Still, in the first place, this terrible failure underlines the guilt of their leaders who must accept first responsibility for the rejection of Jesus Messiah. And, in the second place, this failure explains the suspension of national privilege to which the horrors of the Jewish War so graphically pointed.

3.4   Conclusion

In retrospect, then, the wider Matthean narrative seems designed to leave a dramatic imprint on the reader's reception of the trilogy. From the preceding narrative, and indeed from within the trilogy itself, the reader is given ample reason to conclude that the judgement announced by Jesus will be directed solely against the Jewish leaders. Matthew's story, however, is still far from complete. As the evangelist draws the narrative to conclusion, the evidence he presents implicates not merely the leaders, but also the nation, in the guilt arising from Jesus' death. The leaders have successfully entangled the people in their plot to kill Jesus. Yielding to their leaders, all the people demand his death (27.20–26). From the standpoint of the evangelist, the people have become partners with their leaders in the murder of the prophets. They have spilled the innocent blood of the householder's son (21.37–39, cf. 26.63, 64; 27.40, 43, 54).

Consequently all the righteous blood shed upon the earth will come not only upon the Jewish establishment (23.35), but also upon *this generation* (23.36).

Nevertheless, it will not do to find in this trilogy, with many from the ancient church, the simple replacement of Israel with the Gentiles,[113] nor, with some more recent interpreters, a categorical rejection of Israel that views mission to Israel as a thing of the past.[114] Matthew's portrait of the nation is more nuanced than either of these interpretations would suggest. Here the distinction that this narrative draws between the leaders and the people becomes especially important. If the crowds have been swept into the evil plot conceived by their leaders, chief responsibility lies with the leaders. They have manipulated the people. Their opposition to Jesus is considered (cf. 12.14; 22.15; 27.1: συμβούλιον ἔλαβον), consistent, and malicious. These diverging portraits, then, serve to emphasise the distinctive culpability of the establishment. Perhaps, however, they also have a secondary function. M. A. Powell's discussion of 'sympathy' as a literary effect is relevant here:

> Like empathy, sympathy is viewed by narrative critics as a lit-erary effect created by the implied author. One of the simplest means of arousing the reader's sympathy for a character is to attribute such sympathy to another character with whom the reader has come to empathize. As a general rule, the reader of a narrative will care the most about those characters for whom the protagonist cares the most. This is because the protagonist is usually one character with whom the reader experiences some degree of empathy.[115]

Powell proceeds to illustrate this with reference to the reader's response to the Marcan disciples. Though the Marcan disciples are characterised by persistent failure, the reader still cares about them in a way that he does not about the Jewish opponents, because *Jesus cares for them*. The texts that we have examined here suggest that precisely the same thing could and should be said about the Jewish crowds in Matthew's Gospel.[116]

From the earliest stages of his narrative, the evangelist moulds his portrait of the religious authorities in light of their final rejection of Jesus. But the sharply diverging portrait of the people suggests that, while Matthew intends to elicit no sympathy for the Jewish establishment that has turned its people against Jesus, he intends just that for the masses for whom he still holds out hope.[117]

The wider Matthean narrative suggests that the judgement announced in the trilogy (and, in particular, in The Tenants and The Wedding Feast) cannot be restricted to the leadership – the people have been implicated. Again, the larger story encourages the reader to find reference here both to the events of AD 70 and to the suspension of national privilege to which they graphically point. But suspension of privilege does not mean suspension of mission. Matthew's portrait of the crowds, the lost sheep of the house of Israel, seems designed to evoke the same responses from the reader as it did from the reader's Master: compassion and ministry.

4

JESUS AND THE NATIONS: CHARACTERISATION, PLOT AND THE RECEPTION OF MATTHEW 21.28–22.14

Each of the parables in this trilogy rehearses the story of Yahweh and Israel. This much seems clear. Whether the nations also have a role in these stories is perhaps less certain. Of whom shall the ἔθνος, to whom the kingdom is transferred, be composed (21.43)? To whom is the final invitation in the parable of the Wedding Feast extended (22.8–10)? Traditionally, Matthean scholars have found in the former an allusion to the church and in the latter veiled reference to the Gentile, or at least universal, mission, but this consensus has recently been challenged.[1] In this chapter we continue the task begun in chapter 3 of bringing the evidence of the wider narrative to bear on these parables. Here, however, we turn our attention to the narrative's characterisation of the nations and to the development of the 'Gentile sub-plot' in Matthew's story, asking in both instances how the patterns of the wider narrative help to shape the reader's reception of this trilogy of parables.

4.1　The view at the end: the nations and the narrative conclusion (28.16–20)

For most stories, last scenes are of first importance, and this story offers no exception. We have noted the importance of the Passion Narrative for Matthew's portrait of Israel. The final stages of the story are no less important for the narrative's characterisation of the nations. Indeed, at 28.16–20 several of the most important motifs that have been planted like seeds throughout this narrative finally bear fruit and receive climactic articulation.[2] Narrative critics have disputed the precise significance of 28.16–20 in the plot of Matthew's story,[3] but few contest the fact that these verses represent the climax of this narrative's portrait of the nations and of Gentile mission. Because of the importance of endings in narratives, and because this ending directly addresses the Gentile question, our study of this particular plot line begins with the pericope that draws it to conclusion. Subsequently we turn to examine the development of this

Gentile sub-plot in the earlier portions of the narrative, but always bearing in mind the conclusion towards which it is moving. To borrow Ricoeur's terminology, we shall be interested in 'apprehending the well-known end as implied in the beginning and the well-known episodes as leading to this end'.[4]

In these closing words of the Gospel stands the commission, rich with Old Testament echoes, that the risen Jesus leaves with his disciples. And at the heart of this charge stands the command to make disciples of all the nations (πορευθέντες οὖν μαθητεύσατε πάντα τὰ ἔθνη; 28.19).[5] The inferential οὖν,[6] however, points the reader back to the opening words of Jesus' commission, which supply the grounds for the command to make disciples: ἐδόθη μοι πᾶσα ἐξουσία ἐν οὐρανῷ καὶ ἐπὶ [τῆς] γῆς (28.18b). Universal mission arises from universal authority — that which has now been granted to Jesus.[7] Moreover, reference to worship of Jesus (28.17), his universal authority (28.18), and the allegiance he receives from all the nations (28.19) recalls Daniel 7.14 where all of these things are predicated of one like a Son of Man (Dan. 7.13).[8] Thus, it is as the exalted, and so vindicated, Son of Man that Jesus receives cosmic authority and commands a mission to all the nations, whose worship and obedience is rightfully his (cf. Dan. 7.27).[9]

Even as Jesus' declaration of the universal extension of his authority echoes Daniel 7, so the charge to universal mission recalls the language of the Abrahamic covenant. In Jesus, son of Abraham (cf. 1.1), God's promise that all nations would be blessed through Abraham's descendants (Gen. 12.1–3, cf. Gen. 18.18; 22.18; 26.4) finds fulfilment.[10] The mission of the followers of this son of Abraham is now rightly universal. Nor is this connection between Israel's king and the fulfilment of the promises granted to Abraham unprecedented in Israel's sacred writings. In a clear echo of these promises granted to Abraham, the psalmist declares that all nations will be blessed through the ideal king, the son of David (72.17 (LXX 71.17)). Read along these lines, it was not merely through the sons of Abraham but, more specifically, through the son of David that all nations would find blessing.[11]

In these verses, then, missiological concerns are Christologically grounded. As son of Abraham (Gen. 18.18; 22.18), son of David (Ps. 72.17) and Son of Man (Dan. 7.14), Jesus extends his commission to πάντα τὰ ἔθνη who, as his disciples, will inherit the blessing promised to Abraham and submit to his universal lordship (28.20).

Fittingly, the last words in this narrative belong to Jesus himself. By these words, Jesus rescinds his earlier prohibition of a mission to the nations (10.5, cf. 15.21–28). All the nations, now equally the object of the church's mission, are to be embraced by Jesus' followers.[12] This is where the narrative portrait of the Gentiles ends. We turn now to a consideration of how it arrived here as we trace the story of the nations through the earlier portions of the narrative.

4.2   In retrospect: the Gentile sub-plot (1.1–28.15)

Matthew 1.1–17

If it is true that last words play an especially important role in determining the reader's final impressions of an entire narrative, then it is also true that 'first words and first acts have peculiar power in shaping the perceptions of readers'.[13] In what follows we look at the beginning of Matthew's story, but from the vantage point of the end.

Jesus' genealogy is significant for this story's Gentile sub-plot in at least three ways. Ἰησοῦ Χριστοῦ, this narrative's opening line tells us, is υἱοῦ Δαβὶδ υἱοῦ Ἀβραάμ. If our reading of 28.16–20 is correct, then first, by its declaration that Jesus is the 'son of Abraham,' the narrative anticipates its conclusion. God had promised to Abraham, whose name itself declared his paternity over many nations (Gen. 17.1–8, cf. 1 Macc. 12.19–21), that through his descendants all the nations of the earth would find blessing (e.g., Gen. 12.1–3). God's promise will be fulfilled through Jesus the son of Abraham.[14]

Second, Jesus is also the 'son of David'. Here J. Kingsbury's comments are typical: 'Just as the title "Son of Abraham" characterizes Jesus as the one in whom the Gentiles will find blessing, so the title "Son of David" characterizes Jesus as the one in whom Israel will find blessing.'[15] Perhaps, however, this contrast is too neat. No doubt the chief significance of this language lies in establishing Jesus' royal pedigree, but the linking of the promises made to Abraham with those made to David in both Jewish and Christian writings may suggest that the distinction Kingsbury proposes is overdrawn.[16] Jer. 33.14–26 looks forward to the days when God will grant to Israel and Judah all the promised blessings. A righteous branch from David's line will arise and, thereafter, David will never lack a descendant upon the throne of Israel nor will there fail to be levitical priests who minister to the Lord (33.15–21). Instead, in a clear echo of his promise to *Abraham* (Gen. 22.17), God declares: 'Just as the host of heaven cannot be numbered and the sands of the sea cannot be measured, so I will increase the offspring of my servant *David* and the Levites who minister to me' (Jer. 33.22). The Targum to Psalm 89 makes this link more explicit. Whereas the MT reviews God's covenant with David ('I made a covenant with my chosen one, I swore to my servant David . . .'),[17] the Targum identifies *Abraham* as the chosen one of the first clause: 'I made a covenant for Abraham my chosen one, I swore to David my servant . . .'[18] What God promised David was to establish his descendants (זַרְעֲךָ/τὸ σπέρμα σου) forever, and to build his throne for all generations (Ps. 89.5). Probably, as M. Wilcox suggests, it was the fact that both Abraham and David were promised enduring *seed* (Gen. 17.7 et al., cf. 2 Sam. 7.12) that prompted the Targumist to introduce the reference to Abraham here.[19] Moreover, as we have seen, Psalm 72.17 identifies the Davidic king as the seed of Abraham through whom all the nations will be blessed. So, too, does *Testament of Levi* 8.14–15.[20] All of this suggests the possibility that it is not only as son of Abraham but also as son of David that Jesus brings to the nations the blessing promised to Abraham.

Third, by the inclusion of four women in Jesus' genealogy who are probably to be regarded as Gentiles,[21] the narrator highlights earlier Gentile inclusion among God's people and anticipates the future, full-orbed Gentile inclusion that this narrative will announce.[22]

Matthew 2.1–12

In this narrative, Jesus' first encounter with the nations comes while he is still a young child. The 'Magi from the east' are characterised by their actions, by God's actions, by their speech and by analogy. They journey to Jerusalem and there inquire about the birth of the new king (2.1–2). Directed to Bethlehem, they follow the star they had seen in the East to the child before whom they prostrate themselves (2.9–11). They mark their exit from the narrative stage by obeying the divine guidance that is granted them (2.12). These are noble foreigners indeed.

It is not only *their* actions, however, that places the narrative's stamp of approval upon them. When they are warned in a dream not to return to Herod, the reader recognises the sovereign hand of Israel's God (2.12, cf. 1.20). In retrospect, the star that precedes them (2.2, 10) and the knowledge of a king born in Israel (2.2) must also be attributed to divine guidance. The God of Israel acts on their behalf.

The Magi speak only once, but their speech reveals the purpose of their journey to Israel: they have come to bow before the one who has been born king of the Jews (2.2).

Finally, the Magi are portrayed over against Herod (2.3, 7–8, 12, 13–19), all Jerusalem (2.3) and all the chief priests and elders of the people

(2.4–6). Unlike Herod and all Jerusalem (2.3),[23] the idea of the Jewish king's birth brings the Magi profound joy (2.10). Unlike all the chief priests and elders of the people, they are ignorant as to the birthplace of the young child. Nevertheless, unlike these Jewish leaders, the Magi overcome their ignorance and seek the child out (2.11). Unlike Herod, their desire to pay homage to the young king is genuine (2.3, 11, cf. 2.7–8, 12–19). Unlike Herod and the Jewish leaders, they hear from Israel's God (2.12, cf. 2.2, 10). In all of these ways, the narrative portrait of these foreigners is most positive.

If the references to Abraham and the Gentile women in the genealogy (1.1–17) hint at the significance that the Messiah's birth will have for the nations, then that hint finds an echo here as foreign Magi bow before the young king. From the vantage point of the end, the Magi are but the first of a great multitude from all nations who will bow before Israel's Messiah.[24]

Matthew 3.7–10

There is no explicit reference to the Gentiles here, but there is, on the lips of John the Baptist, the dual warning that descent from Abraham will offer no protection in the coming judgement,[25] and that God is able to raise up 'from these stones' children to Abraham. If God did the impossible in raising up a nation from Abraham, a lifeless rock, and from Sarah, a barren quarry (Isa. 51.1–2, cf. Rom. 4.17), then surely he could bring forth sons from stones once more.[26] What counts, then, as God's reign is about to be inaugurated, is not ethnic origin but the production of 'fruit worthy of repentance'. There is, as yet, no assurance that God *will* raise up other children to Abraham, but the possibility is now raised explicitly. In retrospect, of course, this uncertainty vanishes. The Baptist's warning becomes an adumbration of Gentile inclusion.[27] God will raise up other children to Abraham. The resurrected Lord of the church will commission his followers to a mission to all the nations (28.18–20), and 'in the acceptance of the gospel by them as well as by Israelite believers Abraham has become, in Paul's words, "the father of us all" (Rom. 4: 16)'.[28]

Matthew 4.12–16

By taking up residence in Capernaum, Jesus fulfils the promise of Isaiah 8.23–9.1 where Galilee is Γαλιλαία τῶν ἐθνῶν.[29] For Zebulun and Naphtali – Galilee of the Gentiles – the rod of their oppressor will be broken (Isa. 9.4) because a child has been born, the Davidic king (Isa. 9.6–7). But if the advent of the son of David promises to 'Galilee of the Gentiles' relief *from* the Gentiles in Isaiah, in Matthew's narrative it signals relief *for* the Gentiles. The fact that Jesus' ministry *to Israel* is based in 'Galilee of the Gentiles' promises that the significance of his arrival will extend beyond Israel.[30] Reviewing the end of the story, the reader recalls that it is in Galilee that Jesus commissions the eleven to a mission to the nations (28.16–20), and that here, as there, Gentile blessing has a Christological foundation. Here, Jesus brings light to Galilee of the *Gentiles* precisely because he is *Israel's* Messiah (Isa. 9.1–7).

Matthew 4.24

Jesus' ministry, though apparently restricted to Israel, makes an impact outside of Israel. His fame spreads throughout the whole of Syria.

Matthew 5.13–16

Perhaps it is not incidental that as Jesus was a light (4.12–16), so are his disciples and that, as Galilee of the Gentiles witnessed his light (4.15–16), so the disciples are a light for the *world*[31] and salt of the *earth*. Throughout the narrative, the ministry of Jesus and his disciples is much more limited in scope. Only after 28.16–20 can the latent universalism in these sayings be fully appreciated.[32]

Matthew 5.47

We have already had occasion to observe that this narrative typically paints a favourable portrait of the Gentiles. Matthew 5.47, however, is the first in a series of texts that break this pattern. At 5.46–47 ἐθνικοί (5.47) is parallel to τελῶναι (5.46) and both terms function pejoratively – even tax gatherers and Gentiles love and greet those who love and greet them.

Matthew 6.7, 32

At 6.7, ἐθνικοί once more bears negative connotations. Unlike the Gentiles who suppose that they will be heard on account of their many words, Jesus' disciples are not to babble in prayer. Again, at 6.32, the Gentiles (but now τὰ ἔθνη) function as negative examples. Unlike these pagans, followers of Jesus must not worry about daily provisions since their heavenly father knows their needs (6.31–32).

Matthew 8.5–13

The centurion's actions, his speech, Jesus' speech, and the contrasting example of Jesus' encounters in Israel all help shape the reader's perception of this man. In his approach to Jesus and the plea he issues on behalf of his servant (8.5–6), the centurion begins to demonstrate the faith around which this story revolves. And, if the centurion's cry for Jesus' help testifies to his faith, then the words he utters bear witness to its profundity. Since, like Jesus, he lives 'under authority', he understands that Jesus need not be present to heal his servant. When the centurion speaks, Rome speaks. When Jesus speaks, God speaks. The power of God does not depend upon Jesus' location any more than the power of Rome depends upon the centurion's.

The man's remarkable faith elicits an equally remarkable response from Jesus: 'from no one in Israel have I found such faith'.[33] The centurion in this story is thus juxtaposed with those in Israel. That his faith surpasses all that Jesus has met in Israel both commends him and censures Yahweh's people whose opportunity far exceeded his. Moreover, Jesus insists, this centurion is not alone: he will be among the many Gentiles[34] who will come from the east and west and sit at table with Abraham and Isaac and Jacob in the kingdom of heaven, while the sons of the kingdom are evicted (8.11–12). By the time the centurion's story concludes on the note that his servant has been healed, his faith has become paradigmatic for the faith that receives both healing and final salvation from the hand of God.[35]

John's ominous warning, then, gives way to Jesus' sober assertion:[36] the axe that lies poised *will* fall and 'unfruitful trees' among Abraham's sons will be cut down (3.8, 10, cf. 8.12). Are we also to conclude that the many who come from east and west are new children that God has raised up to Abraham (3.9, cf. 8.11)?[37]

The imagery upon which this saying draws is intriguing. Two observations seem relevant. First, 'many will come from east and west' surely recalls a series of Jewish texts that employ similar language either in anticipation, or in celebration, of the regathering of God's exiled people.[38] That the same language now envisions the inclusion of the nations poignantly demonstrates that the lines of demarcation for Yahweh's people are being dramatically redrawn. But, second, these same texts often depict this regathering as the return of Israel's children, of Yahweh's *sons* and *daughters*. Isaiah 43.5–7 is typical:[39]

> Do not fear, for I am with you;
> I will bring your offspring from the east,
> and from the west I will gather you
> I will say to the north, 'Give them up',
> and to the south, 'Do not withhold;
> bring my sons from far away
> and my daughters from the end of the earth –
> everyone who is called by my name,
> whom I created for my glory,
> whom I formed and made'.

In Isaiah 49.22 (cf. 49.12), the nations are granted a role in this regathering:

> Thus says the Lord God:
> I will soon lift up my hand to the nations,
> and raise my signal to the peoples;
> and they shall bring your sons in their bosom,
> and your daughters shall be carried upon their shoulders.

It is striking that when Matthew's narrative takes up the image of the return of God's people from exile and applies it to the nations, Israel's sons are also present – only, however, to be excluded (8.12)! While they no longer bring Israel's sons and daughters, the nations do come from east and west. Yahweh's (and Abraham's?) other children will come home.

For the first time in this narrative the reader learns both that many Gentiles will participate in the eschatological reign of God and that at least some in Israel will instead face eschatological judgement. What was previously only implicit and potential (3.7–10) here becomes explicit and actual. But, as before, Abraham's name is associated both with the exclusion of some from within Israel and the inclusion of some from without. Viewed through the lens of the narrative's conclusion, these many from east and west do not sit at table with the Patriarchs in the kingdom because the nations have gathered in eschatological pilgrimage to Zion, but because the followers of Jesus have taken his eschatological message from Zion to the nations.[40]

Matthew 10.5–6

After detecting in the preceding narrative repeated anticipations of Gentile inclusion, the reader is abruptly reminded that these earlier incidents were just that – anticipations. There is, as yet, no mission to the nations. On the contrary, here Jesus explicitly prohibits the twelve to go either to the Gentiles or to the Samaritans. Fittingly, as disciples of one who comes to shepherd God's people Israel (2.6), their mission, like his (cf. 15.24), is exclusively to the lost sheep of the house of Israel. In retrospect, the reader recognises that this prohibition was temporary and has now been explicitly rescinded. From a salvation–historical perspective, the mission to the nations awaited Jesus' exaltation to universal lordship (28.16–20).[41]

Matthew 10.14–15

Matthew 10.14–15 is the first in a group of texts in which Jesus compares the fate of unfaithful Israel with that of the Gentiles at the coming judgement. Here he declares that those cities in Israel that reject the message of his disciples will face a judgement worse even than Sodom and Gomorrah.

Matthew 10.18

Set in the wider context of the Matthean mission discourse, 10.18 forms part of a lengthy consideration of the hostility that this mission to Israel, commanded in 10.6, will provoke. The apostles will be handed over to councils and scourged in synagogues[42] but also, curiously, led before kings and governors as a testimony to them 'and to the Gentiles'.[43] Once more the subsequent narrative makes all things clear. 10.18 looks beyond the immediate future[44] where a Gentile mission has been explicitly forbidden (10.5) to the post-resurrection mission to the nations, inaugurated at 28.16–20.

Matthew 11.20–24

At 11.20–24, references to 'Tyre and Sidon' and to 'Sodom' punctuate Jesus' indictment of Chorazin, Bethsaida and Capernaum. Granted similar opportunity, even these notorious centres of Gentile wickedness would have repented.[45] Reference to these Gentile cities functions here principally to help characterise the cities of Galilee. They are evil and ripe for judgement.

Matthew 12.15–21

Jesus withdraws in the face of the Pharisees' resolution to put him to death (12.15, cf. 12.14), but great crowds[46] follow him. He heals all their sick, but also warns them not to make him known (12.15–16) in order that Isaiah's prophecy might be fulfilled (12.17). The citation identifies

Jesus as the servant of Isaiah 42, upon whom God puts his Spirit. He will announce justice[47] to the nations and, although he will not argue or cry out, he will bring justice to victory. In his name will the nations hope.[48] As in 28.16–20, Gentile mission – here only implicit – depends upon the nature of Jesus' Messianic vocation. Blessing for the nations becomes the inevitable consequence of Jesus' assumption of the role of Yahweh's servant.

Matthew 12.38–42

At 12.38–42, reference to Gentiles once more illustrates the culpability of Jesus' contemporaries: unlike the men of Nineveh who repented at Jonah's preaching and the Queen of the South who travelled from the ends of the earth, this generation has neither repented nor sought out Jesus' wisdom, though his greatness eclipses both Jonah's and Solomon's. As in 10.14–15 and 11.20–24, the Gentiles – even the worst of them – compare favourably with Jesus' contemporaries. But each text has less to say about the Gentiles than about Israel.[49] Her rejection of the Messiah has elicited the judgement of her God.

Matthew 13.31–32, 38

Are we to find here, in Jesus' reference to the birds, an allusion to the Gentiles who make their nest in the kingdom's branches (13.31–32)?[50] More obviously, the field in which the sons of the kingdom and the sons of the evil one are planted, awaiting the harvest, is ὁ κόσμος (13.38). In the days preceding the end, ethnic boundaries will be irrelevant.

Matthew 15.21–28

The Canaanite[51] woman is marked by her persistent search for help for her suffering daughter, and by her conviction that Jesus can provide what she so desperately desires. After Jesus meets her first plea with silence (15.23) and the request of the twelve with the assertion that his mission is restricted to Israel's lost sheep (15.24), she nevertheless repeats her cry for help (κύριε, βοήθει μοι; 15.25). Following Jesus' final, and harshest rebuff, she concedes Israel's salvation–historical primacy, but proceeds to ask for secondary blessing (15.27). Finally Jesus acknowledges what the reader has already learned: she is a woman of remarkable faith (15.28). In the end, Jesus answers this faith by granting her wish – her daughter is healed. It is not, however, only her tenacious faith that is noteworthy. Like both the Magi and the centurion, the narrative's characterisation of this woman achieves greater impact by means of the stark contrast that the other characters in this context supply.[52] While the Jewish leaders offer hypocritical worship (15.7–8) and false teaching (15.9), while they are scandalised by Jesus' teaching (15.12) and perversely blind (15.14), and while the disciples remain dull and without understanding (15.16),[53] the Canaanite woman sees – as the blind leaders do not – that Jesus is the Son of David (15.22), bows before him in homage (15.25) and refuses to be scandalised by Jesus' steadfast focus upon Israel (15.24–27).

Once more the narrative presents a most positive portrait of a Gentile character (cf. 2.1–12; 8.5–13).[54] Like Jesus, the reader can hardly help but be won over by the Canaanite woman; and the composite portrait of these Gentiles who encounter Jesus becomes still more favourable. None the less, Jesus' interaction with this woman is exceptional. He is sent only to the lost sheep of the house of Israel.

The appeal of the Canaanite woman becomes, for Jesus, an occasion to articulate both the exclusive nature of his own mission (15.24, cf. 10.5–6) and Israel's salvation–historical primacy (15.26). In the end, the woman's faith wins Jesus' answer to her request (15.28), but no hint that this salvation–historical focus upon Israel is temporary.[55] Nevertheless, from the vantage point of the end this woman, like the centurion, foreshadows the many from all the nations who would turn to Jesus in faith,[56] and who, like the Magi, would yield to him the worship that is rightfully his. Finally, if this pericope highlights the exclusiveness of Jesus' mission to his people, then it also underlines Israel's guilt. What this pagan woman was forced to contend for so strenuously was freely extended to Israel, but in the end largely rejected. This rejection would elicit God's judgement – a judgement that would also hold great import for the nations.

Matthew 18.17

At 18.17, Jesus declares that the persistently unrepentant brother is to be treated as a Gentile and a tax collector (ὥσπερ ὁ ἐθνικὸς καὶ ὁ τελώνης). As in 5.47, 6.7, 32 (but there τὰ ἔθνη), ἐθνικός is used pejoratively and, as in 5.47, is parallel with τελώνης.

Matthew 20.24–28

Matthew 20.24–28 is the last in a series of pejorative references to the nations. Unlike the rulers of the nations (οἱ ἄρχοντες τῶν ἐθνῶν),[57] Jesus' followers' greatness is marked by service, Jesus himself having established the pattern.

How do these texts help shape the reader's developing perception of the Gentiles in Matthew's story? For D. Sim they 'unambiguously betray an anti-Gentile perspective', and suggest that 'the world of the Gentiles is a patently foreign place to be avoided at all costs'.[58] But this reading does justice neither to the fundamental importance of the Gentile mission in this narrative nor to these texts themselves. With respect to these texts, several observations are in order. First, each of these pejorative uses is found on the lips of Jesus. Second, these expressions do seem to tally with Jesus' virtually exclusive focus on Israel and his expressed reluctance to minister to any other than the lost sheep of the house of Israel (cf. 8.7, and especially 15.24, 26). Third, twice in these texts ἐθνικός stands parallel to τελώνης. In both instances τελώνης also functions pejoratively; the Christian reader must abandon the way of life associated with tax collectors. But this scarcely means that, in this narrative, Jesus is not interested in ministry to tax collectors. Quite the opposite is true (cf. 9.9–13; 10.3; 11.16–19; 21.28–32). Fourth, while the textual tradition shows that these expressions were potentially offensive,[59] nevertheless it is also true that occasionally, outside of the Jesus tradition, these expressions could be employed in early Christian literature.[60] In these instances, however, τὰ ἔθνη is emptied of ethnic connotation and refers simply to those who do not know God – pagans as opposed to Christians (and Jews?). That these expressions can stand in parallel with τελώνης in the Matthean narrative suggests similar connotation here. Finally, it is surely significant that the commission that charges the eleven to make disciples of all the nations also comes from Jesus' lips (28.16–20). All of this suggests that Jesus is not instructing his followers to reject Gentiles (or tax collectors). Instead this narrative both underlines the importance of Gentile mission and typically presents these Gentiles as pagans in need of evangelisation.

Matthew 24.9–14

Matthew 24.9–14 stands near the beginning of the Olivet Discourse. Here Jesus warns his disciples that in the days before the end they will be hated by all the nations[61] because of his name (24.9, cf. 10.22). 24.14 declares that 'this gospel' will be proclaimed in all the world as a testimony to all the nations and then the end will come. Though the disciples will face opposition from the nations, the nations will none the less be the beneficiaries of their proclamation of the kingdom. 24.14 constitutes an important turning point in the development of this storyline: for the first time in this narrative, the universal mission of the church finds explicit articulation. While the prohibition of 10.5–6 has not yet been counter-manded, 28.16–20 lies just around the corner.

Matthew 24.29–31

Most often these verses are understood to refer, in rather literal fashion, to the climactic cosmic events that will mark 'the end of this age' (cf. 24.3). On this reading verse 30 describes the parousia of the Son of Man and verse 31 the eschatological gathering of the elect (cf. 13.30, 40–43, 49–50). An alternative reading, however, seems recently to be gaining momentum.[62] While I cannot defend this interpretation here in any detail, I do want to register my support and make one or two observations before turning to discuss briefly the significance of these verses for the developing storyline we are tracing. On this interpretation, the apocalyptic language of verse 29 does not point to literal cosmic chaos but instead to God's dramatic intervention in human history, in the form of national judgement. Verse 30 once more employs apocalyptic language, this time the language of Daniel 7.13–14, to highlight the vindication of the Son of Man.[63] The coming judgement upon the nation that has rejected God's Anointed will offer public vindication of Jesus Messiah. In a manner reminiscent of 8.11–12, verse 31 employs the imagery of the regathering of the exiles (cf. LXX Deut. 30.4; Zech. 2.6 (LXX 2.10); Isa. 27.13) to highlight the universal mission upon which Jesus' followers will embark.[64]

Two important factors favour this reading. First, this interpretation takes seriously the tight narrative connection between chapters 23 and 24. The indictment that chapter 23 records rises as a crescendo towards the climactic verdict of verses 35–36: 'so that upon you may come all the righteous blood shed on earth . . . Truly I tell you, all this will come upon this generation' (ἀμὴν λέγω ὑμῖν, ἥξει ταῦτα πάντα ἐπὶ τὴν γενεὰν ταύτην). Jesus' lament over Jerusalem and the barren temple (23.37–39) gives way to his prediction of the temple's destruction (24.1–2) which, in turn, elicits the disciples' twofold question that this discourse answers (24.3). Significantly, shortly after the verses we have been discussing (24.29–31), Jesus declares: 'Truly I tell you, this generation will not pass away until all these things have taken place' (ἀμὴν λέγω ὑμῖν ὅτι οὐ μὴ παρέλθῃ ἡ γενεὰ αὕτη ἕως ἂν πάντα ταῦτα γένηται; 24.34). The echo of 23.36 is deliberate and obvious. At 23.36 'all these things' certainly refers to the judgement that will overtake unfaithful Israel within the generation. One would expect to find similar significance in the repetition at 24.34.[65]

Second, the Jewish antecedents for the apocalyptic language of these verses should lead us to expect just this sort of reading. They function in the prophets to herald not some sort of cosmic collapse that signals the end of the space–time universe, but rather the historical intervention of Israel's God to judge the nations (cf., e.g., Isa. 13.10; 34.4–5; Ezek. 32.7–8; Joel 2.10).[66]

One more seldom noticed feature[67] of these verses may both lend support to this reading and have significance for this narrative's Gentile sub-plot. 24.30 reads: καὶ τότε φανήσεται τὸ σημεῖον τοῦ υἱοῦ τοῦ ἀνθρώπου ἐν οὐρανῷ, καὶ τότε κόψονται πᾶσαι αἱ φυλαὶ τῆς γῆς . . . Upon seeing the sign of the Son of Man in heaven, all the families of the earth will mourn. πᾶσαι αἱ φυλαὶ τῆς γῆς is a particularly interesting phrase. Here, as in Revelation 1.7, πᾶσαι αἱ φυλαὶ τῆς γῆς becomes the subject of κόψονται in a citation that already conflates Daniel 7.13 and Zechariah 12.10, 12.[68] Since the phrase is found only four times[69] in the LXX – three times depicting the recipients of the universal blessing that comes via Abraham (Gen. 12.3, cf. Gen. 28.14; Ps. 71.17[70]) and once of the pilgrimage of the nations to Jerusalem to worship Yahweh (Zech. 14.17) – but has clearly become part of early Christian tradition, allusion to the universal blessings of the Abrahamic covenant seems probable. Earlier I argued for an allusion to Genesis 12.3 at 28.19, suggesting that God's promise to Abraham of blessing for all the nations was now finally being fulfilled in the universal mission commissioned by the risen Jesus. If this interpretation of 28.19 is correct, then the apparent allusion to that same promise here may prepare the reader to find reference to the universal mission here as well. On the reading presented above, reference to this mission comes in the immediately succeeding verse (24.31). Israel's rejection of Messiah elicits both judgement and blessing – judgement for the nation, but blessing for the nations.

Matthew 26.13

Jesus' pronouncement at 26.13 concludes the story of his anointing at Bethany. There is no explicit mention of the Gentiles here but, in a manner reminiscent of 24.14 which does speak expressly of a mission to all nations, Jesus refers to the proclamation of 'this gospel' throughout the whole world. The presence of such a mission is once more assumed – all that awaits is its inaugurating command.

Matthew 26.28, cf. 20.28

Here, at the Last Supper, Jesus declares: 'this is my blood of the covenant, which is poured out for many for the forgiveness of sins' (26.28). The words recall both 20.28 and 1.21. Jesus came not to be served, but to serve, and to give his life as a ransom for many. He came to save his people from their sins. Surely the πολλῶν encompasses all the beneficiaries of his saving death. After Jesus' charge to universal mission (28.16–20), this must include Gentiles.[71] Must not λαός (1.21), which initially seemed restricted to Israel (cf. 2.6), in retrospect also be broadened to include disciples from all nations?[72]

Matthew 27.1–28.15

Unlike the earlier portion of the narrative, Jesus confronts a number of Gentiles in the passion narrative and, in contrast to the preceding examples, these encounters are not uniformly positive. The first, and most prominent, of these comes when Jesus meets Pilate.

Jesus before Pilate

As all the chief priests and elders of the people bind Jesus and hand him over to Pilate (27.1–2), the reader senses the ominous beginning to the fulfilment of Jesus' passion predictions (20.18–19, cf. 16.21–23; 17.9–13, 22–23). Before the governor Jesus acknowledges that he is the king of Israel (27.11, cf. 26.25) but, to Pilate's astonishment, refuses to answer the charges brought against him by the chief priests and elders (27.11–14).[73] In accord with custom, and understanding that the Jewish leaders had arrested Jesus because of envy, Pilate offers to release one prisoner to the crowd – Jesus or the notorious prisoner Barabbas (27.15–18).[74] Against the dark picture of the Jewish leaders that the narrative continues to paint, Pilate's attempt at a mediating intervention casts him quite favourably.

As Pilate sits in judgement, he receives a message from his wife who, troubled by a dream, urges him to have nothing to do with 'this righteous man' (27.19). Earlier dreams in this narrative have, without exception, been the source of divine revelation and, with the exception of Joseph's first dream, have all been designed to protect Israel's young king.[75] Here, too, the dream centres on Israel's king, now a man, and here, too, the recipient of the dream aims to intervene and save him. But, even as the wife of the pagan governor hears from God and testifies to Jesus' innocence, the chief priests and elders persuade the people to demand Barabbas's release and Jesus' execution (27.20). Her actions contribute to the narrative characterisation of Jesus – he suffers innocently – and of the leaders – they doggedly pursue their long-standing intention to destroy Jesus, here manipulating the crowds to achieve their evil purpose. But, in marked contrast to them, this pagan woman hears from God and seeks to rescue Jesus, and her actions contribute to the developing narrative characterisation of the Gentiles.

When the crowds ask for the release of Barabbas and the crucifixion of Jesus, Pilate objects, asking what evil Jesus has done. But the crowds only intensify their demand for blood. Once more, over against the crowds and, most especially, the leaders who stand behind the crowds, the pagan governor seeks to defend Jesus. Sensing that a riot is imminent, Pilate consents to give the crowds the execution they demand while seeking to absolve himself of responsibility for it. Read against the background of Israel's sacred texts,[76] the unfolding events suggest that 'the world is now upside down'.[77] Declaring himself 'innocent of the blood of this righteous man',[78] Pilate has Jesus flogged and hands him over to be crucified. But, while the pagan governor follows biblical precedent in declaring Jesus' innocence, Yahweh's people, for whom the ritual was designed to purge the guilt of innocent blood (cf. Deut. 21.1–9), gladly accept the responsibility that Pilate scrambles to avoid (27.20–26).

At this juncture in the narrative, two themes seem to be central. First, Jesus suffers unjustly. His is innocent blood (27.4). He is righteous (27.19). He has done no evil (27.23). Second, the Jewish leaders and their people are guilty of shedding this innocent blood (27.25, cf. 21.33–46; 23.29–36; 27.3–10). The narrative portrait of Pilate and his wife seems to function principally to underline these two dominant motifs. Nevertheless, the attentive reader cannot but note that, in comparison with the Jewish leaders and, in the end, even the crowds, the Gentile governor (who repeatedly defends Jesus), and certainly his wife, are characterised in much more favourable light. If, however, Pilate's culpability pales by comparison, it would be an overstatement to claim that the narrative absolves him of responsibility.[79] In the end the governor fails to heed his wife's warning. Indeed, he fails to govern,[80] yielding instead to the wishes of the mob.

Jesus and the soldiers

Before taking Jesus to the place of execution, the soldiers of the governor lead him into the praetorium and there abuse him, bowing in mock homage before the one they hail derisively as 'king of the Jews' (cf. 20.18–19). Here the Gentiles in Matthew's narrative afford no contrast to the Jewish leaders. Instead, they follow the lead of the scribes and elders in spitting upon Jesus, striking him, and hailing him contemptuously by titles that are rightly his (cf. 26.67–68).[81] At Golgotha, the soldiers offer Jesus wine mixed with gall, cast lots for his clothing, post the accusation above his head, 'This is Jesus, the king of Israel,' and, sitting down, keep watch over Jesus (27.33–37).

Nevertheless, this same group of soldiers, having witnessed the portentous events that accompanied Jesus' death are terrified[82] and declare, 'Truly this was the son of God' (27.54). Does the narrative, then, rehabilitate these Gentiles?[83] At very least the reader must note that, in two ways, this response now places the soldiers in starkest contrast to the Jewish leaders with whom they have earlier been linked. First, their confession echoes the words just uttered in derision by the chief priests, with the scribes and elders: εἶπεν γὰρ ὅτι θεοῦ εἰμι υἱός (27.43, cf. 26.63–66).[84] But if the words are similar, the intent is not, as ἀληθῶς (27.54) indicates: the condemning taunt of the leaders becomes a confession of truth on the lips of the soldiers.[85] Second, the supernatural portents that have elicited the soldiers' counter-assertion of the leaders' charge[86] provoke no such change of heart from the Jewish establishment. Instead, they turn their attention to securing Jesus' tomb (27.62–66).

For many, the Christological confession of the centurion and his cohorts at 27.54 foreshadows the Gentile inclusion in which this narrative has shown consistent interest. Even if the narrative is concerned chiefly with Christology here, this conclusion seems secure. As at 8.11–12, the lines of demarcation for God's people are being redrawn. But the narrative does not simply portray a reversal of fortunes – Gentile inclusion at the expense of Jewish exclusion. Beside the Gentile soldiers stand the Jewish women who remain faithful to Jesus to the end (27.55–56, 61; 28.1–10). 'This mixture of Jews and Gentiles is a preview of the *ekklesia* to be formed in Jesus' name.'[87]

After Jesus' death and burial, a final group of soldiers makes its appearance in the narrative, assigned to guard his tomb (27.62–66). But in the scene charged with irony that follows, the soldiers who were to protect against the theft of the corpse themselves become like dead men (28.4) while the corpse is raised to life, 'just as he said' (28.6). The Jewish leaders bribe the pagan soldiers to say that Jesus' disciples stole his body, and the lie is spread (28.15), but they only 'did as they were taught' (28.15). Once more the chief blame is laid at the feet of the perverse Jewish leaders.

4.3 Summary

What can we say, then, of the portrait of the Gentiles that emerges from this narrative? First, collectively, Gentiles are simply portrayed as pagans who do not know Israel's God and, therefore, are not to be imitated. But even at a collective level, when viewed alongside Israel, the culpability of the nations pales by comparison. Second, the individual portraits of the Gentiles that appear in this narrative differ dramatically. As we have seen, they are not all painted with one brush so that, without exception, Gentile characters become exemplars of faith and devotion. Nevertheless, typically, they are presented most sympathetically with the result that the reader naturally embraces them. Moreover, these individuals are consistently cast alongside either the Jewish leaders or the crowds and, against this backdrop, even the poorest of Gentile figures fares well.

The plot of this narrative makes it clear that the favourable characterisation of the Gentiles is not incidental. Instead, this deliberate and sustained contrast prepares the reader both for the judgement that is about to fall upon Israel and the subsequent blessing for the nations. The redefinition of the people of God, with the consequent inclusion of many from among the nations, functions as a narrative thread that is woven intricately throughout the fabric of the entire story, but becomes explicit only at the end. 28.16–20 marks both the conclusion and the climax of the Gentile sub-plot. Here, in the Gospel's final words, Jesus commissions his followers to a mission that encompasses all nations. Looking back over the narrative from this vantage point, the reader sees evidence of deliberate design in the development of this sub-plot. This narrative:

(1)   Anticipates the inclusion of the Gentiles in the people of God from its earliest lines (e.g., 1.1–17; 2.1–12; 3.7–10; 4.12–16);

(2)   Warns that descent from Abraham will offer no protection to the barren in the coming judgement, but equally insists that God is able to raise up other children to Abraham (3.7–10);

(3)   Explicitly asserts that the sons of the kingdom will be replaced at the Messianic banquet in the coming kingdom (8.11–12);

(4)   Envisions a day of universal mission (24.14; 26.13); and, finally,

(5)   Commissions Jesus' followers to engage upon this mission to all the nations (28.16–20).

4.4   Gentiles and the reception of the trilogy (21.28–22.14)

The parable of The Two Sons (21.28–32)

The parable of The Two Sons tells a story that is about neither the nations nor individual Gentiles. Jesus' application of the parable, moreover, makes no allusion to the Gentile peoples. Nevertheless, set within the context of this trilogy, The Two Sons makes a contribution to the wider narrative's Gentile sub-plot in at least two ways. First, like The Tenants and The Wedding Feast, this parable rehearses the story of Yahweh and his people with particular focus on the failure of Israel's leaders and the subsequent recomposition of the people of God.

Second, The Two Sons takes up this motif of the recomposition of Yahweh's people by means of a conscious glance backward to 3.1–10 and, in so doing, prepares the ground for the more fundamental reconstitution of God's people towards which the second and third parables in the trilogy will point. 21.28–32 answers to 3.1–10 in several respects. The two texts mark John the Baptist's entrance to and exit from the narrative stage. In 3.1–10, John enters into conflict with the Pharisees and Sadducees. 21.28–32, set in the midst of a conflict between Jesus and the Jewish leaders, reports a parable that depicts their rejection of the Baptist's message from God. In the former, the people came to John in repentance (3.1–6). In the latter, tax gatherers and prostitutes respond in repentance and faith (21.32). In the former, John charges the Jewish leaders to repent (3.8). In the latter, Jesus notes their stubborn failure to repent (21.32).[88] In the former, John threatens eschatological punishment (3.10). In the latter, as Jesus reviews the leadership's response to the Baptist, John's threat yields to the certainty of Jesus' declaration (21.31). Jesus' parable, then, functions as an affirmation of the Baptist's proclamation: as the eschatological people of God is constituted, the only effective criterion for membership is fruit worthy of repentance (3.8–10, cf. 21.31b–32). In the context of Jesus' ministry, this entails both the inclusion of repentant tax-gatherers and prostitutes and the exclusion of the unrepentant religious elite. But application of this same criterion would entail an even more fundamental redrawing of the lines of membership for Yahweh's people, a redrawing to which both The Tenants and The Wedding Feast devote attention.[89] Repentant Gentiles would join the tax collectors and prostitutes in displacing Israel's elite.

The parable of The Tenants (21.33–46)

The parable of The Tenants becomes the second in this series of three stories about Yahweh and Israel. But, as we noted in our introduction to this chapter, whether the story is exclusively about Israel is much less certain. 21.43, a critical verse on any reading of the Matthean parable, interprets 21.41 where the Jewish leaders pronounce a terrible judgement on the wicked tenants (themselves! cf. 21.45). The vineyard to be taken from those evil men is the kingdom of God. The new tenants are an ἔθνος who produce the fruits of the kingdom. But exactly who composes this new ἔθνος?

A. Saldarini is representative of a growing number of scholars who find in ἔθνος reference to a new group of leaders for Israel.[90] He summarises his conclusions as follows:

> The ordinary meaning of *ethnos* that fits Matthew's usage is that of a voluntary organisation or small social group. The Matthean *ethnos* is a small subgroup, whose exact make-up is not specified. The narrative criticizes the Jewish leadership for rejecting God's message brought by his accredited messenger, Jesus. The parable assumes that the vineyard (Israel), though it has been badly managed, can be given to other tenants (leaders) who will make it bear fruit (21:41). Thus the *ethnos* bearing (literally 'making'), fruit (21:43) is a new group of tenants (that is, leaders of Israel) who will give the owner his share of the fruits at the appropriate time (21:41). Those who are rejected, the previous leaders, are a group who do not act appropriately by producing fruit for the owner. The vineyard, Israel, remains the same; subgroups within Israel are blamed or praised. The *ethnos* thus is a group of leaders, with their devoted followers, that can lead Israel well.[91]

Saldarini offers an extended defence of this reading, in part by seeking to establish the broad semantic range that ἔθνος has in both classical and Hellenistic periods, in part by appealing to the background of such texts as Isaiah 3 and 5, and in part by offering his own reading of the parable.

Although few will accept all of Saldarini's interpretations of ἔθνος in the various texts he cites,[92] equally few will contest that the word can be employed in a variety of senses. The relative prominence of these uses in the biblical writings is another question! If it is true that in the Hellenistic period the singular ἔθνος can be used to refer to a guild, a social class, etc., in addition to a *nation*,[93] then it is also true that *nation* or *people* is by far the most common sense of the word in Israel's sacred writings. The LXX exhibits a remarkable consistency in this regard.[94] Surely the writings of Israel's sacred texts should be given precedence over the pagan poets and philosophers in supplying the background against which Matthew's story should be read. But, if this is the case, is it really true that '[t]he *ordinary* meaning of *ethnos* that fits Matthew's usage is that of a voluntary organization or small social group'?[95]

In Matthew's narrative, when ἔθνος occurs in plural form it consistently refers to the Gentiles or the nations.[96] Unfortunately the use of ἔθνος in 21.43 represents one of only three singular occurrences of the word in this narrative. But in the other two instances (both at 24.7), as its use in the LXX would have led us to expect, the word simply means *nation*. All of this seems to suggest that 'the ordinary meaning of *ethnos* that fits Matthew's usage' is not 'voluntary organization or small social group' but simply 'nation'.

I find Saldarini's reading of the relationship of the leaders and the people in Isaiah 3 and 5 equally unconvincing. Chapter 5 returns to a discussion of these texts.

Most problematic, however, is the failure of his reading to take seriously the wider Matthean narrative. Both the characterisation of the Gentiles within the narrative and this story's Gentile sub-plot, which together underline both the judgement that Israel's failure provokes and the subsequent blessing for the nations, undermine Saldarini's interpretation. Set in the context of the wider narrative that we have explored, it is difficult to avoid finding in this reference to a new nation of tenants an allusion to the *trans-ethnic* composition of the new people of God. Surely those from among the nations who will embrace 'this gospel of the *kingdom*'[97] (24.14), and those from east and west who will sit at table with Abraham and Isaac and Jacob in the *kingdom* (8.11), will be among the new tenants to whom the *kingdom* is given (21.41, 43). Nevertheless, as the preceding parable reminds us, the people who compose this ἔθνος are not simply Gentiles as opposed to Jews; this nation is defined along ethical and not ethnic lines (21.31b-32, cf. 21.41, 43). But the fact that this people is not defined along ethnic lines does suggest that the judgement that has fallen on the tenants has national implications for Israel. She has surrendered the national privilege that was hers. The door to the reign of God is thrown open wide to all the nations.

Even if this conclusion is secure, and I think it is, one might still wonder (with Saldarini) about the appropriateness of employing ἔθνος – nation – to describe a community *without ethnic boundaries*. Probably, as many scholars[98] have suggested, ἔθνος serves as a signal that this new people will *include* Gentiles and not merely a Jewish remnant. But perhaps more is involved. Perhaps, given the fact that the parable rehearses the story of Yahweh's dealings with Israel, ἔθνος is calculated to recall earlier salvation–historical texts that employ similar terminology.[99] I suggest that reading Matthew 21.43 against the backdrop of these texts proves most illuminating.

We have already had occasion in this chapter to refer to the first of the relevant LXX texts. Genesis 12.1–3 records Yahweh's call of Abraham. There, as we have seen, Yahweh promised to bless all the families of the earth by Abraham (Gen. 12.3). But God's first promise was to make

Abraham into a great nation: καὶ ποιήσω σε εἰς ἔθνος μέγα ... (Gen. 12.2). The first echo[100] of these promises comes in chapter 18. In the context of his plans to judge Sodom, Yahweh reaffirms his design for Abraham: Αβρααμ δὲ γινόμενος ἔσται εἰς ἔθνος μέγα καὶ πολύ καὶ ἐνευλογηθή-σονται ἐν αὐτῷ πάντα τὰ ἔθνη τῆς γῆς (Gen. 18.18). An important explanation follows immediately: Abraham will instruct his sons to pre-serve the ways of the Lord by doing righteousness and justice (ποιεῖν δικαιοσύνην καὶ κρίσιν!) in order that the Lord might bring to Abraham all that he has promised. At Genesis 22.18 *Abraham's* obedience becomes the basis for another repetition of the promise and, at Genesis 26.4, for the reaffirmation of the promise to Isaac: καὶ ἐνευλογηθήσονται ἐν τῷ σπέρματί σου πάντα τὰ ἔθνη τῆς γῆς.

Genesis 28.3 and 35.11 trace the promise of a nation of heirs from Isaac to Jacob (καὶ ἔσῃ εἰς συναγωγὰς ἐθνῶν; 28.3, cf. 35.11: ἔθνη καὶ συναγωγαὶ ἐθνῶν ἔσονται ἐκ σοῦ, καὶ βασιλεῖς ἐκ τῆς ὀσφύος σου ἐξελεύ-σονται), and with Jacob the storyline that we have been tracing makes a significant advance. On his way towards Egypt and a reunion with Joseph, Jacob receives from the Lord the assurance that it is in Egypt that Yahweh will make him into a great nation (μὴ φοβοῦ καταβῆναι εἰς Αἴγυπτον· εἰς γὰρ ἔθνος μέγα ποιήσω σε ἐκεῖ . . .; Gen. 46.3).[101]

The Exodus narrative returns to this motif as God brings Israel out of Egypt as a great multitude in accord with his promises to Abraham and to Jacob (Exod. 1.7–10, cf. 12.37–38). When, in the third month after their departure from Egypt, Israel comes to the wilderness of Sinai, Yahweh instructs Moses to declare to the people: 'Now therefore, if you obey my voice and keep my covenant, you shall be my treasured possession out of all the peoples (ἔσεσθέ μοι λαὸς περιούσιος ἀπὸ πάντων τῶν ἐθνῶν). Although the whole earth is mine, you will be for me a kingdom of priests and a holy nation'[102] (βασίλειον ἱεράτευμα καὶ ἔθνος ἅγιον; Exod. 19.5–6). In the context of the conquest of the nations that stands on the horizon, these words are echoed in Exodus 23.22.[103]

While still at Sinai, with Moses on the mountain, the people turn in rebellion against God and worship the calf that Aaron had fashioned from the gold of their jewellery (Exod. 32.1–6). Thus provoked, the Lord declares to Moses: 'Now leave me alone that my anger may burn against them and that I may destroy them. Then I will make you into a great nation' (ἔθνος μέγα; Exod. 32.10). In response to Moses' entreaty, the Lord relents and spares the people (Exod. 32.11–14). But it is noteworthy that if the Lord's wrath has been so ignited against his people that he will destroy them, even then his purpose to raise a great nation from Abraham – here potentially through Moses – will not be thwarted.

In the succeeding chapter, Moses asks to see the Lord in order that he may know the Lord, that he may continue to find favour with him, and that he may know that this great nation (τὸ ἔθνος τὸ μέγα τοῦτο) is Yahweh's people (Exod. 33.13).[104] Echoes of these motifs reverberate throughout the Pentateuch.[105]

The importance of this terminology in Israel's founding narratives, the inauguration of her salvation–historical story, can hardly be denied. In each of the texts we have surveyed, the very existence and identity of the people is at issue. Read against the backdrop of these texts and of the wider Matthean narrative, the provocative ἔθνος at Matthew 21.43 underscores both God's faithfulness to Abraham and the unfaithfulness of his people Israel.

God had purposed to bless Abraham and make him into a great nation, a nation whose children would preserve the ways of the Lord in righteousness and justice, a nation who would embrace the covenant and thus become the treasured possession of her God, a kingdom of priests, a holy nation. But Abraham's children have spurned the covenant. Instead of embracing righteousness and justice, they have spilled the innocent blood of the prophets (Matt. 21.33–46; 22.1–7; 23.29–36). Finally, this generation has filled up the measure of their fathers, murdering Yahweh's son and his ambassadors (21.37–39; 23.29–36; 27.19–26). They have elicited their God's judgement. No longer a kingdom of priests and a holy nation, the kingdom is taken from them and given to a nation who will return to Israel's God the fruits of repentance and righteousness that are rightfully his (21.41, 43, cf. 21.28–32). But has Israel's unfaithfulness nullified Yahweh's promise to Abraham? Apparently not, if the wider Matthean narrative is to guide us.

The strategic allusions in this narrative to the promises made to Abraham in connection with the inclusion of the nations among God's people suggest that here too (Matt. 21.43) the promise of the future incorporation of the Gentiles should be read against the background of the Abrahamic covenant (Gen. 12 et al.). But, whereas earlier we argued that the promises of Genesis 12.3[106] were in view, here allusion would be to the ἔθνος of Genesis 12.2.

I have already suggested that the reader meets the end of the narrative in the beginning when, in the first line of this story, Jesus is introduced as υἱοῦ Ἀβραάμ (1.1). In fulfilment of God's promises to the patriarch, he brings blessing to all the nations as the son of Abraham (28.16–20; cf. 24.30–31). At 3.7–10, to which The Two Sons has pointed the reader, the Baptist warns of the impending judgement against which only fruit worthy of repentance will provide protection. All barren trees will be

Table 3

1.1	3.7–10	8.11–12	21.28–32	21.33–46	22.1–14	28.18–20
	Judgement Threatened (3.7–10)	Judgement Assured (8.12)	Judgement Assured (21.31b)	Judgement Assured (21.41, 43)	Judgement Enacted (22.7)	
	Abrahamic descent offers no safeguard (3.9)	Sons of the kingdom (and of Abraham) evicted (8.12)	Disobedient leaders (sons of Abraham) excluded (21.31b)	Old tenants (sons of Abraham) destroyed (21.41)	First invited (sons of Abraham) destroyed (22.7)	
	Fruit of repentance necessary (3.8, 10)		Repentance Refused (21.32)	Necessary Fruit Absent (21.41, 43!)		
Jesus . . . son of Abraham (1.1)	New children for Abraham? (3.9)	Many from East and West – new children for Abraham! (8.11)	Tax gatherers and prostitutes gain entrance (21.31b–32)	New tenants/ἔθνος – new children for Abraham! (21.43)	New guests invited – new children for Abraham! (22.8–10)	Promise to Abraham answered; blessing for πάντα τὰ ἔθνη (28.18–20)

cut down and burned (3.8, 10). Abrahamic descent will be of no avail. Instead God, who will not be unfaithful to his promises, is able to raise up new children to Abraham (3.9). As we have seen, 8.11–12 returns to several of these motifs. The Baptist's threat of judgement is replaced by Jesus' sober promise of the same (8.12). Abrahamic descent, as John had warned, will prove insignificant as the sons of the kingdom are cast out into outer darkness (8.12). But in their place come many from east and west – new sons for Abraham (8.11). As Table 3 illustrates, each of the parables in this trilogy also revisits several of these motifs.

If judgement was threatened at 3.7–10, then here in the parable of The Tenants, as at 8.11–12 and 21.28–32, it is promised (21.41, 43). Moreover, this judgement will fall precisely because the Jewish leaders have failed to heed the Baptist's warning. They have failed to yield to God the fruit that is rightfully his and that alone could turn aside his judgement (21.34, 41, 43, cf. 3.8, 10). They are barren sons of Abraham, but the vineyard is not deserted. Instead, it is let to other tenants (21.41), a new ἔθνος (21.43), who will give back to God the fruits he demands. If a backward glance to 3.7–10 suggests both that judgement will fall upon Abraham's descendants (3.9), and that it will fall precisely because they have persisted in their barrenness (3.8, 10), is it not likely that the new tenants also correspond to the other children of Abraham of whom John spoke (3.9, cf. 8.11)?[107] Probably we should conclude that in these new tenants, this new ἔθνος, God is raising up new descendants for Abraham, as the Baptist averred he could.[108] A forward glance to 28.16–20, with its emphasis on God's faithfulness to his promises to Abraham, lends further credence to this reading. If this is the case, then we are not far from the conclusion that not only will all nations be blessed through Abraham and his descendants (Gen. 12.1–3; 18.18; 22.18; 26.4; Ps. 72.17), but also that many from the nations will help compose *the* great ἔθνος that God promised to make from Abraham (Gen. 12.2, cf. 17.6 (LXX), 18.18). The nations who are blessed by their interaction with the nation in the end are incorporated into that nation! Sadly, many of the original citizens lose their heritage.[109]

The parable of The Wedding Feast (22.1–14)

Linked as tightly as it is to the parable of The Tenants, it is not surprising that many of the points of contact between The Tenants and the wider narrative re-emerge here. Once more Israel's failure and the judgement it elicits receive accent. Like The Tenants, The Wedding Feast tells the story of a repeated mission that is repeatedly and violently spurned

(22.3–6, cf. 21.34–39), and, as in The Tenants, this violent rejection of Yahweh's messengers summons a violent reprisal (22.7, cf. 21.41, 43). Once more, however, the story is not only of failure and judgement, but also of subsequent blessing. As in The Tenants, so in The Wedding Feast the failure of those first confronted with this mission leads to the inclusion of their replacements (22.8–10, cf. 21.41, 43). As there would be new tenants, so there are replacement guests at the feast.

Once more, if the reader brackets the wider narrative, it is difficult to be certain what to make of these replacement guests. Perhaps they are the lost sheep of the house of Israel, marginal characters held in disdain by the Jewish establishment (cf. 21.28–32).[110] The logic of the story, however, in which all the guests first invited are dead and in which the objects of the final mission are ὅσους ἐὰν εὕρητε (cf. 22.10, συνήγαγον πάντας οὓς εὗρον), perhaps points to a distinction more fundamental than between elite and marginal.

The placement of this parable in this trilogy surely favours this latter alternative. The carefully crafted parallels between the two stories suggest that this parable is to be interpreted in close connection with The Tenants. If, as we have suggested, The Tenants alludes to Israel's loss of privilege and to the *trans-ethnic* composition of the new nation, then presumably The Wedding Feast alludes to the abolition of the earlier restrictions on the mission of Jesus' followers (10.5, cf. 15.24). As we have seen, the wider narrative only confirms this reading. 22.8–10 announces, in veiled parabolic fashion, the future universal mission upon which God's servants will embark. The invitation to the wedding feast is now to be offered indiscriminately (22.9, cf. 28.19). Here the narrative both anticipates, and offers theological justification for, the climactic pronouncement of 28.16–20. Gentile inclusion arises from Israel's failure. This latter point is established nowhere more clearly than in these two parables.[111] Israel's failure provokes the recomposition of Yahweh's people, but this recomposition nevertheless underlines Yahweh's faithfulness to the covenant promises made to Abraham. If elsewhere universal mission depends upon the universal authority that awaits Jesus' resurrection and exaltation (28.16–20), these two conditions are not unrelated – the one (Israel's failure) leads to the other (Jesus' exaltation) by way of the cross.[112]

4.5   Conclusion

The positive characterisation of the Gentiles in deliberate and sustained contrast to Israel (or sub-groups within Israel) prepares the reader for the judgement that is about to fall on God's people and the blessing that awaits the nations. The Gentile sub-plot confirms this expectation, telling the story of the inclusion of all nations among God's people in fulfilment of his promises to Abraham. The judgement of the wicked tenants and first invited guests, together with the subsequent blessing of the new tenants/ἔθνος and the replacement guests that these parables present, is to be understood against this wider narrative backdrop. The fruit of repentance becomes the mark of Yahweh's eschatological people. The nation is judged. The nations are included in the reconstituted people of God.

The conclusion, defended in chapter 1, that the Synoptic parables are components of the evangelists' wider communicative action has prompted the investigation of the wider narrative presented in these last two chapters. By focusing, respectively, upon Israel and the nations, I have attempted to establish – at least in part – the narrative background against which these salvation–historical parables must be heard if we aim to hear them as the evangelist intended. I argued in chapter 3 that the characterisation of Israel that emerges from the wider narrative makes it difficult to restrict the judgement that these parables announce to the Jewish establishment. The nation is indicted. In this fourth chapter, our exploration of Matthew's characterisation of the nations and of the 'Gentile sub-plot' both suggest that the evangelist intends, in this trilogy, an allusion to the many from among the nations who will join Israel's faithful as Abraham's children.

With this narrative backdrop in place, the remainder of this study turns to a careful examination of the parables themselves. Both chapters 5 and 6 will attempt to isolate the responses that the evangelist hoped to elicit from his readers, but, whereas chapter 6 offers a redactional reading that focuses upon the author, chapter 5 presents a narrative-critical reading that pays special attention to the reader.

5

A NARRATIVE-CRITICAL READING
OF THE TRILOGY

If chapters 1 and 2 were devoted, respectively, to questions of method and of the origin of the trilogy, and chapters 3 and 4 to exploring the role that the wider narrative plays in shaping the reader's response to these parables, then chapters 5 and 6 shift the focus to the trilogy of parables itself. This chapter offers a narrative-critical reading of these parables. In accord with the conclusions drawn in chapter 2, I make a conscious attempt here to read the parables as a *trilogy* and, in line with the argument developed in chapter 1, I attempt to elucidate the responses that the trilogy seems *designed* to evoke from the *reader*. In this regard, I shall be especially interested in the *inclusive* nature of these parables.

In his 1990 monograph D. Howell suggests that Matthew's narrative is an 'inclusive' story in that it invites its readers 'to appropriate and involve themselves in the story and teaching of the Gospel'.[1] Howell turns from this observation to formulate the questions that set the agenda for his study: 'Who is "included" in Matthew's story and how are they "included"? Are literary techniques used which help structure a reader's response to the story and its message? If so, how do they function?'[2] These questions will also occupy my attention. In this chapter I examine the nature of the evangelist's rhetoric and seek to isolate the responses that this rhetoric seems designed to elicit.[3]

We have already seen that these parables offer important salvation–historical insight, taking up the story of Yahweh's dealings with Israel. But, from the vantage point of the response of the reader envisioned by the evangelist, the withdrawal of the kingdom from Israel and the inclusion of the nations do not represent the sole – or even the prin-cipal – focus of the trilogy. Instead, the chief focus of these parables is paraenetic. The parables build towards a hortatory climax at 22.11–14.

5.1 The Two Sons (21.28–32)

The narrative setting

Matthew 21 opens on the ominous note that Jesus is approaching Jerusalem. Since the first of his passion predictions the reader has known that Jerusalem is the city of Jesus' destiny (16.21, cf. 20.18–19). Perhaps surprisingly, then, he enters the city to the acclamation of the crowds (21.1–11). Once inside the city, however, conflict reigns. Jesus enters the temple, drives out those conducting business in its precincts, heals the blind and the lame and accepts the praise of the children. Indignant, the chief priests and scribes confront Jesus (ἀκούεις τί οὗτοι λέγουσιν;) but, unrepentant, he leaves them and spends the night in Bethany (21.12–17).

As he returns to Jerusalem the next morning, in an act reminiscent of Israel's prophets, Jesus curses a barren fig tree and it withers immediately (21.18–22). Back inside the city and the temple, the Jewish leaders confront him once more, explicitly challenging his authority. To their question (ἐν ποίᾳ ἐξουσίᾳ ταῦτα[4] ποιεῖς; καὶ τίς σοι ἔδωκεν τὴν ἐξουσίαν ταύτην;) Jesus responds by posing his own question (τὸ βάπτισμα τὸ Ἰωάννου πόθεν ἦν; ἐξ οὐρανοῦ ἢ ἐξ ἀνθρώπων;). As we shall see, these two questions form the primary background against which this parable must be heard. Jesus' counter-question effectively foils the Jewish leaders – he need not explicitly reveal the source of his authority (21.27). His question also becomes the occasion for the Jewish leaders' frank, albeit private, admission (21.25) that helps shape the following parable. As the crowds' estimate of John had earlier saved him (cf. 14.5), so now their allegiance to the Baptist rescues Jesus (21.26). But the reader has already learned that, like John's, this reprieve will only be temporary (17.9–13).

The parable proper

The dispute about the Baptist initiated in 21.23–27 continues here. In Matthew's narrative the people persistently embrace John as a prophet of Israel's God.[5] With equal consistency, however, the Jewish establishment sets its face against him. As such 21.28–32, the narrative's final reference to John's encounter with Israel, unfolds according to type.

Τί δὲ ὑμῖν δοκεῖ; introduces The Two Sons and alerts the reader, as it had the Jewish leaders before him, that he is being invited to pass judgement. From the outset of the trilogy, then, the reader is entangled in the concerns of the stories about to unfold.[6]

The parable itself is simple and succinct. A man with two sons instructs first one, and then the other, to work in his vineyard. The first son immediately expresses assent,[7] but his ready agreement proves mere lip-service; he never does make it to the vineyard.[8] By contrast, the second son initially dismisses his father's request,[9] but subsequently changes his mind and sets off to work.

Two features invite comment. First, sons figure prominently in each of the parables in this trilogy but, in distinction from this parable (ἄνθρωπος εἶχεν τέκνα δύο; 21.28), The Tenants and The Wedding Feast feature only one son, namely, Jesus (υἱός; 21.37; 22.2). In this context Matthew's narrative reserves υἱός for metaphorical references to 'the Son'.[10]

Second, the setting for the work envisioned is a vineyard. For McNeile, '"[w]ork in the vineyard" is only the scenery of the parable; obedience alone is the point at issue.'[11] But probably it is not incidental that this trilogy of parables about Yahweh and Israel opens with a story set in a vineyard. Without exception, metaphorical references to God's vineyard in the LXX point to his people, Israel.[12] Identifying the father in this story as God, the reader naturally associates this vineyard with Israel.[13]

At 21.31 Jesus' question (τίς ἐκ τῶν δύο ἐποίησεν τὸ θέλημα τοῦ πατρός;) invites the judgement that will draw the parable proper to conclusion. The question is reminiscent of 7.21. In both instances 'doing the will of the father' distinguishes those who enter the kingdom from those who do not. 12.50 is similar: there the same criterion isolates Jesus' true followers. At 18.14 the will of the father – that none of these little ones should perish – implicitly charges readers to reclaim lost sheep, as their father would.[14] Elsewhere, once in the garden in Jesus' prayer (26.42), and once in the prayer Jesus taught (6.10), the reader learns that submission to the father's will is to be expressed in prayer. In this narrative, then, 'the will of the father' has a definite hortatory function. Even Jesus' prayer in the garden (26.42) takes on this function because of the inclusion of the identical phrase in the model prayer (6.10). Like Jesus, his followers are to pray for *and submit to* the will of the father. The question that Jesus puts to the Jewish leaders, then, both recalls earlier and anticipates later treatments of the nature of true discipleship. The parable has a paraenetic function;[15] and if at the story level Jesus' question is addressed to the Jewish leaders, then at the discourse level it invites a verdict from the reader.

As important as questions are from the standpoint of the reader's involvement, however, more fundamentally the reader is *included* in this trilogy of parables simply because they are effective stories. Contemporary reader-response critics were hardly the first to point out the remarkable capacity Jesus' parables have to involve the reader in their concerns. For Dodd, they '[*arrest*] the hearer by [their] vividness or strangeness . . . *leaving the mind in sufficient doubt about its precise application to tease it into active thought*'.[16] As we noted above, E. Fuchs argued that Jesus' parables function as *language events* (*Sprachereignisse*) for those with ears to hear. The hearer is drawn into the world of Jesus' parables and *interpreted by them*.[17] R. Funk insisted that the parable remains open until the listener, caught up in the story, renders the requisite judgement.[18] All of these observations are attempts to describe the capacity that Jesus' stories have to *strike home* to the hearer in ways that theological argument seldom can.

As Matthew's narrative portrays it, at one level at least, this happens to the Jewish leaders. They enter into the story's concerns and, at its conclusion, offer the judgement that the story's logic demands. What is more important for our purposes, however, is that similar things also happen to subsequent hearers. Swept into the world of the story, they, too, must render judgement.

As they will in the parable of The Tenants (21.41), the Jewish leaders issue their verdict – the second son has done the will of the father. Their answer gives way to Jesus' counter-response as the narrative turns from the parable to its application.

The parable's application

Like David when confronted with Nathan's story of the rich exploiter (2 Sam. 12.1–6), the Jewish leaders declare the obvious verdict. Like Nathan, Jesus points his finger of judgement at the Jewish leaders: 'You are the man!' (2 Sam. 12.7). The tax collectors and prostitutes[19] precede you into the kingdom of God. While Jesus' words themselves 'neither imply nor deny that those addressed would finally reach the Kingdom',[20] since they are followed by 21.32 and set in the context of this trilogy (cf. 21.40–41, 43; 22.6–8), the reader must take προάγουσιν here in an exclusive sense.[21] Unlike the tax collectors and prostitutes, whom they despise, the Jewish leaders will not find entrance[22] into the kingdom.

If 21.31c declares Jesus' sentence against the Jewish leaders, then 21.32 grounds that decree in the nature of the religious authorities' guilt. John 'came in the way of righteousness' but, while the tax-gatherers and prostitutes welcomed his message, the Jewish leaders refused to believe him. The sense of the parable now becomes evident. Like the first son, in spite of an affirmation of intent, the Jewish leaders have failed to do the will of the father and consequently are excluded from the kingdom.

On the other hand, like the second son, the religious outcasts enter the kingdom because, in spite of their initial reluctance, they have believed the Baptist and so done the will of the father. The father in the story is not the Baptist but God himself – the God to whom Jesus' adversaries profess allegiance, but whose appeal on the lips of the Baptist they have rejected. The people are vindicated. The authorities are condemned. The Baptist was a prophet of the God of Israel.

The way of righteousness

While the general thrust of the parable's interpretation seems clear enough, perhaps the same cannot be said for its components including, especially, the phrase ἐν ὁδῷ δικαιοσύνης. In a 1992 essay, D. Hagner refers to a trend among Matthean scholars to take each of the seven occurrences of δικαιοσύνη in Matthew as referring to the ethical conduct that is demanded of those who wish to follow Jesus.[23] Hagner's essay probably represents the most recent, sustained rejection of this trend. He concludes that at 21.32 gift and not demand is in view and that we should take this phrase to mean 'the way of God's salvation'.

The main lines of his argument may be summarised as follows. First, it is wrongheaded to insist that any writer consistently use a word in precisely the same sense.[24] Second, while (ה)צדק and its LXX counterpart δικαιοσύνη occur with a variety of senses in the OT, '[a]mong the most important of these meanings is found in the reference to the eschatological salvation and vindication brought to the people of God. This sense of the word is particularly prominent in the prophets.'[25] Third, at 3.15 where δικαιοσύνη is also used in a context in which the Baptist figures prominently, ethical righteousness cannot be in view.[26] Fourth, unlike Luke, elsewhere Matthew 'does not stress John as a preacher of righteousness'.[27] Fifth, with respect to 21.32 itself, what is at stake in this context is 'going into the kingdom of heaven [sic]'.[28] Moreover, something of a counterpart to ὁδὸς δικαιοσύνης may be found at 22.16, ἡ ὁδὸς τοῦ θεοῦ. Finally, and most importantly for his case, '[t]he emphasis of immediate context is not upon the practice of righteousness but upon receiving the gospel; not upon doing, but upon believing'.[29]

In spite of Hagner's careful defence of a salvation–historical understanding of δικαιοσύνη at 21.32, I think that here, as elsewhere in this narrative, the word refers to ethical conduct.

As Hagner rightly notes, δικαιοσύνη does occur in a variety of senses in the LXX[30] – not least with reference to *God's* saving activity[31] but also to the *human* conduct that conforms to God's standards.[32] And, of course, Matthew need not employ the word consistently. Perhaps, however, it is suggestive that, while the phrase 'the way[s] of righteousness'[33] is relatively common in Jewish and early Christian texts, nowhere else does it refer to the way of eschatological deliverance. Instead, the phrase always describes the human practice of righteousness.[34] We might expect to find it used in similar manner here. Nevertheless, as Hagner insists, the use of (ה)צדק/δικαιοσύνη in these texts is broad enough that any firm conclusions about the meaning of ἐν ὁδῷ δικαιοσύνης must await our study of Matthew's story itself.

Examination of the context of 21.32 prompts the reader to affirm what Hagner denies, namely, that emphasis does fall upon doing, upon the practice of righteousness, and not merely upon believing. As we have seen, the parable's application identifies the religious authorities as the son whose promise to work was never transformed into action, and the tax collectors and prostitutes as the son who finally obeyed his father and went to work in the vineyard. We might summarise this as follows.

(1)   The chief priests and elders (the son who failed to do the father's will) fail to enter because they rejected God's appeal; they did not believe the Baptist.

(2)   The tax gatherers and prostitutes (the son who did the father's will) enter the kingdom because they responded to God's appeal; they believed the Baptist.

In this context, then, doing the will of the father is closely linked with believing the Baptist. Is 'the father's will' to be identified with faith, which secures entrance to God's kingdom? Or is 'believing the Baptist' a concrete illustration of the obedience (doing the father's will) that marks those who enter the kingdom? If the use of similar language elsewhere in Matthew's story is any guide, then surely the reader must opt for the latter alternative.

We have already had occasion to refer to 7.21–23,[35] but once again it becomes important. As here, so there, those who finally enter God's kingdom are those who do the will of the father. Mere profession of allegiance is of no value. At 7.21–23 doing the will of the father means obeying Jesus' teaching.[36] Surely this is the point once more in 12.50 where the reader learns, in Hagner's words: 'The disciples of Jesus are his true family because they follow his teaching. The essence of discipleship is doing τὸ θέλημα τοῦ πατρός μου τοῦ ἐν οὐρανοῖς . . . The will of the Father is the righteousness taught by Jesus and is inseparable from the dawning of the kingdom and discipleship to Jesus.'[37]

Those who would enter God's kingdom must obey God. In failing to heed the appeal made by God through his servant, the Baptist, the chief priests and elders of the people have illustrated their disobedience and sealed their fate.[38] If believing the Baptist comes into special focus in 21.32, it is probably because here Jesus indicts the Jewish leaders with their own words (cf. 21.25). As we shall see, Matthew's emphasis on the necessity of obedience to God for entrance to the kingdom also finds expression in the remaining two parables of the trilogy.

One final observation about the context in which 21.32 is set may be important. The first reference to John in this context comes in 21.25, which, with its question about John's baptism, directs the reader back to Matthew 3 where the evangelist introduces the Baptist. As the herald of the imminent reign of heaven, John charges Israel to 'prepare the way of the Lord' *by* returning to her God in repentance (3.2–3).[39] He confronts the Jewish leaders coming to his baptism, warning them to produce fruit worthy of repentance (3.8) since every tree that does not produce good fruit is cut down and thrown into the fire (3.10). In this narrative, then, the Baptist *is* a preacher of righteousness.[40] His message is Jesus' message (cf. 4.17; 7.19). He calls his generation to a way of life that flows out of genuine repentance.[41]

If a close analysis of the context of Matthew's reference to the ὁδὸς δικαιοσύνης suggests an ethical understanding of righteousness here, then the use of δικαιοσύνη elsewhere in the Gospel points in the same direction.[42] Perhaps the most important parallel comes at 5.20 since there, as here, the reader confronts an 'entrance saying'; there, as here, the narrative contrasts the Jewish leaders with those who enter the kingdom; and there, as here, δικαιοσύνη plays a central role in distinguishing those who enter from those who do not. 5.17–19 addresses the problem of Jesus' relationship to the law and the prophets (5.17–18) and the consequent (οὖν) responsibility his followers have to observe the commandments (5.19). 5.20 supplies the grounds (γάρ) for 5.19 by appealing to the prospect of their future entrance to or exclusion from the kingdom: 'For I say to you that unless your righteousness (δικαιοσύνη) greatly surpasses that of the scribes and Pharisees, you will surely not enter the kingdom of heaven.' At issue, then, is the abiding validity of the law. 5.19 calls for conduct that conforms to God's standards. 5.21–48 elucidates that manner of the obedience for which Jesus calls. All of this suggests that at 5.20 also δικαιοσύνη refers to ethical righteousness.[43]

The careful reader, then, has every reason to find in δικαιοσύνη at 21.32 reference to ethical righteousness, to the manner of living that conforms to God's standards.[44] Set in the midst of their escalating conflict with Jesus, the indictment of the chief priests and elders receives polemical accent here. Although John came calling for righteousness,[45] they failed to believe him (καὶ οὐκ ἐπιστεύσατε αὐτῷ). The threefold reference to 'believing the Baptist' in 21.32 links the application to the earlier admission of the chief priests and elders, places their indictment upon their own lips (cf. 21.25), and contrasts them unfavourably with the despised tax collectors and prostitutes. As we have seen, this is entirely consistent with the portrait of the Jewish leadership that is painted throughout this narrative. In rejecting this ethical way and the God who demands it, the Jewish leadership has effectively excluded itself from his kingdom.

But there is inclusion as well as exclusion in this story. From the vantage point of the establishment, Jesus' declaration could hardly have seemed less than scandalous. For them, Jesus' *association* with tax gatherers and sinners was offensive (9.9–13, cf. 11.16–19). But the reader has been offered a dramatically different perspective. This earlier characterisation also leaves its mark on the reader's reception of the parable.

Characterisation and reader response: the marginal characters and the Baptist

J. Anderson isolates five major groups of characters that populate Matthew's story: the crowds, the disciples, the Jewish leaders, the supplicants, and the Gentiles.[46] But by the time the reader of Matthew's Gospel finds reference – in Jesus' explanation of The Two Sons – to the tax gatherers and prostitutes that precede the chief priests and elders into the kingdom, she senses the affinity that they share with members from each of Anderson's character groups, save the Jewish leaders. What unites these characters is their 'marginal' status. Moreover, their prominence in Matthew's narrative is such that, while most of them can be identified with other character groups, they themselves none the less form a recognisable group of characters. Like the other major character groups in the narrative, they are characterised chiefly by their response to Jesus and by his response to them.

In this narrative, Jesus consistently embraces those people who stand on the fringes of Jewish society. This is perhaps most clearly demonstrated in Jesus' healing ministry. The series of incidents recorded in chapters 8 and 9 is particularly instructive. There Jesus heals, successively, a leper (8.2–4), a Gentile's servant (8.5–13), a woman (8.14–15), many who were demon possessed and all the sick (8.16–17), two demoniacs (8.28–34), a paralytic (9.2–8), a woman plagued by a perpetual haemorrhage (9.20–22), a ruler's deceased daughter (9.18–19, 23–26), two blind men and a dumb demoniac (9.32–34). Of these, perhaps only the official whose daughter Jesus raises from the dead (9.18–19, 23–26) stands as an exception to this cast of otherwise marginal characters. Nor can these events be dismissed as isolated or incidental.[47] Jesus' healing of the blind and the lame, the lepers and the deaf, and even the dead, stands as an index of his Messianic vocation (11.2–6).

Moreover, it is not only by healing those in desperate need that Jesus demonstrates his commitment to the marginal in Israel. He also displays the mercy that is of fundamental importance to Israel's God[48] by welcoming tax gatherers and sinners at his table, so extending his offer of forgiveness (cf. 9.1–8) and invitation to discipleship to sinners in need of pardon (9.10–13). That Jesus designates one of these an apostle (9.9, cf. 10.3) only accentuates the posture he adopts towards Israel's outcasts. This stance provokes the opposition both of the Pharisees – self-appointed guardians of Israel's purity – and, more broadly, of 'this generation'[49] who dismiss Jesus as 'a glutton and a drunkard, a friend of tax gatherers and sinners' (11.19).

What he models by acts of healing and by extension of table-fellowship to sinners, Jesus explicitly affirms in his teaching: the poor are the recipients of his proclamation (11.6); a child becomes a tutor for the disciples (18.1–5, cf. 19.13–15); and the tax gatherers and prostitutes enter God's kingdom (21.31b–32).

The marginalised are not the only characters in Matthew's narrative that Jesus consistently embraces, but they are distinctive; what sets them apart is the consistency with which they embrace him.

The Gentile Magi are the first 'outsiders' whose response to Jesus is recorded in this narrative (2.1–12). We have already had occasion to note the favourable characterisation they receive. Here we recall only the stated purpose of their journey: 'to pay him homage' (2.2, cf. 2.11). They become the first in a series of marginal characters in this narrative to bow before Jesus. In each of these texts the evangelist's rhetoric helps move the reader towards the worship of Jesus.[50] But worship is not the only response towards which the marginal characters in Matthew's narrative lead the implied reader. The leper who guides the reader towards worship of Jesus at 8.2–4 also displays a remarkable faith (κύριε, ἐὰν θέλῃς δύνασαί με καθαρίσαι), and faith is perhaps the dominant trait of the marginalised in Matthew's story.

Matthew's account of the healing of the leper gives way, in 8.5–13, to the story of another 'outsider' – the Gentile centurion of Capernaum who has come to Jesus on behalf of his paralysed servant. It is, as we have seen, a story about faith. The narrative presents this centurion engaged in dialogue with Jesus. Several decades ago, H. J. Held demonstrated that the Matthean miracle stories are punctuated by conversations in which request and answer are connected, often by means of a catchword, with the result that the faith displayed in these narratives may be described as a praying faith.[51] Understood this way, these miracle stories function as models for the reader designed to elicit the same kind of believing prayer.[52]

At 8.11–12, however, the faith in view is not so much 'praying faith' as 'saving faith'. The Gentile centurion thus stands as a promise of what faith may secure from the hand of the Lord, in terms both of temporal help and of final salvation, but also as a warning of the fate to which the absence of faith must inevitably lead. The implied reader, then, finds in this text not merely an historical witness to Jesus' healing power, but also, and primarily, an implicit call to a faith in Jesus that finds salvation here and hereafter.[53]

If worship and faith are the dominant responses towards which this cast of marginal characters move the implied reader, they also elicit from the sympathetic reader service (8.14–15, cf. 26.6–13; 27.55–56, 57–61; 28.1–7), obedience (9.9, cf. 4.18–22), understanding (27.29, 54, cf. 11.25–27) and humility (18.1–5). Here we restrict comment to the last of these. In reply to the disciples' question about relative greatness (18.1), Jesus calls a child (18.2) and makes him a model of the humility required for both entrance to and greatness in the kingdom (18.3–4). The reader must *become* one of the marginal!

For the reader, as for Jesus, the marginalised in Israel become the objects of welcome acceptance and of fruitful ministry. Indeed, this is precisely what Jesus commands (9.8; 18.5, cf. 19.13–15); but these marginal characters also become guides for the reader, modelling appropriate responses to Jesus.

Returning to The Two Sons, what distinguishes the tax collectors and prostitutes from the chief priests and elders is that, in embracing the way of righteousness, the former have done the will of the father. As elsewhere in this narrative, the performance of righteousness becomes the criterion for entrance into the kingdom. As such, even if the chief emphasis here is polemical, for the reader the repetition of this ethical criterion becomes implicitly hortatory. Like the parable proper, the application holds paraenetic import for the reader. Here, following the lead of the despised tax collectors and prostitutes, he must, in repentance, embrace the way of righteousness. Entrance to the kingdom is at stake.

The characterisation of the Baptist in this narrative only reinforces this implicit paraenesis. That the reader will locate John firmly in the Hebrew prophetic tradition seems obvious. This is the consistent witness of Matthew's narrative, endorsed by the testimony of the narrator (3.3), of Jesus (11.7–11; 17.9–13), of the Scriptures (3.3, 11.10), and accepted by the people (14.5, cf. 21.26). This narrative portrait of John as Yahweh's prophet underscores the significance of his proclamation. Having acknowledged the Baptist's prophetic role, the reader must come to terms with John's message. Earlier we noted John's insistence that only fruit worthy of repentance (3.8) would turn aside the imminent judgement (3.10). John's demand becomes, for the reader, a divine decree. For the reader, as for the marginal, believing the Baptist entails the pursuit of the righteousness that flows from genuine repentance.[54]

Curiously, the application does not conclude with the simple but telling contrast between the religious authorities' unbelief and the sinners' faith. Instead, the indictment continues: ὑμεῖς δὲ ἰδόντες οὐδὲ μετεμελήθητε ὕστερον τοῦ πιστεῦσαι αὐτῷ. That this concluding sentence underlines the special culpability of the Jewish leaders seems clear. The tax gatherers and prostitutes met John's message of righteousness with repentance. Witnessing this, the Jewish leaders were afforded a second opportunity to heed the invitation of the Father.[55] Perhaps of equal importance, however, by underlining this second opportunity for repentance, this parable (or rather its application) anticipates the development of the same motif in The Tenants (cf. 21.34, 36) and The Wedding Feast (cf. 22.3, 4).

Earlier I suggested that the two questions of 21.23, 25 were particularly important for the interpretation of our parable. When the chief priests and elders evaded Jesus' question, he turned to the parable and, on his way to answering their question about his authority (21.33–46), answered his own about John's. John's authority came from heaven; to reject him was to reject the God who made his appeal through him (21.31b–32).

This short parable, then, reviews the story of the Baptist's encounter with Israel. John comes as a prophet of the God of Israel (21.31b–32) and meets with a genuine repentance that leads to pardon from the people, on the one hand, and a stubborn rejection that leads to condemnation from the leaders, on the other.[56]

The parable of The Two Sons is, first of all, polemical. The Jewish leaders' professed allegiance to God has been exposed as mere pretence by their refusal to respond to his appeal, now placed on the lips of his servant the Baptist. But the judgement that Jesus pronounces on the Jewish leaders has both eschatological and ecclesiological significance. While the tax gatherers and prostitutes enter the eschatological kingdom, the religious elite remain outside, excluded by their persistent refusal to obey the Father. And, like 7.21–23, the parable warns the reader that profession is no substitute for performance: the people of God is composed exclusively of those who do the will of the Father.

5.2 The Tenants (21.33–46)[57]

The parable proper

The initial charge (21.33a)

Ἄλλην παραβολὴν ἀκούσατε introduces The Tenants, links it to the first of the trilogy's parables and, perhaps already, prepares the reader for both the polemical and the paraenetic notes that will feature prominently in this story.

As we have already noted,[58] this is not the first time that this narrative employs ἀκούω in parabolic contexts. At the conclusion of both the parables of The Sower (13.9) and of The Tares (13.43), Jesus issues the charge: ὁ ἔχων ὦτα ἀκουέτω. By issuing the call to hear *after* he has spoken, Matthew's Jesus invites the hearers – in the first instance the crowds (cf. 13.2–3) and in the second his disciples (cf. 13.36), but in both cases also the subsequent hearers of this Gospel – *to move beyond hearing* to understanding and obedience (cf. 13.23–24, 51–52). In the case of The Sower, Matthew's narrative repeats this challenge by reiterating the exhortation to listen (Ὑμεῖς οὖν ἀκούσατε τὴν παραβολήν; 13.18) at the outset of the parable's *explanation* where, presumably, the call to *understanding* is most appropriate. Again, at the conclusion of this interpretation, hearing is linked with understanding (ὁ τὸν λόγον ἀκούων καὶ συνιείς). It is the one who hears and understands who bears fruit. In this narrative, hearing in its fullest sense can never be separated from obeying.[59] The one who does not bear fruit does not hear and understand. Finally, at 15.10 a similar charge (ἀκούετε καὶ συνίετε), addressed to the crowd, prefaces Jesus' parabolic utterance about the nature of defilement (15.11).

Having confronted the call to understand and obey the message of The Sower at 13.18 (Ὑμεῖς οὖν ἀκούσατε τὴν παραβολήν), the reader is prepared to find a similar exhortation in the echo of this charge at 21.33 (Ἄλλην παραβολὴν ἀκούσατε). Unlike 13.18, however, 21.33 is addressed to Jesus' adversaries. Most obviously, the phrase issues a challenge to the Jewish leaders. But, at another level, this introduction also addresses subsequent hearers and so calls *them* to an understanding that bears fruit in obedience. This was precisely the function of the similar introduction at 13.18.

This point is only underscored when we remember that the Gospel was almost certainly designed for aural reception.[60] In such a setting it would be most natural for listeners to find themselves addressed in such phrases as 'Let anyone with ears listen!' (13.9, 43); 'Listen and understand' (15.10); and 'Listen to another parable' (21.33, cf. 13.18). If this is so, then here also the trilogy turns towards subsequent hearers. Here listeners are *included* by direct address.

The setting: a vineyard, its owner, and his tenants (21.33b)

The remainder of verse 33 sets the scene against which the story is told. Having planted a vineyard, the owner let it out to tenant farmers[61] and departed. The vocabulary of this verse is marked by a number of clear echoes of Isaiah 5.2 (LXX), which reads: καὶ φραγμὸν περιέθηκα καὶ ἐχαράκωσα καὶ ἐφύτευσα ἄμπελον σωρηχ καὶ ᾠκοδόμησα πύργον ἐν μέσῳ αὐτοῦ καὶ προλήνιον ὤρυξα ἐν αὐτῷ· καὶ ἔμεινα τοῦ ποιῆσαι σταφυλήν, ἐποίησεν δὲ ἀκάνθας. The obvious allusions to Isaiah 5 point the reader back to Isaiah's Song of the Vineyard, which, in spite of notable differences,[62] shares with Jesus' story of the vineyard several important motifs. Both stories tell the story of Yahweh's dealings with Israel. Both point to his gracious initiative in this relationship. In both stories, Yahweh waits for fruit[63] from Israel and finds none. Again, in both stories the failure of Israel's leaders has dramatic implications for the people, upon whom judgement also falls (Isa. 5.7, cf. 3.13–15). Perhaps, then, the reader is to find in this allusion to Isaiah's parable a hint that, radical as this parable must have seemed to many pious Jews – Christian or otherwise – the roots of its message could be found in their own Scriptures. Certainly this would suit the parable's polemical design and it is a point to which the parable will return (21.41–42).

Perhaps, however, the specific allusions to Isaiah's Song have additional significance. For most scholars, the hedge, the tower and the winepress seem to have no metaphorical import in a story whose details often do.[64] Here *Targum Isaiah* 5.1b–2, 5 becomes important:

> *My people*, my beloved *Israel, I gave them a heritage* on a *high* hill *in* fertile *land*. And I *sanctified them* and I *glorified them* and I *established them as the plant of a* choice vine; and I built *my sanctuary* in *their* midst, and I even *gave my altar to atone for their sins; I thought that they would do good deeds, but they made their deeds evil* . . . And now I will tell you what I *am about to do* to my *people*. I will *take up my Shekhinah from them*, and *they* shall be for *plundering*; I will break down *the place of their sanctuaries*, and *they will be* for trampling.[65]

In the Targum, then, the tower has become the temple, the wine-vat has become the altar,[66] and the song as a whole has become a prediction of the temple's destruction. The uncertainties surrounding the dating of the Targums mean that, as it relates to Jesus' parable, in itself *Targum Isaiah* 5 is intriguing, but perhaps little more. Already in 1984, however, C. Evans argued that the appearance of similar tower symbolism in *1 Enoch* 89[67] suggests that it is plausible 'that the tower symbolism had already found its way into the emerging targumic tradition prior to the synoptic tradition.'[68] The recent publication of 4Q500 has strengthened this case. Both Evans and G. Brooke have argued that 4Q500 contains several allusions to Isaiah 5 and, once more, links Isaiah's vineyard with the temple. Evans concludes: 'These additional points of coherence strongly suggest that the cultic interpretation preserved in the Targum predates the New Testament.'[69]

If indeed we accept these proposals, the relevance for Jesus' parable becomes obvious. Set in the context of a dispute with the Jewish establishment in the temple (cf. 21.23), in the wake of his symbolic cleansing of the temple (21.12–17), and just prior to his prediction of the destruction of the temple (24.2, cf. 21.40–41; 22.7), The Tenants places the cult and not merely the nation at the forefront from the outset of its story.[70] And already the parable prepares the reader for the judgement its conclusion will declare (cf. 21.41).

The tenants and the servants: rebellion and murder (21.34–36)

Matthew 21.34–36 details the landowner's attempts to collect his fruit (τοὺς καρποὺς αὐτοῦ) at harvest (ὅτε δὲ ἤγγισεν ὁ καιρὸς τῶν καρπῶν). Reference to the harvest sets the stage for the encounter between the tenants and the householder, but the careful selection of vocabulary prepares the reader already to think at the metaphorical level. Earlier in this narrative, ἐγγίζω has been employed in salvation–historical contexts. In its first three occurrences the kingdom is its subject and the phrase of which it is a part summarises John's, Jesus', and the disciples' proclamation: the long awaited kingdom has drawn near (3.2, cf. 4.17; 10.7). At 21.1, ἐγγίζω signals Jesus' fateful approach to Jerusalem. Subsequently, the hour of Jesus' betrayal (26.45) followed by the betrayer himself (26.46) draw near. Elsewhere in Matthew's story, then, where ἐγγίζω is used, it is first the kingdom and then the death of Jesus that approaches.

καιρός is admirably suited for use in salvation–historical contexts but its use in this narrative is often more mundane.[71] But significantly, in its two occurrences in this parable, καιρός is closely linked with καρπός (21.34, 41). Elsewhere, Matthew consistently uses καρπός metaphorically, a use already firmly rooted in the LXX.[72] Like literal fruit from a tree, this metaphorical fruit is also produce, but now the produce of a person's life. In this narrative, good fruit consists of doing[73] the will of the Father, which is now expressed in the teaching of Jesus. The opening clause of verse 34 at once sets the stage for the heart of the story and anticipates its conclusion at verse 41.

At harvest-time, then, the householder sent his servants (τοὺς δούλους αὐτοῦ) to collect his fruit. But these servants received only violence from the hands of the tenants: one was beaten, another killed and another stoned (21.35). τοὺς δούλους αὐτοῦ (21.34, 35, cf. 21.36: ἄλλους δούλους) recalls the common LXX phrase, οἱ δοῦλοι αὐτοῦ οἱ προφῆται.[74] Reference to their violent fate echoes a common Jewish motif and anticipates 23.37: Ἰερουσαλὴμ Ἰερουσαλήμ, ἡ ἀποκτείνουσα τοὺς προφήτας καὶ λιθοβολοῦσα τοὺς ἀπεσταλμένους πρὸς αὐτήν. 23.37 effectively removes any doubt that may linger about the identity of the servants – they are the prophets.[75] Already in Matthew's story, the reader is reminded of the rejection of the prophets that Israel's Scriptures had chronicled;[76] and if this portrait signals the identity of the prophets, then, implicitly, it also signals the identity of their master.

In answer to this violence, the owner countered by sending a second, larger,[77] group of servants, but the earlier scene was repeated. καὶ ἐποίησαν αὐτοῖς ὡσαύτως brings the discussion of the servants to a conclusion in economical fashion and crisply underlines the fact that this second group meets the same fate as their earlier counterparts. It is the fate that the prophets have always suffered at the hands of God's people.[78]

In a narrative that has repeatedly (and recently) underlined both John the Baptist's prophetic vocation (11.9–10; 14.5; 21.26) and his rejection (3.7–10; 11.16–19; 21.23–32) and execution (14.1–12, cf. 17.10–13), the reader naturally locates John in this line of rejected prophets. He has confronted the Jewish establishment with a message from Yahweh and Israel's history has been re-enacted. As successor to the prophets' ministry to Israel, the Baptist has also become a successor to their destiny. But, successor to the prophets though he may be, more importantly for Matthew's narrative, John is precursor to the Messiah.

The tenants and the son: rebellion and murder (21.37–39)

At 21.37–39 the focus shifts from the servants to the son. After[79] the dramatic failure of the previous missions, the householder now sends his son, expecting that he will be granted respect (21.37), but the appearance of the son becomes, for the tenants, only an occasion to seize his inheritance.[80] Casting him out of the vineyard, they kill him also (21.38–39).

Having already identified the householder as God, the reader naturally identifies his son as Jesus.[81] The final clause of 21.37 (ἐντραπήσονται τὸν υἱόν μου) underlines for the reader the singular culpability of the tenants. Even the appearance of the owner's son cannot turn them from the evil path they have chosen. Instead, their perversity is only extended. In their murder of the heir outside of the vineyard (21.39), the reader finds only thinly veiled allusion to the execution of Jesus outside of the city (27.31–33, cf. John 19.17, 20; Heb. 13.12).[82]

Earlier, we suggested that the reader would locate John the Baptist with the prophets who meet with rejection and death at the hands of the tenants. Throughout this narrative, the striking parallels between John and Jesus highlight an important component of Jesus' Messianic vocation. Like John, Jesus comes as a prophet calling Israel to return to her God in repentance in light of the imminent dawn of his kingdom (3.2, cf. 4.17); and, like the Baptist, Jesus joins the long train of Yahweh's prophets who meet with rejection and violence from Yahweh's people (21.34–39, cf. 14.1–12; 17.9–13). This trilogy gives expression to this polemical motif with signal clarity.

If, however, these parallels underline the prophetic nature of Jesus' Messianic vocation, then the startling discontinuities between the two alert the reader to the ways in which Jesus – in person and mission – eclipses John (3.11, cf. 9.14–17; 11.2–15). The situation is no different when we turn to these parables. In the parable of The Tenants, the reader learns once more of Jesus' impending fate: like John, the prophet Jesus from Nazareth (21.11, cf. 21.46) will die at the hands of the Jewish establishment (21.37–39). But if, as elsewhere in Matthew's narrative, Jesus walks the path that the forerunner had previously walked, then, as elsewhere, he does so in a manner that transcends his predecessor. Whereas John meets his destiny as δοῦλος θεοῦ, Jesus meets his as υἱὸς θεοῦ.[83]

Like John, Jesus is a prophet and more than a prophet. Unlike John, Jesus is Messiah, God's Son – ὁ ἐρχόμενος whose sandals the Baptist is not worthy to carry (3.11). The remarkable parallels between John and Jesus in Matthew's narrative underline, polemically, the common fate that would await both forerunner and Messiah, but these repeated parallels also serve to accent the differences between the two. Jesus is like John, but even greater:[84] John is the Christological witness; Jesus is the Christ.

The tenants and the owner: reprisal (21.40–41)

At verse 40 the narrative turns from its rehearsal of the tenants' rebellion to consider the master's response to their murderous defiance: 'When the master of the vineyard comes, what will he do to those tenants?'[85] The temporal clause that prefaces the question is intriguing. Two important factors encourage the reader to detect here a secondary allusion to AD 70. First, the answer provided by the Jewish leaders in 21.41 (κακοὺς κακῶς ἀπολέσει . . .) seems an apt reference to the events surrounding the Jewish war.[86] More importantly the final parable of the trilogy contains an unmistakable echo of 21.40–41. There 'those murderers' are destroyed, but their city is also burned (22.7). If, as seems likely, this alludes to the destruction of Jerusalem in AD 70, then it becomes natural to find a similar allusion here where God's judgement on Israel for the rejection of his servants is also in view.[87]

At 21.41 the Jewish leaders answer Jesus' question, so forging one more link with The Two Sons by issuing their own condemnation (cf. 21.31). For the reader, the portrait of a group of leaders perversely blind to their own sin continues to emerge.[88] κακοὺς κακῶς . . . αὐτούς emphasises both the evil nature of the tenants and their terrible fate. By their persistent pursuit of the son's destruction, the Jewish leaders seal their own.

The sentence, moreover, refers to replacement as well as destruction. The vineyard will be leased to another group of *tenant farmers* (ἄλλοις γεωργοῖς). ἐκδίδωμι recalls 21.33 (the only other occurrence of the word in Matthew's narrative), and perhaps highlights the fact that, like the first tenants, their replacements remain only farmers responsible to the vineyard owner.

The Jewish leaders' response to Jesus' question concludes with a relative clause that 21.34 had anticipated. Like a double-edged sword it recalls the failure of the first tenants even as it highlights the condition upon which the new tenants retain possession of the vineyard: the new tenants will give back to the owner the fruits of the vineyard. Here the reader feels as if he is in familiar territory as the narrative returns to a favourite motif. Earlier I suggested that, in this narrative, good fruit consists of doing the will of the Father. Perhaps 7.15–27 demonstrates this most clearly. In this context, one other feature of the use of the word in Matthew's story may be observed, namely, its connection with judgement. Already at 3.10 in the Baptist's preaching, the reader learns that the production of good fruit is the one thing that turns aside judgement. This theme is developed in 7.15–20. 7.19 echoes 3.10 but the preceding verses supply the underlying logic. Just as a tree's produce betrays the nature of the tree, so the products of a person's life unveil the nature of her character. What one does reveals who he is. Failure to produce good fruit can only point to a faulty tree (7.17–18), the kind that is cut down and cast into the fire (7.19). At 7.21 the metaphor is lifted: only those who do the will of the Father enter the kingdom. 12.33–35 explains why the Pharisees, who have just charged Jesus with being in league with Satan (12.22–24ff.), are unable to say what is good. Once again, the pericope is concerned with judgement and, once again, a person's 'fruit' – now his words – becomes the criterion of judgement (12.36–37). Outside of The Tenants, καρπός appears for the final time at 21.19 where Jesus, in a symbolic pronouncement of judgement, curses the fig tree: 'May no fruit ever come from you again.' As often in Matthew's narrative, the absence of fruit provokes judgement.[89]

If the final clause of verse 41 returns to a prominent motif in this narrative, then it also echoes Psalm 1.3. καρπός occurs frequently in the LXX, referring both to literal and to metaphorical produce of various sorts,[90] but only at Psalm 1.3 does one find anything like the concentration of words found here in this relative clause – the echo is surely intentional.[91] Psalm 1.3 describes the blessed who delight in the law of the Lord: καὶ ἔσται ὡς τὸ ξύλον τὸ πεφυτευμένον παρὰ τὰς διεξόδους τῶν ὑδάτων, ὃ τὸν καρπὸν αὐτοῦ δώσει ἐν καιρῷ αὐτοῦ. The parallels between the two relative clauses are striking.

If, however, 21.41 recalls Psalm 1.3, the subtle differences between the two texts may also be significant. ἀποδώσουσιν, which with αὐτῷ replaces δώσει, is common in this narrative, often used as part of its emphasis on reward. Here, however, it is not God who 'gives back' but his new tenants. The fruit which the new people produce must be given back to the one to whom it rightfully belongs (cf. τοὺς καρποὺς αὐτοῦ, v. 34). The obedience for which God calls is only that which is rightfully his. Where Psalm 1.3 has ἐν καιρῷ αὐτοῦ, Matthew 21.41 has ἐν τοῖς καιροῖς αὐτῶν. Here, for the only time in this narrative,[92] καιρός is plural. If this difference is significant, perhaps here *seasons* subtly suggests that there is not just one harvest time for these new tenants. Similarly καρπός is now plural as seems appropriate in a metaphorical reference to the various products of a person's life that obedience to God requires.

This echo of Psalm 1.3 calls the reader's attention to the wider psalm with the sharp distinction it draws between the two ways and their destinies. Those who are blessed (v. 1), the righteous (v. 6), like trees that yield fruit in season, prosper in whatever they do (v. 3). On the contrary, the godless (v. 4), the sinners (v. 5), are like the chaff, which the wind drives from the face of the earth (v. 4) – the way of the godless will perish (v. 6). The failure of the first tenants to yield fruit marks them as those who walk not the first path, but the second.[93] Their judgement is only to be expected. The Scriptures require it. Like the earlier allusion to Isaiah's vineyard story, the allusion to Psalm 1 seems designed in part to underline that what Jesus was here declaring – the replacement of Israel as God's people – actually has its basis in Israel's Scriptures.

The (self-) indictment elicited from the Jewish leaders, then, functions polemically. The pronouncement itself – laced with bitter irony, coming as it does from the leaders themselves – highlights both the evil nature and the terrible fate of Jesus' adversaries. But in the relative clause that brings the pronouncement to its conclusion, polemics and paraenesis join hands. This depiction of the new tenants at once underlines the failure of the old tenants and reminds their replacements that God's demands have not changed. What serves as a note of condemnation for the one acts as a warning for the other. Once more, then, this trilogy fixes its gaze upon the reader and, once more, the purpose is hortatory. The new people of God, like the old, must give back to him fruit in season.

The parable's interpretation and application (21.42–46)

The stone saying: vindication (21.42)

If 21.41 alluded to the Israel's Scriptures in support of the verdict rendered against the tenants, then in 21.42 allusion yields to quotation as Jesus appeals to Psalm 117.22–23 (LXX) in defence of the same judgement. The polemical 'Have you never read in the Scriptures' (cf. 21.16) introduces the citation. Jesus finds support for the verdict declared by the Jewish leaders in the Scriptures but ironically, as he turns the text against them, he makes it plain that they have not understood their own writings. The lord of the vineyard is not content to bring vengeance on his son's murderers. He proceeds to vindicate and exalt the rejected son.[94]

If we were justified earlier in finding allusion to the temple in Jesus' reference to the tower that was built in the vineyard (as in *Tg. Isa.* 5.2), then this saying becomes marked by a more obvious anti-temple sentiment and its connection to the parable becomes more obvious.[95] The Targum, as we noted above, announces the destruction of the temple. In this context, probably the reference to a new cornerstone likewise implies the destruction, or at least the replacement, of the existing temple.[96]

The parable's interpretation: transferral (21.43)

Matthew 21.43 interprets the parable's significance. As διὰ τοῦτο suggests, verse 42 provides the basis from which the inferential conclusion of

verse 43 may be drawn.[97] Echoing, as it does, the judgement declared by
the Jewish leaders in verse 41, this pronouncement likewise cuts sharply
in two directions.

With the metaphor now lifted, Jesus indicts the Jewish leadership. As
in verse 41 where those who sought to destroy the son face destruction,
so here those who rejected the stone are rejected. The use of the so-
called theological passive (ἀρθήσεται) implies that, as it was the Lord
who vindicated the rejected stone, so, too, it is God who has wrested[98]
the kingdom from the Jewish leaders (ἀφ᾽ ὑμῶν).[99]

The striking reference to the kingdom of *God* (as opposed to the kingdom *of heaven*, which is typical of this narrative) establishes another link
with the preceding parable (21.31). And if it is God who has taken the
kingdom, then it is God who has given it again.[100] The apologetic note
rings loud and clear: God himself has wrenched the kingdom from the
builders who rejected the stone of his choice and has transferred it to a
new ἔθνος.[101]

Furthermore, if the narrative underlines the divine sanction granted this
new people, then it also devotes attention to its composition. The kingdom
is transferred to a nation producing its fruits (ἔθνει ποιοῦντι τοὺς καρποὺς
αὐτῆς). I have already argued at length that the wider narrative encourages
the reader to find in ἔθνος here an allusion to the *trans-ethnic* community
of believers who replace the *nation* of Israel as subjects of the reign of
God. It will not do to identify this ἔθνος, on the one hand, merely as a
new leadership group for Israel or, on the other, simply as the Gentiles
who displace the Jews. This nation that God raises up in faithfulness to
his promises to Abraham is defined along ethical – not ethnic lines, and,
as in verse 41, this ethical description of the new people functions both
as an indictment of those now rejected and as a warning to those who
would not be rejected. Once again, polemics and paraenesis are closely
linked.

Not surprisingly, then, the principal features of the parable surface
again as 21.43 offers interpretation. With simple clarity, Jesus underlines
once more the guilt of the Jewish leaders and its consequences. And,
once more, the reader's attention is drawn to God – this judgement can
only be attributed to him. Again the narrative's ecclesiological concern
surfaces. If God's judgement has meant exclusion for some, then it has
meant inclusion for others. And while the boundary lines of this people are
remarkably redrawn, there is continuity in terms of God's demand – the
people of the kingdom must produce its fruits. Yet again, this paraenesis
addresses the reader.

The narrative conclusion (21.45–46)[102]

Matthew 21.45–46 permits the reader to view the first two parables of the triad from the vantage point of the Jewish leadership. Καὶ ἀκούσαντες ironically recalls Jesus' introduction to the parable (Ἄλλην παραβολὴν ἀκούσατε). Granted this 'inside view', the reader learns that, at one level, the Jewish leaders *have heard* Jesus' parables. They understand well that these parables are about them.[103] They have been granted leading roles in Jesus' stories. They are the son who gladly agrees to work in the vineyard, but never arrives. They are the tenants who murder the Son. They are the builders who reject the stone of God's choice. At a more fundamental level, however, their hearing fails. They become classic examples of those who look without seeing.[104] Their deficiency is not intellectual but moral. Instead of bearing fruit in obedience, they are only hardened in their opposition to Jesus. Only fear of the people, who consider Jesus a prophet, prevents them from seizing him immediately. This explanatory clause (ἐπεὶ εἰς προφήτην αὐτὸν εἶχον) effectively distances the crowds from their leaders. More importantly, it also echoes 14.5 and 21.26 where it referred to John, thus reminding the reader once more that the path marked out for Jesus is the one that John has already walked (17.9–13, cf. 14.1–12). It is the way of a prophet (cf. 21.11).[105]

Thus, this is in the first place a story about Israel's leaders and her God. The vineyard (21.33), its produce (21.34), the servants (21.34) and the son are his (21.37). The rebellion is theirs (21.34–39, 45, 46). Their own Scriptures pronounce judgement on them (21.33, 41, 42). Nor is it only the Scriptures that declare this verdict. So perversely blind are they to their own sin that they actually pronounce their own condemnation (21.40–41). They have failed to give back to God the obedience that was rightfully his and have provoked his judgement (21.41, 43). But it is also a story about a new group of tenants whose distinguishing feature is that they yield to God the obedience that is rightfully his (21.41, 43). As such, it is a story about the reader who, having stood on the receiving end of the paraenesis that is implicit throughout, has himself been drawn into the world of the story.

5.3   The Wedding Feast (22.1–14)

At 22.1 the spotlight shifts from the Jewish leaders back to Jesus as he resumes his parabolic address. As we shall see, The Wedding Feast revisits the central motifs of the earlier parables but also extends them as the trilogy moves towards its climax.

The invitation to the feast: polemics and salvation-history
(22.1–10)

The invitation twice extended: Matthew 22.2–4

From the outset, the reader notes the obvious links to the earlier parables
of the trilogy. Like The Two Sons and The Tenants, this story concerns
the kingdom (but now ἡ βασιλεία τῶν οὐρανῶν). The use of ἄνθρωπος
(followed by an appositive) and of ὅστις echoes 21.33 (cf. also 21.28).
The appearance of the son recalls the prominence of the sons in the two
previous parables and, especially, in The Tenants.[106] The central role
granted to the son in the preceding parable prepares the reader to identify
him here; here too the son is the Son.[107] That it is a wedding feast in his
honour is especially appropriate in a narrative that twice presents Jesus
as bridegroom.[108]

Nor are these links limited to the introduction. ἀπέστειλεν τοὺς δούλους
αὐτοῦ reproduces exactly the phrase from 21.34. Here the servants are
commissioned to call the invited guests to the feast. As the tenants rebuffed
the servants' attempt to collect the householder's fruit (21.35), so here the
guests refuse the king's invitation (22.3). καὶ οὐκ ἤθελον ἐλθεῖν at once
underlines this stubborn obstinacy and anticipates 23.37, where a similar
phrase stands at the heart of Jesus' climactic lament over Jerusalem.

Having once been declined, the king dispatches a second group of
servants bearing the same invitation (22.4).[109] Once more the repetition
is striking – πάλιν ἀπέστειλεν ἄλλους δούλους duplicates the report of
the second mission in The Tenants (21.36). These exact echoes of 21.34,
36 prepare the reader to find here, as there, reference to the repeated
missions of *the prophets* (τοὺς δούλους αὐτοῦ) to Israel. The natural
identification of the king as God only strengthens this suspicion. But the
parable's developing storyline will give the reader reason to modify this
preliminary conclusion.

Rejection and reprisal: Matthew 22.5–7

As the first of the two sons twice rejected the opportunity to repent (21.32),
and as the first tenants twice refused to surrender the fruit of the vineyard
(21.34, 36), so here the guests twice spurn the invitation to the wedding
feast (22.3, 5). The first group of guests simply ignores the king's envoys
and returns to daily routines (22.5), but the indifference of the first (22.5)
quickly gives way to the violence of the rest as they seize, mistreat and
murder the king's servants (22.6). Derrett finds no inherent implausibility

either in the fact that *all* of those originally on the king's guest list refuse his invitation, or in their violent mistreatment of his messengers,[110] but surely the boundaries of credibility are exceeded on both counts. In Lambrecht's words, 'Such conduct is completely out of proportion. The narrative, as it were, springs open. The hearers cannot but look for an allegorical sense.'[111] What is more, the narrative's developing storyline encourages the reader to arrive at the same conclusion.[112] The verbal echoes that link this part of the parable to The Tenants[113] also signal the more important conceptual echoes of the earlier story. As The Tenants had earlier underscored Israel's rejection of the prophets, so here once more The Wedding Feast oversteps the boundaries of plausibility to highlight the Jewish rejection of God's servants. And if 22.6 tightens the parallels to the preceding parable, then, of course, it also prepares for the massive retaliation narrated in 22.7.

In anger the king answers the slaying of his servants with a slaughter of his own, commissioning his armies to execute his wrath against the murderers of his servants and their city (22.7). Once more the points of contact, both verbal and conceptual, with the preceding parable are obvious. Just as the vineyard owner will answer the murder of his servants and his son by *destroying those* tenants, so now the king in his fury *destroys those*[114] murderers who have killed the bearers of his invitation to the royal wedding feast.

In this parable, however, even the destruction of the murderers does not exhaust the king's fury; he also commissions the destruction of their city. For many scholars, this reference to the burning of the city can only be understood as a thinly veiled allusion to the destruction of Jerusalem in AD 70 – an *ex eventu* prophecy.[115] Some, however, remain unconvinced. In 1972, B. Reicke issued the following charge: 'An amazing example of uncritical dogmatism in New Testament studies is the belief that the Synoptic Gospels should be dated after the Jewish War of AD 66–70 because they contain prophecies *ex eventu* of the destruction of Jerusalem by the Romans in the year 70.'[116]

Not surprisingly, then, the debate as to whether Matthew 22.7 does, in fact, represent an *ex eventu* prophecy has occupied most of the scholarly discussion of this verse;[117] but, whether the verse is *ex eventu* or not,[118] two important considerations encourage the reader to find an allusion to the destruction of Jerusalem at 22.7. First, this narrative does depict the sacking of Jerusalem as God's punishment upon *this generation* of Jewish people for their violent rejection of his servants. This point is established most clearly at 23.29–24.2. Second, the striking similarities between 23.29–24.2 and 22.6–7 suggest that, already here, the destruction of Jerusalem is in view.

In 23.29–33, Jesus charges the Jewish leaders with the same murderous rejection of God's servants that characterised their fathers and, ironically,[119] challenges them to fill up the quota of the nation's sins. On the heels of this challenge, Jesus explains[120] that he is providing them with an opportunity to do just that as he sends to them prophets and wise men and scribes (23.34). In rejecting and murdering Jesus' servants, the Jewish leaders invoke upon themselves divine punishment for the cumulative guilt of their nation. ὅπως ἔλθῃ . . . (23.35) recalls διὰ τοῦτο (23.34) and presents this accumulation of guilt and the consequent outpouring of judgement as the purpose for which the servants of Jesus are sent. 23.36 echoes the verdict of 23.35: *all these things* will come upon *this generation.*

Four times previously, the reader of this narrative has confronted this expression (ἡ γενεὰ αὕτη) as Jesus indicts *this generation.* In the first three instances (11.16; 12.41, 42), the phrase describes those who, having been confronted with God's direct appeal through Jesus, have nevertheless refused to repent and thus have only condemnation awaiting them at the final judgement.[121] The fourth pronouncement (12.45) is rather more general but, falling fast on the heels of 12.41–42, eschatological overtones seem natural here too. Thus far in the Gospel, then, the reader has been prepared to think of the judgement that *awaits this generation* as an eschatological one. Nor is this notion absent from this text.[122]

Read against the backdrop of the wider narrative, however, the parable of The Tenants – which rehearses this same theme of the repeated rejection of God's servants – has established the fact that God's judgement on this generation has already invaded this age. By her persistent rebellion, Israel has forfeited her position as the people of God and another ἔθνος has been installed (21.41, 43).

Matthew 23.37–24.2 suggests likewise that, while the final punishment of this generation awaits the age to come, once more in anticipation of that, God's judgement will enter this age. The passage at 23.37–38 reports Jesus' lament over unrepentant Jerusalem whose house is forsaken and desolate. Following the puzzling pronouncement of verse 39, which is perhaps best viewed as a conditional prophecy,[123] Jesus leaves the temple and, when his disciples draw attention to its buildings, declares: 'Truly I tell you, not one stone will be left here upon another; all will be thrown down' (24.2). At 24.34 Jesus declares that *this generation* will not pass away until *all these things* – almost certainly including the temple's destruction – take place (cf. 23.36). The destruction of the temple signals God's judgement on rebellious Israel for the rejection of his servants which spans her history, but which is brought to completion by *this generation* in their murderous rejection of Jesus' servants. This is not to say that this judgement executed upon Jerusalem exhausts the divine punishment. As we have already noted, an eschatological sentence awaits this generation – ἡ κρίσις τῆς γεέννης (23.33). AD 70 is a precursor.

If 23.29–24.2 instructs the reader that the destruction of Jerusalem comes as God's punishment upon his people for the rejection of his servants including, finally, the servants sent by Jesus, then the striking similarities between 23.29–24.2 and 22.6–7 encourage her (in retrospect) to find reference to the destruction of Jerusalem already in the earlier text. Both texts highlight the repeated initiative taken by God in calling his people (22.3–4; cf. 23.37). Both texts underline the persistent, wilful rejection with which his people greet this initiative (22.3–6, cf. 22.37).[124] In both texts the people not only reject God's appeal, but also mistreat and murder[125] his servants (22.6, cf. 23.34). In both texts, God responds in judgement (22.7, cf. 23.35–24.2). In both texts, God's judgement centres on their city (22.7, cf. 23.37–24.2). Given these similarities and the fact that this trilogy focuses on the implications of the decisive failure of the Jewish nation to receive God's servants, it is difficult to avoid the conclusion that the reader should find an allusion to the destruction of Jerusalem already at 22.7.[126]

These verses align this parable with The Tenants with the result that the deuteronomistic outlook that marks that parable finds prominent expression here too. Things have not changed in Israel. This generation of God's people, like those before it (cf. 21.33–46), has rejected and murdered God's servants, the bearers of his invitation to the great feast, and so has invoked his judgement.

Furthermore, if the parallels between 23.29–24.2 and this parable lead the reader to conclude that 22.7 alludes to the destruction of Jerusalem, they also make it clear that it is the treatment of *the servants that Jesus sends* that finally brings the rebellious nation's sin to full measure and calls forth the judgement of God upon city and nation. If we conclude, then, that 22.7 points to the destruction of the city, we should probably also conclude that at least the second group of servants (22.4) represents *Christian* servants.[127]

Commenting on the identification of the servants, Hare writes: 'The problem is to determine whether the two sets of servants mentioned in verses 3 and 4 represent the prophets of the old and new dispensations respectively or signify only pre-Christian messengers.'[128] On the basis of 23.34ff., Hare opts for the former alternative. However, the close similarities between this parable and 23.29–37 so firmly secure the identification of the second group of servants that I think that the problem is rather to determine whether the two sets of servants mentioned in verses 3 and 4 represent the prophets of the old and new dispensations respectively or signify only *Christian* messengers. One might argue that the decisively different role played by the son in the two parables prepares the reader for a different interpretation of the servants. Whereas in the earlier parable, the son appears after the servants and, like them, is rejected and murdered, here he is present from the outset as the bridegroom and the natural picture is the Messianic banquet; most naturally, these servants do not precede Jesus.[129] Perhaps, if we are to distinguish between the two groups, we should think, first, of the pre-paschal and, second, of the post-paschal missions of the disciples. Interestingly, the echo of 22.3 at 23.37 describes the response of 'Jerusalem' to Jesus' mission.

Like The Two Sons and The Tenants, The Wedding Feast depicts the rejection of God's servants. But, for the reader, the servants in this final parable no longer belong to a different era. The fact that the Jewish establishment has set itself against not only Baptist and Messiah, but also Messiah's servants means that, whereas in the first of the trilogy's parables the reader aligned himself with the marginal characters over against the elite, in the second and especially the third parable, she identifies with the prophets themselves. The Jewish establishment continues to persecute Yahweh's messengers, but now these messengers are members of the community (22.4–6, cf. 23.34). They now stand where John and the prophets before him stood. Like the Baptist, they have attached themselves to the kingdom and, like the Baptist, they have felt the fury of the violence that has been hurled against that kingdom (11.12, cf. 10.17, 23; 23.34). In his relationship with the Jewish leaders, John has become a model of courageous discipleship for the community. And John's example also offers consolation. If, like John and the prophets before him, Jesus' followers are persecuted because of righteousness, they are blessed. Their reward is great. Theirs is the kingdom (5.10–12).

The parable concerns itself, then, with the rejection of God's servants – most especially, those commissioned by Jesus (22.2–6) – and with the retaliation that comes as God's decree (22.7), but also with the invitation to the feast issued once more (22.8–10). This redirected invitation itself invites discussion.

The invitation redirected: Matthew 22.8–10

Having disposed of his murderous subjects, in 22.8–10 the king turns his attention again to the wedding feast. Once more the note of eschatological readiness is sounded – the banquet is ready; and once more the guilt of those first invited is underlined – they were not worthy (22.8).[130]

Since the guests first invited were unworthy (and are now dead!), the king commissions[131] his servants to invite another contingent of guests to the feast. The inferential οὖν makes the redirected mission the direct consequence of the first guests' unworthiness. The points of contact with 21.41 and, especially, 21.43 are obvious and important. In both cases, Israel's persistent rejection of God's servants leads directly (cf. the function of διὰ τοῦτο [21.43] with οὖν [22.9]) to her loss of privilege. The Jewish rejection of the Christian missionaries is of a piece with her rejection of the prophets and the Son. If this last rejection has finally filled the cup of Israel's rebellion (cf. 23.32), then it is nevertheless the persistent rejection of God's servants throughout her history – prophets, Son, and now the Son's ambassadors – that has led to her rejection,[132] and the subsequent inclusion of the Gentiles.

While, as we have argued,[133] this third invitation to the feast depicts the Gentile mission,[134] probably the reader is not to conclude that, from the perspective of this narrative, the Gentile mission awaits the destruction of Jerusalem. Against this stands the programmatic statement of 28.19, announced by Jesus immediately after the resurrection. Instead, the desolation of the city stands as dramatic symbol of the judgement of God that has fallen against his people, as a result of which her privileged status has been forfeited and the invitation to the great wedding feast extended to all.

Matthew 22.10 is transitional, linking the two main parts of the parable. In succinctly reporting the events of this third (now successful) invitation, it brings the first part of the parable to its conclusion and prepares for the subsequent inspection of the wedding guests in 22.11–13. In accord with their commission, the king's servants gather all whom they find[135] with the result that the hall is filled. But now a further qualification is added; they have found and gathered πονηρούς τε καὶ ἀγαθούς. On this phrase Bornkamm comments:

> The characteristically Matthaean thought that the coming judgment applies even to the disciples . . . is also expressed in the parables of the vineyard and the marriage feast . . . The same, with express reference to the congregation, is also stated by the closing scene of the parable of the marriage feast, which

Matthew adds (22.11–13), but so does the expression πονηρούς τε καὶ ἀγαθούς already, which occurs in 22.10, and which, like the closing parables of ch. 13, points towards the final separation, and finally so does the concluding sentence in 22.14, which is so characteristic of Matthew: 'Many are called but few are chosen.'[136]

These words have proved especially influential. Indeed, it is difficult to find a writer who fails to comment here on Matthew's concern for the church as a *corpus mixtum*.[137] But, while preparing for the judgement scene depicted in 22.11–14, perhaps the πονηρός/ἀγαθός language is also polemical in design. So unworthy are the first guests that they are now replaced by people gathered indiscriminately, πονηρούς τε καὶ ἀγαθούς (cf. 21.31b–32). In any case, gathering gives way to inspection in 22.11–14.

The inspection at the feast: eschatology and ethics (22.11–14)

With the banquet hall finally filled, the king undertakes an inspection of the guests.[138] Finding a man inappropriately clad, the king questions him about the absence of his wedding garment, but the man's silence is telling – he can offer no excuse. With this examination, the focus of the story shifts from Israel, her rejection of Messiah's emissaries and her own consequent rejection, to the Christian community, *her* future judgement and the potential rejection of *her* members. If in the parable of The Tenants, polemics and paraenesis join hands as the parable reaches its climax (especially vv. 41, 43), then here, in the parable of The Wedding Feast, the polemic of the earlier portion of the parable yields to paraenesis as the parable – and the trilogy – draws to its conclusion. As is typically the case in Matthew's narrative, the paraenesis has an eschatological rooting.

Bauckham argues that the social significance of the wedding garment in the world of the narrative is often ignored: 'Wearing festal garments indicated one's participation in the joy of the feast. To appear in ordinary, soiled working clothes would show contempt for the occasion, a refusal to join in the king's rejoicing . . . Once again, this is no ordinary act of dishonor to a host but a matter of political significance.'[139] Guests would be expected to arrive in 'clothes that were both longer than those worn by ordinary people on working days and also newly washed.'[140] Poor people would often borrow garments for such occasions.[141] All of this may be true and may supply important local colour, but it is nevertheless also true that earthly kings do not sentence their rebellious subjects to hell, as this king does (22.13)! As Bauckham notes, 'the king's final words leave the narrative world of the parable and adopt conventional imagery for hell (cf. Matt. 8:12; 13:42, 50) . . . It brings the reader abruptly face to face with the story's religious message by concluding it in terms that already move into interpretation.' The story itself begs to be read at another level, as indeed it has been throughout the church's history.[142]

Numerous suggestions have been made as to the identification of the wedding garment: the Holy Spirit;[143] charity;[144] justification;[145] 'the festive garment of joy';[146] repentance;[147] righteousness;[148] good works.[149] What does seem clear is that 22.11–13 warns the reader to prepare for the eschatological judgement.[150] Moreover, both the wider narrative and this trilogy itself have shaped the reader's perception of this judgement and so guide her understanding of this metaphorical reference. In this narrative the final judgement is, from first to last, a judgement of works (12.36–37, cf., e.g., 16.27; 24.45–51; 25.31–46). Similarly, those who enter the kingdom are those marked by surpassing righteousness (5.20), who do the will of the Father (21.28–32!, cf. 7.21–27; 12.46–50), who give back to him the fruits of obedience that are rightfully his (21.41, 43!, cf. 3.8–10; 7.15–20; 12.33–37). Whether, then, we describe this wedding garment as the fruits of repentance, or righteousness, or good works, or, with Chrysostom, 'life and practice', is probably of little consequence. For the reader, the king's inspection at the feast highlights the ethical imperative of the gospel. Eschatology motivates ethics.

Verse 13 turns to consider the fate of the man who lacks this garment woven in 'life and practice'. Employing several images for final condemnation common to this narrative, the king banishes the guilty man from his banquet hall.[151] Like the tares separated from the wheat (13.30), this man, too, is bound, but whereas their destination is the furnace of fire (13.42), he is bound for the outer darkness.[152] 'There,' the king solemnly declares, 'people will weep and gnash their teeth' (22.13).[153] Three times in this narrative, these last two images of judgement appear together. Perhaps it is noteworthy that in the first instance, in a saying that also envisages the eschatological feast, it is the *Jewish* sons of the kingdom who are evicted (8.12), while here and at 25.30 the warning is applied to those within the Christian community. The warning first directed against the Jewish sons becomes an especially appropriate warning for Christian sons at the climax of a trilogy that has focused on Israel's rebellion and her subsequent rejection. If earlier in this parable Jerusalem's destruction stands as a concrete demonstration of her rejection by God, then here this rejection of elect Israel serves as graphic warning that the members of the nation that has supplanted her (21.43) are not exempt from the fate she has met. They, too, must yield to God the obedience that is rightfully his (21.41, 43, cf. 22.11–13). Yet again the trilogy's paraenesis is aimed at the reader.[154]

The parable concludes at 22.14 with the crisp, explanatory saying: 'For many are called, but few are chosen.' In a provocative 1990 article that builds upon the earlier interpretation of E. Boissard, B. Meyer argues, noting the absence of the comparative forms of the adjective in both Hebrew and Aramaic, that πολλοί and ὀλίγοι function here as correlative comparatives and that the saying means: More, i.e. all, are called, but less, i.e. not all, are chosen.[155] Meyer correctly notes that elsewhere Jesus (and Matthew) uses very different, and more positive, language, as he envisages those who will be saved,[156] and he demonstrates clearly both the existence of this semitising idiom and the fact that πολλοί/ὀλίγοι are used in this way in the LXX.[157] But this is not the only way that the πολλοί/ὀλίγοι contrast functions in the LXX. More commonly, in contexts in which they stand in opposition to one another, πολύς and ὀλίγος function as ordinary positive adjectives,[158] as they do elsewhere in this narrative.[159] Matthew 7.13–14 is especially important in this regard since there too Jesus addresses the issue of final salvation. Meyer dismisses this text with the following comment: 'But that paraenetic text, besides putting the accent on human behaviour rather than on God's judgment, does not, in fact, allude to a positive "few".'[160] The similarities between the two texts are, however, closer than Meyer allows. Both texts offer paraenesis in the light of the coming judgement. Just as the warning that many bypass the narrow gate (7.13b–14) underlines the urgency of finding it (7.13a), so here the sober statement that few are chosen (22.14) highlights the importance of preparing the garments required at the eschatological banquet (22.11–13). And since, in both contexts, it makes fine sense to take the adjectives in their usual positive sense, we should be cautious about finding in either another example of the semitising idiom. Moreover, the more natural Greek sense of the words of 7.13–14 and 22.14 accords well with the theology that emerges from this narrative. In the end, of course, the reader of Matthew's Gospel will have to balance this portrait with the others it offers of final salvation, but here he must let it have its intended impact.

Nor, if we reject Meyer's solution, do we need to resort to the exegetical gymnastics he rightly denounces in order to defend 'the common but inherently improbable view that this "generalizing conclusion" attached to part two of the parable relates only to part two.'[161] The reader knows all too well that many have rejected the invitation to the wedding feast (22.2–10), and, as 22.11–13 (cf. 7.21–23) insist, even accepting the invitation to the feast is no guarantee of final admittance. 'Between call and election lies the concrete worthy or unworthy life which will be judged by God.'[162] The saying relates to both parts of the story and draws the parable, in its entirety, to its intended conclusion.

The parable of The Wedding Feast is both polemical and salvation–historical, but it is also paraenetic and, in support of this, eschatological. Israel's massive failure and corresponding rejection stands as a poignant warning against presumption on the part of the members of a community that fully expect to attend the Feast that she declined.

5.4   Conclusion

The story that is taken up in this trilogy is Israel's story. The reign of heaven has been inaugurated and Messiah has come, but things in Israel – disturbingly – remain much as they were before. Under the leadership of shepherds who have deserted their flock (9.36) and of blind guides (15.14–15), she has become a barren tree (21.18–22), failing to give back to God the obedience that is rightfully his. Nowhere is this more evident than in Israel's stubborn refusal to hear the voice of her God in the repeated pleas of his prophets that echo down throughout her history (21.34–36), now graphically illustrated in her rejection and mistreatment of the Baptist (21.38–32, cf. 14.1–12; 17.9–13). Even John's execution, however, does not exhaust the evil rebellion of Yahweh's people. Israel's history of rejecting and killing Yahweh's prophets will culminate finally in the murder of Messiah and the prophets he commissions (21.37–39; 22.4–6, cf. 23.34). A barren fig tree of her own volition, Israel will remain barren by divine decree – she will never again bear fruit (21.19, cf. 21.41, 43). Responsibility for all of this must be laid, first of all, at the leaders' feet. Their stubborn rejection of Yahweh's servants – Baptist, Messiah and Messiah's prophets – bears witness to the perversity that has rendered them prime candidates not to lead God's people but to face his wrath (3.7–10, cf. 21.31b–32, 41–43; 22.6–7).

This trilogy, however, is not only polemical or salvation–historical. Indeed, from the vantage point of the response of the reader envisioned by the evangelist, these concerns, if essential, are not primary. Instead, several lines of evidence converge to suggest that these parables function chiefly to call the reader to faithful obedience to Yahweh and to his son Jesus in the wake of Israel's dramatic failure.

First, the position of 22.11–14 favours this conclusion. If, as I have argued, these three parables are to be read as a trilogy, then 22.11–14 functions as the conclusion not merely of The Wedding Feast, but also of the entire trilogy. It is striking that, as the trilogy reaches its conclusion – indeed its climax – and turns most obviously to address the reader, here paraenesis supplants polemic.

Second, as we have seen, at several points the trilogy anticipates its paraenetic climax. With the tax gatherers and prostitutes, the reader embraces the message of Yahweh's prophet, the Baptist. But John's message is one of repentance and righteousness (21.31b–32, cf. 3.7–10). The echoes of the development of these hortatory motifs in the wider narrative resound for the reader. Only the son who does the will of the Father enters the kingdom (21.28–32, cf. 7.21–27). The second of the trilogy's parables opens with the charge to hear (and obey!). The importance of this charge becomes apparent when, drawing upon another familiar hortatory motif, The Tenants instructs the reader (even as it indicts the Jewish leadership) that the new tenants of the vineyard must give back to the owner the fruit that is rightfully his (21.34, 41, 43). In the Two Sons and The Tenants, paraenesis accompanies polemic.

Third, as Schweizer has argued, the wider structure of chapters 21–25 supports this conclusion. One need not accept the details of his outline to find persuasive his proposal that both 21.23–22.14 and 22.15–25.46 move from dispute with Israel's leadership, indictment of the nation, and pronouncement of sentence(s) against her, to paraenesis aimed at the church. For Schweizer, as we have seen,[163] 21.23–27 (cf. 22.15–46) presents Israel's trial; 21.28–32 (cf. 23.1–32) the verdict; 21.33–46 (cf. 23.33–36) the sentence; 22.1–10 (cf. 23.37–24.2), the execution of this sentence; and 22.11–14 (cf. 24.3–25.46) the climactic exhortation, reserved for the church. Probably these distinctions are too neat. Each of the parables in the trilogy pronounces the verdict against Israel's leaders – and by extension, against the nation – and each of the parables declares a sentence. Nevertheless the general pattern Schweizer identifies is secure. Both 21.23–22.14 and 22.15–25.46 move from indictment of the nation to paraenesis for the reader. In both cases, the paraenesis aimed at the reader stands in the final, climactic, position. The earlier, polemical and salvation–historical motifs are, of course, important, but the structure of the narrative suggests that this trilogy, like 22.15–25.46, is calculated to do more than convince the reader of Israel's guilt, more even than underline the legitimacy of the new ἔθνος, though doubtless it does both. Instead, these parables repeat the story of Israel's failure as a warning to the reader and to the *nation* to which she belongs. This *nation*, too, will render account to God.

Fourth, the prominent role that is granted to the final judgement in exhorting the reader towards faithful discipleship elsewhere in this narrative at least prepares the reader for its similar function here. In a narrative whose five major discourses each conclude with promises of future reward or warnings of final judgement (7.21–27, cf. 10.37–42; 13.47–50; 18.34–35; 24.36–25.46), it is perhaps not surprising that this trilogy should end on a similar note.

Finally, Matthew's redaction of the parables in this trilogy offers corroborating evidence; but this, of course, anticipates the discussion in chapter 6, to which we now turn.

PART THREE

The trilogy in redaction-critical perspective

6

THE TRILOGY IN REDACTION-CRITICAL PERSPECTIVE

The reading of the trilogy offered in chapter 5 concentrated on the trilogy's rhetoric and the inclusion of the reader. In this chapter our focus shifts from reader and rhetoric to author and composition. Like the wider narrative to which it belongs, this trilogy of parables is marked by an intriguing combination of old and new, of tradition and redaction. Here we examine the manner in which the old has been made new, offering not so much a redaction-critical reading of the trilogy as a discussion of the distinctive emphases that arise from this redaction. An examination of the sources upon which the evangelist drew in composing this trilogy introduces the chapter and lays the foundation for the subsequent discussion of the distinctive treatment they receive at his hand. But, although my approach shifts dramatically, my interest in the responses that the evangelist intended to elicit from his readers remains central.

6.1   The sources of the parables

The Two Sons

The three parables that compose the trilogy pose distinctive challenges to a redaction-critical investigation. The Two Sons is unique to Matthew and there is little agreement about the sources that stood behind the Matthean parable. For Jülicher, the parable proper was an authentic word of the authentic Jesus.[1] Jeremias concurred with this judgement and attributed the story to 'the special Matthaean material'.[2] For Van Tilborg, as we have noted, both this story and the trilogy in which it now stands are pre-Matthean.[3] On the other hand, H. Merkel and R. Gundry are representative of those who have argued that the parable was composed by the evangelist himself.[4] Scholarly opinion is once more divided over the relationship of the parable's application in 21.32 to Luke 7.29–30.[5]

My attempt to isolate Matthew's special contribution to the parable begins with an examination of the parable in the light of the distinctive vocabulary of the wider Gospel.⁶ The following words and phrases from The Two Sons invite special attention: Τί ὑμῖν δοκεῖ; δύο; προσέρχομαι; ὁ δὲ ἀποκριθεὶς εἶπεν; ὕστερος; τὸ θέλημα τοῦ πατρός; λέγουσιν; λέγει αὐτοῖς ὁ Ἰησοῦς; δικαιοσύνη.

As we noted in our earlier discussion of the trilogy, while δοκέω itself is not especially Matthean (Matt. 10×; Mark 2×; Luke 10×), the introductory question (τί ὑμῖν δοκεῖ) occurs six times in Matthew but nowhere else in the Synoptic tradition.⁷ The question occurs both in uniquely Matthean material (17.25; 21.28) and in pericopes paralleled in Luke (18.12) and Mark (22.17, 42; 26.66). Most probably, then, the evangelist himself is responsible for this introduction.⁸

προσέρχομαι is decisively Matthean. Of its eighty-six occurrences in the NT, fifty-one are found in Matthew, five in Mark and ten in Luke. In perhaps forty instances Matthew employs the word when it is absent from the Marcan or Lucan parallels.⁹ It is difficult to avoid the conclusion that here also, at 21.28 and 21.30, its presence is to be attributed to Matthean redaction.¹⁰

Similarly we can be reasonably confident that we are seeing the hand of the evangelist at work when we meet the construction ὁ δὲ ἀποκριθεὶς εἶπεν at 21.29–30. ἀποκρίνομαι itself is common throughout the Synoptic tradition, but it occurs most frequently in Matthew (55×; Mark 30×; Luke 46×). Similar observations could be made of the formulaic 'answering, he said' (Matt. 45×; Mark 16×; Luke 37×). More importantly, while this formula appears in various forms in each of the three Gospels,¹¹ twice in this parable we meet the preferred Matthean construction – ὁ δὲ ἀποκριθεὶς εἶπεν (Matt. 19×; Mark 2×; Luke 6×).¹²

ὕστερος occurs only eight times in the Synoptic tradition, but seven times in Matthew. Three times (21.29, 32; 25.11) ὕστερος appears in pericopes that are unique to Matthew, once Matthew alone employs the word in a traditional Q pericope (4.2), and three times he inserts it into material he inherits from Mark (21.37; 22.27; 26.60). As such, its use here may also come from Matthew's hand.

Both θέλημα and πατήρ occur more frequently in Matthew than in either Mark or Luke, but the margins are not great.¹³ In the Synoptic tradition, however, τὸ θέλημα τοῦ πατρός is uniquely Matthean.¹⁴ Outside of this phrase, θέλημα occurs only twice in Matthew; in both instances, the Father is explicitly addressed in prayer (6.10, cf. 26.42) and the content of the prayer is identical (γενηθήτω τὸ θέλημά σου).¹⁵ Thus in each of its six Matthean occurrences, θέλημα is explicitly the will *of the Father*. This phrase also we can safely attribute to the evangelist.

The asyndetic use of λέγει/ουσιν in the historical present also features prominently in Matthew. In contrast to Mark and Luke, where this construction appears but once and twice respectively, twenty-eight occurrences punctuate the Matthean narrative, none of which is demonstrably traditional.[16] Similarly the phrase λέγει αὐτοῖς ὁ Ἰησοῦς occurs infrequently in Mark and never in Luke, but commonly introduces Jesus' responses in Matthean dialogues.[17]

Seven of the eight uses of δικαιοσύνη in the Synoptic tradition occur in Matthew,[18] and, given the importance of the concept of righteousness in Matthean thought,[19] its presence here is probably due to Matthean redaction.[20]

Of the nine words and phrases highlighted above, I think it probable that in this parable eight are in fact redactional in origin here: only δύο is equally likely to be traditional.[21] Vocabulary analyses, however, do not constitute the only way forward in detecting the work of the evangelist. We turn, secondly, to a consideration of the links between this parable and the others in this trilogy.

Links to the other parables in the trilogy

If, as I have argued, the evangelist himself has forged this trilogy, then probably he is also responsible for many of the verbal and conceptual parallels that feature prominently in these parables. Table 4 shows the impressive list of words and phrases in The Two Sons that find echoes in one of the two later parables.[22] Some of these parallels are clearly more significant than others but they can hardly all be dismissed as incidental. I judge as most significant, and likely to be intentional echoes: λέγουσιν; λέγει αὐτοῖς ὁ Ἰησοῦς; λέγω ὑμῖν ὅτι; and ἡ βασιλεία τοῦ θεοῦ. Of course, one might maintain that it was their presence in the traditional parable of The Two Sons that prompted Matthew to fashion the parallels that now stand in the subsequent parables but, while this possibility cannot be dismissed, we shall see that there are good reasons in each case to conclude that already here we see the evangelist's hand at work.

Moreover, these verbal echoes only underscore the more important conceptual parallels. Several motifs link The Two Sons to The Tenants or The Wedding Feast. Like the parables that follow, The Two Sons begins with a man of authority – here a father – taking the initiative by issuing some sort of command or invitation (21.28–29, cf. 21.33–34; 22.1–4). As in The Tenants and The Wedding Feast, the invitation goes out repeatedly (21.32, cf. 21.34–39; 22.3–4).[23] Does the fact that in the first story we meet this motif only in the application suggest we see the

Table 4

Word/Phrase	The Two Sons	The Tenants	The Wedding Feast
τίς/τί	21.28, 31 (No par)	21.40 (Matt. par Mark)	
ἄνθρωπος	21.28 (No par)	21.33 (Matt. par Mark)	22.2 (No par or Matt. par* Luke), 22.11 (No par or Matt. [+] Luke)
εἶχεν	21.28 (No par)	21.38 (Matt. diff Mark), 21.46 (Matt. diff Mark)	22.12 (No par or Matt. [+] Luke)
πρῶτος	21.28, 31 (No par)	21.36 (Matt. diff Mark)	
εἶπεν	21.28, 29, 30 (No par)	21.38 (Matt. par Mark)	22.1 (No par or Matt. par Luke), 22.4 (No par or Matt. par* Luke), 22.13 (No par or Matt. [+] Luke)
ἀμπελῶν	21.28 (No par)	21.33, 39, 40, 41 (all Matt. par Mark)	
ἀποκριθεὶς εἶπεν	21.29, 30 (No par)		22.1 (No par or Matt. diff Luke)
οὐ θέλω	21.29 (No par)		22.3 (No par or Matt. diff Luke)
ὕστερον	21.29, 32 (No par)	21.37 (Matt. diff Mark)	
ἀπῆλθεν	21.29, 30 (No par)	21.36 (Matt. diff Mark)	22.5 (No par or Matt. diff Luke)
ὡσαύτως	21.30 (No par; cf. also 20.5)	21.36 (Matt. diff Mark)	
κύριος	21.30 (No par)	21.40 (Matt. par Mark) 21.42 (Matt. par Mark)	
ποιέω	21.31 (No par)	21.36 (Matt. diff Mark), 21.40 (Matt. par Mark), 21.43 (Matt. [+] Mark)	22.2 (No par or Matt. par* Luke)

λέγουσιν	21.31 (No par)	21.41 (Matt. diff Mark)
λέγει αὐτοῖς ὁ Ἰησοῦς	21.31 (No par)	21.42 (Matt. diff Mark); λέγει also appears at 21.45 (Matt. diff Mark)
λέγω ὑμῖν ὅτι	21.31 (No par)	21.43 (Matt. [+] Mark)
ὑμᾶς	21.31	21.43 (Matt. [+] Mark)
ἡ βασιλεία τοῦ θεοῦ	21.31 (no par)	21.43 (Matt. [+] Mark)
ἦλθεν	21.32 (No par or Matt. diff Luke)	21.40 (Matt. par* Mark)
πρός + accus.	21.32 (No par or Matt. diff Luke)	21.34 (Matt. par Mark) 21.37 (Matt. par Mark)
ὁδός	21.32 (No par or Matt. diff Luke)	
ἰδόντες	21.32 (No par or Matt. diff Luke)	21.38 (Matt. diff Mark)

	λέγει – 22.8 (No par or Matt. par* Luke), 22.12 (No par or Matt. [+] Luke)
	22.2 – ἡ βασιλεία τῶν οὐρανῶν (No par or Matt. diff Luke (ἡ βασιλεία τοῦ θεοῦ))
	22.3 (No par or Matt. diff Luke)
	22.9 (No par or Matt. diff Luke) 22.10 (No par or Matt. par Luke)
	22.11 (εἶδεν; no par or Matt. [+] Luke)

evangelist's hand here (21.32c)? Again, in each of the stories, the man's plea is rejected and his ambassadors despised (21.30–32, cf. 21.35–39; 22.3–6). In The Two Sons, however, reference to ambassadors is again restricted to the application where the reader learns that the Father has made his appeal through his servant, the Baptist (21.32). In the first two parables, Jesus invites the Jewish leaders to pronounce judgement on the guilty (themselves) and they oblige (21.31a–b, cf. 21.40–41). Here, as in the parables that follow, this judgement excludes the guilty from the kingdom (21.31b, cf. 21.41, 43; 22.7–8) but also includes, in a remarkable reversal, a scandalous replacement cast: tax gatherers and prostitutes, a new ἔθνος, people gathered from the streets, evil as well as good (21.31, cf. 21.43; 22.9–10). Yet again, this reversal only becomes apparent in the concluding application of The Two Sons (21.31b–32).

Almost without exception, then, the important parallels that bind The Two Sons to The Tenants and The Wedding Feast do not stand in the parable itself, but rather in the concluding application (21.31b–32). Having already concluded that the evangelist was responsible for joining the three parables, and for forging a series of echoes that lend a distinctive unity to the trilogy, I think it probable that Matthew himself is largely responsible for the current shape of the application.

If the series of links within the trilogy points towards Matthean redaction, then connections to the wider Matthean narrative also betray the hand of the evangelist.

Links to the wider Matthean narrative

In our earlier discussion of the formation of the trilogy,[24] I noted that the most important of the trilogy's links to the wider narrative that betray the evangelist's hand comes at 21.32. There οὐκ ἐπιστεύσατε αὐτῷ echoes the words of the chief priests and elders from the preceding pericope (21.25) and turns their admission into a powerful self-indictment. If Matthew is responsible for the formation of the trilogy, then 21.32 affords clear evidence of the manner in which he aligns the first of these parables to the Marcan narrative framework.

Two Matthean parallels suggest that we may also see the evangelist's hand in the introduction of the Baptist at 21.32: ἦλθεν γὰρ Ἰωάννης. At 11.18, where the Lucan parallel reads: ἐλήλυθεν γὰρ Ἰωάννης ὁ βαπτιστής[25] (Luke 7.33), Matthew again has ἦλθεν γὰρ Ἰωάννης, a phrase which appears in only these two texts in the Synoptic tradition. At 17.12, Matthew once more prefers the aorist tense over the perfect when describing John's arrival: where Mark has καὶ Ἠλίας ἐλήλυθεν (9.13), his text reads: Ἠλίας ἤδη ἦλθεν.

Probably we should also detect a third echo of the earlier Matthean narrative in the words ἐγώ, κύριε followed by ἐποίησεν τὸ θέλημα τοῦ πατρός (21.30–31). As at 7.21–23 (cf. 12.46–50), what secures entrance to the kingdom is not mere words of allegiance (κύριε κύριε (7.21, 22; par Luke; cf. also 25.11)), but active obedience (ποιῶν τὸ θέλημα τοῦ πατρός (7.21; diff Luke)). That this phrase, which is almost certainly redactional at 7.21, should here be attributed to the evangelist only confirms our earlier analysis of Matthew's distinctive vocabulary.

Finally, we note a link to the wider narrative of Matthew's Gospel that consists of a distinctive stylistic trait of the evangelist. We have previously had occasion to refer to the evangelist's 'predilection for forming or enlarging conversations'.[26] Both here and in The Tenants, λέγουσιν introduces the response of Jesus' adversaries to his query that establishes the significance of the story and that, in turn, gives way to Jesus' counter-response (λέγει αὐτοῖς ὁ Ἰησοῦς . . .). In both instances, we see evidence of Matthew's redactional hand (21.31, cf. 21.40–41).[27]

The use of a Q saying?

Before concluding our discussion of the evangelist's redactional shaping of the parable, we turn to one final question. Did Matthew make use of the tradition that stands behind Luke 7.29–30? The question is difficult but, in spite of the obvious differences between the two texts, it seems likely that the two evangelists did draw upon a common source here. First, these differences are partly explained by the redactional fingerprints that both evangelists have left on these texts.[28] Second, Luke 7.29–30 stands in the midst of a section in that Gospel united by its focus on the Baptist. Matthew includes a comparable section at 11.2–19. He records close parallels to the Q material located at Luke 7.18–28 and at 7.31–35 but, apart from this parable, not 7.29–30.[29] Third, although verbal parallels between the two texts are few, some may be isolated: οἱ τελῶναι (Matt. 21.31, 32, cf. Luke 7.29); Ἰωάννης (Matt. 21.32, cf. Luke 7.29); δικαιοσύνη/δικαιόω (Matt. 21.32, cf. Luke 7.29); αὐτῷ/οὗ = the Baptist (Matt. 21.32, cf. Luke 7.30).[30] Fourth, ἦλθεν γὰρ Ἰωάννης (21.32) may suggest that Matthew frames this verse under the influence of the Q material that immediately follows this saying in Luke (Matt. 11.18, cf. Luke 7.33). Fifth, important conceptual parallels mark the two accounts. At the heart of both sayings stands the contrast between the marginalised Jews and the Jewish elite in their response to the Baptist.

In both the Matthean and Lucan sayings, rejecting John means rejecting God.

The two passages as they now stand are very different. Nevertheless, Matthew was familiar with the Q material that surrounds Luke 7.29–30, this material does seem to have left its mark on his introduction to 21.32, and the two sayings are marked by the same dominant concerns. These considerations favour the conclusion that Matthew was familiar with this (Q) material and adapted it for use in this parable. Given the differences that currently mark the two sayings, however, this conclusion must be held tentatively.

Conclusion

Matthew's redaction.   The story in its current form is thoroughly Matthean – evidences of Matthew's hand are scattered throughout the parable. Nevertheless, it is also true that the nature of the evidence that points to Matthean redaction differs noticeably when we move from the parable (21.28–31b) to its application (21.31c–32). In the story proper, evidence of redaction is limited largely to the evangelist's distinctive vocabulary. By contrast, when we turn to the application, in addition to distinctively Matthean vocabulary, we meet links to both the second and third parables in the trilogy as well as to the wider narrative of the Gospel and, probably, see the results of Matthew's handling of the Q saying that stands behind Luke 7.29–30.

The question of sources.   What can we say of the prior history of the parable itself and not merely of the Matthean editing? I have already argued that the parable did not form part of a pre-Matthean literary tradition that had already linked it with the other two members of the trilogy. Beyond this we can only speak tentatively. The parable may well have appeared in writing for the first time in the text of Matthew's Gospel. This would account for its Matthean flavour from beginning to end. However, I think it more likely that the parable circulated earlier in an oral form than that it is to be attributed to Matthew's compositional creativity, since it does not seem to be the parable itself so much as its application that links the story to its current context. Perhaps the oral circulation of the story may also account for some of the confusion that surrounds the text.[31] Nevertheless it is difficult to deny that the evangelist could have composed the parable out of dominical fragments (i.e., 7.21–23). Conceivably, the parable could even have already existed in a prior, written, tradition, but if so, having been reworked so thoroughly by Matthew, there are few places where we could be confident we are encountering this tradition.

If these conclusions are modest and hesitant, I take some consolation that the ability confidently to isolate the evangelist's sources remains less important for our purposes than to be able to detect the evangelist's redactional hand at work in the shaping of the parable. Before turning to a discussion of the significance of this redaction, we shift our attention to the sources that lay behind The Tenants and The Wedding Feast.

The Tenants

Since each of the Synoptic evangelists includes the story of The Tenants, a redactional study of this parable confronts challenges that differ in important respects from those a similar study of The Two Sons must tackle. Even here, however, some uncertainty about sources remains. In recent decades, several scholars have questioned the priority – in whole or in part – of the Marcan form of this parable. In his 1983 monograph, K. Snodgrass argued that Matthew's version of this parable is prior.[32] In the course of the following discussion of the evangelist's redactional shaping of the trilogy, I occasionally turn aside to respond to the main lines of Snodgrass's argument and defend the conclusion that, in terms of literary relationships, Mark's version of the parable is prior.

The Wedding Feast

Its relationship to the Lucan parable of The Great Supper

Matthew's parable of The Wedding Feast does have a parallel of sorts in the Lucan parable of The Great Supper (14.16–24), but their relationship has long been the subject of scholarly dispute. On the one hand, the main details of the plot are very similar. A man prepares to host a great feast but, the preparations having been completed, the invited guests *all* refuse his invitation. In anger, he extends an invitation to those whose names had not appeared on the first guest list and his hall is finally filled. Equally important, many of the significant differences between the Matthean and Lucan parables underline themes that are characteristic of the respective narratives. In short, the modifications are understandable.[33] Not surprisingly, then, one group of scholars concludes that a common source underlies the parable in its two canonical forms.[34]

On the other hand, only rarely do the two stories agree verbally and, as A. Harnack pointed out, while the two stories follow the same general plot line, marked differences remain. In Matthew the host is a king (God), and the feast is a wedding feast given in honour of his son (Christ). Several servants (as opposed to Luke's single servant) are sent out with invitations. In Matthew the first invited are invited twice (once in Luke), the second time by other servants. While Luke places far greater stress on the excuses offered by the first invited, only Matthew reports that some of them mistreated and murdered the bearers of the king's invitation. In Matthew's story alone, the king retaliates by sending his armies against those murderers, destroying them and burning their city. Finally, the story of the man without a wedding garment is unique to Matthew.[35] Of course, the parables are also set in entirely different contexts (cf. Luke 14.1ff.). These considerations have led other scholars to conclude either that the two parables are similar stories told on different occasions[36] or that the evangelists had access to different versions of the story.[37]

Since the evangelists freely arrange traditional material, and since most of the differences in a list like Harnack's can be explained readily in terms of redactional considerations, the most significant obstacle that stands in the way of assigning the parables to the Q tradition is their striking lack of verbal agreement. To my knowledge, C. Blomberg has offered the most detailed analysis of the vocabulary of these parables.[38] On the basis of his analysis, Blomberg concludes that the Matthean and Lucan 'Supper' parables do not spring from a common source.

His argument, however, is weakened by one or two important flaws. First, Blomberg measures the parables found only in Matthew and Luke against the same standard he employs with those found in the Triple Tradition where, typically, he records the verbal agreement present between Luke and Mark. But the situations are *not* quite comparable since, if the parables found only in Matthew and Luke do come from the Double Tradition, both of the evangelists (potentially) have been active in editing their source. Here, then, we should expect a lower measure of verbal agreement, at least in some instances, than when comparing either Matthew's or Luke's adaptation of Mark with the Marcan pericope itself. A more suitable analysis would compare the verbal agreement found between Matthew and Luke in parables of the Triple Tradition with the verbal agreement found in the parables reported only by the two evangelists since, in both cases, there would (potentially) be a middle factor involved, Mark in the case of the Triple Tradition and Q in the case of the Double Tradition. But the data available for comparison here are very limited. Leaving aside the interpretation of The Sower and the parable of The

Mustard Seed, which seems also to have been in the Double Tradition, we are left with the parables of The Sower and of The Tenants.

This leads to our second criticism. While it is perhaps unfair to criticise Blomberg too harshly at this point, since he sets up the Lucan parables as a 'test case', one wonders how compelling his case can be until it is set within the context of the tendencies of the wider Synoptic tradition. The sayings in the Triple Tradition seem to offer appropriate material against which to measure the significance of the very limited degree of verbal agreement in the parables under examination, since we are still dealing with reports of Jesus' teaching, and since, if we grant some form of Marcan priority, we have in place a middle factor that may be comparable to the source(s) with which Matthew and Luke worked in the sayings of the Double Tradition. A survey of the sayings in the Triple Tradition reveals a wide divergence in the degree of verbal agreement between Matthew and Luke. The agreement always surpasses that found in these two parables but the gap is not always large,[39] and the sheer variation in the range of verbal agreement should caution us against dismissing prematurely the notion of a common source for our parables. Nor can a purely statistical comparison take into account the adaptation that has obviously taken place as the Matthean parable has been aligned with the others in this trilogy.

In the end, we cannot be certain about the sources that lie behind the Matthean and Lucan 'Supper' parables. Since the most significant differences can be attributed to Lucan and, especially, Matthean redaction, in my view it remains plausible to think that a common source does stand behind the two canonical stories; but, in any case, there is little in my argument that depends upon this conclusion since the main lines of Matthean redaction can be isolated without precise knowledge of prior sources. Before turning to such an examination, we pause briefly to consider the origin of verses 11–14.

The wedding garment: the origin of 22.11–14

If it is true that modern scholarship is divided over the relationship of the Matthean and Lucan parables, then it is also true that no consensus exists as to the origin of Matthew 22.11–14, for which there is no Lucan counterpart. A minority of scholars insists that the parable as it stands represents an original unity.[40] More often one meets either the conclusion that these verses come from a separate parable that Matthew has reworked and incorporated,[41] or that they come from the evangelist's own hand.[42]

Once more a certain judgement seems elusive. On the one hand, the presence of typical Matthean vocabulary in these verses is undeniable,[43] and the evangelist returns here to a favourite motif – the final judgement. On the other hand, within these verses the greatest concentration of 'Matthean' vocabulary is found at verse 13, but the distinctively Matthean phrases found here are elsewhere inserted into traditional contexts;[44] this should make us cautious about finding Matthean creation here.[45] Perhaps the most that we can say with confidence is that, whatever their origin, in their current form these verses are thoroughly Matthean.

From this analysis of sources, we turn in the remainder of this chapter to consider the distinctive shape that Matthew gives to this trilogy.

6.2   The redactional shaping of the trilogy

In an important discussion of The Wedding Feast, W. Trilling drew attention to two different redactional tendencies – paraenesis and polemics – and attributed them to distinct stages in the redaction of the Gospel. The final stage, for which the evangelist himself was responsible, consisted of a polemical rewriting of the entire document.[46] Shortly thereafter, R. Dillon argued for a similar tradition-history for The Tenants. Dillon proposed that The Tenants and The Wedding Feast were linked by paraenesis especially suitable to a baptismal *Sitz im Leben* 'prior to the polemical design of the final redactor'.[47] I am less confident than either Trilling or Dillon that we can isolate various *stages* of redaction through which Matthew's narrative has passed, but it is true that more than one redactional tendency can be isolated in the parables of this trilogy. In what follows, I seek to trace the distinctive polemical, theocentric, salvation–historical and paraenetic emphases that emerge from this trilogy.

The polemical rewriting of the trilogy

The Two Sons

As it now stands, the parable of The Two Sons is thoroughly Matthean. If however, as I think, the parable itself was traditional, then Matthew probably inherited a parable whose principal function was paraenesis. This emphasis has not been eliminated. In the redactional application to John, however, the evangelist employs this paraenesis against the Jewish leaders. Their professed allegiance to God has been exposed by their rejection of his appeal, now placed on the lips of his servant the Baptist. So blind are they to their plight, they pronounce their own indictment

(21.31b). While the impious tax gatherers and prostitutes enter the eschatological kingdom, the pious religious elite remain outside, excluded by their persistent refusal to obey the Father (21.31c–32). The parable has become polemical.

In a brief discussion in chapter 5, I suggested that, since metaphorical references to God's vineyard in the LXX consistently point to Israel, and since The Two Sons is the first of three parables about God and Israel, it would be natural for the reader to associate this vineyard with Israel.[48] The presence of several interesting links to Isaiah's parable of The Vineyard (Isa. 5.1–7) only encourages this association.

First, the parable of The Tenants, which immediately follows The Two Sons, unambiguously directs the reader to the Isaianic parable. Linked as closely as these parables are, The Tenants' clear allusion to the vineyard of God's people in Isaiah 5 establishes the plausibility of finding a similar reference here.

Second, both here and in Isaiah's parable, judgement is pronounced because of the absence of righteousness. Speaking through the prophet, Yahweh declares: ἔμεινα τοῦ ποιῆσαι κρίσιν, ἐποίησεν δὲ ἀνομίαν καὶ οὐ δικαιοσύνην ἀλλὰ κραυγήν (Isa. 5.7). Here Jesus issues a similar indictment: ἦλθεν γὰρ Ἰωάννης πρὸς ὑμᾶς ἐν ὁδῷ δικαιοσύνης, καὶ οὐκ ἐπιστεύσατε αὐτῷ. Like Israel of old, Jesus' contemporaries have rejected the way of righteousness.[49]

Third, both Isaiah and Matthew draw special attention to the failure of Israel's leaders. In the context of Isaiah's indictment of the vineyard, the prophet stresses both the special culpability of Israel's leaders and the judgement that awaits them (Isa. 3.14). We meet similar motifs in the redactional application to this parable: 21.31b pronounces judgement on the Jewish leaders and 21.32 explains the nature of their guilt. Moreover, the link to Isaiah 3.14 is verbal as well as conceptual. At 21.23, where the nature of Jesus' authority is challenged, Mark's 'the chief priests and the scribes and the elders' becomes 'the chief priests and elders of the people' as Matthew identifies the Jewish leaders. In so doing, he modifies his Marcan tradition in two ways (see Table 5): reference to the scribes is eliminated,[50] and the 'elders' become 'the elders of the people', a phrase that occurs here for the first time in Matthew's Gospel and only four times in the Synoptic tradition.[51] That both of these modifications align the text of 21.23 with the text of Isaiah 3.14 perhaps suggests the influence of the earlier text here.

If we conclude that already here in The Two Sons the reader is to find allusion to Isaiah 5, then presumably this link to the prophetic texts serves to align the chief priest and elders with an earlier

Table 5

LXX Isaiah 3.14	Mark 11.27	Matthew 21.23
αὐτὸς κύριος εἰς κρίσιν ἥξει μετὰ τῶν πρεσβυτέρων τοῦ λαοῦ καὶ μετὰ τῶν ἀρχόντων αὐτοῦ Ὑμεῖς δὲ τί ἐνεπυρίσατε τὸν ἀμπελῶνά μου καὶ ἡ ἁρπαγὴ τοῦ πτωχοῦ ἐν τοῖς οἴκοις ὑμῶν;	Καὶ ἔρχονται πάλιν εἰς Ἱεροσόλυμα. Καὶ ἐν τῷ ἱερῷ περιπατοῦντος αὐτοῦ ἔρχονται πρὸς αὐτὸν οἱ ἀρχιερεῖς καὶ οἱ γραμματεῖς καὶ οἱ πρεσβύτεροι	Καὶ ἐλθόντος αὐτοῦ εἰς τὸ ἱερὸν προσῆλθον αὐτῷ διδάσκοντι οἱ ἀρχιερεῖς καὶ οἱ πρεσβύτεροι τοῦ λαοῦ λέγοντες·

generation of evil leaders in Israel. Like their forebears, they are ripe for judgement.

The Tenants

Unlike The Two Sons, the traditional parable of The Tenants was already polemical. Nevertheless, Matthew sharpens this polemic. The most obvious and important of Matthew's polemical modifications appear in the later stages of the story, but already the earlier portion prepares the way.

As Matthew tells the story, the householder sends his servants to collect his share of the harvest when the season of fruits (ὁ καιρὸς τῶν καρπῶν) had drawn near. Although Mark does not speak of a *season of fruits*, both καιρός and καρπός form part of his vocabulary at 12.2. Most scholars conclude that Matthew simply reworked this traditional material.[52]

It is possible, however, that another Marcan tradition played an equally important role in the shaping of this Matthean phrase. Earlier in this chapter, it is the absence of καιρός that is particularly interesting. In the Marcan Cursing of the Fig Tree, the evangelist explains why Jesus found nothing but leaves on the tree in question – it was not the season for figs (Mark 11.13). Matthew omits Mark's curious explanatory comment (21.19), perhaps precisely because it is curious and, potentially, casts Jesus in a bad light.[53] But if, in the Marcan account, the comment stands as a signal to the reader of the symbolism involved in Jesus' action,[54] then perhaps, in part, the reason Matthew omits it is also tied to symbolism – now the symbolism that pervades this part of *his* story. If, as seems likely, the fig tree stands as a symbol of Israel in Matthew,[55] perhaps, in anticipation of this parable which laments the failure of Israel to produce fruit, Matthew omits the Marcan explanation and reintroduces it, in slightly modified form, here at the outset of the parable. Far from being out of season, it was high time for both fig tree and tenants to yield fruit. In any case, as we shall see, this modification prepares for the important redactional conclusion to verse 41.

Although the point can easily be overstated, there is also a polemical heightening in Matthew's depiction of the reception of the servants.[56] In contrast to the Marcan account, here from the beginning the servants sent to collect their master's fruit are not only mistreated but also murdered (21.35–36).

More important is the series of polemical modifications that begin at 21.40 as Jesus invites the response of the Jewish leaders to his story. Here Matthew advances Mark's later reference to the farmers (τοῖς γεωργοῖς) and adds ἐκείνοις, which he earlier omitted (21.38, cf. Mark 12.7). As a consequence, the objects of the owner's reprisal become explicit – Mark's 'what will he do?' becomes, more specifically, 'what will he do *to those farmers*?' Matthew's redaction concentrates attention squarely on the wicked tenants and underlines his polemical interest.

Jesus' question gives way to the Jewish leaders' response at 21.41, but the polemic continues. In Matthew, unlike Mark, the Jewish leaders answer Jesus' question (so issuing their own condemnation) and the traditional polemic is intensified. This modification typifies Matthean style,[57] links The Tenants to The Two Sons (cf. 21.31), and underlines the guilt of the Jewish leaders by emphasising once more their perverse blindness to their own sin.[58] But what the Jewish leaders actually say is equally important. Mark's τοὺς γεωργούς (Mark 12.9) – having been included in the preceding question (21.40) – gives way to κακοὺς κακῶς . . . αὐτούς, which stresses both the culpability of the tenants and their terrible fate, already terrible in Mark. Matthew retains Mark's ἀπόλλυμι – the only traditional word in the opening clause – and reproduces it in the next parable at 22.7 where, as we have seen, he alludes to the destruction of Jerusalem. Probably he already hints at that destruction here.[59] Matthew has again intensified an already polemical tradition.

The Jewish leaders' response to Jesus' question concludes with a uniquely (and characteristically[60]) Matthean relative clause that the evangelist's redaction in 21.34 had anticipated – the season of fruit had come (21.34), but the tenants remained unfruitful (21.41). As elsewhere in this Gospel, so here the absence of fruit provokes judgement. In an earlier discussion of this text, I suggested that this clause echoes Psalm 1.3. Probably the intended function of the allusion was at least partly polemical: only judgement can await those tenants who fail to yield fruit. The Scriptures require it.[61]

The polemic continues at 21.42 but, after his redactional introduction,[62] Matthew follows Mark's citation of Psalm 117.22–23 (LXX) exactly. Verse 21.43, by contrast, is unique to Matthew and offers his interpretation of the parable. Here Jesus indicts the Jewish leadership in plain language: God will take the kingdom from them (ἀφ' ὑμῶν) and give it to a nation (ἔθνει) that – unlike them – produces its fruits.

It is immediately striking that the kingdom seized from the Jewish leaders is the kingdom *of God* and not the typically Matthean kingdom of heaven.[63] Since the phrase (kingdom of God) is emphatically *not* Matthean in style, not a few commentators attribute 21.43 to prior tradition.[64] But, first, clear markers of Matthean style and interest remain.[65] Second, the evangelist changes what appears in his sources as kingdom of God consistently enough[66] that any departure from that pattern would surely be intentional, whether the phrase originated from his hand or not. Third, as Trilling has noted, while Matthew's Gospel shows clear preference for *kingdom of heaven*, it nevertheless also displays considerable diversity here – in at least twelve instances βασιλεία remains unqualified, or is qualified by something other than οὐρανῶν.[67] Fourth, the 'theocentric' focus that marks Matthew's redaction of this parable provides contextual reason for the evangelist's departure from his typical vocabulary in 21.43. The change suits the polemical point being made: in turning against his servants and his son, the Jewish leaders have turned against their God, so invoking his judgement – the withdrawal of *his* kingdom. Finally, the phrase may have been chosen, in part, to establish another link with the preceding parable (21.31).[68] Matthew 21.43 echoes 21.41 (with its distinctively Matthean shape), interprets the Matthean parable, and returns – as we have seen – to some of the most important themes of the wider Gospel. All of this suggests, I think, that 21.43 comes from Matthew's pen. In any case, by shaping it as he has, the evangelist makes it distinctively his.

Finally, Matthew's narrative conclusion also manifests a polemical intensification. From its position at the end of Mark's summary, the evangelist advances the fact that the Jewish leaders understand the polemical intent of Jesus' parable. Matthew both expands and alters the Marcan clause as he moves it forward. The redactional καὶ ἀκούσαντες[69] introduces the Matthean sentence and ironically recalls the evangelist's introduction to the parable (Ἄλλην παραβολὴν ἀκούσατε).[70] The Jewish leaders do perceive the intent of Jesus' parable, but their *hearing* nevertheless fails as their opposition to Jesus only intensifies. Moreover, unlike Mark, Matthew specifically identifies the Jewish leaders here and, whereas earlier in the chapter he had linked the scribes (21.15) and elders of the people (21.23) with the chief priests, here it is the Pharisees who join them (21.45). The Jewish leadership thus stands united against Jesus and together feels the sting of his indictment. Finally, what is implicit in Mark becomes explicit in Matthew. Jesus' parables are no longer merely against the Jewish leaders, as in Mark; they are about them. They not only condemn them; they portray them. They are the disobedient son, the murderous tenants, the builders who reject the stone of God's choice and so evoke his judgement. Each of these modifications highlights the guilt of the Jewish leaders. Matthew's polemic outstrips Mark's.

The Wedding Feast

As in The Tenants, so here Matthew extends the polemical features that already marked the traditional parable. This polemical intensification first becomes apparent at 22.6–7. Even if one concludes that Matthew and Luke are working from different sources, or report stories told on separate occasions, it is difficult to avoid the conclusion that 22.6–7 should be attributed to Matthean redaction. The clear verbal and conceptual links to The Tenants present here suggest that they have been formed under the influence of the preceding parable.[71]

Like the guests invited to the Lucan supper (Luke 14.17–21), all of the Matthean guests refuse the invitation (22.3–5). Unlike the Lucan guests who offer various excuses for their absence, the first of the Matthean guests simply ignore the king's envoys.[72] Gundry thinks that already here Matthew's handling of the excuses is designed to intensify the guilt of the Jewish leaders.[73] More probably, Matthew dismisses extraneous details in this part of the narrative as he moves eagerly towards the insertion of verses 6–7, which dominate this part of his story.[74]

Verse 6 introduces the most dramatic redactional development in this part of the story. While Luke's invited guests continue to offer apologies, in Matthew indifference (22.5) yields to violence as the remaining invitees abuse and murder the bearers of the king's invitation (22.6).[75] In the preceding chapter, I argued that the developing storyline encourages the reader to find allusion here to the events of the Jewish war. This conclusion probably receives corroboration here from the otherwise curious insertion of verses 6–7 into the parable. Even if we conclude that the royal sacking of a city is merely a topos, we must still account for its presence here. If we were right in concluding that Matthew sees the destruction of Jerusalem as God's punishment of his rebellious people for the rejection of his servants (cf. 23.29–24.2), then the suggestion that the evangelist thinks here of this destruction offers the most reasonable explanation.

The passage at 22.8–10, with its redirected invitation, once more underscores the guilt of those first invited – they were not worthy. Their rebellion (and consequent execution) leads directly to the extension of the invitation to a new cast of guests.[76] As in The Tenants (cf. 21.41, 43), Israel's persistent rejection of her God's servants elicits his judgement. Verse 10 succinctly reports the events of this redirected invitation: the king's servants gather all whom they find so that, as in the Lucan story, the hall is filled. But here a further qualification is added; they have found and gathered evil and good. Verse 10 obviously prepares the reader for the judgement scene depicted in verses 11–14,[77] but the πονηρός/ἀγαθός language is also polemical in design. So unworthy are the first guests, they are now replaced by people gathered indiscriminately, πονηρούς τε καὶ ἀγαθούς.

The parable Matthew inherited was already polemical – *all* the guests refuse the invitation to the feast and are subsequently replaced by those originally bypassed. By his insertion of verses 6–7, however, the evangelist intensifies the polemic. Now the guests are guilty not only of slighting the host, but also of murdering his messengers. Israel's history has been repeated (cf. 21.33–46).

The theocentric rewriting of the trilogy

More than once we have had occasion to observe that each of the parables in this trilogy tells the story of Yahweh and his people Israel. Each of the parables features a central character that points metaphorically to Israel's God. In The Two Sons, ignoring the appeal of the *father* leads to exclusion from the kingdom of *God*. In The Wedding Feast, the king is the only actor whose presence is constant throughout the story. He gives a feast celebrating his son's wedding, dispatches his servants to call the invited guests, answers the violence of the first invited with a violence of his own, commissions his servants to invite a new assembly of guests and finally conducts an inspection to ensure that the guests who arrive at the feast are appropriately clad. One's response to this king's invitation elicits either blessing or punishment. Once more, entrance to God's reign is at stake.

It is, however, in The Tenants above all that Matthew's *redactional* focus upon Israel's God becomes apparent. This theocentric focus is first evident at 21.33. There Mark's ἀμπελῶνα ἄνθρωπος ἐφύτευσεν becomes the more typically Matthean ἄνθρωπος ἦν οἰκοδεσπότης ὅστις ἐφύτευσεν ἀμπελῶνα.⁷⁸ If, however, the addition of οἰκοδεσπότης accords with Matthean style, its presence here should not be dismissed as mere stylistic preference. Here Matthew offers an early hint that the vineyard owner will be granted special prominence in his parable.

At 21.34 two redactional modifications highlight the role of the householder. First, Mark's δοῦλον becomes τοὺς δούλους αὐτοῦ, which recalls the common LXX phrase, οἱ δοῦλοι αὐτοῦ οἱ προφῆται.⁷⁹ But, more than this, the addition of αὐτοῦ is the first of five redactional insertions of αὐτοῦ in the space of five verses, the first four of which seem designed, like the expanded description in verse 33, to draw attention to the master of the house and especially to emphasise his authority.⁸⁰ Second, λαβεῖν τοὺς καρποὺς αὐτοῦ replaces Mark's cumbersome ἵνα παρὰ τῶν γεωργῶν λάβῃ ἀπὸ τῶν καρπῶν τοῦ ἀμπελῶνος. Whereas in Mark τοῦ ἀμπελῶνος qualifies ὁ καρπός, in Matthew the qualifying genitive is once again αὐτοῦ. The fruit is now not merely fruit of the vineyard, but fruit that belongs to the householder.⁸¹ This was, of course, true, but implicit, in the Marcan version, but what is explicit is still only anticipatory, pointing forward to the important redactional clause at the end of 21.41.

The theocentric focus of the Matthean parable may be observed once more at 21.37 where, following the Marcan story, the evangelist turns his attention from the servants to the son. One modification is especially noteworthy. υἱός is now qualified by αὐτοῦ rather than ἀγαπητός. K. Snodgrass suggests that, by describing the son as ἀγαπητόν and pointing out that he came ἔσχατον, Mark has provided two important Christological hints. For him, the absence of these two features from the Matthean story⁸² suggests that Matthew's version of the parable is prior, since neither Matthew nor the early Church wanted to play down Christology.⁸³

The absence of ἀγαπητός from the Matthean story is striking.⁸⁴ In the entire Synoptic tradition, outside of this parable, ἀγαπητός is found only at Matthew 12.18 and the various reports of the Baptism and Transfiguration.⁸⁵ In Matthew, as in Mark, the voice from heaven describes Jesus as ὁ υἱός μου ὁ ἀγαπητός at both the Baptism (3.17) and Transfiguration (17.5). In addition, Matthew inserts ὁ ἀγαπητός μου redactionally into the citation of Isaiah 42 at 12.18. The Christological significance of the word for Matthew, as for Mark and Luke, can hardly be denied.⁸⁶

In my view, however, an appeal to Matthean priority creates more problems than it solves. Examples of typical Matthean redaction extend throughout this parable. Nor is it the case that there are no markers of Matthean redaction in this verse. Most significantly, this is the fourth time in the space of four verses that αὐτοῦ has been uniquely Matthean (cf. 21.34 [2×]; 21.35). In each case, the presence of αὐτοῦ seems significant. In the first three instances, they draw attention to the landowner – the servants are *his* and the fruit is *his*. Since this emphasis also reappears in the important and uniquely Matthean pronouncement of judgement in 21.41b, it seems probable that the presence of αὐτοῦ here is again due to Matthean redaction and, once more, is intended to direct our attention to the landowner, and thus towards God.[87] Whereas *beloved* son focuses attention on the *son*, *his* son seems to call attention to the father. Snodgrass objects that neither Matthew nor the early church would ever play down Christology, but probably we should not expect the developing tradition *always* to grant equal or greater prominence to Christological concerns (or indeed to score the Christological point in precisely the same manner) and to subordinate all other concerns at every point.

I think that it is reasonable to conclude that Matthew's redaction subtly shifts the focus here from the son to the father and that most probably this has to do with the unique purposes for which the evangelist tells this story again. As he has done since the first verse of the parable, the evangelist draws attention to the vineyard owner, and, while there is a subtle shift in focus, if the identity of the householder is secure – as it surely is – then, as it relates to the son's identity, αὐτοῦ points in the same direction as ἀγαπητός, which is not needed to ensure the metaphorical connection here.[88] The Christological point is made more subtly than in Mark, but it is made. After Easter, at least, the son's identity is obvious.[89]

Several of the distinctively Matthean redactional motifs converge at 21.41. Not surprisingly, the evangelist's special interest in the householder surfaces here once more. As I noted above, 21.41c echoes Psalm 1.3. Matthew, however, inserts ἀποδώσουσιν αὐτῷ in place of the Psalm's δώσει. As at 21.34, the fruit of the vineyard belongs to *him*. Failure to produce this fruit elicits judgement.

Probably this distinctive 'theocentric' emphasis that runs through the parable is related to the polemical intensification we have observed: the vineyard is *his* (21.33); the fruit is *his* (21.34); the servants are *his* (21.34); the son is *his* (21.37); the rebellion is *theirs* (21.34–39, 45, 46). The tenants' refusal to yield fruit in response to the missions of the servants and the son, their treatment of the servants and even the son is, essentially, wicked rebellion against the owner himself – the kind of rebellion that demands the sort of judgement pronounced in 21.41 and interpreted in 21.43: the kingdom of *God* will be taken from them. Matthew's theocentric focus functions principally as support for his polemical point.

The salvation–historical rewriting of the trilogy

The Two Sons

Each of the parables in this trilogy also bears witness to Matthew's distinctive salvation–historical interest. Earlier I noted the polemical nature of the parable's redactional application, but the polemic directed against the chief priests and elders also has salvation–historical import: Israel's elite are displaced by tax gatherers and prostitutes in the *kingdom of God*. Moreover, by placing this vineyard parable in the context of this trilogy, the evangelist at least raises the question of whether the reader should find secondary allusion to the many Gentiles in the son whose initial 'no' to God gives way to repentance and obedience.[90]

The Tenants

Even as Matthew has intensified Mark's already polemical rendering of The Tenants, so his redactional hand has left its stamp on the parable's salvation–historical message. The parable's first verse signals Matthew's awareness of and interest in its salvation–historical significance. As we have seen, the vocabulary of this verse (21.33, cf. Mark 12.1) features several distinct echoes of Isaiah 5.2 (LXX). Matthew's redaction is interesting because in two instances his modification of Mark's word order makes the resulting Matthean word order more nearly follow Isaiah's: Mark's ἀμπελῶνα ἄνθρωπος ἐφύτευσεν becomes Ἄνθρωπος . . . ἐφύτευσεν ἀμπελῶνα (cf. Isa. 5.2: ἐφύτευσα ἄμπελον); and καὶ φραγμὸν . . . περιέθηκεν replaces Mark's καὶ περιέθηκεν φραγμὸν (cf. Isa. 5.2: καί φραγμὸν περιέθηκα). Further, Matthew's insertion of ἐν αὐτῷ once again agrees with Isaiah against Mark. The significance of these changes is difficult to determine since, in the remainder of the verse, Matthew is content to follow Mark's word order when once again he could have tightened the links to Isaiah's parable.[91] At least Matthew, no less than Mark, directs the reader's attention back to Isaiah's vineyard parable. Like Isaiah, Jesus tells a story about Israel and her God.[92]

Earlier we noted that at 21.34 Mark's δοῦλον becomes τοὺς δούλους αὐτοῦ, recalling the common LXX phrase, οἱ δοῦλοι αὐτοῦ οἱ προφῆται. At 21.35 τοὺς δούλους αὐτοῦ is redactional again, replacing Mark's αὐτόν. A second alteration confirms the evangelist's special interest in this phrase as he describes the servants' fates. Matthew condenses this part of the Marcan account,[93] but adds to the Marcan tradition ὃν δὲ ἐλιθοβόλησαν. The addition of λιθοβολέω anticipates 23.37:

Ἰερουσαλὴμ Ἰερουσαλήμ, ἡ ἀποκτείνουσα τοὺς προφήτας καὶ λιθοβολοῦσα τοὺς ἀπεσταλμένους πρὸς αὐτήν. By his redaction, Matthew
tightens the metaphorical reference to the prophets. The story is about
Israel's past.

The vocabulary of 21.39 is entirely Marcan, but Matthew rearranges the
Marcan order so that, whereas in Mark the son is murdered and then cast
out of the vineyard, in Matthew the expulsion precedes the execution.[94]
Probably, like Luke, Matthew intends to align the details of the story with
the events surrounding Jesus' passion.[95] The story is not merely about
Israel's past.

Matthew's salvation–historical interest surfaces again in his redaction
of 21.40–41. As in Mark (cf. Isa. 5.4), Jesus asks how the vineyard owner
will answer the rebellion of the tenants. The Matthean form of Jesus'
question, however, includes important modifications: ἐλεύσομαι comes
forward from Jesus' *answer* to the question in Mark and, following the
redactional ὅταν, prefaces the question with a temporal clause: '*When* the
master of the vineyard *comes*.' In chapter 5, I suggested that here Matthew
alludes to AD 70. Both the uniquely Matthean κακοὺς κακῶς (21.41) and
the redactional echo of 21.40–41 at 22.7 favour this conclusion. *Matthew
fills in the details of Mark's salvation–historical outline* – the judgement
that Jesus announces is given visible expression in the events of the Jewish
war.

At 21.43,[96] perhaps the most important verse in the pericope from a
Matthean perspective, salvation–historical concerns are paramount. The
verse, which interprets the Matthean parable, is unique to Matthew and
should probably be attributed to Matthean redaction in its entirety.[97] I have
argued above[98] that this verse announces both the salvation–historical loss
suffered by Israel and the consequent salvation–historical gain bestowed
upon the nations. The nations have been included in the nation that God
had promised to raise up from Abraham. Henceforth, Abraham's children
(and Yahweh's) are marked by ethical and not ethnic traits. In typical
Matthean fashion, the significance of Jesus' parabolic statement is laid
bare. It is difficult to imagine a more dramatic salvation–historical import
than Matthew finds in this parable.

The Wedding Feast

Salvation–historical concerns are equally prominent in The Wedding
Feast. In particular, 22.6–7 – together with the placement of the parable in this trilogy – leave a distinctive Matthean stamp on the salvation–
historical portrait that emerges from this story. If we were correct in

finding here allusion to the events of the Jewish war, then this parable presents the destruction of Jerusalem as the visible expression of the divine judgement that these parables declare; but, as we noted in earlier discussion, these verses also shape the salvation–historical portrait that emerges from the earlier portion of the parable.

Like Luke's story, Matthew's is a kingdom story about a man who gave a feast; unlike Luke, the kingdom is now the kingdom of heaven, the man is a king, and the feast is a wedding feast for his son. Matthew's hand is evident both in his selection of vocabulary and in the links that he forges with the parable of The Tenants. ὡμοιώθη ἡ βασιλεία τῶν οὐρανῶν ἀνθρώπῳ βασιλεῖ (22.2) is thoroughly Matthean. The introductory formula is found elsewhere only at 13.24 and 18.23 in the entire Synoptic tradition.[99] Moreover, the use of ἄνθρωπος, followed by an appositive, and of ὅστις both typify Matthean style and link this parable to the preceding one.[100] The role of the son in The Tenants (21.37–39) prepares for his (redactional) appearance here: here, too, the son is the Son.

The invitation issued to the wedding guests (22.3)[101] has once more been modified under the influence of the preceding parable. ἀπέστειλεν τοὺς δούλους αὐτοῦ reproduces the Matthean redaction in 21.34 as the singular servant of the traditional stories (Mark 12.2, cf. Luke 14.17) yields to the many in the Matthean parables.[102] As in The Tenants, the failure of the first mission[103] provokes a second:[104] πάλιν[105] ἀπέστειλεν ἄλλους δούλους duplicates the redactional phrase from the earlier parable (21.36) and, in echoing his *summary* of the Marcan sending in the preceding parable, the evangelist *expands* the 'sending' motif in this parable; in Luke only one servant is sent once to the guests first invited. But Matthew is not merely echoing this motif from the earlier parable. Here, as I suggested above,[106] he is concerned to isolate a different group of servants. If 22.7 alludes to the destruction of Jerusalem, then the servants of 22.4 (and probably 22.3) are the prophets and wise men and scribes that Jesus commissions (cf. 23.34). It was Israel's rejection of them, finally, that filled up the 'measure of their fathers' (23.32).

As we have already noted, like The Tenants, The Wedding Feast tells the story not only of a salvation–historical exclusion, but also of an inclusion. The invitation to the great feast must now be carried to other people. Once more the single servant of the traditional story is multiplied in the hands of the evangelist as the king's new servants are commissioned to bear the invitation to the feast.[107] As in Luke, a new cast of guests replaces those first invited, but by his inclusion of The Wedding Feast in this trilogy, Matthew makes it clear that, for him, these guests include men and women from all the nations. After 21.43, it can hardly mean less. Here the evangelist anticipates the programmatic commission at 28.18–20.

At 22.11–14, Matthew's salvation–historical sketch leaps forward to the end of history, but his focus here is not so much salvation–historical as paraenetic, and it is Matthew's distinctive emphasis on paraenesis to which, finally, we turn.

The paraenetic rewriting of the trilogy

The Two Sons

The Two Sons features an important paraenetic component, recalling Jesus' earlier teaching that entrance to the kingdom is reserved for those who *do the will of the father* (7.21; Matt. diff Luke). This language is distinctively Matthean and, even if we conclude that the evangelist inherited a traditional parable to which he appended the present application, most probably Matthew himself has forged this echo. Likewise in the application, where salvation–historical and polemical concerns are admittedly most prominent, reference to *the way of righteousness* (21.32) recalls the characteristically Matthean employment of δικαιοσύνη in hortatory contexts earlier in this Gospel.[108] In The Tenants, Matthew's redaction only underlines the distinctive paraenetic thrust he envisions for this trilogy.

The Tenants

The opening words of The Tenants signal Matthew's paraenetic interest. In chapter 5 I suggested that, at the discourse level, the parable's initial charge ("Αλλην παραβολὴν ἀκούσατε) calls subsequent hearers to obey the parable. Redactional observations lend confirmation to this suggestion.[109] "Αλλην παραβολὴν ἀκούσατε replaces Mark's καὶ ἤρξατο αὐτοῖς ἐν παραβολαῖς λαλεῖν (12.1) and, as we have seen, recalls Matthew's introduction to the interpretation of The Sower (13.18). There ὑμεῖς οὖν ἀκούσατε were unique to Matthew. In Mark, Jesus calls the crowds to listen at the outset of the parable ('Ακούετε; 4.3). Matthew, however, omits the word and relocates it to 13.18 where, at the outset of the parable's *explanation*, he finds the call to *understanding* and *obedience* most appropriate.

Matthew's use of ἀκούω in 13.10–17 confirms this reading. In Mark, as in the first part of the Isaianic text (6.9–10) to which Jesus refers, hearing is, in the first instance, limited to physical perception and, in the second, contrasted with understanding. This is consistent with his use of the word in the following interpretation of the parable (4.13–20). Each of the four groups described *hear* (4.15, 16, 18, 20), but hearing alone constitutes an inadequate response to the message of the kingdom, which must be welcomed and so bear fruit (4.20).

Matthew's expansion of this part of the Marcan narrative (13.10–17, cf. Mark 4.10–12) features nine occurrences of ἀκούω, the first two of which are found at 13.13 and are traditional (cf. Mark 4.12). The first, ἀκούοντες, reproduces the Marcan form exactly and, as it did in Mark, describes mere physical perception. As Matthew has replaced ἵνα with ὅτι in its second occurrence in this verse, the verb is now indicative rather than subjunctive in mood. But, more significantly, by inserting the negative particle οὐκ before ἀκούουσιν and changing the negative that precedes συνίουσιν to οὐδέ, Matthew has transformed ἀκούουσιν so that, whereas in Mark it stands in opposition to συνίουσιν, here it is instead roughly synonymous with it.

ἀκούω appears three more times in Matthew's quotation of Isaiah 6.9–10. In the first of these (13.14), as in Mark, it is directly contrasted with συνίημι. Similarly, in its second appearance, the hearing is that accomplished only by ears that are particularly dull (καὶ τοῖς ὠσὶν βαρέως ἤκουσαν; 13.15). However, in its final use in the quotation, ἀκούω is once again parallel to συνίημι (καὶ τοῖς ὠσὶν ἀκούσωσιν καὶ τῇ καρδίᾳ συνῶσιν . . .). Mark's summary of Isaiah 6.9–10 excludes this portion of that text.

Matthew's version of the Q saying paralleled at Luke 10.23–24 accounts for the final four appearances of ἀκούω in this pericope. The first of these stands in a uniquely Matthean clause (καὶ τὰ ὦτα ὑμῶν ὅτι ἀκούουσιν; 13.16) that seems designed to align this saying with its current Matthean context.[110] The remaining three occurrences are found in an identical form in Luke's version of the saying. In each case, the use of ἀκούω is entirely positive. Unlike those whose ears are heavy of hearing (13.15), Jesus' disciples are blessed because their ears really do hear (13.16). To them is granted the privilege of hearing withheld from God's servants of previous generations (13.17).

Matthew's use of ἀκούω in this pericope is less consistent than Mark's. Whereas for Mark, here and in the following interpretation of the parable, hearing, at least without further qualification, consistently describes an inadequate response to the spoken word,[111] for Matthew the same word may point either to *mere* hearing or to the hearing that takes root as understanding. However, when Matthew's use of ἀκούω describes an inadequate response, he is at that point indebted to either Mark (13.13a) or Isaiah (13.14, 15a). Conversely, whenever Matthew uses the word to mean more than mere hearing he has imported this sense into this Marcan context, whether by means of editing Mark (so 13.13b), of extending the Isaianic quotation (13.15b), or of introducing and (probably) editing a tradition that he shares with Luke (13.16–17). Here hearing means understanding.

In this context, one final redactional modification invites comment. Mark describes the seed that was sown on good soil as those who hear the word and accept it (παραδέχονται) and bear fruit (4.20). Both Matthew and Luke replace Mark's παραδέχονται – the Matthean substitute is συνίημι.[112] For Matthew it is the one who hears and understands who bears fruit. Hearing in its fullest sense can never be separated from obeying.

Matthew's use of ἀκούω in 13.3–24, then, suggests that Ὑμεῖς οὖν ἀκούσατε τὴν παραβολὴν τοῦ σπείραντος (13.18) issues a call to understand and obey. Probably its intended function is similar here at 21.33;[113] this accords well with the distinctive role granted to ethical exhortation in the Matthean parable.

Three redactional alterations highlight this distinctive ethical exhortation that comes to the fore in the concluding judgement pronounced by the Jewish leaders (21.41). First, ἐκδώσεται replaces δώσει. The change from δίδωμι to ἐκδίδωμι recalls 21.33,[114] and perhaps underlines the tentativeness with which the replacements possess the vineyard. The second modification points in the same direction. Mark's ἄλλοις becomes ἄλλοις γεωργοῖς. The vineyard is leased – not *given* as in Mark – to another group of *tenant farmers*. They replace the first farmers but remain only farmers responsible to the vineyard owner. Like the first farmers, their response to him will determine his response to them.[115] In the third modification, however, we may observe the most important of these paraenetic alterations. In chapter 5 we noted that the Matthean relative clause that concludes 21.41, with its emphasis on the necessity of the production of fruit, recalls the important earlier hortatory employment of this motif in Matthew's Gospel.[116] God demands of the new tenants precisely what he demanded of their predecessors. Here we need only note that the relative clause in its entirety is unique to Matthew. As the Matthean parable is drawn to conclusion, the guilt of the first tenants is depicted not only in terms of their rejection of Yahweh's prophets, but also – and more explicitly – in terms of failing to produce the fruit that the householder requires. This is only reinforced when the thin veil of this imagery is removed in the Matthean interpretation at 21.43: the kingdom will be given to an ἔθνος that *produces the fruits* of the kingdom. That Matthew chooses to issue the polemical verdict in this manner strongly suggests that paraenetic concerns have become as important as polemical ones here.[117] The new tenants, like the old, must give back to God the fruit of obedience that is rightfully his. As we have seen, Matthew only underlines this critical point as the trilogy reaches its climax.

The Wedding Feast

In the preceding chapter, I noted that, whereas in The Tenants polemics and paraenesis join hands as Matthew interprets the parable (21.41, 43), in The Wedding Feast the polemic of the earlier portion of the parable yields to paraenesis as the parable (and the trilogy) draws to its conclusion. Once more we need only note that this paraenetic conclusion is uniquely Matthean. The traditional parable was both polemical – outlining the failure of the guests first invited to attend the great feast – and salvation–historical – describing the replacement of these guests. In Matthew's hands the polemic has been intensified – the first invited murder the king's envoys – and the salvation–historical focus sharpened – the king answers their rebellion by burning their city and inviting other guests to his feast. Nevertheless, in spite of Matthew's polemical and salvation–historical interests, in his hands the parable reaches its climax with paraenesis that seems to have been absent from the traditional parable.

6.3   Conclusion

What, then, can we say about the response that Matthew intended to elicit from his readers by his redactional shaping of the trilogy? If we may judge by his manipulation of his tradition, the evangelist wanted them to understand the nature and gravity of Israel's (and most especially Israel's leaders') failure. Matthew intensifies an already polemical tradition. But Matthew's redaction focuses on not only Israel's leaders, but also Israel's God. This theocentric focus serves, on the one hand, to explain the judgement that this trilogy declares – the Jewish establishment is guilty of rebellion against its God – and, on the other, to justify the extension of Israel's privilege to the nations. The parables have a sharp salvation–historical focus. But the response Matthew envisions is not merely cognitive. The unique focus upon paraenesis implores the reader not to repeat Israel's dramatic failure, but to prepare for the eschatological banquet by yielding to God the obedience that is rightfully his.

7

CONCLUSIONS

7.1   Method

This study has attempted to demonstrate the validity of the proposal that redaction- and narrative-critical approaches to the Gospels can function as effective allies in addressing the intended meaning of the Gospel narratives and the responses they elicited from their first readers.

Narrative critics have distanced themselves from redaction critics in several ways. At two important points, I have defended a mediating position. First, whereas redaction criticism has typically been a cognitive, author-oriented discipline, and narrative criticism has focused on the text and its affective impact on the reader, I have argued that careful attention to the author and the reader (or to the cognitive and the affective domains) are not mutually exclusive. Following the lead of speech-act theorists, I have suggested that, in addition to propositional content, speech-acts – whether verbal or written – have both illocutionary and perlocutionary force. On this model of communication, questions may be posed about both the intended meaning and the intended function of written texts – questions embracing both author and reader, both what a text means and what it does. Accordingly, this study has repeatedly returned to one question: 'What does the text suggest that the evangelist intended to elicit from his readers by way of response?'

Second, narrative critics have typically denounced the fragmentation of the Gospel narratives that is too often the accompaniment of redaction criticism, and have instead emphasised – rightly, in my view – the integrity of the Gospel narratives. On the other hand, I think they have wrongly underestimated, or ignored, the secondary nature of this integrity. An approach to the Gospels that aims to uncover the response[s] that the evangelists wished to elicit from their readers can only benefit from a careful analysis both of the rhetorical strategies employed in the 'final form' of the Gospels, and of the evangelists' manipulation of their tradition in the construction of this 'final form'. This conclusion justifies both redaction- and narrative-critical analysis.

When we turn to the parables, this problem of the fragmentation of the Gospel narratives has been exacerbated, in the aftermath of A. Jülicher's seminal work, by the tendency to concentrate scholarly energies upon the reconstruction of the parables of Jesus at the expense of sustained scrutiny of the final forms of the parables; but the Synoptic parables are both texts worthy of investigation in their own right and integral parts of the evangelists' wider communicative actions. If this is so, then two important conclusions follow: first, the primary question for the interpreter of the *Synoptic parables* must be 'how might the *evangelist* have expected this story to be heard?' rather than 'how might *Jesus* have expected this story to be heard?'; second, these stories must be read against the backdrop of the wider narrative that the respective evangelists have created. Surely this is all the more true when we are dealing with a parable like The Tenants that patently tells a story that is picked up and filled out by the wider narratives in each of the Synoptic Gospels. If these conclusions are accepted, then future study of the evangelists' parables must devote greater attention to their location and function in Gospels' unfolding plots, and to the role played by the wider narrative in shaping the reader's reception of these parables. Narrative criticism has an important role to play in the rehabilitation of the parables as they stand in the Gospels.

7.2   Matthew's trilogy of parables: 21.28–22.14

I have attempted to contribute to this rehabilitation by an examination of the carefully crafted trilogy of parables at Matt 21.28–22.14. Each of the parables in this trilogy – like Matthew's Gospel itself – tells a story about Yahweh and his people. They beg to be read against the backdrop that Matthew's wider story provides.

The nation

This wider story, I have argued, places a distinctive stamp on these parables. Matthew's narrative portrait of Jesus' encounter with Israel suggests that he did not intend the judgement that this trilogy declares to be restricted to the Jewish leadership. Instead, the nation itself is indicted. 'This generation' is guilty of rejecting God's climactic appeal (11.16–19, cf. 12.38–42, 43–45; 16.1–4; 23.34–36; 24.34). Confronted by Israel's Messiah, 'all the people' have called for his execution (27.20–26).

Nevertheless, the distinct characterisation of the various sub-groups within Israel does not allow the reader to conclude that all Israelites are equally culpable. Israel's marginalised are consistently portrayed in a favourable light; and at the heart of the new ἔθνος (21.43) that this trilogy announces stands a group of *Jewish* disciples who have embraced Israel's Messiah (cf. 19.28).

The crowds are presented in ambivalent terms. On the one hand, they follow Jesus in great numbers (e.g., 4.25; 8.1; 12.15) and embrace him as a prophet of Israel's God (16.13–14, cf. 21.11, 46); they are the recipients of his compassion (9.36; 14.14; 15.32), his proclamation (e.g., 4.23; 9.35) and his healing (e.g., 4.23–24; 8.16; 9.35). On the other hand, their spiritual obduracy constitutes them unable genuinely to hear Jesus' message (13.13–15, cf. 13.2; 13.34–35, cf. 13.36) and, in the end, manipulated by their leaders, they demand his death (27.20–26). It is not merely the Jewish leaders who have spilled the innocent blood of the vineyard owner's son (cf. 21.37–39).

If, however, Jesus' execution is not *solely* the responsibility of the Jewish authorities, it is nevertheless *supremely* theirs. From the outset of the narrative, the Jewish leaders have set themselves up as the allies of the Herods (17.9–13, cf. 2.1–23; 14.1–12; 16.21) and of Satan himself (4.1–11, cf. 16.1; 19.3; 22.18, 35) and, thus, as the mortal enemies of Jesus. Not only have they persistently sought his destruction (12.14, cf. 21.46; 26.3–5; 27.20–26); they have also consistently sought to turn the nation against Jesus (9.32–34, cf. 12.22–24; 27.20–26; 28.11–15). There is no ambivalence in this picture: final responsibility for Israel's rejection of her Messiah must be laid at their feet.

From Matthew's vantage point, Israel – under the leadership of blind guides – has re-enacted her tragic history of repudiating Yahweh's servants by violently rejecting Yahweh's son the Messiah (and his messengers). Re-enactment though it may be, this rebellion is a climactic re-enactment, bringing Israel's sins to full measure and eliciting the decisive judgement of her God. Israel's sons and daughters who have failed to do the will of the Father will be excluded from the kingdom (21.31b–32, cf. 3.7–10; 8.11–12). More dramatically, the kingdom will be taken from the nation and given to another ἔθνος (21.41, 43). As a *nation*, Israel has ceased to be the people of God. This judgement is given dramatic historical expression in the events of the Jewish war (22.6–7).

Nevertheless, the recognition that, for Matthew, Israel has ceased to be the people of God hardly suggests that the evangelist no longer envisions a mission to the *people* of Israel. Matthew's characterisation of the crowds seems designed to evoke the reader's sympathy, and may imply that he continues to envision and engage in just such a mission. In any case, this narrative plainly presents a continuing mission to Israel (cf. 23.34) after, and as part of the fulfilment of, Jesus' command to universal mission (28.18–20). Matthew sets himself polemically against the leaders of the nation that (he believes) has executed her Messiah and so abandoned her God. He also dares to hope for the day when many of Israel's sons and daughters will yet embrace Israel's Messiah (23.39), and in that hope engages in a continued mission to her.

The nations

Matthew's narrative, of course, also evinces sustained interest in the fate of the nations. Collectively, Gentiles are portrayed as pagans in need of evangelisation. Even here, however, their culpability pales vis-à-vis 'this generation' in Israel, which has rejected its Messiah (10.14–15, cf. 11.20–24; 12.38–42). Individual Gentiles are typically portrayed much more favourably. The Magi (2.1–12), the centurion at Capernaum (8.5–13) and the Canaanite woman (15.21–28) all take the initiative to seek out Jesus. Each of them bows before Jesus and, from the vantage point of the end, becomes an adumbration of the many from east and west who will offer worship to Israel's Messiah.

The passage at 28.16–20 draws Matthew's 'Gentile sub-plot' (and the Gospel itself) to its grand conclusion. Granted universal authority as risen Lord, Jesus commissions his followers to a universal mission, rescinding his earlier prohibition of mission outside of Israel (10.5–6, cf. 15.24). All the nations (πάντα τὰ ἔθνη; cf, e.g., Gen. 12.3; 18.18) will be blessed by Jesus, the son of Abraham (cf. 1.1). In retrospect, the earlier portions of this narrative clearly anticipate this conclusion. Warning the Jewish establishment of the necessity of producing fruit worthy of repentance, John the Baptist insists that God is able to raise up children to Abraham 'from these stones' (3.7–10). In the midst of a mission characterised by its exclusive focus upon Israel, Jesus takes the Baptist's warning a step further. The Gentile centurion becomes paradigmatic of the many from east and west who will sit at table with Abraham and Isaac and Jacob, while the sons of the kingdom are cast out (8.11–12).

The trilogy is thus set in the midst of a narrative that devotes careful attention to the move from an exclusive mission to Israel to a universal mission to all the nations; and to the eviction of unfaithful Jewish sons from the kingdom and their replacement with many from among the nations. In such a context, it is difficult to avoid the conclusion that when Jesus refers to a new ἔθνος to which the kingdom will be transferred

(21.43), and to a new, inclusive mission (22.8–10), Matthew's readers are to find reference to Gentile inclusion in the reconstituted people of God, and to universal mission respectively.

However I have also suggested that Matthew's provocative reference to the ἔθνος to whom the kingdom will be granted (21.43) may deliberately recall the salvation–historical promises granted to Abraham (Gen. 12.2) and traced throughout Israel's founding narratives. Since this Gospel opens by linking Jesus with Abraham (1.1), closes with an allusion to God's promise to the patriarch that all nations would find blessing in his seed (28.16–20) and twice explicitly associates Abraham with the exclusion of some Israelites from the kingdom and their replacement by other 'children' (3.7–10; 8.11–12), such a notion would hardly have been foreign to the evangelist. Read against the background of both the wider Matthean narrative and Israel's sacred texts, Matthew 21.43 suggests that the nations have not only been blessed by Abraham's descendants; by yielding allegiance to Israel's Messiah, they have also *become* part of that nation that God promised he would raise from Abraham. Sadly, many of Abraham's own heirs, having rejected Jesus Messiah, find themselves rejected, evicted from the kingdom, and excluded from this promised ἔθνος.[1]

If this proposal is accepted, then, although Matthew stops short of designating the Messianic community the 'true Israel', he does present this new *nation* as the legitimate heir of God's promises to Abraham, thus underlining both God's faithfulness to his promises to the patriarch, and the continuity of this *nation* with historic Israel. However, the discontinuity is equally pronounced. Israel has been indicted. God's kingdom has been withdrawn. A new ἔθνος has risen in its place.

The reader

Against this backdrop that the wider Matthean narrative provides, chapters 5 and 6 of this book turned to focus directly on the trilogy of parables. The trilogy features a series of progressions. The three parables tell the stories, respectively, of Israel's rejection of John, Jesus and Jesus' messengers. The first proclaims the exclusion of the Jewish elite from the kingdom, the second announces the transfer of the kingdom, the third points to the visible historical expression of this judgement. The parables also tell a story of inclusion: Israel's marginalised (21.31b–32), a trans-ethnic community (21.43) and men and women from all nations (22.8–10) constitute the replacement cast. The echoes that run through these parables underscore not so much the repetition of events as the recurrence of motifs, effectively placing an exclamation point over the evangelist's polemical, salvation–historical and theocentric interests.

Chapters 5 and 6 – which examined, respectively, the rhetoric of the narrative and the evangelist's manipulation of his tradition – have demonstrated that, as important as polemical and salvation–historical concerns are to this trilogy, they do not exhaust its concerns. Indeed, from the vantage point of the response envisioned by the evangelist, these concerns, if essential, are not primary. Instead the parables build towards the paraenetic climax of the trilogy recorded at 22.11–14. Having embraced the Messiah that Israel has repudiated, this ἔθνος has positioned herself (or rather, been positioned) in Israel's stead as the people of God; but the parables are as much about the responsibilities incumbent upon the people of God as the replacement of Israel per se. From the evangelist's standpoint, this new nation is composed of those who do the will of the Father (21.28–32); who give back to the God of Israel the fruit that is rightfully his (21.33–44); who come to the wedding feast dressed in garments woven 'in life and practice' (22.2–14). The new nation is defined along ethical and not ethnic lines. Israel's failure has become a sober warning to all who expect to attend the feast that she declined.

This trilogy of parables bears eloquent witness to the sophistication of the evangelist's literary achievement. If I am right, Matthew has taken three parables from separate sources and has woven them into an impressive unity. He has both highlighted the parallels that marked the traditional parables, and extended this parallelism. By means of a series of verbal parallels that echo through this trilogy, he has signalled the convergence of motifs that both binds these stories together and grants to them a new rhetorical force. This achievement is all the more impressive if, as I think, Matthew has worked within the constraints of the traditional Jesus material. He has not written these parables *de novo*.

Nor is this literary sophistication evident only in the striking relationship between these parables. Instead, in the hand of the evangelist, these parables have become integral to the wider story he tells. Standing at a critical juncture in the Gospel narrative, these stories propel the plot towards its inevitable climax. Their polemical posture only intensifies the resolve of Jesus' opponents, who aim to destroy him (21.46). At the same time, at the discourse level, they instruct the reader by picking up themes that have been central to the story from its opening lines and by anticipating (and offering theological justification for) the narrative's conclusion. Indeed, they look beyond the boundaries of the plotted story to the judgement that is about to fall upon Israel for the rejection of her Messiah, to the mission that will occupy the new nation that rises in her place and, climactically, to the final judgement.

Clearly then, this trilogy also testifies to the evangelist's theological vision and to his pastoral impulse. Confronted with her God's climactic appeal, Israel has once more turned a deaf ear. As Matthew sees it, the nation has been indicted, and men and women from all nations have joined Israel's faithful in the reconstituted people of God. But, as we have had repeated occasion to observe, Matthew's interests in this trilogy are not only polemical and salvation–historical. Instead, writing as a pastor, Matthew calls his readers to faithful allegiance to Israel's God (and to Jesus his Son), in the conviction that this obedience is the distinguishing characteristic of God's people in all ages.

APPENDIX
THE TEXT OF THE PARABLE OF THE
TWO SONS

Every verse in the parable of The Two Sons is dotted with textual problems. The most significant, however, is the string of variants that runs through verses 29–31. Although UBS[4] lists five variant readings in these verses, three principal alternatives may be isolated, as Table 6 indicates.[1] Readings 1 (NA[27] et al.) and 2 (NA[25] et al.) introduce the two sons in differing order but they agree that the son who eventually repents and sets out to work has done the father's will. By contrast, the third reading pronounces a blessing upon the son who *only promises* to work in the vineyard. We begin our discussion with this distinctive third reading.

Reading 3

Though not accepted today by any major critical text or translation, this third reading has not been without eminent proponents. J. R. Michaels has offered one of the most distinctive defences of this reading.[2] He notes first that the parable proper (21.28–31a; 'saying vs. doing') and its interpretation (21.31b–32; 'belief vs. lack of belief') lack correspondence, but that the interpretation is closely linked in theme to 21.23–27. Second, no less than three key words in the parable are ambiguous. In each case, Michaels abandons the usual understanding, noting that the resulting sense brings the parable into close connection with its context. μεταμέλεσθαι can describe repentance but also a regret that falls short of repentance. Since several of the MSS (e.g. D, e, sy[s]) that state that the Jewish leaders did 'repent' (21.32) also condemn the 'repentant' son, Michaels concludes that we should find reference only to regret and not to genuine repentance here (cf. 27.3). Similarly, ἀπέρχεσθαι tells us only that one son departed (21.29) while the other did not (21.30), but whether this departure implies obedience – that he went to the vineyard – or not, we can only learn from the context. Michaels concludes it does not. Finally, ὕστερον can mean either 'later' or 'too late' and he prefers the latter; 21.32c should then be taken to mean: 'And you, when you saw it, regretted

Table 6

	Reading 1	Reading 2	Reading 3
1st Son's response	οὐ θέλω, ὕστερον δὲ μεταμεληθεὶς ἀπῆλθεν.	ἐγώ (ὑπάγω Θ f¹³ 700 pc), κύριε (- Θ) καὶ οὐκ ἀπῆλθεν.	οὐ θέλω, ὕστερον δὲ μεταμεληθεὶς ἀπῆλθεν εἰς τὸν ἀμπελῶνα.
2nd Son's response	ἐγώ, κύριε, καὶ οὐκ ἀπῆλθεν.	οὐ θέλω, ὕστερον (δὲ Θ f¹³ 700 pc) μεταμεληθεὶς ἀπῆλθεν.	ἐγώ, κύριε, καὶ οὐκ ἀπῆλθεν.
Which of the two did the will of the father?	ὁ πρῶτος.	ὁ ὕστερος (ἔσχατος Θ f¹³ 700 pc).	ὁ ἔσχατος.
Manuscript evidence	(א) C L W (Z) Δ 0102 0281 f¹ 33 𝔐 f q vg^ww sy^p.h sa^mss mae Hier^mss	B Θ f¹³ 700, al (lat) sa^mss bo Hier^mss	D it sy^s.(c)
Modern translations	KJV, RV, ASV, NAB, JB, NJB, GNB, NIV, RSV, NRSV	NASB, New World, NEB, REB	
Modern commentators	Zahn (1903) Plummer (1915) Allen (1922) Lagrange (1948) Lohmeyer (1956) Schniewind (1956) Filson (1960) Grundmann (1968) Albright and Mann (1971) Benoit (1972) Hill (1972) Schweizer (1975) K. and B. Aland (1987) Bonnard (1992) Gnilka (1992) Hare (1993) Metzger (1994) Gundry (1994) Hagner (1995) Langley (1996) Davies and Allison (1997) Luz (1997)	Westcott and Hort (1896) Weiss (1898) Riggenbach (1922) Schmid (1951) Gaechter (1963) Kretzer (1971) Green (1975) Weder (1978) Maier (1980) Carson (1984) Patte (1987)	Lachmann (1842) Merx (1902) Wellhausen (1904) Hirsch (1951) Michaels (1968) Schulz (1976)

later (i.e., too late) because you did not believe him.'³ In defence of a slightly modified form of reading 3, then, Michaels proposes the following textual history.

1.　　　The parable of The Two Sons circulated as an independent unit in the tradition.
2.　　　Matthew used it in connection with 21.31b–32 (rather than perhaps 7.21) with the result that the emphasis shifted from 'saying vs. doing' to 'futile regret'.
3.　　　The ambiguity of μεταμεληθεὶς ἀπῆλθεν (v. 29) resulted in the later inclusion of εἰς τὸν ἀμπελῶνα in some MSS, so reversing the shift in emphasis created by the evangelist's redaction. This reversal both obscured the evangelist's understanding of the parable ('futile regret') and gave it once more its traditional significance ('saying vs. doing').
4.　　　Most MSS either changed the elders' reply from ὁ ἔσχατος to ὁ πρῶτος or else rearranged the order of the two sons to fit ὁ ἔσχατος.

Michaels's argument is intriguing but fails to convince. His understanding requires that we follow reading 3 in its surprising answer to Jesus' question (21.31) and in its omission of the negative from 21.32, but *not* in its understanding of μεταμέλεσθαι or ἀπέρχεσθαι, since εἰς τὸν ἀμπελῶνα, which follows ἀπέρχεσθαι on this reading, ensures positive connotations for both of these words. In the face of two other well-attested readings that both make fine sense, it seems unnecessarily desperate to appeal to a reading that finds support in no extant MS.⁴

J. Wellhausen offered a more conventional defence of reading 3.⁵ In spite of its comparatively weak MS support, Wellhausen contended that we should accept this reading as original since it is clearly the most difficult, and since it most easily accounts for the rise of the other two readings (the scribes responding to what they deemed the obvious need to correct the Jewish leaders' misguided reply). Strictly speaking, the Jewish leaders were not mistaken. Instead, sensing that Jesus was spinning this parable against them, they *deliberately* supplied the wrong answer in order to short-circuit Jesus' indictment.⁶ The text at 21.31b–32, then, does not supply the application of the parable, but instead Jesus' angry response to the Jewish leaders' perverse obstinacy.

For many scholars, however, this third reading is not only the hardest reading but is also so difficult as to be nonsensical.⁷ Not only is the point of the parable spoiled; of equal importance, there is no hint in

Jesus' counter-response that the Jewish leaders have supplied the wrong answer.[8]

What is not often noted is that this third reading also undermines the subsequent Matthean narrative.[9] In the Matthean version of The Tenants, which immediately follows The Two Sons, Jesus again concludes his parable with a question. There, as we have seen, the question draws attention to the declaration of the judgement that must fall upon the wicked tenants (21.40, cf. Mark 12.9). In Mark and Luke, Jesus answers the question himself but, in Matthew, the Jewish leaders pronounce judgement on the wicked tenants (themselves; 21.41, cf. Mark 12.9; Luke 20.16). How likely is it that Matthew (alone!) would have the Jewish leaders pronounce their own indictment in 21.41, if immediately prior (21.31) he had portrayed them as too crafty to do the same? The third reading, then, not only supplies what is manifestly the wrong answer to Jesus' question, but also subverts the Matthean narrative.

In spite of the fact that text critics and Matthean specialists alike[10] continue to credit an anti-Jewish or anti-Pharisaic sentiment for the rise of reading 3, such a conclusion is most unlikely, since the same MSS[11] that supply the 'wrong' answer to Jesus' question in 21.31 also omit the negative (οὐδέ (B et al.) or οὐ (א et al.)) in 21.32. This minor change holds major significance. The Jewish leaders are here granted entrance to the kingdom, the repentance of Israel's marginal having finally moved them to repentance. προάγουσιν (21.31) must now be understood in a temporal – instead of an exclusive – sense. This is hardly an anti-Jewish or anti-Pharisaic reading. On the contrary, the leadership is rehabilitated![12] Against Wellhausen, then, this reading does not underscore the perversity of the Jewish leaders, nor does the acknowledgement that it is the most difficult afford it decisive support.

Readings 1 and 2

If the third reading can be set aside as secondary, deciding in favour of one of the first two readings is extraordinarily difficult. Both receive external support from early and important witnesses.[13] And the internal evidence seems to point in different directions.

On the one hand, transcriptional probabilities favour reading 1. W. Allen[14] listed five factors that would have made it natural to transpose the order of reading 1, which he judged original:

(1)   It might be argued that if the first son went, there was no occasion to summon the second;[15]

(2)   the fulfilment of the command forms an unexpected climax to
        the story;

(3)   it was natural to identify the disobedient son with the Jew, the
        obedient son with the Gentile. Along this line of interpretation
        the latter should come last in chronological order;[16]

(4)   the ὕστερον of v.[29] may have had some influence in causing this
        verse to be placed after v.[30];

(5)   further, v.[32] may have suggested the change of order. 'John came,
        and you did not believe' = οὐκ ἀπῆλθε; 'the toll-gatherers and
        harlots believed' = μεταμεληθεὶς ἀπῆλθε.

Most of these suggestions, however, offer little genuine assistance.
(4) can, I think, be safely set aside as inconsequential. In so far as (2) and
(5) are significant, they are offset by the recognition that one could as
easily envision a situation in which these considerations influenced the
author and not the later copyists.[17]

That (1) can similarly be turned on its head is demonstrated by the
argument posited by (among others) both Wellhausen and K. and B.
Aland who, like Allen, favour reading 1. They insist that if the first son
had declared himself ready to work, the father would have had no reason
to issue the same charge to the second son.[18] For them, the story only
holds together if the first son (initially) rejects the father's plea (note that
both Allen's and Wellhausen's argument rest upon the *assumption* that
the father has work in the vineyard for only one of his sons).[19] Thus,
for Allen, the logic of the story (the first son *must* (say yes but) *not go
to work* to give his father a reason to summon his brother) may have
prompted later scribes to alter reading 1 to reading 2. For Wellhausen
and the Alands, the logic of the story (the first son *must say no* to give
his father a reason to summon his brother) shows that reading 1 must be
original. Although both of these are attempts to support reading 1, they
succeed only in showing that this type of argument cannot prove decisive
here – such arguments brandish a two-edged sword.[20]

Allen's third suggestion – (3) above – is the most significant. From
early on, the parable was interpreted along salvation–historical lines.[21]
Prima facie, however, the Matthean Jesus does not appear to be concerned at all in this parable with the order of Jew and Gentile in salvation
history, addressing rather the contrasting lot of the Jewish leaders and
the marginalised of their own race in the wake of their response to the
message of the Baptist (21.31b–32). It is not difficult to imagine that,
if reading 1 were original, the transposed order could have arisen in the
scribal tradition out of concern for a correct salvation–historical sequence.

Nevertheless I think that important intrinsic considerations point towards a more likely solution.

If transcriptional probabilities favour the first reading, intrinsic probabilities quite consistently favour the second.[22] Unlike most contemporary scholars, Westcott and Hort found in the 'salvation–historical order' intrinsic support for reading 2. For them, readings 1 and 2 were distinguished by the fact that:

> against all biblical analogy [reading 1] would make the call of the Jews on the larger scale, and of the chief priests and elders on the smaller, to follow after that of the Gentiles and of the publicans and harlots respectively.[23]

In a 1926–7 article, W. M. Macgregor suggested that it is not only the salvation–historical order but also the typical order in which the characters in Jesus' parables appear – the respectable appearing first and giving way to the unlikely – that supports the sequence outlined in reading 2.[24] Derrett added a third observation: since in the application the Jewish leaders appear first, we would expect them to in the story as well.[25] Like the transcriptional probabilities considered above, however, none of these considerations is decisive.

However, one important line of evidence which, to my knowledge, has not previously been brought to bear on this problem but which has repeatedly surfaced in this study,[26] lends important support to reading 2. The remarkable conceptual and verbal alignment that characterises these parables favours the second reading because it would establish one more significant parallel that extends throughout the trilogy.

We have had repeated occasion to note the presence of these parallels and need only pause here briefly to review the most significant of these:

1. Each of the parables begins with an invitation or command issued by a man of authority (who represents God) (21.28, cf. 21.33–34; 22.2–3).

2. In each of the parables the invitation goes out repeatedly (21.32, cf. 21.34–37; 22.3–4, 8–9).

3. In all three stories, the invitation is repeatedly spurned and the man's ambassadors despised (21.30, 32, cf. 21.35–39; 22.3–6).

4. Each of the parables also includes characters who obey the command or accept the invitation (21.29, cf. 21.41c, 43; 22.10).

5. All three parables pronounce judgement on the unfaithful (21.31b–32, cf. 21.41–43; 22.7).

6.   All three parables announce the replacement of the unfaithful
          with a scandalous cast that nevertheless yields to the man's
          wishes (21.31b–32, cf. 21.41, 43; 22.8–14).

As we have seen, however, it is not merely the conceptual parallels
that mark these parables but also the manner in which these parallels are
achieved that is worthy of note. I have argued above that Matthew has
adapted the parable of The Two Sons – especially its application – to align
it with the other parables in the trilogy;[27] and that this same redactional
tendency to highlight the parallelism that marks these parables can be
observed in both The Tenants and The Wedding Feast.[28] The repeated
invitation is a case in point. In each of the three parables, those guilty
of disobedience twice spurn the command of their God. If this is in
itself significant, underlining the deliberate and persistent nature of their
refusal, then it is also significant that Matthew's redaction is responsible
for the harmonisation achieved here. The Marcan parable of The Tenants
reports the sending of three separate servants followed by 'many others' to
collect the fruit of the vineyard (Mark 12.2–5). As we have seen, Matthew
abbreviates the Marcan account at this point, reporting only two missions
(Matt 21.34–36). By contrast, Matthew appears to *extend* the traditional
sending motif in The Wedding Feast. Whereas Luke reports the sending
of one servant once to extend the call to those first invited to the banquet
(Luke 14.16–21), Matthew again tells of a twofold mission twice rejected
(22.2–5). Equally significant, this motif of a double rejection also surfaces
in The Two Sons, *even though it forms no part of the parable proper*.
In the application, however, the evangelist adds that the Jewish leaders
missed a second opportunity to repent and obey when they witnessed the
repentance of the tax gatherers and prostitutes; here Matthew anticipates
the dual rejection of The Tenants and The Wedding Feast.[29] Clearly,
Matthew takes pain to correlate these parables. In the latter two parables,
the redacted storyline allows the evangelist to extend the parallelism to
the verbal level: ἀπέστειλεν τοὺς δούλους αὐτοῦ (21.34, cf. 22.3); πάλιν
ἀπέστειλεν ἄλλους δούλους (21.36, cf. 22.4); τοὺς δούλους αὐτοῦ . . .
ἀπέκτειναν (21.35, cf. 22.6); and these parallels are only representative of
the many verbal echoes that bind these parables together.[30] The evangelist
has aligned the parables in this trilogy repeatedly by underlining the links
that were present in the traditional stories and by forging new ones.

    All of this is directly relevant to the textual problem at hand. In this con-
text, it is surely significant that one of the two principal variants creates
still another important link to the second and third parables in the trilogy, while the other produces a notable exception. Given the evangelist's

demonstrable interest in underlining (and strengthening) the parallel motifs that characterise these parables, he is more likely to be responsible for the reading that finds an echo in the parables that follow. In the trilogy's other parables, both the tenants to whom the vineyard is first leased and the guests to whom the invitation is first extended reject the repeated initiatives of the vineyard owner and the king. Only subsequently does the reader learn of other tenants who will give back to the owner the fruit that is rightfully his, and of other guests who will accept the king's invitation to the feast. In both instances, then, *the failure of the first leads to their indictment, and subsequent opportunity for the second*. In The Two Sons, this is precisely the sequence in reading 2 where the first son expresses assent, but fails to go to the vineyard to work. If we accept this reading, then here – as in the several instances noted above – The Two Sons anticipates subsequent developments in the two parables to follow. Reading 1, on the other hand, would mark a significant departure from the evangelist's clear preference for the correlation of the parables, since on this reading the *first* called finally obeys and enters the kingdom, while the *second* fails to do the father's will and is condemned.

We are left, then, with the common problem that intrinsic considerations point in one direction and transcriptional probabilities point in another. The plausible suggestion that an early scribe might have transposed the order of the original reading in an attempt to reflect the 'correct' salvation–historical order stands in favour of the first reading. The author's demonstrable attempt to underline and increase the parallelism that runs through these parables stands firmly in favour of the second. The decision is not easy but I suggest that the weight of intrinsic probabilities here makes the second reading more likely to be original. Later scribes *may* have been interested in 'correcting' the salvation–historical sequence here,[31] but, if the argument presented above in chapter 2 is correct, then the evangelist *was* keenly interested in the links between these parables and made a concerted effort to highlight them. It would be surprising if he failed to take advantage of another opportunity to do the same here.

If indeed the second reading was original, how might the other readings have emerged? B. Metzger suggests that the rise of the third reading might be 'due to copyists who either committed a transcriptional blunder or who were motivated by anti-Pharisaic bias'.[32] We have already seen, however, that the MSS that witness this third reading also agree in omitting the negative particle in 21.32 (so attributing repentance to the Jewish leaders) and thus can hardly be accused of an anti-Pharisaic bias. The transformation of the negation in verse 32 also makes it difficult to attribute the rise of reading 3 to an accidental transcriptional blunder – more probably there is a relationship between these two distinctive readings at verses 29–31 and verse 32. In any case, the distinctiveness of reading 3 suggests that it cannot be dismissed as a mere conflation of readings 1 and 2.

In an important (but often neglected) essay, J. Schmid argues that: (1) reading 3 arose as the deliberate work of a scribe with a distinctive understanding of the parable; and (2) the rise of this reading formed an intermediate stage in the textual history of the parable (between readings 2 and 1).[33] Reading 3, he thinks, grew out of the confusing relationship between the parable and its application.[34] A scribe mistakenly thought that the father in the story represented the Baptist, and proceeded to identify the Jewish leaders as the 'no-saying' son (in line with their response to John), and the tax gatherers and prostitutes as the son who said 'yes'. This would explain the elimination of the negative particle in 21.32. Since the parable makes it clear that the son who said 'no' (i.e., the Jewish leaders on this reading) subsequently repented, repentance could hardly be denied to the Jewish leaders in the application (21.32) – thus the removal of the negative particle.

The resulting parable was obviously flawed, however, and invited further correction that resulted in a third distinctive reading (reading 1, he thinks).[35]

Naturally, Schmid's conjecture can neither be proved nor disproved. I think, however, that it does offer both a plausible explanation for the omission of οὐδέ in 21.32, and a reasonable account of the rise of the three distinctive readings of this parable,[36] and so demonstrates that reading 3 may well have formed the intermediate stage between readings 1 and 2, whichever was original.

To my mind, however, Schmid is unable to provide any compelling reason that reading 2 is to be preferred. He acknowledges that the original that reading 3 altered could have been either 1 or 2 but, with Westcott and Hort, concludes that the religious reality depicted strongly favours the originality of reading 2.[37] Although we have seen that such arguments can hardly prove decisive, I think that his instinct was correct – reading 2 is original – and that the argument from the design of the trilogy mounted here offers important intrinsic evidence in favour of this conclusion.

Conclusion

While transcriptional probabilities offer strong support for the third reading – it is certainly the most difficult reading and, as such, nicely explains the rise of the two other principal variants – this support is more than offset by intrinsic probabilities. The reading is indeed so difficult as to be almost nonsensical. Moreover, it flies in the face of the developing Matthean narrative. To the force of these intrinsic considerations must be added the limited external evidence, which likewise militates against this third option.

Both of the first two readings receive significant external support. Transcriptional probabilities favour reading 1, but intrinsic probabilities offer strong support for reading 2. On balance, reading 2 seems more likely than reading 1 to be original. Although the most difficult, reading 3 seems least likely to be original.

NOTES

1 Introduction: of authors, readers and approaches to the parables

1. In addition to source, form and redaction criticism which the standard commentators continue to employ (see, e.g., W. D. Davies and Dale C. Allison, *A Critical and Exegetical Commentary on the Gospel According to Saint Matthew* (ICC; 3 vols.; Edinburgh: T. & T. Clark, 1988–97)), one thinks here not only of narrative, reader-response and social-scientific criticism, but also of discourse analysis, feminist criticism and deconstruction, of rhetorical and canonical criticism, and now even of autobiographical (cf. *Semeia* 72 (1995)) and post-colonial criticism (cf. *Semeia* 75 (1996)).
2. See, e.g., Stephen C. Barton, *Discipleship and Family Ties in Mark and Matthew* (SNTSMS 80; Cambridge University Press, 1994), 16–22; David D. Kupp, *Matthew's Emmanuel: Divine Presence and God's People in the First Gospel* (SNTSMS 90; Cambridge University Press, 1996), xiii–xiv.
3. Cf. Anthony C. Thiselton, *New Horizons in Hermeneutics* (London: Harper-Collins, 1992), 471, on the impact of literary criticism on biblical studies more broadly: 'The turn towards literary theory in biblical studies constitutes one of the three most significant developments for biblical hermeneutics over the last quarter of a century.'
4. See, e.g., Mark Allan Powell, *What is Narrative Criticism?* (Minneapolis: Fortress, 1990), 10; cf. Kupp, *Matthew's Emmanuel*, 22–7.
5. On the importance of defining interpretive aims, see esp. R. Morgan, with J. Barton, *Biblical Interpretation* (Oxford University Press, 1988), 7, 215, 221; Thiselton, *New Horizons*, 499–502.
6. 'Reconceiving Narrative Criticism', in *Characterization in the Gospels: Reconceiving Narrative Criticism* (ed. David Rhoads and Kari Syreeni, 13–48, JSNTSup 184; Sheffield Academic Press, 1999), 23.
7. See, e.g., David Rhoads and Donald Michie, *Mark as Story: An Introduction to the Narrative of a Gospel* (Philadelphia: Fortress, 1982), 3; Dorothy Jean Weaver, *Matthew's Missionary Discourse: A Literary Critical Analysis* (JSNTSup 38; Sheffield: JSOT, 1990), 25–6.
8. See, however, the seasoned methodological reflections in Graham N. Stanton, *A Gospel for A New People: Studies in Matthew* (Edinburgh: T. & T. Clark, 1992), 23–53.

9. David B. Howell, *Matthew's Inclusive Story: A Study in the Narrative Rhetoric of the First Gospel* (JSNTSup 42; Sheffield: JSOT, 1990), 21–4, 31–3, offers a typical expression of this sentiment.

10. Cf. J. Anderson's interesting admission: 'In Gospels studies since [the completion of her thesis in 1983] the problems as well as the possibilities of these approaches have been revealed. Several criticisms have been particularly telling. One is that the rallying cry of the Gospels as wholes, the Gospels as unified narratives, is just as much an *a priori* presupposition as previous assumptions that they were not' (*Matthew's Narrative Web: Over, and Over, and Over Again* (JSNTSup 91; Sheffield: JSOT, 1994), 7). Like beauty, unity is sometimes found in the eye of the beholder: '[r]eading for unity is . . . criticism's second nature' (Merenlahti and Hakola, 'Reconceiving Narrative Criticism', 28).

11. Powell, *What is Narrative Criticism?*, 7.

12. See the discussion of authorial intention that follows on pp. 8–13.

13. R. T. Fortna, *The Fourth Gospel and Its Predecessor* (Edinburgh: T. & T. Clark, 1988), 8–9, imagines a situation not unlike this for the first readers of John's Gospel.

14. See further Thiselton, *New Horizons*, 210–11, 475–6, citing Wordsworth: 'we murder to dissect'; J. D. Kingsbury, 'Review of *A Gospel for a New People*, by Graham N. Stanton', *JTS* 44 (1993), 649.

15. On the ambiguities surrounding the use of the terms *history* and *fiction*, see V. Philips Long, *The Art of Biblical History* (Grand Rapids: Zondervan, 1994), 58–63.

16. Robert M. Fowler, *Let the Reader Understand: Reader-Response Criticism and the Gospel of Mark* (Minneapolis: Fortress, 1991), 79.

17. Ibid., 80; but see also his more restrained comments on p. 64.

18. B. C. Lategan, 'Some Unresolved Methodological Issues', in *Text and Reality: Aspects of Reference in Biblical Texts*, by B. C. Lategan and W. S. Vorster, 3–25 (Atlanta: Scholars Press, 1985), 22.

19. Howell, *Matthew's Inclusive Story*, 26–30, drawing upon W. S. Vorster, 'Meaning and Reference: The Parables of Jesus in Mark 4', in *Text and Reality: Aspects of Reference in Biblical Texts*, by B. C. Lategan and W. S. Vorster, 27–65 (Atlanta: Scholars Press, 1985), 60.

20. Cf. J. D. Kingsbury, 'Reflections on "The Reader" of Matthew's Gospel', *NTS* 34 (1988), 458.

21. See now the collection of essays in Richard Bauckham (ed.), *The Gospels for All Christians* (Grand Rapids: Eerdmans, 1998), which offers a spirited challenge to the consensus that the Gospels were written for specific communities. Cf. Luke Timothy Johnson, 'On Finding the Lucan Community: A Cautious Cautionary Essay', *SBLSP* 16 (1979), 87–100; Eugene E. Lemcio, *The Past of Jesus in the Gospels* (Cambridge University Press, 1991), 24.

22. F. Watson, *Text and Truth* (Grand Rapids: Eerdmans, 1997), 33–69; cf. Watson, 'Toward a Literal Reading of the Gospels', in *The Gospels for All Christians* (ed. Richard Bauckham, 195–217, Grand Rapids: Eerdmans, 1998). On the historical interests of the evangelists, see further Graham N. Stanton, *Jesus of Nazareth in New Testament Preaching* (Cambridge University Press, 1974), 137–71; C. F. D. Moule, 'Jesus in New Testament

Kerygma', in *Essays in New Testament Interpretation* (Cambridge University Press, 1982), 45–9; Lemcio, *The Past of Jesus*.

23. See Thiselton, *New Horizons*, 351–58, and Watson, *Text and Truth*, 34, 55–7, on the role of emplotment in both fictional and historical narrative.

24. Cf. M. Sternberg, *The Poetics of Biblical Narrative: Ideological Literature and the Drama of Reading* (Indiana University Press, 1985), 25; emphasis added.

25. See further ibid., 23–35, to which I am indebted for the argument developed above; the citation comes from p. 25. Cf. Merenlahti and Hakola, 'Reconceiving Narrative Criticism', 33–46.

26. Powell, *What is Narrative Criticism?*, 58, 66–7. Powell's subsequent writings seem to temper this position; see, e.g., 'Narrative Criticism', in *Hearing the New Testament: Strategies for Interpretation* (ed. Joel B. Green, 239–55, Grand Rapids: Eerdmans, 1995), 240; 'Toward a Narrative-Critical Understanding of Matthew', in *Gospel Interpretation: Narrative-Critical and Social–Scientific Approaches* (ed. J. D. Kingsbury, 9–15, Harrisburg: Trinity Press, 1997), 13.

27. Similarly Merenlahti and Hakola, 'Reconceiving Narrative Criticism', 40–2.

28. Cf. M. Hooker, 'In his own Image?' in *What About the New Testament? Essays in Honour of Christopher Evans* (ed. M. Hooker and C. Hickling, 28–44, London: SCM, 1975) 30, 36–41, for a critique of the unwarranted scepticism in some redaction-critical circles regarding the evangelist's interest in history, and her scepticism about the speculative nature of *Sitz im Leben* reconstructions.

29. See Thiselton, *New Horizons*, 58–63, for a survey of these developments and Jane P. Tompkins (ed.), *Reader-Response Criticism: From Formalism to Post Structuralism* (Baltimore: Johns Hopkins University Press, 1980), for an introductory series of essays that charts the rise of the reader in literary-critical circles. Cf. also B. F. Meyer, 'The Challenges of Text and Reader to the Historical-Critical Method', *Concilium* 1 (1991), 3–12; Kevin J. Vanhoozer, *Is There a Meaning in this Text? The Bible, the Reader and the Morality of Literary Knowledge* (Leicester: Apollos, 1998).

30. Powell, *What is Narrative Criticism?*, 96.

31. Howell, *Matthew's Inclusive Story*, 38–43; the citation comes from p. 38. Similarly John A. Darr, *On Character Building: The Reader and the Rhetoric of Characterization in Luke–Acts* (Louisville: Westminster/John Knox, 1992), 17–20.

32. R. M. Fowler, 'Reader-Response Criticism: Figuring Mark's Reader', in *Mark and Method: New Approaches in Biblical Studies* (ed. Janice Capel Anderson and Stephen D. Moore, 50–83, Minneapolis: Fortress, 1992), 51.

33. So also T. Longman, *Literary Approaches to Biblical Interpretation* (Grand Rapids: Academie, 1987), 61–7.

34. R. G. Mills, 'Redaction Criticism in Matthean Studies: A Literary Critical Defence', Ph.D. thesis, University of Otago (1997).

35. On *point of view* see B. Uspensky, *A Poetics of Composition* (trans. V. Zavarin and S. Wittig, Berkeley: University of California Press, 1973) and S. S. Lanser, *The Narrative Act: Point of View in Prose Fiction* (Princeton University Press, 1981), 184–222.

36. So, e.g., J. D. Kingsbury, *Matthew as Story* (2nd edn, Philadelphia: Fortress, 1988), 33.
37. So Howell, *Matthew's Inclusive Story*, 161.
38. Rhoads and Michie, *Mark as Story*, 39. W. C. Booth, *The Rhetoric of Fiction* (2nd edn, University of Chicago Press, 1983), 20, makes a similar point about the pervasive influence of the author's point of view.
39. Booth, *Rhetoric*, 436; emphasis original. Perhaps we should also add, in light of our previous discussion of history and fiction, that for Booth *the rhetoric of fiction* is not restricted to fiction; cf. *Rhetoric*, 407.
40. Norman R. Petersen, *Literary Criticism for New Testament Critics* (Philadelphia: Fortress, 1978), 58; Kingsbury, *Matthew as Story*, 3.
41. Cf. Mark Allan Powell, 'Characterization on the Phraseological Plane in the Gospel of Matthew', in *Treasures New and Old: Recent Contributions to Matthean Studies* (ed. David R. Bauer and Mark Allan Powell, 161–77, Atlanta: Scholars Press, 1996), 163.
42. On the control of distance, see esp. Booth, *Rhetoric*, 243–66. Cf. also W. Iser, 'The Reading Process: A Phenomenological Approach', in *Reader-Response Criticism: From Formalism to Post Structuralism* (ed. Jane P. Tompkins, 50–69, Baltimore: Johns Hopkins University Press, 1980), 65, for whom the reader's identification with characters in the story is a 'strategem by means of which the author stimulates attitudes in the reader'.
43. Cf. Howell, *Matthew's Inclusive Story*, 44–5.
44. See esp. Janice Capel Anderson, 'Double and Triple Stories, The Implied Reader, and Redundancy in Matthew', *Semeia* 31 (1985), 71–89, on the use of repetition and, on commentary as a rhetorical device, see Booth, *Rhetoric*, 169–209. On p. 200 Booth summarises his preceding discussion: 'So far we have considered only commentary which is about something clearly dramatized in the work. The authors have simply tried to make clear to us the nature of the dramatic object itself, by giving us the hard facts, by establishing a world of norms, by relating particulars to those norms, or by relating the story to general truths. *In so doing, authors are in effect exercising careful control over the reader's degree of involvement in or distance from the events of the story, by insuring that the reader views the material with the degree of detachment or sympathy felt by the implied author*' (emphasis added).
45. Booth, *Rhetoric*, 138; see further pp. 71–6; 211–21; Seymour Chatman, *Story and Discourse: Narrative Structure in Fiction and Film* (London: Cornell University Press, 1978), 147–51.
46. So Kingsbury, *Matthew as Story*, 38. Here I prefer Booth's version of the implied reader (which is ultimately in the text) over Iser's (which arises out of the interaction between a real reader and the text; cf. W. Iser, *The Implied Reader: Patterns of Communication in Prose Fiction from Bunyan to Beckett* (Baltimore: Johns Hopkins University Press, 1974); *The Act of Reading: A Theory of Aesthetic Response* (London: Routledge & Kegan Paul, 1978)) as both more useful heuristically and more satisfying theoretically.
47. Cf. Howell, *Matthew's Inclusive Story*, 210: 'Thus, to speak of the implied reader is in a sense, to speak of the embodiment of *the response Matthew was aiming at* when he composed his Gospel' (emphasis added). See also pp. 41–9, and cf. Rhoads and Michie, *Mark as Story*, 1; Darr, *Character Building*, 32.

48. Kingsbury, *Matthew as Story*, 147–60; similarly, the world of the narrative may function as an index of the world of the evangelist (cf. Kingsbury, 'The Reader', 459). Powell, *What is Narrative Criticism?*, 97, adds that the implied author may likewise serve as an index of the real author.
49. *Pace* Mills, 'Redaction Criticism', 248–76.
50. Stephen D. Moore, *Literary Criticism and the Gospels* (London: Yale, 1989), 12–13, 55, makes the same point.
51. Similarly ibid., 77.
52. E. Struthers-Malbon, 'Narrative Criticism: How Does the Story Mean?' in *Mark and Method: New Approaches in Biblical Studies* (ed. Janice Capel Anderson and Stephen D. Moore, 23–49, Minneapolis: Fortress, 1992), 35, states matter-of-factly: 'Narrative criticism seeks to avoid the "intentional fallacy" of redaction criticism.' Powell, *What is Narrative Criticism?*, 29, voices similar concerns, but is happy to pursue the intention of the *implied author*.
53. Cf. Meyer, 'Text and Reader', 9–10; Thiselton, *New Horizons*, 559–62; Watson, *Text and Truth*, 118–19; Vanhoozer, *Is There a Meaning?*, 222, 230, 239, 246, 248, 250–3.
54. Thiselton, *New Horizons*, 560.
55. As narrative critics have been quick to point out: cf., e.g., R. M. Fowler, 'Who is "the Reader" in Reader Response Criticism?', *Semeia* 31 (1985), 19–20; similarly, Howell, *Matthew's Inclusive Story*, 25.
56. For an introduction to speech-act theory, see J. L. Austin, *How to Do Things With Words* (Oxford: Clarendon, 1962); for recent application of these principles to biblical hermeneutics, see, e.g., Anthony C. Thiselton, 'Reader-Response Hermeneutics, Action Models, and the Parables of Jesus', in *The Responsibility of Hermeneutics* (ed. Roger Lundin, Anthony C. Thiselton and Clarence Walhout, 79–126, Grand Rapids: Eerdmans, 1985), 79–126 (esp. 100–1, 107); *New Horizons*, 283–307, 358–68, 597–604; Watson, *Text and Truth*, 98–103; Vanhoozer, *Is There a Meaning?*, 198–280 (esp. 208–14).
57. The history of the interpretation of Jesus' parables has been told repeatedly and well and need not be repeated here. See, e.g., G. V. Jones, *The Art and Truth of the Parables: A Study in their Literary Form and Modern Interpretation* (London: SPCK, 1964); N. Perrin, *Jesus and the Language of the Kingdom* (London: SCM, 1976); W. S. Kissinger, *The Parables of Jesus: A History of Interpretation and Bibliography* (London: Scarecrow, 1979); P. Dschulnigg, 'Positionen des Gleichnisverständnisses im 20. Jahrhundert', *TZ* 45 (1989), 335–51; C. L. Blomberg, *Interpreting the Parables* (Leicester: Apollos, 1990); 'The Parables of Jesus: Current Trends and Needs in Research', in *Studying the Historical Jesus: Evaluations of the State of Current Research* (ed. Bruce Chilton and Craig A. Evans, 231–54, Leiden: Brill, 1994); K. R. Snodgrass, 'From Allegorizing to Allegorizing: A History of the Interpretation of the Parables of Jesus', in *The Challenge of Jesus' Parables* (ed. Richard N. Longenecker, 3–29, Grand Rapids: Eerdmans, 2000).
58. The second volume was completed in 1899; a second edition was published in 1910.
59. C. H. Dodd, *The Parables of the Kingdom* (London: Nisbet & Co. Ltd., 1935; reprint, 1941); see, e.g., pp. 26, 31–2, 111–53.

60. J. Jeremias, *The Parables of Jesus* (3rd edn, trans. S. H. Hooke, London: SCM, 1954; reprint, 1955); see esp. pp. 20–88.
61. Perrin, *Language of the Kingdom*, 101.
62. Cf., e.g., J. Drury, 'The Sower, the Vineyard, and the Place of Allegory in the Interpretation of Mark's Parables', *JTS* 24 (1973), 367–79; J. W. Sider, 'Rediscovering the Parables: The Logic of the Jeremias Tradition', *JBL* 102 (1983), 61–83; B. Gerhardsson, 'If We Do Not Cut the Parables Out of Their Frames', *NTS* 37 (1991), 321–35; I. H. Jones, *The Matthean Parables: A Literary and Historical Commentary* (Leiden: Brill, 1995), 68–81.
63. Cf., e.g., C. W. Hedrick, *Parables as Poetic Fictions: The Creative Voice of Jesus* (Peabody, MA: Hendrickson, 1994), 3–4; W. R. Herzog, *Parables as Subversive Speech: Jesus as the Pedagogue of the Oppressed* (Louisville: Westminster/John Knox, 1994), 3–4.
64. Admittedly, the search for authentic Jesus material elsewhere in the Synoptic tradition offers a clear parallel to Jeremias's search for 'the very words of Jesus' in the parables, and so makes this observation somewhat artificial. Nevertheless, the degree to which this agenda has dominated the scene in parables scholarship justifies the distinction.
65. Of course redaction-critical tools were regularly employed in the reconstruction of earlier stages of the tradition.
66. Notable exceptions include J. D. Kingsbury, *The Parables of Jesus in Matthew 13: A Study in Redaction-Criticism* (London: SPCK, 1969); C. E. Carlston, *The Parables of the Triple Tradition* (Philadelphia: Fortress, 1975); J. R. Donahue, *The Gospel in Parable: Metaphor, Narrative and Theology in the Synoptic Gospels* (Philadelphia: Fortress, 1988); J. Lambrecht, *Out of the Treasure: The Parables in the Gospel of Matthew* (Louvain: Peeters, 1992).
67. See now W. Carter and J. P. Heil, *Matthew's Parables: Audience-Oriented Perspectives* (Washington: The Catholic Biblical Association of America, 1998).
68. Cf. Dodd, *Parables*, 13, who followed Jülicher in concluding 'not that the allegorical interpretation is in this or that case overdone or fanciful, but that the parables in general do not admit of this method at all'. Elsewhere, however, Dodd can temper this conclusion; cf. ibid., 21. For a succinct summary of Jülicher's position, see Dschulnigg 'Gleichnisverständnisses', 336–7.
69. Cf., e.g., D. O. Via, *The Parables: Their Literary and Existential Dimension* (Philadelphia: Fortress, 1967), 4–10; Perrin, *Language of the Kingdom*, 92–3; B. B. Scott, *Hear Then The Parable: A Commentary on the Parables of Jesus* (Minneapolis: Fortress, 1989), 43–4; Hedrick, *Poetic Fictions*, 8.
70. P. Fiebig, *Altjüdische Gleichnisse und die Gleichnisse Jesu* (Tübingen: Mohr, 1904); *Die Gleichnisreden Jesu im Lichte der rabbinischen Gleichnisse des neutestamentlichen Zeitalters. Ein Beitrag zum Streit um die 'Christusmythe' und eine Widerlegung der Gleichnistheorie Jülichers* (Tübingen: Mohr, 1912).
71. Cf. Scott, *Hear Then The Parable*, 16.
72. Ibid., 7–13.
73. Cf. M. Boucher, *The Mysterious Parable* (Washington: The Catholic Biblical Association of America, 1977), 12: 'Every kind of speech called *parabolē* in the NT appears also in the OT.'
74. Cf. esp. Drury, 'The Place of Allegory', 374–9.

75. Similarly Donahue, *Gospel in Parable*, 12; Jones, *Matthean Parables*, 78–9. Other writers to challenge the basic distinction that Jülicher drew between parable and allegory include M. Black, 'The Parables as Allegory', *BJRL* 42 (1960), 273–87; R. E. Brown, 'Parable and Allegory Reconsidered', *NovT* 5 (1962), 36–45; J. D. M. Derrett, 'Allegory and the Wicked Vinedressers', *JTS* 25 (1974), 426–32; H. J. Klauck, *Allegorie und Allegorese in Synoptischen Gleichnistexten* (Münster: Aschendorff, 1978); B. H. Young, *Jesus and His Jewish Parables: Rediscovering the Roots of Jesus' Teaching* (New York: Paulist, 1989); Blomberg, *Interpreting the Parables*.

76. E. Fuchs, *Studies of the Historical Jesus* (trans. Andrew Scobie, London: SCM, 1964), 207–28 (esp. 219–22); cf. A. C. Thiselton, 'The Parables as Language-Event: Some Comments on Fuch's Hermeneutics in the Light of Linguistic Philosophy', *SJT* 23 (1970), 437–68.

77. See E. Jüngel, *Paulus und Jesus* (Tübingen: Mohr, 1962), and E. Linnemann, *Parables of Jesus* (trans. John Sturdy, London: SPCK, 1966).

78. Fuchs, *Historical Jesus*, 211.

79. Cf. Jüngel, *Paulus und Jesus*, 135.

80. Thiselton, 'Parables as Language-Event', 439 n. 1, rightly notes, however, that it is a misleading oversimplification to suggest that Jülicher was *only* interested in the cognitive function of Jesus' parabolic teaching. See, e.g., D. A. Jülicher, *Die Gleichnisreden Jesu* (2nd edn, Tübingen: J. C. B. Mohr, 1910), I:105.

81. Thiselton, 'Parables as Language-Event', 439; cf. pp. 464–5; Austin, *Words*, 45.

82. Cf. Thiselton, 'Parables as Language-Event', 439 n. 2.

83. So also Boucher, *Mysterious Parable*, 30; *contra*, e.g., Perrin, *Language of the Kingdom*, 105–6.

84. Cf. Blomberg, 'Current Trends', 231–2.

85. Via, *Parables*, ix–25; cf. Hedrick, *Poetic Fictions*, 86–7, who has argued a line that is in some ways reminiscent of Via. For Hedrick, however, the general first-century background of these stories is much more important than it was for Via: Jesus' fictive accounts would have been understood as an assault on Judaism's shared fictions.

86. Scott, *Hear Then The Parable*, 41–2; cf. p. 56.

87. Here Scott echoes the emphasis of his predecessors, but the rationale offered varies; cf., e.g., R. W. Funk, *Language, Hermeneutic, and the Word of God* (New York: Harper and Row, 1966), 214; Via, *Parables*, 52–7; Perrin, *Language of the Kingdom*, 134.

88. Scott, *Hear Then The Parable*, 45.

89. *Contra*, e.g., Via, *Parables*, 52–7; 70–107; Hedrick, *Poetic Fictions*, 26–35.

90. See, e.g., A. N. Wilder, *Early Christian Rhetoric: The Language of the Gospel* (London: SCM, 1964), 80–1, 92; Funk, *Language,* 133–62; J. D. Crossan, *In Parables: The Challenge of the Historical Jesus* (New York: Harper and Row, 1973), 10–16.

91. Scott, *Hear Then The Parable*, 47.

92. Funk, *Language*, 133; cf. R. Bultmann, *The History of the Synoptic Tradition* (trans. John Marsh, Oxford: Blackwell, 1963; reprint, 1972), 198.

93. The near blanket dismissal of the applications that accompany the Synoptic parables (cf. Scott, *Hear Then The Parable*, 17) and the regular denigration

of allegory (Scott's more moderate position notwithstanding) are two cases in point. Scott himself acknowledges that the sharp distinction between allegory and parable cannot be sustained, but nevertheless quickly denies the presence of allegory in Jesus' parables on the questionable evidence that Thomas affords, buttressed by an appeal to Jülicher (*Hear Then The Parable*, 43–5). For an even-handed discussion of the problems of Thomas's order vis-à-vis the Synoptics, and possible echoes, in Thomas, of redactional elements from the Synoptics, see C. Tuckett, 'Thomas and the Synoptics', *NovT* 30 (1988), 132–57.

94. Scott, *Hear Then The Parable*, 41–2.
95. This problem of context is an extraordinarily important one to which Scott devotes insufficient attention. Although I cannot develop this argument here, it seems to me that context plays a decisive role in shaping the reception of enigmatic utterances of all sorts.
96. See Moore, *Literary Criticism*, 71–107, and Fowler, 'Reader-Response Criticism', for introductions to the reader-response criticism of the Gospels.
97. For an introduction to 'deconstruction', a post-structuralist approach to texts that shares some common interests with reader-response criticism, see J. Culler, *On Deconstruction: Theory and Criticism After Structuralism* (Ithaca: Cornell University Press, 1982); for its application to Gospels studies see, e.g., S. Moore, 'Deconstructive Criticism: The Gospel of the Mark', in *Mark and Method: New Approaches in Biblical Studies* (ed. Janice Capel Anderson and Stephen D. Moore, 84–102, Minneapolis: Fortress, 1992); S. Moore, *Poststructuralism and the New Testament: Derrida and Foucault at the Foot of the Cross* (Minneapolis: Fortress, 1994); and, for an important theological critique, see now Vanhoozer, *Is There a Meaning?*
98. Cf. Snodgrass, 'History of Interpretation', 11.
99. See also Thiselton, 'Reader-Response Hermeneutics', for an assessment of the value of reader-response hermeneutics for the study of the parables.
100. When, throughout the course of the study, I refer to the *readers* that the evangelist envisioned, I use the term loosely, recognising that in all probability the intended recipients of the Gospels would have been *hearers*, the Gospels having been designed for public reading. Occasionally, I make this explicit, referring to the Gospel's *hearers*. See Stanton, *New People*, 73–6; B. B. Scott and M. E. Dean, 'A Sound Map of the Sermon on the Mount', in *Treasures New and Old: Recent Contributions to Matthean Studies* (ed. David R. Bauer and Mark Allan Powell, 311–78, Atlanta: Scholars Press, 1996).

2   Matthew's trilogy of parables: 21.28–22.14

1. Chrysostom, *Homilies on the Gospel of Saint Matthew 68.1* (*NPNF*[1] 10:415).
2. B. Weiss, *Das Matthäus-Evangelium* (7th edn, Göttingen: Vandenhoeck & Ruprecht, 1898), 373.
3. Ibid., 365, 369–70, 373.

4. Willoughby C. Allen, *A Critical and Exegetical Commentary on the Gospel According to Matthew* (3rd edn, ICC; Edinburgh: T. & T. Clark, 1912; reprint, 1922), 235.

5. Ibid., 226.

6. A. Plummer, *An Exegetical Commentary on the Gospel According to S. Matthew* (London: Robert Scott, 1909; reprint, 1915), 294; Plummer thought that all three parables came from the Logia.

7. Ibid., 294.

8. E. Klostermann, *Das Matthäusevangelium* (2nd edn, Tübingen: Mohr, 1927), 169, 173.

9. Ibid., 175.

10. A. H. McNeile, *The Gospel According to Matthew* (London: Macmillan, 1915), 306; cf. 313.

11. Trilling assigned the banquet parables to the Q tradition; cf. 'Zur Überlieferungsgeschichte des Gleichnisses vom Hochzeitsmahl Mt 22, 1–14', *BZ* 4 (1960), 263.

12. Ibid., 252, 254–5, 263.

13. Ibid., 252–4; 257–8.

14. Ibid., 262 n. 30.

15. Ibid., 263.

16. Ibid., 252.

17. Ibid., 254–5.

18. Ibid., 254–5.

19. Ibid., 255.

20. Ibid., 255.

21. Ibid., 263.

22. Ibid., 264; cf. Trilling, *Das Wahre Israel: Studien zur Theologie des Matthäus-Evangeliums* (3rd edn, Munich: Kösel, 1964), 84.

23. *Homilies on the Gospel of Saint Matthew* 69.1 (*NPNF*[1] 10:422).

24. S. Van Tilborg, *The Jewish Leaders in Matthew* (Leiden: Brill, 1972), 47; for the Table, see pp. 47–8 n. 3.

25. O. H. Steck, *Israel und das gewaltsame Geschick der Propheten: Untersuchungen zur Überlieferung des deuteronomistischen Geschichtbildes im Alten Testament, Spätjudentum und Urchristentum* (Neukirchen-Vluyn: Neukirchener, 1967), 297–316.

26. Van Tilborg, *Jewish Leaders*, 46–9.

27. Ibid., 47–63; see esp. p. 52.

28. Ibid., 46.

29. E. Schweizer, 'Matthäus 21–25', in *Orientierung an Jesus: Zur Theologie der Synoptiker* (ed. Paul Hoffmann, 364–71, Freiburg: Herder, 1973); the article is reprinted in Schweizer, *Matthäus und seine Gemeinde* (Stuttgart: KBL Verlag, 1974), 116–25, and he returns to the discussion in a 1989 *Festschrift* for W. Trilling ('Auf W Trillings Spuren zu Mt 22,1–14', in *Christus bezeugen* (ed. Karl Kertelge, Traugott Holtz and Claus-Peter März, 146–9, Leipzig: St. Benno, 1989)).

30. Schweizer, 'Matthäus 21–25', 365.

31. E. Schweizer, *The Good News According to Matthew* (trans. David E. Green, Atlanta: John Knox, 1975), 401–2, 420.

32. Schweizer, 'Matthäus 21–25', 366–7; cf. Schweizer, *Matthew*, 400–3.

33. Schweizer, 'Matthäus 21–25', 367–71.
34. A. Ogawa, 'Paraboles de l'Israël véritable? Reconsidération critique de Mt. xxi 28 – xxii 14', *NovT* 21 (1979), 121–49. Cf. Ogawa, *L'histoire de Jésus chez Matthieu: La signification de l'histoire pour la théologie matthéenne* (Frankfurt: Peter Lang, 1979), 179–95.
35. Ogawa, 'L'Israël véritable?', 143–4.
36. Ibid., 144–5; cf. R. Walker, Die *Heilsgeschichte im ersten Evangelium* (Göttingen: Vandenhoeck & Ruprecht, 1967), 91–3.
37. Ogawa, 'L'Israël véritable?', 140–1.
38. Ibid., 149.
39. Ibid., 128–30; 136–7; 140–2, 44.
40. Ibid., 138–9, 149.
41. Lambrecht, *Treasure*, 89–142.
42. Ibid., 100.
43. Ibid., 119–20.
44. Ibid., 118.
45. Ibid., 100.
46. Ibid., 137.
47. Ibid., 136.
48. Cf. Lambrecht, *Treasure*, 92, 100.
49. Ibid., 100.
50. Ibid., 136.
51. Ibid., 102–3; cf. R. Hummel, *Die Auseinandersetzung zwischen Kirche und Judentum in Matthäusevangelium* (Munich: Kaiser, 1966), 25.
52. Jones, *Matthean Parables*, 371, 389.
53. Ibid., 405, 412.
54. Ibid., 371–412 passim.
55. Later in his commentary, Luz underlines the close ties between 21.23–27 and 21.28–32; cf. Luz, *Das Evangelium nach Matthäus* (EKKNT; 3 vols., incomplete; Zürich: Benzinger, 1985–97), III:205.
56. Luz, *Matthäus*, III:196–7; cf. Luz, *The Theology of the Gospel of Matthew* (trans. J. Bradford Robinson, Cambridge University Press, 1995), 118–21.
57. R. A. Edwards, *Matthew's Story of Jesus* (Philadelphia: Fortress, 1985), 74–8.
58. Kingsbury, *Matthew as Story*, 82–3; cf. Kingsbury, 'The Parable of the Wicked Husbandmen and the Secret of Jesus' Divine Sonship in Matthew: Some Literary–Critical Observations', *JBL* 105 (1986), 643–55.
59. Howell, *Matthew's Inclusive Story*, 151.
60. Ibid., 152.
61. The book, *Matthew's Parables: Audience–Oriented Perspectives*, is a joint effort, written by W. Carter and J. P. Heil, but Carter is responsible for the treatment of this trilogy.
62. Carter and Heil, *Matthew's Parables*, 147.
63. Carter and Heil, ibid., 1, describe their approach as 'audience-oriented': '[O]ur central focus concerns what happens as the gospel's audience interacts with the parables in their present form and in their current placement *within* the plot of Matthew's gospel.'
64. Ibid., 159–60.

65. Ibid., 175 n. 66.
66. Ibid., 148.
67. See esp. ch. 5.
68. If, as in 1.17, we take Χριστοῦ to be titular; alternatively, we meet the names of three important figures in the salvation–historical story that this narrative will relate.
69. 4.23–25 would then serve as a transition leading into the sermon.
70. However, Matthew's fondness for triads does not prevent him, on occasion, from turning a traditional grouping of three into two (e.g. 13.57, cf. Mark 6.4, 18.8, cf. Mark 9.34–37; perhaps 8.18–22, cf. Luke 9.57–62). Cf. C. L. Mitton, 'Threefoldness in the Teaching of Jesus', *ExpTim* 75 (1964), 228–30.
71. See D. C. Allison, 'The Structure of the Sermon on the Mount', *JBL* 106 (1987), 423–45; Davies and Allison, *Matthew*, I:61–72; 86–87; cf. further Allen, *Matthew*, lxiv–lxv; M. D. Goulder, *Midrash and Lection in Matthew* (London: SPCK, 1974), 26; D. A. Hagner, *Matthew 1–13* (WBC 33A; Dallas: Word, 1993), lii; Luz, *Matthew 1–7*, 38; J. Moffat, *An Introduction to the Literature of the New Testament* (3rd edn, Edinburgh: T. & T. Clark, 1918), 257.
72. Luz's list is illustrative and not comprehensive. Though not included here, he argues forcefully, as we have seen, that the parables at 21.28–22.14 form a trilogy. 'Examples', he maintains, 'can be increased at will' (*Matthew 1–7*, 38).
73. Davies and Allison, *Matthew*, I:61–2.
74. Cf. 5.21, 27, 34, 38, 43.
75. Allison, 'Structure', 432.
76. Ibid., 433.
77. See Davies and Allison, *Matthew*, I:63–4, for their outline of the entire sermon.
78. + λέγων if, at 13.33, we follow ℵ C L M U Θ 118 f^{13} 28 157 788 1346 h (l) q vg^{mss} sa^{ms} mae; cf. 13.24, 31.
79. Davies and Allison, *Matthew*, I:62.
80. Thomas, however, has versions of both The Hidden Treasure (*Gos. Thom.* 109) and The Pearl (*Gos. Thom.* 76).
81. In the case of The Mustard Seed, however, Luke places it in a different context (Luke 13.18–19). Probably the parable was also found in Q. Both the nature of the agreements between Matthew and Luke over against Mark and the fact that, in both Matthew and Luke, the same Q parable follows immediately support this conclusion.
82. Davies and Allison, *Matthew*, I:62, 65.
83. Ibid., 70.
84. Luz, *Matthew 1–7*, 38. Davies and Allison, *Matthew*, I:134–5, concur, with the exception of the Sermon, which they contend is patterned on the three traditional pillars of Simeon the Just. For a discussion of triads as a feature of Jesus' teaching, see Mitton, 'Threefoldness'. For the place of triads in Jewish writings, see Delling 'τρεῖς', *TDNT* VIII: 217–19, and J. Neusner, *Torah from the Sages. Pirke Avot: A New American Translation and Explanation* (Chappaqua, NY: Rosell, 1984), 23–4, 28–32, 39–44, 71–9, 99, 112–14, 137–41.

85. L. T. Johnson, *The Gospel of Luke* (Collegeville, MN: The Liturgical Press, 1991), 187.
86. Van Tilborg, *Jewish Leaders*, 49. Throughout this study, I use the following 'tags' in comparing the use of particular words and constructions employed by the evangelists:

> No par = neither of the other two Synoptic evangelists has a parallel to the pericope in which this word (phrase, construction, etc.) is found.
>
> Matt. par Mark (Matt. par Luke, etc.) = Matthew uses the word in a pericope paralleled in Mark who also employs this term.
>
> Matt. diff Mark (Matt. diff Luke, etc.) = Matthew uses the word in a pericope paralleled in Mark, but Mark lacks the specific term.
>
> Matt. [+] Mark (Matt. [+] Luke, etc.) = Matthew uses the word in a pericope paralleled in Mark, but Mark lacks the entire sentence in which the term stands.
>
> Matt. < Mark (Matt. < Luke, etc.) = Mark uses the item in material paralleled in Matthew, but Matthew lacks that specific term.

87. Van Tilborg, *Jewish Leaders*, 49–50.
88. Ibid., 49.
89. Ibid., 50. He notes that the presence of τότε and of συμβούλιον ἔλαβον also betray the evangelist's hand. Van Tilborg cites the following texts as evidence that συμβούλιον ἔλαβον is redactional here: Matt. 12.14; 22.15; 27.1, 7; 28.12; Mark 3.6; 15.1. In fact, the evidence is more decisive than this list of texts might suggest. While συμβούλιον does appear in these two Marcan texts, συμβούλιον ἔλαβον appears five times in Matthew but nowhere else in the NT or LXX:

> The use of συμβούλιον in Matthew:
> NT: 8×
> Matt.: 5×
> 2×: Matt. par Mark (12.14; 27.1)
> 2×: No par (27.7; 28.12)
> 1×: Matt. diff Mark (22.15)
> Mark: 2×
> Luke: 0×
> συμβούλιον ἔλαβον
> 2x: No par (27.7; 28.12)
> 3x: Matt. diff Mark (12.14; 22.15; 27.1)

90. Van Tilborg, *Jewish Leaders*, 50.
91. At Luke 10.36, Luke does come close to employing the Matthean formula.
92. Van Tilborg, *Jewish Leaders*, 50 n. 1, claims that the expression may be found in the LXX, but only in the 'typically Greek books, such as Esther, Tobias, Macc 1–4.' But, while δοκέω appears in a number of constructions in these books, the Matthean question formula is not one of them. Esther 1.19 is typical: εἰ οὖν δοκεῖ τῷ βασιλεῖ προσταξάτω βασιλικόν, καὶ γραφήτω . . . Perhaps 4 Macc. 11.16 approaches the distinctive Matthean usage as nearly as any: ὥστε εἴ σοι δοκεῖ βασανίζειν μὴ μιαροφαγοῦντα βασάνιζε (cf., similarly, 1 Macc. 15.20; 4 Macc. 11.5 (A)).

93. So also, e.g., D. Hill, *The Gospel of Matthew* (London: Marshall, Morgan and Scott, 1972), 297; Davies and Allison, *Matthew*, III:166; Luz, *Matthäus*, III:207 n. 22. Van Tilborg, *Jewish Leaders*, 50, and Jones, *Matthean Parables*, 391, think that the question may well have introduced the parable in the pre-Matthean tradition. In defence of this conclusion Jones observes that 'the Particle δὲ [*sic*] in 21:28 . . . has parallels in the MSS at 18:12' (Ibid., 274 n. 332 (i)). Indeed at 18.12 D does include δέ, just as several omit it at 21.28 (Y Θ *f*¹³ 788 1346); to my knowledge no witnesses include the particle in the remaining four occurrences (in addition to NA²⁷, see R. J. Swanson, *New Testament Manuscripts: Matthew* (Sheffield Academic Press, 1995), 168, 173, 207, 215, 220, 273). This is not surprising since both at 18.12 and 21.28, over against 17.25, 22.17, 42, and 26.66, the question introduces a new pericope. Contrast, e.g., 22.41–42: ἐπηρώτησεν αὐτοὺς ὁ Ἰησοῦς λέγων· τί ὑμῖν δοκεῖ περὶ τοῦ χριστοῦ;

94. Similarly Luz, *Matthäus*, III:207.

95. So already Weiss, *Matthäus*, 367. It is true, however, that Matthew does use this phrase to introduce the following parable (22.1). Elsewhere he shows some preference for the phrase; of the six times it occurs in Matthew, only at 13.3 is it demonstrably traditional (although its appearance in 22.1 was probably influenced by Mark 12.1). Presumably Mark means to describe the manner of Jesus' speech. Mark employs the same expression at 3.23, 4.2 and 4.11, but in none of these texts does the phrase introduce a single parable. In the LXX, aside from Ps. 77.2, which Matthew cites at 13.35, the phrase is found only at Sir. 38.34; 45.15, 17.

96. ἄλλην παραβολήν

Matt.: 4×

1×: No par (13.24)
2×: Matt. diff Mark (13.31; 21.33)
1×: Matt. diff Luke (13.33)

Mark: 0×

Luke: 0×

97. See our earlier discussion at p. 37.

98. So also Kingsbury, *Parables*, 12–13. Jones, *Matthean Parables*, 372 n. 97, remains unconvinced.

99. *Contra* Van Tilborg, *Jewish Leaders*, 50, for whom the presence of ἀκούσατε makes a redactional origin improbable.

100. Van Tilborg, *Jewish Leaders*, 50.

101. ἀκούσας/ἀκούσαντες: Matt.: 21×; Mark: 12×; Luke: 10×.

102. Cf. pp. 109–10; 148.

103. See the discussion of the use of ἀκούετε καὶ συνίετε in 13.12–23 in ch. six, 156–8.

104. ὄχλος (Singular): Matt.: 19×; Mark: 37×; Luke: 25×. ὄχλοι (Plural): Matt.: 31×; Mark: 1×; Luke: 16×.

105. Similarly, e.g., McNeile, *Matthew*, 313.

106. Van Tilborg, *Jewish Leaders*, 51.

107. Moreover, while the combination of οἱ ἀρχιερεῖς καὶ οἱ Φαρισαῖοι is unusual, elsewhere, in a pericope unique to the First Gospel (27.62), the evangelist

links them together once more. The combination appears nowhere else in the Synoptics and, elsewhere in the NT, only at John 7.32; 11.47, 57; 18.3.

108. Jones, *Matthean Parables*, 400.
109. Ibid., 400 n. 228; similarly Van Tilborg, *Jewish Leaders*, 52, for whom the use of πάλιν and παραβολαῖς is 'rather irrelevant'.
110. Van Tilborg, *Jewish Leaders*, 51–2.
111. Only at 13.35, where Matthew quotes Ps. 77.2 (LXX), does this phrase occur in a construction from which an indirect object is absent. Perhaps the tendency toward this word order in Matthew is due in part to the influence of this LXX text where ἐν παραβολαῖς, immediately following the verb, precedes the object. For the use of λέγων after παραβολή, see 13.3, 24, 31; Luke 12.16, 15.3.
112. Cf. esp. 13.10, 13, 34 where, in each case, the phrase is probably to be attributed to Matthean redaction under the influence of Ps. 77.2, quoted in 13.35.
113. V. Hasler, 'Die königliche Hochzeit, Matth 22, 1–14', *TZ* 18 (1962), 28, thinks that Matthew prefers the plural παραβολαῖς here because he has combined two separate parables.
114. Cf. esp. 11.25 and 28.5, but also 15.15 and 17.4. See further BAGD, s.v. ἀποκρίνομαι, 2.

3   Jesus' encounter with Israel: the nation, its leaders and their people

1. See esp. Stanton, *New People*, 77–84, on the use of σύγκρισις as a rhetorical strategy in ancient texts. See also S. Rimmon-Kenan, *Narrative Fiction: Contemporary Poetics* (London: Methuen, 1983) on the use of analogy in characterisation.
2. In chs. 3 and 4, however, I typically assign redactional observations to footnotes.
3. Cf. also D. Senior, *The Passion of Jesus in the Gospel of Matthew* (Wilmington, DE: Michael Glazier, 1985), 21; Howell, *Matthew's Inclusive Story*, 240.
4. πάντας τοὺς ἀρχιερεῖς καὶ γραμματεῖς τοῦ λαοῦ (2.4); 5 × in Matthew ὁ λαός stands in the genitive case qualifying some group of Jewish leaders – elsewhere always οἱ ἀρχιερεῖς καὶ [οἱ] πρεσβύτεροι (21.23; 26.3, 47; 27.1) – each time, it would seem, underscoring the relationship between the leaders and their people. Perhaps it is not incidental that in each case a plot against Jesus' life lies within the immediate context.
5. Cf. 17.9–13, where the characterisation of the Jewish leaders is achieved by a backward glance to 14.1–12. There, responsibility for John's death was clearly laid at Herod Antipas's feet. At 16.21 the reader learned of the parallel role that the religious leaders would play in Jesus' execution. In ch. 17, however, Antipas and the religious leaders apparently unite as the mortal foes of both prophet and Messiah: just as *they* have done to John, so also *they* will do to Jesus (17.12). See also W. Trilling, 'Die Täufertradition bei Matthäus', *BZ* 2 (1959), 274–5.

6. Probably we should not, with A. Saldarini, *Matthew's Christian–Jewish Community* (University of Chicago Press, 1994), 28, find reference here only 'to a specific part of the people of Israel, namely, those who are in need of leadership and care'.

7. Bezae omits πᾶσα (2.3), perhaps, as Davies and Allison, *Matthew*, III:237 n. 36, note, because elsewhere in Matthew, with the possible exception of 3.5, Ἱεροσόλυμα is a neuter plural. On Matthew's portrait of Jerusalem, see P. W. L. Walker, *Jesus and the Holy City: New Testament Perspectives on Jerusalem* (Grand Rapids: Eerdmans, 1996), 25–56.

8. Matthew's treatment of his sources here suggests that the stark contrast he draws between the people and their leaders is anything but accidental. In 3.1–6 Matthew follows Mark; Luke omits this pericope. 3.7–10 records a traditional Q saying that appears in nearly identical wording at Luke 3.7–9. In Luke, however, the addressees are the *crowds* going out to be baptised by John. As such: Mark paints a picture of a people very responsive to the Baptist's ministry; the Lucan Baptist censures the crowds, warning them to prepare for the coming judgement; Matthew takes over Mark's positive portrait of the people, incorporates the Q saying but, unlike Luke, has the Baptist censure only the Pharisees and Sadducees. Juxtaposed as they are, both the indictment of the leaders and the positive portrait of the crowds receive emphasis.

9. Δ Θ f¹ *pc* (cf. vg^mss) insert πάντες before οἱ ὄχλοι; 998 and Eus replace οἱ ὄχλοι with πάντες.

10. Redactional considerations are interesting here as well: 7.28–29 represents Matthew's adaptation of Mark 1.22, where Mark reports the response in the Capernaum synagogue to Jesus' teaching. Placing this Marcan material in a different context, Matthew modifies Mark's report by making two additions: (1) by adding οἱ ὄχλοι Matthew changes the subject from the synagogue congregation to the crowds, thus eliminating the possibility that the leaders echo the people's response; (2) by adding αὐτῶν (both the absence of αὐτῶν (a harmonising corruption?; cf. Mark 1.22) and the addition of καὶ οἱ Φαρισαῖοι (a natural complement; cf. Matt. 5.20; 12.38; 23.2, 13, 15, 23, 25, 27, 29) in some witnesses appear to be secondary), Matthew changes Mark's 'the scribes' to 'their scribes' in a manner reminiscent of his frequent characterisation of the synagogues as *their* synagogues (4.23; 9.35; 10.17; 12.9; 13.54; 23.34 (ὑμῶν)). If the synagogues have become foreign institutions, the scribes have become foreign leaders. See further Stanton, *New People*, 97, 127–31.

11. See also Powell, 'Characterization', 161–77, who notes that the contrast between the rhetoric of the religious leaders when they speak *to* Jesus and when they speak *about* him contributes to their overall characterisation as hypocrites.

12. As perhaps in Mark (2.7).

13. Subsequently the reader will learn that this evil charge of blasphemy finds an echo in the accusation that justifies Jesus' execution (26.65–66); cf. Kingsbury, *Matthew as Story*, 118.

14. ἐφοβήθησαν, the more difficult reading, is to be preferred over ἐθαύμασαν. See B. Metzger, *A Textual Commentary on the Greek New Testament* (2nd edn, Stuttgart: German Bible Society, 1994), 20.

15. Whereas in Mark's conclusion, *all* were amazed and glorified God, in Matthew it is specifically the *crowds* who have this response.
16. Hos. 6.6, cf. 1 Sam. 15.22; Ps. 40.6; Prov. 16.7 (LXX); Heb. 10.5.
17. That the verb is set in the third person (ἐκβάλλει τὰ δαιμόνια; *he* casts out demons) suggests that the Pharisees address the crowds instead of Jesus.
18. 9.34 in its entirety is missing from some witnesses: in addition to D a k sy^s and Hilary of Poitiers, listed by NA^{27}, J. N. Birdsall, 'A Note on the Textual Evidence for the Omission of Matthew 9.34', in *Jews and Christians* (ed. James D. G. Dunn, 117–22, Tübingen: Mohr, 1992), 117–19, notes that the poet Juvencus (*c.* AD 330) and the Arabic Diatessaron omit the verse. Birdsall emphasises the antiquity of the omission and insists that a few witnesses 'in outlying borders of the early church' (119), which agree against the rest, may indeed preserve the original form of the text, but leaves open the resolution of this problem. T. Zahn, *Das Evangelium des Matthäus* (Leipzig: Deichert, 1903), 386, rejects the verse as an interpolation (similarly Allen, *Matthew*, 98; Klostermann, *Das Matthäusevangelium*, 84). H. J. Holtzmann, *Die Synoptischen Evangelien* (Leipzig: Engelmann, 1863), 182, thought that the logic of the narrative required some aspersion linking Jesus to Beelzebul before 10.25 (similarly Luz, *Matthäus*, II:62 n. 2; Metzger, *Textual Commentary*, 20). But as Klostermann, *Das Matthäusevangelium*, 84, countered, this argument can be reversed. Nevertheless, the verse should probably be regarded as authentic. Stanton, *New People*, 175–6, notes both that the manuscript support for 9.34 is impressive and that it differs from the Matthean parallels at 10.25 and 12.24, 27 (as well as from Mark 3.22, the only Marcan parallel) and consequently should probably not be regarded as a harmonising corruption. One additional feature of Matthew's Gospel should be noted, which also favours the inclusion of 9.34. As I argue in this chapter, the evangelist characteristically draws a sharp contrast between the crowds and the Jewish leaders, especially in response to the deeds of Jesus; 9.34 fits this pattern.
19. J. M. Gibbs, 'Purpose and Pattern in Matthew's Use of the Title "Son of David"', *NTS* 10 (1964), 458.
20. This sharp contrast between the people and the leaders is again distinctively Matthean; cf. Mark 3.22; Luke 11.14–15.
21. On 'inside views' see esp. Booth, *Rhetoric*, 115–16, 245–9.
22. Matthew 9.36 is based upon Mark 6.34; 9.37–38 is Matthew's version of a Q saying also recorded at Luke 10.2. Notable differences in Matthew's account include: (1) Mark's πολὺν ὄχλον becomes τοὺς ὄχλους; (2) Matthew adds ἐσκυλμένοι καὶ ἐρριμμένοι to Mark's description of the crowds.
23. Cf. 12.38–42, 43–45; 16.1–4; (17.14–20); 23.34–36; 24.34 and their Synoptic parallels. On the significance of the motif in Q, see C. Tuckett, *Q and the History of Early Christianity* (Edinburgh: T. & T. Clark, 1996), 165–207.
24. Having been handed over (4.12), John is now in prison (11.2–6).
25. Similarly S. McKnight, 'A Loyal Critic: Matthew's Polemic with Judaism in Theological Perspective', in *Anti-Semitism and Early Christianity: Issues of Polemic and Faith* (ed. Craig A. Evans and Donald A. Hagner, 55–79, Minneapolis: Fortress, 1993), 71 n. 59: for Matthew 'this generation' has a 'Pharisaic cast'. Cf. 12.38–42, 43–45; 16.1–4; 23.34–36. These observations also speak against Lührmann's thesis that 'this generation' almost becomes a *terminus technicus* for the nation of Israel in its entirety (*Die Redaktion der Logienquelle* (Neukirchen-Vluyn: Neukirchener, 1969), 30, 32–43, 93).

See the important modifications to this thesis for which Tuckett, *Q and the History*, 196–201, argues. See also E. Lövestam, *Jesus and 'this Generation': A New Testament Study* (Stockholm: Almqvist & Wiksell, 1995), who argues that ἡ γενεὰ αὕτη is, in the first place, a pejorative reference to the moral and spiritual evil of the people that aligns them with the generation of the flood (e.g., Gen. 7.1: בַּדּוֹר הַזֶּה [LXX: ἐν τῇ γενεᾷ ταύτῃ]) and, especially, with the generation of the wilderness (e.g., Deut. 1.35, הַדּוֹר הרה הַזֶּה). In my view, however, Lövestam's attempt virtually to empty the phrase of chronological significance proves unsuccessful. Fluid and even secondary though it may be in some instances, in each of its Matthean occurrences contextual features isolate its temporal import: it refers to Jesus' and Matthew's contemporaries.

26. So Stanton, *New People*, 364–77.
27. Similarly C. Deutsch, *Hidden Wisdom and the Easy Yoke: Wisdom, Torah and Discipleship in Matthew 11.25–30* (JSNTSup 18; Sheffield: JSOT, 1987), 40–2.
28. On the role of 'doublets' in Matthew's narrative, see esp. Anderson, *Narrative Web*, 175–89.
29. Similarly Anderson, *Narrative Web*, 177–9.
30. Once more (cf. 9.34) the Pharisees refer to Jesus in the third person (οὗτος), thus making it plain that their accusation is directed toward the crowds and not Jesus himself; so also Davies and Allison, *Matthew*, II:335. On the textual problem in 12.24, see the brief note in Luz, *Matthäus*, II:118 n. 2.
31. Similarly Gibbs, 'Son of David', 463; Davies and Allison, *Matthew*, II:334, however, find such a reading 'a bit over-subtle'.
32. Perhaps it is not incidental that they come from Jerusalem. Earlier, in Jerusalem, the chief priests and scribes of the people had been associated with the murderous Herod (2.4).
33. τὸν λόγον (ℵ¹ B D Θ 579 700 892 *pc* it sy^s.c.p.hmg co; Ir^lat Or Eus) is replaced in a number of witnesses by either τὸν νόμον (ℵ*.2 C 073 *f*^13 *pc*; Ptol) or τὴν ἐντολήν (L W 0106 *f*^1 33 𝔐 lat sy^h; Cyr). See Metzger, *Textual Commentary*, 31.
34. Cf. Isa. 60.21; 61.3; CD 1.7; 1QS 8.5; 11.8; Rom. 2.19; and R. T. France, *Matthew* (TNTC; Grand Rapids: Eerdmans, 1985), 244.
35. Cf. Luz, *Theology*, 68. On the textual problem, see Metzger, *Textual Commentary*, 31–2; Swanson, *Matthew*, 145.
36. See p. 199 n. 105.
37. See p. 199 n. 106; whereas, in Mark (10.1), Jesus teaches the crowds, in Matthew (19.2) he heals them.
38. Cf. 16.1; 22.18, 35.
39. Diff Mark.
40. Both ὄχλος (21.8) and ὄχλοι (21.9) are unique to Matthew, as is τῷ υἱῷ Δαυίδ (21.9).
41. So, e.g., Kingsbury, *Matthew as Story*, 80–1.
42. Both 21.10b, which answers to 2.3, and 21.11 are unique to Matthew.
43. In favour of the suggestion that Matthew thinks here of the 'prophet like Moses' (Deut. 18.18), see D. Allison, *The New Moses: A Matthean Typology* (Edinburgh: T. & T. Clark, 1993), 248–53.

44. Cf. 2 Sam. 5.6–8 LXX.
45. 21.14–15, with the healings of the blind and the lame, the acclamation of the children, and the indignant response of the chief priests and scribes, are unique to Matthew.
46. Matthew places an acknowledgement of their fear of the crowd on the lips of the Jewish leaders (21.26); in Mark it is an explanatory comment added by the evangelist (11.32); ὡς προφήτην replaces the awkward Marcan expression (ὄντως ὅτι προφήτης ἦν) and echoes 14.5, where the motif is unique to Matthew.
47. Though, of course, Matthew also introduces the Pharisees here.
48. As representatives of those who find reference in this trilogy to a judgement against Israel and not merely her leaders, we note: J. Calvin, *A Harmony of the Gospels Matthew, Mark and Luke* (3 vols., ed. David W. Torrance and Thomas F. Torrance, Carlisle: Paternoster, 1972), III:21–2; Weiss, *Matthäus*, 370; Zahn, *Matthäus*, 625; J. Schmid, *Das Evangelium nach Matthäus* (Regensburg: Pustet), 1959, 305–7; Trilling, *Das Wahre Israel*, 62–5, 84–5; Carlston, *Parables*, 43–4; Schweizer, *Matthew*, 414; Senior, *Passion*, 119–21; P. Bonnard, *L'Évangile Selon Saint Matthieu* (3rd edn, Geneva: Labor et Fides, 1992), 316–17; D. Hagner, *Matthew 14–28* (WBC 33B; Dallas: Word, 1995), 623.
49. J. Andrew Overman, *Church and Community in Crisis: The Gospel According to Matthew* (Valley Forge, PA: Trinity Press, 1996), 303. Similarly, with variations: K. Tagawa, 'People and Community in the Gospel of Matthew', *NTS* 16 (1970), 161; O. L. Cope, *Matthew: A Scribe Trained for the Kingdom of Heaven* (Washington: The Catholic Biblical Association of America, 1976), 85–6; K. R. Snodgrass, *The Parable of the Wicked Tenants* (Tübingen: Mohr, 1983), 90–4; 'Recent Research on the Parable of the Wicked Tenants: An Assessment', *BBR* 8 (1998), 192–3; A.-J. Levine, *The Social and Ethnic Dimensions of Matthean Social History: 'Go nowhere among the Gentiles...' (Matt. 10:5b)* (Lewiston, NY: Mellen, 1988), 208–11; D. J. Harrington, *The Gospel of Matthew* (Collegeville, MN: The Liturgical Press, 1991), 302–4; N. T. Wright, *The New Testament and the People of God* (London: SPCK, 1992), 76; R. H. Gundry, *Matthew: A Commentary on His Handbook for a Mixed Church under Persecution* (2nd edn, Grand Rapids: Eerdmans, 1994), 430; Saldarini, *Christian–Jewish Community*, 44–5, 60–2, 81, 245 n. 68; Kupp, *Matthew's Emmanuel*, 91, 95, 213; Davies and Allison, *Matthew*, III:189–90; Carter and Heil, *Matthew's Parables*, 163–5.
50. J. A. Overman, 'Matthew's Parables and Roman Politics: The Imperial Setting of Matthew's Narrative with Special Reference to His Parables', *SBLSP* 34 (1995), 433.
51. The crowds only make an appearance in Matthew's version of this pericope.
52. On the notoriously difficult 23.2–3a, I agree with Luz, *Theology*, 122: 'That the disciples must "do everything they tell you to do" (23:2) is, of course, an example of hyperbole that, rhetorically, reaffirms the main thrust of Matthew's Gospel, the emphasis on practice over theory. In reality some of the prophecies of woe (e.g. 23:23–26) harbour different doctrinal emphases.'
53. Matthew 23.14 is probably secondary, inserted under the influence of Mark 12.40 or Luke 20.47 (so, e.g., Metzger, *Textual Commentary*, 50); but cf. J. M. Ross, 'Floating Words', *NTS* 38 (1992), 153–4.

54. On the question of the Second Temple Jewish mission to the Gentiles, see S. McKnight, *A Light Among the Nations: Jewish Missionary Activity in the Second Temple Period* (Minneapolis: Fortress, 1991) and, on this verse, esp. pp. 106–8.

55. Cf. J. Gnilka, *Das Matthäusevangelium* (HTKNT 1; 2 vols., Freiburg: Herder, 1986, 1992), II:296.

56. See above pp. 53–4, and 192–3 n. 25.

57. Understanding ἕως ἄν to signal a conditional prophecy; see D. C. Allison, 'Matt. 23:39 = Luke 13:35b as a Conditional Prophecy', *JSNT* 18 (1983), 75–84; Stanton, *New People*, 247–55.

58. B* *pc* omit καὶ ἀποκτείνωσιν.

59. Only Matthew supplies this setting; in general, most of 26.3–4 is unique to Matthew (diff Mark) and most of 26.5 follows Mark. And whereas Mark (followed by Luke) identifies the Jewish leaders as chief priests and scribes, Matthew refers to them as chief priests and elders *of the people* (the witnesses, however, are marked by considerable variation here; under influence from Mark, 𝔐 it sy$^{p.h}$ insert οἱ γραμματεῖς between οἱ ἀρχιερεῖς and οἱ πρεσβύτεροι; W inserts οἱ Φαρισαῖοι in the same place; B* omits τοῦ λαοῦ).

60. Note that Jesus has just declared that he will be delivered up to be crucified *during* the Passover (26.2).

61. So also J. P. Heil, *The Death and Resurrection of Jesus: A Narrative–Critical Reading of Matthew 26–28* (Minneapolis: Fortress, 1991), 24–25.

62. Cf. Matt. 2.4; 21.23; 26.3; and 27.1. Mark now identifies the leaders as chief priests and scribes and elders.

63. See further Heil, *Matthew 26–28*, 52–3.

64. So McNeile, *Matthew*, 393.

65. So F. W. Beare, *The Gospel According to Matthew* (Oxford: Blackwell, 1981), 516.

66. So Hagner, *Matthew 14–28*, 788. Cf. John 18.3, 12.

67. Kingsbury, *Matthew as Story*, 4. Cf. R. T. France, *Matthew: Evangelist and Teacher* (Grand Rapids: Academie, 1989), 225, who draws a careful distinction between the historical events and the narrative development: while, historically, it must remain dubious that the same people who heralded Jesus' entrance to the city now, days later, call for his crucifixion, at the narrative level, the movement of the crowds from 'sympathetic detachment to active hostility' is undeniable.

68. Mark's ὄχλος becomes, in Matthew, ὄχλος πολύς (26.47). At 26.55 τοῖς ὄχλοις replaces Mark's αὐτοῖς.

69. πάντες is a Matthean addition (27.22; diff Mark). Among the other notable redactional alterations in the Matthean account, we observe: (1) as is often the case, Mark's singular ὄχλον becomes plural (ὄχλους) in Matthew (27.20); (2) Mark's chief priests become, in Matthew, chief priests and elders (27.20); (3) Mark's ἀνέσεισαν becomes, in Matthew, ἔπεισαν (27.20); (4) Matthew adds τὸν δὲ Ἰησοῦν ἀπολέσωσιν (27.20).

70. The tumult among the people that the Jewish leaders had feared and that had prompted them to decide *not* to arrest Jesus during the feast (26.5) does in fact erupt. But, very different from the one they envisaged, they have provoked it and it achieves their purposes.

71. All three texts are unique to Matthew.

72. Howell, *Matthew's Inclusive Story*, 119.
73. Diff Luke (11.50–51).
74. So א L W f^1f^{13} 33 𝔐 lat sy[p.h] sa[mss] mae bo; A Δ pc aur f h alter the order: τούτου τοῦ δικαίου; 1010 pc bo[ms] conclude with τοῦ δικαίου, omitting τούτου. NA[27] follows B D Θ *pc* it sy[s] (sa[mss]) Or[lat] which omit τοῦ δικαίου. Deciding which reading is original is more difficult here than most have imagined. On the one hand, it is easy to imagine the insertion of δίκαιος by a pious scribe eager to underscore Jesus' innocence, but difficult to find a motivation for its deletion if δίκαιος were original. This consideration proves decisive for Metzger, *Textual Commentary*, 56–7. On the other hand, in view of the similar endings of the words in question, an accidental omission 'by scribal leap' (so Davies and Allison, *Matthew*, III:590 n. 52) is not improbable. Moreover, as we have seen, the presence of δίκαιος here would certainly tally with the distinctive Matthean predilection for this term in this part of his narrative. See also Gundry, *Matthew*, 564–5.
75. Each of these references to 'innocent blood' is unique to Matthew.
76. The correspondence is even more striking in B which, like Matthew, reads ἀθῷος in place of καθαρός.
77. Verses 46 and 47 are present in Theodotion but absent from the Old Greek.
78. The charge Daniel lays against the first of the two elders is also noteworthy; cf. Sus. 52–53.
79. T. B. Cargal, '"His Blood be upon us and upon our Children": A Matthean Double Entendre?', *NTS* 37 (1991), 101–12, finds a more subtle irony here; perhaps too subtle. He argues for the presence of a double entendre, which 'differs from most forms of irony in that the two levels of meaning are not opposed to one another' (110). At one level, the evangelist does insist that the Jewish nation is at least partly responsible for the innocent Jesus' death. At another level, however, Matthew 'introduced a sacrificial view of Jesus' blood which would allow for the "forgiveness of [the] sins" (Matt. 26. 28) of "his people" (Matt. 1. 21). They have "sinned [against] innocent blood" (Matt. 27. 4), but Matthew still prays that God will forgive "the guilt of innocent blood in the midst of thy people Israel" (allusion to Deut. 21. 8) by the application of Jesus' blood upon them and their children (Matt 27. 25)' (112). As we note above, the connections to both 1.21 and 26.28 are important here. But since, from the earliest stages of his story, the evangelist has made it plain that descent from Abraham is no substitute for fruit worthy of repentance and will offer no protection in the coming judgement (3.7–10), and since, from at least ch. 21 onward, the narrative grants so prominent a place to the terrible consequences of the rejection and murder of Yahweh's servants the prophets, it is difficult to find a plea for national forgiveness here as Jesus' execution unfolds.
80. Saldarini, *Christian–Jewish Community*, 32–3; similarly H. Kosmala, 'His Blood on Us and on Our Children (The Background of Matt. 27, 24–25)', *ASTI* 7 (1970), 98. For Saldarini the crowds represent the people of the Jewish community, both in Jesus' day and in Matthew's. They are portrayed in positive, if sometimes ambivalent, terms because Matthew envisions a continued ministry to them, hoping to attract them to his brand of Judaism. The people in Matthew's Gospel are indicted only when linked to their leaders. As such, Israel's leaders, but not Israel herself, are rejected in Matthew's Gospel. I am generally sympathetic to most of what Saldarini wants to say

about the Matthean crowds. Nevertheless, he seems unwilling to grapple with
the failure of the crowds at the climax of Matthew's story. Earlier treatments
of the crowds in this Gospel have reached diverging, and sometimes fanciful, conclusions. Van Tilborg devoted a chapter of his 1972 monograph
to an examination of the crowds. He argued that Matthew's portrait of the
crowds is consistently positive. Since it is not easy to put a positive spin on
27.20–23, this pericope represents the chief difficulty for his reading. But, for
Van Tilborg, 27.20, since it is traditional and not redactional, does not reveal
the evangelist's true stance. Justified criticisms of this sort of employment
of redaction criticism have arisen both from its practitioners and its critics
(cf., e.g., Stanton, *New People*, 41–2, 51–3). Minear, 'The Disciples and the
Crowds in the Gospel of Matthew', *AThR Supplementary Series* 3 (1974),
28–44, noted the special prominence granted to the crowds in Matthew's
narrative and concluded that the evangelist was addressing the lay people
among his contemporaries as Jesus addressed the crowds, and, similarly, envisioned contemporary church leaders, when Jesus spoke to the disciples.
However, this imaginative (and anachronistic) reading stumbles over the fact
that, favourably disposed to the crowds as the evangelist may have been,
his narrative nevertheless depicts them as those to whom the mysteries of
the kingdom have *not* been given, whose hearts have been hardened and
whose spiritual senses have been dulled (13.1–2, 10–15); as those to whom
he speaks only in parables and from whom he withholds explanation (13.34–
36ff.); and, finally, as those who were persuaded by their leaders to demand
Jesus' execution (27.20–26). The same considerations render Gundry's position untenable: for him, the crowds represent the international community of
professing disciples (*Matthew*, 65, 66, 139 and passim). Gundry recognises
the problem and counters, at 13.34, that the crowds comprise false disciples
as well as true (*Matthew*, 269) and, at 27.20, that: '[Transferring the blame
from Pilate to the crowds] adds to the Christianization of Pilate and would
mar Matthew's portraying the crowds as disciples except that they are misled
and thus symbolize the masses in the church who are led into sin by antino-
mian leaders' (*Matthew*, 563). But these responses are desperate expedients.
There is little in the narrative that would prompt the reader to associate the
crowds with the contemporary Christian masses. If the reader is to find correspondence between the crowds and *any* contemporary group, surely it would
be much more natural for that group to be the Jewish masses who have not
yet embraced Jesus as Messiah (so, in addition to Saldarini, T. L. Donaldson,
Jesus on the Mountain: A Study in Matthean Theology (JSNTSup 8; Sheffield:
JSOT, 1985), 208).

81. Similarly McKnight, 'Loyal Critic', 72–3 n. 64.
82. Cf. Deut. 21.1–9; Josh. 2.19; 2 Sam. 1.16; Jer. 26.15; 51.35; for washing
    hands as a symbol of innocence, cf. Deut. 21.1–9!; Ps. 26.6; 73.13; and, for a
    discussion of the biblical background to Matt. 27.24–25, see Kosmala, 'His
    Blood on Us', 94–126.
83. Similarly *T. Levi* 16.3–4; but cf. also 16.5.
84. Both pericopes are unique to Matthew.
85. The irony of their declaration at 27.63–64 is now obvious!
86. Cf. 12.14; 22.15; 27.1, 7.
87. Cf. 15.14; 23.16, 17, 19, 24, 26.
88. Matthew 7.5 would seem to be the exception that proves the rule.

89. Cf. 6.1–6, 16–18; 15.1–9; 22.15–22; 23.1–7, 27–28, 29–36; 28.11–15, cf. 27.62–66.
90. See, e.g., 9.9–13; 12.1–8; 17.9–13; 19.3–9; 21.12–17, 42; 22.23–33, 34–40; 23.23–24.
91. Cf. 26.47–56; 27.3–10.
92. Cf. 15.1–20; 16.1–12; 23.18–22.
93. 23.16–17, cf. 26.3–5, 59–66, 67–68; 27.3–10, 11–14, 15–18; 28.11–15.
94. Cf. 9.1–8, 32–34; 11.28–30; 12.1–8, 9–14, 15–21, 22–30; 21.12–17; 23.4, 23–24.
95. The citation of Hos. 6.6 (cf. 1 Sam. 15.22; Ps. 40.6; Prov. 16.7; Heb. 10.5) and its introduction (πορευθέντες δὲ μάθετε τί ἐστιν) is unique to Matthew. Similarly, Matt. 12.7.
96. See also 16.21–23; 17.9–13, 22–23 (cf. 26.45); 20.17–19 (cf. 26.2); 21.33–46; 23.29–33, 37–39; 26.3–5 (cf. 26.47–56; 27.57–58), 14–15, 59–66, 67–68; 27.1–2, 3–10, 11–14, 15–18, 20–26.
97. Cf. 4.12; 14.13!; 15.21.
98. As the evil generation of the wilderness put God to the test in the face of mighty acts of deliverance (Exod. 17.1–7; Num. 14.22; Deut. 6.16; Ps. 78.18, 41; 95.8; 106.14), so they respond to God's mighty acts in Jesus by putting him to the test (12.38–42; 16.1–4); cf. Lövestam, *'This Generation'*, 21–37.
99. Cf. 10.17–20, 23, 24–28; 11.12(?); 22.1–14; 23.34–36. The persecution that these texts envisage most naturally arises in the context of mission. Some of these texts specifically address a pre-70 context (cf. 22.1–7(?); 23.34–36), but can this be maintained for all of them (5.11–12?)? In any case, even the texts that describe the Jewish opposition that evokes the judgement of AD 70 are significant here. Typically, one of the linchpins in the argument that sees Matthew turning his back on the mission to Israel is the reading of the post-resurrection commission at 28.18–20 that takes πάντα τὰ ἔθνη to refer exclusively to Gentiles (see esp. D. R. A. Hare and D. J. Harrington, ' "Make Disciples of all the Gentiles" (Mt 28:19)', *CBQ* 37 [1975], 359–69, and, for a thorough refutation of their thesis, J. P. Meier, 'Nations or Gentiles in Matthew 28:19?', *CBQ* 39 (1977), 94–102). But it is undeniable that the Matthean narrative envisions a mission that will take place among both Israel and the nations in the years *following* this programmatic commission (23.34–36). Since a mission to Israel continues after the Great Commission, only powerful evidence from the narrative could support this exclusive reading of 28.18–20 and the conclusion that Matthew has abandoned commitment to a Christian mission among Israel.
100. Cf. 3.7–10; 5.20; 12.31–32, 33–37, 38–42, 43–45; 21.28–32, 33–46; 22.1–14; 23.13, 15, 29–33; 24.51(?).
101. Cf. 9.32–34, 36–38; 11.28–30; 12.22–30; 23.5, 13, 15, 16–22, 23–24; 27.20–26; 28.11–15.
102. Cf. 1.21; 2.6; 4.23–24; 8.16–17; 9.9–13, 35, 36–38; 11.1, 28–30; 12.15, 46; 14.13–14, 15–21; 15.29–31, 32–39; 19.1–2; 23.1–7ff., 23.37–39.
103. Cf. 10.5–12, 16–23; 14.15–21; 15.32–39; 17.14–20.
104. See 3.5–6, cf. 11.7 (John); 4.24–25; 7.28–29; 8.1; 9.2–8, 32–34; 12.15; 14.13–14; 15.29–31; 16.13–20; 17.14–18; 19.1–2; 21.1–11; 22.23–33; 26.3–5.

105. Cf. 4.25; 8.1; 12.15; 14.13; 19.2; 20.29; 21.9.
106. Cf. 4.23, 24; 8.16; 9.35; 12.15; 14.14; 15.30; 19.2; 21.14.
107. Cf. 14.5; 21.23–27, 46.
108. Cf. 11.20–24; 13.3–9, 18–23, 24–30, 36–43, 53–58; 20.29–34; 23.37–39; 27.20–26; and the texts that indict 'this generation'.
109. At 13.13 Matthew's ὅτι replaces Mark's ἵνα, placing emphasis on the prior failure of the crowds. See the discussion in Davies and Allison, *Matthew*, II:392.
110. Nevertheless Saldarini, *Christian–Jewish Community*, 232 n. 50, is justified in critiquing Kingsbury who is guilty of exaggeration when he writes: 'Repudiated by *all segments of Israel*, Jesus responds by declaring that Israel has become hard of heart (13:13–15)' (*Matthew as Story*, 73; emphasis added).
111. See Luz, *Theology*, 5, 86, who sees in 13.12 an anticipation of 21.43.
112. Cf. 8.11–12; 10.14–15; 11.20–24; 13.3–9, 18–23; 21.18–22, 33–46; 22.1–10; 27.24–26.
113. So Eusebius, *Dem. ev.* 9.11 (PG 22, 692–3); Ps. Macarius, *Hom. 4.23* (PG 34.389–92); cf. Zeno, *Tractatus* I.13.9; so also, in the modern era, Weiss, *Matthäus*, 370; Dodd, *Parables*, 128; Jeremias, *Parables*, 60; B. Lindars, *New Testament Apologetic: The Doctrinal Significance of the Old Testament Quotations* (London: SCM, 1961), 173–4; G. Strecker, *Der Weg der Gerechtigkeit* (Göttingen: Vandenhoeck & Ruprecht, 1962), 33–4, 110–13; Walker, *Heilsgeschichte*, 79–83.
114. So esp. Walker, *Heilsgeschichte*, 79–83, 114–26; D. R. A. Hare, *The Theme of Jewish Persecution of Christians in the Gospel According to St. Matthew* (Cambridge University Press, 1967), 148–57.
115. *What is Narrative Criticism?*, 57.
116. Powell seems to have missed this point as he scrambles to avoid an anti-Semitic reading of Matthew's Gospel, restricting its referents to the world of the narrative. In my view, Matthew is neither anti-Semitic nor anti-Judaism, but rather sets himself polemically against that branch of Judaism that has rejected its Messiah and so, to his way of thinking, has abandoned its God. See esp. McKnight, 'Loyal Critic'.
117. I do not mean to suggest that the Jewish leaders and the crowds simply *represent* the Jewish leaders and masses contemporary to the evangelist. It may well be, however, that as the evangelist tells his story about Jesus it is, in part, shaped by his experiences with Israel – both her leaders and the masses. Cf. the cautious conclusions that D. A. Carson draws about our capacity to isolate Matthew's *Sitz im Leben* ('The Jewish Leaders in Matthew's Gospel: A Reappraisal', *JETS* 25 (1982), 161–74).

4 Jesus and the nations: characterisation, plot and the reception of Matthew 21.28–22.14

1. See, e.g., Saldarini, *Christian–Jewish Community*, 44–5, 58–64, 78–81; Tagawa, 'People and Community', 161; Cope, *Scribe*, 85–6; Snodgrass, *Wicked Tenants*, 87–95; 'Recent Research', 192–3; Levine, *Matthean Social History*, 206–15; Harrington, *Matthew*, 302–4, 308; Wright, *People of*

God, 76; Gundry, *Matthew*, 430; D. C. Sim, 'The Gospel of Matthew and the Gentiles', *JSNT* 57 (1995), 43 n. 41; Overman, *Church and Community*, 303; Kupp, *Matthew's Emmanuel*, 91, 95, 213; Davies and Allison, *Matthew*, III:189–90; Carter and Heil, *Matthew's Parables*, 163–5.

2. Davies and Allison, *Matthew*, III:687, refer to these verses as 'the grand denouement'. For Stanton, *New People*, 139–40, this is the climax of the Gospel and 'the key to its understanding'.

3. See, e.g., F. J. Matera, 'The Plot of Matthew's Gospel', *CBQ* 49 (1987), 233–53; J. D. Kingsbury, 'The Plot of Matthew's Story', *Int* 46 (1992), 347–56; M. A. Powell, 'The Plot and Subplots of Matthew's Gospel', *NTS* 38 (1992), 187–204; W. Carter, *Matthew: Storyteller, Interpreter, Evangelist* (Peabody, MA: Hendrickson, 1996), 159–75.

4. P. Ricoeur, 'Narrative Time', *Critical Inquiry* 7 (1980), 179. Cf. P. J. Rabinowitz, *Before Reading: Narrative Conventions and the Politics of Interpretation* (Ithaca: Cornell University Press, 1987), 62–3.

5. R. H. Smith, 'Matthew 28:16–20, Anticlimax or Key to the Gospel', *SBLSP* 32 (1993), 600, would characterise this an ecclesiological reading of the Great Commission. He distinguishes between Christological, ecclesiological and ethical readings, only the last of which he finds justifiable in this narrative. The question is one of emphasis – at one level, surely, the reader must not be forced to choose between Christological, ecclesiological and ethical readings. The universal mission that shatters previous 'ecclesiological' boundaries (28.19a) rests squarely upon a Christological foundation (28.18b), and is explained in ethical terms (28.19b–20a). At another level, however, the basic grammar of the sentence suggests that the command to 'make disciples of all the nations' is the central component of this commission. The wider narrative only confirms this reading.

6. οὖν is replaced by νῦν in some MSS (D it) and omitted in others (א A 0148^vid *f*^13 *M* bo^pt; Ir^lat), but receives substantial (B W Δ Θ *f*^1 33 565 892 1241 *ſ* 844 *ſ* 2211 lat sy sa mae bo^pt) support and is probably original. Even if it were omitted it would be difficult to avoid the conclusion that 28.18b supplied the grounds for the commission at 28.19–20.

7. *Pace* L. Gaston, 'The Messiah of Israel as Teacher of the Gentiles: The Setting of Matthew's Christology', *Int* 29 (1975), 37, it is *not* true that '[n]othing really has changed in Matthew's Jesus by this exaltation. The authority he now has, he always had.' To be sure, this narrative has made it clear that Jesus' ministry was marked by a remarkable ἐξουσία, but the 'unlimited, cosmic dimensions' (J. Meier, 'Two Disputed Questions in Matt. 28.16–20', *JBL* 96 (1977), 413) of this new authority make it distinctive.

8. See Davies and Allison, *Matthew*, III:682–3, for discussion of the evidence that leads most Matthean scholars to find allusion to Dan. 7 here. But see also D. R. Bauer, *The Structure of Matthew's Gospel: A Study in Literary Design* (Sheffield: Almond, 1988; reprint, 1989), 111–12.

9. Perhaps Gen. 49.10 also forms part of the background for this text: 'The sceptre shall not depart from Judah, nor the ruler's staff from between his feet, until tribute comes to him; and *the obedience of the peoples* is his.' For first-century application of this text to the Messiah, see 4Q252 (הצדק צמח דויד עד בוא משעה). The LXX, which with the Targums also agrees in reading this Messianically, renders the final clause: καὶ αὐτὸς προσδοκία ἐθνῶν (and he is the expectation of the nations). Cf. Matt. 2.6; *T. Jud.* 21.2; 24.5; Heb. 7.14.

10. Similarly P. O'Brien, 'The Great Commission of Matthew 28:18–20: A Missionary Mandate or Not?', *RTR* 35 (1976), 74–5; Davies and Allison, *Matthew*, III:683. See T. Dozeman, '*Sperma Abraam* in John 8 and Related Literature', *CBQ* 42 (1980), 342–58, for discussion of the use of the promises to Abraham in mission contexts.

11. If the prayers of the psalm express Israel's hopes for the ideal king (perhaps Solomon himself), the hyperbolic language of the psalm lent itself towards Messianic interpretation. Cf. J. L. Mays, *Psalms* (IBC; Louisville: John Knox, 1994), 238.

12. At several points, I shall take issue with D. Sim's reading of Matthew's characterisation of Gentiles. Sim sets his 1998 monograph (*The Gospel of Matthew and Christian Judaism: The History and Social Setting of the Matthean Community* (Edinburgh: T. & T. Clark, 1998)) in the context of recent work on the social setting of Matthew's Gospel and argues that Matthew's community was sectarian, at odds with its parent Judaism, but also with Pauline Christianity and with the Gentile world more broadly.

He argues that Matthew's Gospel betrays both his steadfast allegiance to the Jerusalem church and his resolute opposition to the law-free Pauline mission. Indeed, Matthew's community took no part in the Gentile mission to which his Gospel adverts (*Matthean Community*, 188). On the contrary, the evangelist actually forbids its participation in this mission (7.6). Sim's analysis of Matthew's four 'anti-Gentile' texts (5.46–47; 6.7–8; 6.31–32; 18.15–17) suggests that 'the evangelist's community shunned and avoided its Gentile neighbours' (*Matthean Community*, 229). The positive portraits of individual Gentiles that do occur in Matthew's story probably indicate that some Gentiles had attached themselves to his community, but they would have entered as converts to law-observant Christian Judaism.

For a number of reasons I find Sim's reading unconvincing: (1) His basic approach invites critique. *Presupposing* the existence of the Matthean community, Sim consistently reads the details of Matthew's story about Jesus as if they were transparent for life in the evangelist's community. The success of his reading of 28.19 rests largely upon the absence of explicit references (apart from the prophecy of 24.14 (cf. 26.13) and this command) to Gentile mission. But how much weight can an argument like this carry in a narrative that purports to tell of a Jewish Messiah who deliberately limits his ministry to Israel? (2) Still with questions of method, Sim rightly argues, in relation to the 'anti-Gentile' texts, that material in the Gospel may not be dismissed as merely traditional and in some cases not representing the evangelist's viewpoint. However, one might be forgiven for wondering how different it is to insist, as Sim does, that the texts that envision Gentile mission are not intended for his community (*Matthean Community*, 243–4, cf. 'Gentiles', 41). (3) He has not satisfactorily addressed the manner in which earlier portions of the narrative seem calculated to anticipate the mission that 28.16–20 announces. (4) Sim's monograph addresses a weakness in his 1995 essay ('Gentiles'), which included no treatment of 21.33–45, but 21.43 still receives far less attention than it deserves. (5) He offers an historical reconstruction that has Matthew's community in Antioch suffering persecution from Gentiles along with all other Jews in the city both during the Jewish war and in subsequent years *precisely because they were Jewish*! But the references to persecution from the Gentiles in Matthew (like the persecution from the Jews!) are explicitly said to arise because of the disciples' allegiance to Jesus (10.18; 24.9). It is probably no accident that these texts are set in mission contexts. Most naturally, persecution from the nations implies a mission to those nations that gives rise to the conflict of which the Gospel warns. See further W. G. Olmstead, review of David C. Sim, *The Gospel of Matthew and Christian Judaism, JRH* 25 (2001), 88–90.

13. Smith, 'Matthew 28:16–20', 597. See Rimmon-Kenan, *Narrative Fiction,* 119–22, for a discussion of what M. Perry and his associates referred to as 'the primacy effect', the tendency of that which is encountered first to shape the reader's experience of a narrative.

14. So also, e.g., Kingsbury, *Matthew as Story,* 47; Luz, *Matthew 1–7,* 110, who refers to the 'broad Jewish tradition which sees Abraham as the father of the proselytes'. Cf. Str-B 3:211.

15. Kingsbury, *Matthew as Story,* 47–48; similarly R. E. Brown, *The Birth of the Messiah* (2nd edn, New York: Doubleday, 1993), 68.

16. Cf. Luke 1.30–33, 55, 69–73; Acts 3.25; 13.23; Gal. 3.16; and see esp. M. Wilcox, 'The Promise of the "Seed" in the New Testament and the Targumim', *JSNT* 5 (1979), 2–20.

17. In the LXX (Ps. 88.4) 'my chosen one' (לִבְחִירִי) is now plural: διεθέμην διαθήκην τοῖς ἐκλεκτοῖς μου, ὤμοσα Δαυιδ τῷ δούλῳ μου.

18. Dating the Targums is of course extraordinarily difficult, but in my view the fascinating links between several NT texts and the Targum to Ps. 89 make a pre-Christian origin plausible here. See Wilcox, 'Promise of the "Seed"', to whom I owe this reference and whose translation I have followed.

19. Wilcox, 'Promise of the "Seed"', 3–6.

20. Both the date and interpretation of this text are disputed. M. De Jonge thinks that the Testaments received their present *redacted* form in Christian circles during the latter half of the second century and that Jesus is the king who will arise from Judah, the prophet from the seed of Abraham, who will establish a new priesthood for all the nations (H. W. Hollander and M. De Jonge, *The Testament of the Twelve Patriarchs: A Commentary* (Leiden: Brill, 1985), 82–5, 154; for his earlier view on their composition, see De Jonge, 'Christian Influence in The Testaments of the Twelve Patriarachs', in *Studies on the Testaments of the Twelve Patriarchs* (ed. M. De Jonge, 193–246, Leiden: Brill, 1975), 195–7).

H. C. Kee, following R. H. Charles (*The Testaments of the Twelve Patriarchs* (London: Black, 1908)), maintains that the Testaments are a second-century BC Jewish work (Kee favours an early second century date; Charles dated the document to the late second century [*Twelve Patriarchs,* xv, lvii–lxv]) into which Christian *interpolations* were later inserted (Kee, 'Testaments of the Twelve Patriarchs: A New Translation and Introduction', in *The Old Testament Pseudepigrapha,* vol. I, *Apocalyptic Literature and Testaments* (ed. James H. Charlesworth, 775–828, New York: Doubleday, 1983), 777–8). For Kee the kingship that is granted to Judah and 'immediately defined as a "new priesthood" . . . may allude to the Maccabean priest-kings, with their increasingly secular discharge of the dual role' ('Twelve Patriarchs', 791). See Charles for a proposed emendation of this text and for the suggestion that vv. 14–15 refer to John Hyrcanus, the only man in Israel's history to whom the triple office of prophet, priest, and king was assigned

(*Twelve Patriarchs*, 45; cf. Charles, *The Greek Versions of the Testaments of the Twelve Patriarchs,* Oxford: Clarendon, 1908, 44–5). Cf. Josephus, *B.J.,* 1.2.8.

The clear transfer of promises made to Abraham to the heirs of David in both Ps. 72.17 and Jer. 33.22 suggests that a pre-Christian origin of this saying cannot be discounted. But what is most significant for our purposes here is that, whether of Jewish or Christian origin, once more we find the Davidic king identified as the seed of Abraham who brings blessing to the nations (cf. *T. Sim.* 7.2). If this text is in fact pre-Christian and not the product of subsequent redaction, we have one more striking example of the transfer of Abraham's blessings to David in the Jewish writings. If Christians were responsible either for the composition or later modification of the text, we have another example of Christian thinkers making the same transfer. Either way, the presence of another text which makes this connection between Abraham and David strengthens the case for finding a similar link here in Matthew.

21. Rahab was a Canaanite (cf. Josh. 2) and Ruth a Moabite (cf. Ruth 1.1–4). Of Bathsheba's ethnic origin we know little but, significantly, she is here referred to as τῆς τοῦ Οὐρίου (Matt. 1.6). Uriah was a Hittite (2 Sam. 11.3). Philo (*Virt.* 221) identifies Tamar as a native of Syria–Palestine, while in both *Jub.* 41.1–2 and *T. Jud.* 10.1–2 she is a daughter of Aram. See further J. Emerton, 'An Examination of Recent Structuralist Interpretation of Genesis XXXVIII', *VT* 26 (1976), 90–3; 'Judah and Tamar', *VT* 29 (1979), 403–15; R. Bauckham, 'Tamar's Ancestry and Rahab's Marriage: Two Problems in the Matthean Genealogy', *NovT* 37 (1995), 313–20.

22. So, e.g., M. Luther, *Luther's Works* (ed. Jaroslav Pelikan, vol. VII, *Lectures on Genesis Chapters 38–44*, St. Louis: Concordia, 1965), 35–6. But see also Brown (*Birth*, 71–4) who, although he expresses reservations about this interpretation, apparently regards it as a subordinate motif. Sim, 'Gentiles', 21–3, is less enthusiastic. That this sort of reading would not have been foreign to Matthew's readers is perhaps suggested by an interesting parallel from the book of Ruth. The narrative concludes with a genealogy that identifies the son that was providentially granted to this Moabitess (4.13) as the grandfather of David (4.17, 18–22). In the same context, Ruth is explicitly compared to Tamar (4.12), and the genealogy that ends with David begins with Perez, the son of Tamar and Judah. As Gentiles had been incorporated into the Davidic line, so now fittingly the son of David would bring blessings that would extend beyond the borders of Israel.

23. Cf. Chrysostom, *Homilies on the Gospel of Saint Matthew* 6.6 (*NPNF*[1] 10:40). Davies and Allison, *Matthew*, I:238, object that scholars have overplayed the Jew/Gentile contrast. Instead the pericope is another example of Matthew's penchant for exalting the humble and humbling the exalted.

24. Already Chrysostom, *Homilies on the Gospel of Saint Matthew* 6.1, 2 (*NPNF*[1] 10:36–7) and Augustine, *Sermon* 199.3; 202.1 (*PL* 38, 1028, 1033), understood the Magi as the first-fruits of the Gentiles, an interpretation followed by the clear majority of modern commentators. See, e.g., Luz, *Matthew I–7*, 133, 139; Hagner, *Matthew 1–13*, 27, 31; Brown, *Birth*, 181–3. But, if the Magi represent the first-fruits of the Gentiles, do they also represent the first-fruits of the eschatological pilgrimage

of the nations to Israel (so Donaldson, *Jesus on the Mountain*, 185–6; Davies and Allison, *Matthew*, I:249–50; Brown, *Birth*, 187; Luz, *Matthew 1–7*, 137–8, remains agnostic)? Isa. 60.1–6 and Ps. 72.10–11, 15 (cf. *Ps. Sol.* 17.31; *1 Enoch* 53.1) offer interesting parallels. Of the two texts, the latter is marked by the closest connection to the Matthean account but also is less obviously about an eschatological pilgrimage.

25. Cf. John 8.33–44; Rom. 9.6–9; Justin, *Dial.*, 44.
26. So already Chrysostom, *Homilies on the Gospel of Saint Matthew* 11.3 (*NPNF*[1] 10:69). Similarly, Davies and Allison, *Matthew*, I:308–9.
27. So also, e.g., F. F. Bruce, *The Time is Fulfilled* (Exeter: Paternoster, 1978), 74; Senior, *Passion*, 24. But see also Saldarini, *Christian–Jewish Community*, 42–3, 77.
28. Bruce, *Time*, 74.
29. Matthew departs from LXX Isa. 8.23–9.1 at several points including: (1) the omission of τὰ μέρη τῆς Ἰουδαίας after Galilee of the Gentiles in Matthew (but also absent in the MT); (2) εἶδεν (4.16) replaces ἴδετε (MT רָאוּ); (3) φῶς ἀνέτειλεν αὐτοῖς (4.16) replaces φῶς λάμψει ἐφ' ὑμᾶς (MT אוֹר נָגַהּ עֲלֵיהֶם). (1) is significant if, as seems clear, Matthew's narrative here anticipates the significance Jesus' ministry will have for the nations. (2) and (3) probably reflect the evangelist's eschatological vantage point. In Jesus, the light *has* dawned.
30. Commenting on this text, and the wider prologue, Luz writes: 'Matthew's Prologue is thus not simply the beginning of the Jesus story; it is also, and ultimately, the narrative anticipation of that story' (*Theology*, 29).
31. Cf. Isa. 42.6; 49.6; 51.4; and contrast *T. Levi* 14.2–4.
32. See also Luz, *Matthew 1–7*, 249–52; Stanton, *New People*, 379; S. McKnight, 'Gentiles', in *Dictionary of Jesus and the Gospels* (ed. J. Green and S. McKnight, 259–65, Downers Grove: InterVarsity, 1992), 261.
33. The alternative reading (οὐδὲ ἐν τῷ Ἰσραὴλ τοσαύτην πίστιν), though widely supported, is almost certainly secondary – an assimilation to the parallel at Luke 7.9. See Metzger, *Textual Commentary*, 17.
34. D. Allison is representative of those scholars who have recently challenged the common understanding of this text, which finds reference to Gentiles in the 'many who will come from east and west' (cf. Sanders, *Jesus and Judaism* (London: SCM, 1985), 219–20; Levine, *Matthean Social History*, 107–30; already McNeile, *Matthew*, 105, questioned whether Jesus' saying originally had anything to do with Gentiles). In a 1989 article he argues, based largely on antecedents in Jewish texts, that 'when Jesus referred to people coming from east and west he was probably thinking about the diaspora' ('Who will come from East and West? Observations on Matt 8.11–12/Luke 13.28–29', *IBS* 11 (1989), 159). Again: 'The saying had nothing at all to do with Gentiles. Passed down without a context, it was susceptible of being reinterpreted against the original sense. This unfortunately happened when the author of Matthew placed the logion in the middle of a pericope that contained a Jew/Gentile contrast. The new context suggested the identification of those from east and west with Gentiles' ('East and West', 167). But, for Allison, the fact that 8.11–12 has been reinterpreted because of its placement in its Matthean context does not entail the conclusion that this is how the evangelist himself understood the saying. He hints at this position in his 1989

article and defends it in his commentary. 8.11–12 makes no explicit reference to Gentiles. On the contrary, the saying draws upon imagery from the OT of a return from exile for *Yahweh's people*, but not of an eschatological Gentile pilgrimage. Whenever such a pilgrimage is in view, it is never portrayed in Jewish literature as simultaneously a judgement upon Israel, nor is it ever connected with a feast for the nations. Finally, if the 'sons of the kingdom' refer to Jews as a whole in contrast to Gentiles, the saying 'at least hyperbolically, consigns all of Israel to perdition' (Davies and Allison, *Matthew*, II:27).

Several brief comments can be made by way of response. First, while it is of course true that the πολλοί are not explicitly named Gentiles, 8.10b makes this allusion clear, as exegetes throughout the church's history have understood. Second, the OT and later Jewish texts to which Allison points are in fact instructive, but his argument seems to assume that traditional motifs must be employed in a traditional manner. In its Matthean context, Jesus' announcement surprises – even shocks – and that by design. But the surprise ensues when traditional expectations are reversed. Allison's reading can only be successful when earlier Jewish treatments of these motifs are given hermeneutical priority over the Matthean narrative. Finally 8.11–12, while rhetorically charged, hardly 'consigns all Israel to perdition'. Both the immediate context (cf., e.g., 8.1–4, 14–15; 9.1–8, 9–13) and the wider narrative (4.18–22; 27.55, 56, 61, cf. 28.1–10; 27.57–60) provide examples of faithful Israelites who yield allegiance to Jesus. Some are *promised* roles of importance in the coming kingdom (19.28). Ironically, Allison recognises this and makes some of these same observations in arguing, against Trilling, that, even if he is wrong and the evangelist does think here of Gentiles, that would not rule out a future conversion of Israel (Davies and Allison, *Matthew*, II:31). What is more, for Allison's own interpretation, an absolute exclusion of 'the sons of the kingdom' faces exactly the same problems as it does in the traditional reading. Since he does not wish to suggest that all *Palestinian Jews* will be evicted from the kingdom, only to be replaced by the diaspora, Allison is forced to conclude that the 'many from the east and west' serve primarily as a foil, with the emphasis falling squarely upon 'the miserable lot of those who fail to welcome the Messiah' (Davies and Allison, *Matthew*, II:28). To my mind, none of the lines of evidence that Allison cites is compelling. The narrative context in which 8.11–12 is set clearly makes the centurion representative of the many Gentiles who will sit at table with the Patriarchs at the Messianic banquet.

35. See also R. T. France, 'Exegesis in Practice: Two Samples', in *New Testament Interpretation* (ed. I. H. Marshall, 253–81, Grand Rapids: Eerdmans, 1977), 260–4.

36. But see also Davies and Allison, *Matthew*, II:31, who raise the possibility that 8.11–12 should also be viewed as a prophetic threat – 'a word which speaks of damnation not as a certainty but as a prospect demanding repentance'.

37. Cf. Bruce, *Time*, 62.

38. Ps. 107.3; Isa. 43.5–7; 49.12; Zech. 8.7; Bar. 4.36–37; 5.5–6; *Ps. Sol.* 11.2; cf. LXX Deut. 30.4.

39. In addition to Isa. 43.5–7 and 49.22, see also Bar. 4.36–37; 5.5–6; *Ps. Sol.* 11.2.

40. For discussion of the prophetic expectation of an eschatological pilgrimage of the nations and the possible role it plays in supplying a background for this text see, e.g., B. F. Meyer, *The Aims of Jesus* (London: SCM, 1979), 247; S. Brown, 'The Matthean Community and the Gentile Mission', *NovT* 22 (1980), 196–7; G. R. Beasley-Murray, *Jesus and the Kingdom of God* (Grand Rapids: Eerdmans, 1986), 170–4; Allison, 'East and West', 162–5.

41. So rightly M. Hooker, 'Uncomfortable Words: X. The Prohibition of Foreign Missions (Mt 10.5–6)', *ExpTim* 82 (1971), 363.

42. Gundry, *Matthew*, 192, finds in the Jewish rejection of 10.17 the reason for the expanded mission. 10.17–18 would thus anticipate 21.43. Similarly Stanton, *New People*, 140.

43. In each of these ways, the reader notes in retrospect, the disciple is like his master: cf. 26.47–75; 27.1–2, 26.

44. Cf. especially U. Luz, 'Die Junger im Matthäusevangelium', *ZNW* 62 (1971), 141–71; ET 'The Disciples in the Gospel according to Matthew', in *The Interpretation of Matthew* (ed. Graham Stanton, 98–128, Philadelphia: Fortress, 1983).

45. On Tyre and Sidon, see Isa. 23; Jer. 25.15–29ff.; 27.1–7ff.; 47.1–7; Ezek. 26–28; Joel 3.1–8; Amos 1.9–10; Zech. 9.2–4. References to Sodom (and Gomorrah) abound.

46. Ὄχλοι, however, may not be original. Cf. Metzger, *Textual Commentary*, 26.

47. Both the immediate context, where Jesus defends the cause of justice and mercy against the Pharisees (12.1–13), and the conclusion of the citation ('and in his name will the Gentiles hope') favour taking κρίσις here as *justice* rather than *judgement*. So, e.g., Hagner, *Matthew 1–13*, 338; Gundry, *Matthew*, 229–30; *contra* Luz, *Matthäus*, II:247–8.

48. That this last clause forms a critical part of the citation is evident from the fact that Matthew passes over the first part of Isa. 42.4 to get to καὶ τῷ ὀνόματι αὐτοῦ ἔθνη ἐλπιοῦσιν. Cf. also LXX Isa. 11.10 where the similar clause (ἐπ' αὐτῷ ἔθνη ἐλπιοῦσιν) refers to the Davidic king.

49. So also Senior, *The Gospel of Matthew* (Nashville: Abingdon, 1997), 47.

50. So, e.g., T. W. Manson, *The Teachings of Jesus* (Cambridge University Press, 1951), 133 n. 1; Jeremias, *Parables*, 79 n. 82; Luz, *Theology*, 88.

51. Cf. Donaldson, *Jesus on the Mountain*, 132: 'Matthew calls her a "Canaanite", using the common OT term for Israel's adversaries – and thereby evoking Israel's deeply-engrained fear of and revulsion towards Gentile ways.'

52. So also Edwards, *Matthew's Story*, 57.

53. For Levine, *Matthean Social History*, 159, the faith of the Gentile here, as in ch. 8, stands in contrast not principally to the unbelief of the Jews, but rather to the 'little faith' of the disciples.

54. The links between the Canaanite woman and the centurion (8.5–13) are several: (1) both are Gentiles; (2) both address Jesus as κύριε (8.6, 8, cf. 15.22, 25, 27); (3) both plead for help for members of their household who are suffering terribly (8.6, cf. 15.22); (4) both meet with an initial rebuff from Jesus (8.7, cf. 15.23–26); (5) in dialogue with Jesus, both demonstrate exceptional faith (8.8–9, cf. 15.22–27); (6) both elicit from Jesus comment about their remarkable faith (8.10, cf. 15.28); (7) both receive the healing they request (8.13, cf. 15.28).

55. *Pace* France, *Evangelist*, 234. Because the narrative presents Jesus' encounter with this Gentile as exceptional, because there is as yet no negation of 15.24 (which echoes 10.5–6) and because the text gives little reason to think otherwise, I suspect that the crowds that come to Jesus in 15.30 and are subsequently healed and fed are, as elsewhere in this narrative, *Jewish* crowds; similarly Davies and Allison, *Matthew*, II:563–4; *contra* Zahn, *Matthäus*, 525–7; P. Gaechter, *Das Matthäus-Evangelium* (Innsbruck: Tyrolia, 1963), 505; D. A. Carson, 'Matthew', in *The Expositor's Bible Commentary* (ed. F. Gaebelein, 8: 3–599, Grand Rapids: Zondervan, 1984), 356–9.

56. So also W. R. G. Loader, 'Son of David, Blindness, Possession, and Duality in Matthew', *CBQ* 44 (1982), 578; Anderson, 'Redundancy', 76, 79.

57. On the question of whether Israel should be included among the nations here, Matthean scholars are divided. See, e.g., Meier, 'Nations or Gentiles?', 96, and Saldarini, *Christian–Jewish Community*, 80, for an inclusive reading; Hagner, *Matthew 14–28*, 581, thinks the text refers to rulers of the 'pagan Gentiles'.

58. Sim, 'Gentiles', 25, 30.

59. At 5.47 L W Θ f^{13} 𝔐 h sy^p all read τελῶναι instead of ἐθνικοί. At 6.7 the presence of ἐθνικοί is again disputed. Here B, 1424, sy^c, and mae read ὑποκριταί; so also *Did.* 8.2. Cf. also Justin, *Apol.* I.15.9, where οἱ πόρνοι replaces Matthew's οἱ τελῶναι (5.46): Εἰ ἀγαπᾶτε τοὺς ἀγαπῶντας ὑμᾶς; τί καινὸν ποιεῖτε; καὶ γὰρ οἱ πόρνοι τοῦτο ποιοῦσιν. The pejorative point is scored; the vocabulary is flexible.

60. Cf. Eph. 4.17; 1 Pet. 2.12; 4.13; 3 John 7; Ign. *Trall.* 8.2; Pol. *Phil.* 11.2 (here, however, 'gentes' and qualified by 'qui ignorant iudicium domini').

61. Several MSS omit τῶν ἐθνῶν here (C f^1 1424 *l*2211 1 (sy^s) bo^{ms}), probably under the influence of Mark 13.13 (cf. Matt. 10.22).

62. See, e.g., the following discussions of Matt. 24 and/or Mark 13: R. V. G. Tasker, *The Gospel According to St. Matthew* (Leicester: InterVarsity, 1961), 223–8; R. T. France, *Jesus and the Old Testament* (London: Tyndale Press, 1971), 227–39; *Matthew*, 333–6; S. Brown, 'The Matthean Apocalypse', *JSNT* 4 (1979), 2–27; D. Garland, *Reading Matthew: A Literary and Theological Commentary on the First Gospel* (New York: Crossroad, 1993), 234–9; N. T. Wright, *Jesus and the Victory of God* (Minneapolis: Fortress, 1996), 320–68; K. E. Brower, '"Let the Reader Understand": Temple and Eschatology in Mark', in *The Reader Must Understand* (ed. K. E. Brower and M. W. Elliot, 119–43, Leicester: InterVarsity, 1997), 119–43; C. H. T. Fletcher-Louis, 'The Destruction of the Temple and the Relativization of the Old Covenant: Mark 13:31 and Matthew 5:18', in *The Reader Must Understand* (ed. K. E. Brower and M. W. Elliot, 145–69, Leicester: InterVarsity, 1997), 145–69; cf. G. B. Caird, *New Testament Theology* (ed. L. Hurst, Oxford: Clarendon, 1994), 243–67; 359–66.

63. See esp. France, *Jesus*, 227–39; but also the critique in M. Casey, *Son of Man: The Interpretation and Influence of Daniel 7* (London: SPCK, 1979), 172–8.

64. I do not, however, agree with those Matthean scholars for whom Gentile mission *begins* at AD 70; so, e.g., Walker, *Heilsgeschichte*, 114–26; Hare, *Jewish Persecution*, 148; 154–5; Luz, *Theology*, 120, 127 n. 14, 138–41; *Matthäus*, 3: 243–4. Cf. also McKnight, 'Loyal Critic', 67 n. 45, for whom 'full Gentile inclusion' awaits 'the revoking of Jewish privilege that does not become

visibly demonstrated until 70 CE'. However important the events surrounding the Jewish war proved to be in giving momentum to this mission, in this
narrative, *inauguration* of the universal mission awaits only the universal exaltation of Messiah that is proclaimed immediately after Jesus' resurrection.

65. But cf. Lövestam, *'This Generation'*, 81–7.
66. Cf. Caird, *New Testament Theology*, 249–50.
67. See, however, Brown, 'Matthean Apocalypse', 13–14; M. Wilcox, 'Text
Form', in *It is Written: Scripture Citing Scripture* (ed. D. A. Carson and
H. G. M. Williamson, 193–204, Cambridge University Press, 1988), 201–2;
R. Bauckham, *The Climax of Prophecy: Studies on the Book of Revelation*
(Edinburgh: T. & T. Clark, 1993), 319–22. Of these, only Brown points out
the missiological significance of this allusion for 24.31.
68. See here especially Bauckham, *Prophecy*, 319–22.
69. Cf. also Amos 3.2; the only variation is that φυλή is anarthrous (πασῶν
φυλῶν τῆς γῆς).
70. Here, as we noted above, the blessing comes via the Davidic king who has
inherited God's promise to Abraham.
71. Cf. J. Jeremias, *The Eucharistic Words of Jesus* (trans. Norman Perrin,
London: SCM, 1966), 227–31.
72. The commentators are divided over this question. Luz, *Matthew 1–7*, 121,
e.g., insists that in Matthew λαός always refers to Israel; so also Hare,
Jewish Persecution, 159 n. 4. By contrast, Davies and Allison, *Matthew*,
I:210, identify 'his people' as 'the ecclesia of both Jew and Gentile'; similarly Powell, 'Plot', 196 n. 27. The redefinition of God's people that this
narrative highlights favours the latter reading.
73. Cf. Isa. 53.7; is there also an allusion here to Isa. 52.15?
74. See Metzger, *Textual Commentary*, 56, for an introduction to the interesting
textual problem surrounding the name of [Ἰησοῦν] Βαραββᾶν.
75. Cf. 1.20–21; 2.12, 13, 19, 22.
76. Cf. Ps. 26.6; 73.13; and esp. Deut. 21.1–9; Sus. 46ff. See p. 62 for our
discussion of the striking parallels between the stories of Susanna and Jesus
at this point.
77. Luz, *Theology*, 135 n. 2.
78. See the discussion of the textual problem here in ch. 3, p. 196 n. 74 above.
79. *Contra* Gundry, *Matthew*, 561–4, who makes repeated reference to Matthew's
'Christianizing' of Pilate. As Carson, 'Jewish Leaders', 173–4, rightly notes,
Pilate's 'see to it yourselves' (ὑμεῖς ὄψεσθε; 27.24) recalls the same phrase
at 27.4 (σὺ ὄψῃ), so linking him to the Jewish leaders and perhaps suggesting that, like theirs, his attempt to avoid responsibility for Jesus' death was
unsuccessful.
80. Perhaps Matthew's preference for the term ἡγεμών for Pilate is, in part,
calculated to underline this irony; so Davies and Allison, *Matthew*, III:554.
Probably, it also makes Jesus a model for his followers. Like him, they will
be dragged before governors (10.18); so Gundry, *Matthew*, 552. After this,
Pilate's only appearance in the narrative (aside from a passing reference on
the lips of the Jewish leaders at 28.14) comes after Jesus' execution when, at
the request of the chief priests and Pharisees, he makes a guard of soldiers
available to secure Jesus' tomb (27.62–66).

81. Not surprisingly, Sim, 'Gentiles', 24, emphasises the 'particularly poor light' in which these soldiers are cast. Similarly R. E. Brown, *The Death of the Messiah: From Gethsemane to the Grave* (New York: Doubleday, 1994), 877. But, while this narrative neither condemns the Jews en masse nor extends a blanket exoneration to the Gentiles, perhaps what these observations fail to address is that this is not the last encounter that the reader will have with either the Jewish leaders or these Gentile soldiers. Subsequently their stories take dramatically different turns.

82. ἐφοβήθησαν σφόδρα. At 17.6, the only other place in the NT where these words occur together, ἐφοβήθησαν σφόδρα describes the response of the three disciples on the Mount of Transfiguration to the voice from the cloud that declares: οὗτός ἐστιν ὁ υἱός μου ὁ ἀγαπητός, ἐν ᾧ εὐδόκησα· ἀκούετε αὐτοῦ. In both instances, then, ἐφοβήθησαν σφόδρα describes the fear that follows supernatural displays and in both instances the significance of the event revolves around Jesus' divine sonship. For Gundry, *Matthew*, 578, this connection between the disciples at the Transfiguration and the soldiers at the cross implies the conversion of the latter.

83. So Heil, *Matthew 26–28*, 87.

84. Cf. also the taunt hurled by the passers by at 27.40.

85. See Sim, 'The "Confession" of the Soldiers in Matthew 27.54', *HeyJ* 34 (1993), 401–24, for a fundamentally different interpretation.

86. So, rightly, Kingsbury, *Matthew as Story*, 89.

87. Senior, *Passion*, 176.

88. Differently, Schweizer, *Matthew*, 412: 'In the context of verses 25–26, however, Matthew is trying to say that the people had already made the wrong decision when they rejected John the Baptist, although 3:5 has a rather different message.' But does not the narrative make it clear that the people have *not* rejected the Baptist (21.26, 32)? Like 3.1–12, 21.23–32 arraigns not the people but the leaders.

89. Jesus' explicit application of the parable to the *Jewish* elite vis-à-vis the *Jewish* sinners means that I cannot agree with, e.g., Chrysostom, *Homilies on the Gospel of Saint Matthew* 67.2 (*NPNF*[1] 10:411), that the two sons in our parable represent, in the first place, the Gentile and Jewish peoples. Nevertheless, neither can I agree with the majority of modern scholars for whom the parable makes no contribution to our understanding of the 'Gentile-question' in Matthew's narrative. This parable tells the story of the surprising reversal of marginal and elite *within* Israel as God's eschatological people is constituted. Nevertheless, set in the context of this trilogy, it is difficult to dismiss a secondary salvation–historical allusion to Jews and Gentiles in the two sons' responses to the Father's appeal. Perhaps the Church Fathers' salvation–historical reading is not so far removed from its sense in Matthew's narrative as many contemporary scholars have assumed.

90. Saldarini, *Christian–Jewish Community*, 44–5, 58–64, 78–81; see p. 199 n. 1 for reference to other recent defences of this reading.

91. Saldarini, *Christian–Jewish Community*, 60–1.

92. Cf., e.g., his reading of Acts 24.17; *Christian–Jewish Community*, 245–6 n. 69.

93. See Saldarini, *Christian–Jewish Community*, 60.

94. This is not to deny that there are exceptions to this pattern. Saldarini, *Christian–Jewish Community*, 245 n. 68, points to 1 Macc. 1.34, where he finds in ἔθνος ἁμαρτωλόν reference to an 'evil leadership group' made up of Jews loyal to the Seleucids. Even here, however, the commentators are divided. J. Goldstein, *1 Maccabees* (AB 41; Garden City: Doubleday, 1976), 123–4, 219–20, argues that this ἔθνος ἁμαρτωλόν (cf. Isa. 1.4) is composed at least partly of apostate Jews, probably bolstered by pagan military settlers. J. Bartlett, *The First and Second Books of the Maccabees* (Cambridge University Press, 1973), 26–7, although he likewise finds reference to a garrison made up of both renegade Jews and pagan soldiers, restricts the meaning of ἔθνος ἁμαρτωλόν to Syrian soldiers (similarly REB, *impious foreigners*). For him, the Jewish renegades are the ἄνδρας παρανόμους. Cf. Josephus, *Ant.*, 12.252, 305.

95. Saldarini, *Christian–Jewish Community*, 60; emphasis added.

96. Cf. 4.15; 6.32; 10.5, 18; 12.18, 21; 20.19, 25; 24.9, 14; 25.32; 28.19. As we noted above (p. 198 n. 99), Matthean scholars are divided over whether the important phrase πάντα τὰ ἔθνη (24.9, 14; 25.32; 28.19) should include or exclude Israel. My point here is simply that the term, in its plural form, typically bears ethnic connotations.

97. 1424 g¹ (l) r¹; Eus Cyr all omit τῆς βασιλείας, but its original presence in the text is hardly to be questioned.

98. So, e.g., Senior, *Matthew*, 46.

99. See also R. Swaeles, 'L'Arrière-fond scripturaire de Matt. xxi.43 et son lien avec Matt. xxi. 44', *NTS* 6 (1960), 310–13, for the interesting suggestion that Matt. 21.43–44 allude to Dan. 2.34, 44, and 7.27 (as well as Isa. 8.14). The proposal is plausible, but becomes less attractive if, as I think, Matt. 21.44 is secondary.

100. In Gen. 17 the reader learns of the covenant that God makes with Abraham to make him the father of many nations (καὶ ἐγὼ ἰδοὺ ἡ διαθήκη μου μετὰ σοῦ, καὶ ἔσῃ πατὴρ πλήθους ἐθνῶν; Gen. 17.4, cf. 17.5–6). Indeed, although the covenant would be kept with Isaac, even Ishmael would become a great nation (ἔθνος μέγα; Gen. 17.19–21, cf. Gen. 21.13, 18).

101. See also Gen. 48.4 where Jacob reviews the promises God had made to him in Canaan with Joseph (cf. Gen. 35.11–12); and Gen. 48.19 where he pronounces similar blessing on Manasseh.

102. For evidence that the early Christians viewed themselves in these terms cf., e.g., 1 Pet. 2.9–10; Rev. 1.5–6.

103. The echo of this promise is absent from the MT, which, nevertheless, does make success in the coming campaigns dependent on the people's obedience.

104. Differently MT: וּרְאֵה כִּי עַמְּךָ הַגּוֹי הַזֶּה ('Consider too that this nation is your people.')

105. Cf. Num. 14.12; Deut. 7.6; 9.14; 14.2; 26.5, 19.

106. Cf. Gen. 18.18; 22.18; 26.4.

107. It is at least interesting that *Tg. Isa.* 5.1 reads: '*The prophet said*, I will sing now for *Israel – which is like a vineyard, the seed of Abraham, my friend – my friend's* song for his vineyard' (Chilton's 1987 translation).

108. See now J. Marcus, 'The intertextual polemic of the Markan vineyard parable', in *Tolerance and Intolerance in Early Judaism and Christianity* (ed. Graham N. Stanton and Guy G. Stroumsa, 211–27, Cambridge University

Press, 1998), 219–21, for the suggestion that, in part, the *Marcan* parable of The Tenants answers the question, 'who are Abraham's rightful heirs?'

109. God keeps his promise to Abraham in view of Abraham's faithful obedience (cf. Gen. 22.18; 26.4). By her repudiation of the ways of the Lord, Israel repudiates her covenant relationship (cf. Gen. 22.19; Exod. 19.5–6; 23.22).

110. So Levine, *Matthean Social History*, 211–15; Harrington, *Matthew*, 308 (though he remains open to the possibility that 22.8–10 'may even explain the presence of Gentiles within the Jewish Christian community'); Saldarini, *Christian–Jewish Community*, 63–4. Sim, *Matthean Community*, 158–9; 239–40 (cf. 'Gentiles', 43 n. 41) similarly rejects the conclusion that the third mission alludes to Gentile mission.

111. For discussion of the relationship between Israel's failure and Gentile inclusion as portrayed in The Tenants, cf. Eusebius, *Dem. ev.* 9.11 (PG 22, 692–3); Hooker, 'Uncomfortable Words', 363; Gaston, 'Messiah', 32; Senior, *Passion*, 39–40; Donaldson, *Jesus on the Mountain*, 208–9; Matera, 'Plot', 242–3; Stanton, *The Gospels and Jesus* (Oxford University Press, 1989), 67; *New People*, 140; Heil, *Matthew 26–28*, 87; McKnight, 'Gentiles', 262. On this motif in The Wedding Feast, see W. B. Selbie, 'The Parable of the Marriage Feast', *ExpTim* 37 (1926), 267; Hare, *Jewish Persecution*, 148, 154; D. Marguerat, *Le Jugement dans l' Évangile de Matthieu* (Geneva: Labor et Fides, 1981), 338–40.

112. Nevertheless, the narrative stops short of depicting Israel's failure as a *necessary* condition for Gentile inclusion. From the vantage point of this narrative, perhaps it would be more accurate to describe the failure of Yahweh's people as an *historical* condition – historically, Israel's failure led to the universal mission. 28.16–20 at least hints that Gentile inclusion was part of God's sovereign purpose since Abraham.

5 A narrative-critical reading of the trilogy

1. Howell, *Matthew's Inclusive Story*, 17.
2. Ibid., 17.
3. When Howell refers to Matthew's Gospel as an inclusive story, he also means that there is a sense in which 'the experiences of Matthew's church were inscribed in the narrative' (Ibid., 94). Here, Howell's work has been anticipated by a generation of redaction critics including, most notably, U. Luz. In an important essay Luz argued, against G. Strecker (*Der Weg*), that the disciples of Jesus are not set in an unrepeatable holy past ('Disciples'). Instead, they are transparent so that Matthew's community stands behind his portrait of the disciples. Nevertheless, while the evangelist shaped his story in light of the experiences of his community, he did not eliminate historical markers: 'It is as pupils of the historical Jesus that the disciples become transparent and are models of what it means to be a Christian' ('Disciples', 105). Again, with reference to the two feeding miracles, he writes: 'We must therefore conclude that it is precisely as past historical events that these two miracle-stories become transparent for the present

life of the community' (Ibid., 106). In his recent treatment of Matthew's theology, Luz takes up this motif once more (*Theology*, 66); see also P. Lampe and U. Luz, 'Diskussionsüberblick', in *Das Evangelium und die Evangelien* (ed. Peter Stuhlmacher, 413–31, Tübingen: Mohr, 1983; ET 'Overview of the Discussion', in *The Gospel and the Gospels* (ed. Peter Stuhlmacher, 387–404, Grand Rapids: Eerdmans, 1991)) 424.

Nevertheless, even when speaking of the inclusive nature of Matthew's narrative, Luz's and Howell's chief interests remain distinct. Whereas Luz seems most concerned with the manner in which the events in Matthew's story *reflect* the experiences of his community, Howell focuses instead on the narrative's potential to *embrace* and to *shape* its reader. It is this latter focus that I shall adopt as I turn to examine the inclusive nature of this Matthean trilogy of parables.

4. For J. Wellhausen, *Das Evangelium Matthaei: Übersetzt und Erklärt* (Berlin: Reimer, 1904), 106, it was not Jesus' authority to act (as in the 'cleansing' of the temple) but to *teach* that was challenged here (cf. 7.29). Several recent exegetes have echoed this conclusion, or at least insisted that the fundamental challenge was directed against Jesus' teaching; cf., e.g., Schweizer, *Matthew*, 409; Gnilka, *Das Matthäusevangelium*, II:216; Luz, *Theology*, 118 (but contrast Luz, *Matthäus*, III:209); Jones, *Matthean Parables*, 391. But the reader can hardly forget Jesus' actions in the temple the previous day and, as Plummer, *Matthew*, 293, noted, ταῦτα ποιεῖς naturally suggests that the challenge to Jesus' action is primary.

5. 11.16–19 constitutes the only possible exception to this otherwise consistent portrait. See above the discussion on pp. 53–4; 192–3 n. 25.

6. On the role played by questions in drawing the reader into the concerns of the narrative world, see, e.g., G. Prince, 'Introduction to the Study of the Narratee', in *Reader-Response Criticism: From Formalism to Post-Structuralism* (ed. Jane. P. Tompkins, 7–25, London: Johns Hopkins University Press, 1980), 12–15.

7. Hagner, *Matthew 14–28*, 613, suggests that ἐγώ in ἐγώ, κύριε (21.30) 'is short for ἰδοὺ ἐγώ, i.e., "Here am I" [Heb. הִנֵּנִי, *hinnenî*], a Septuagintal formula of consent.' Jones, *Matthean Parables*, 393 n. 210, citing Sophocles (*Trachiniae*, 1247–8), suggests that it is probably a classicism. Cf. also Jülicher, *Die Gleichnisreden*, II:368–9, and BDF section 441 (2); both suggest that ὑπάγω should be understood; D makes this explicit. Chrysostom, *Homilies on the Gospel of Saint Matthew* 67.2, substitutes ἀπέρχομαι for ἐγώ, κύριε.

8. The textual puzzle here is complex. Against NA[27], I am following the reading of B et al. See the extended defence of this text-critical judgement in the Appendix, pp. 167–76.

9. Here at 21.29 the son's rejection of his father's plea (οὐ θέλω) may anticipate the later rejection of the king's invitation to the wedding feast (οὐκ ἤθελον; 22.3) and the Jewish rejection of Jesus (οὐκ ἠθελήσατε; 23.37), but the parallel is probably more formal than real since, unlike the two later groups, the son's initial rebellion gives way to repentance and obedience.

10. Cf. the Fourth Gospel and, indeed (apart from Rev. 21.7, a citation of 2 Sam. 7.14), the entire Johannine corpus where this distinction is maintained. Believers become τὰ τέκνα τοῦ θεοῦ (John 1.12; 11.52; 1 John 3.1, 2, 10;

5.2); Jesus alone is ὁ υἱὸς τοῦ θεοῦ (e.g., John 1.34, 49; 3.16, 17, 18, 35). Matthew is less consistent; cf. Matt. 5.9, 45.

11. McNeile, *Matthew*, 306. Similarly F. Filson, *A Commentary on the Gospel According to St. Matthew* (London: Black, 1960), 227. But Blomberg, *Interpreting the Parables*, 189, refers to the vineyard as a 'stock symbol for Israel'.

12. See Isa. 3.14; 27.2; Jer. 12.10 (cf. 2.21; 5.10; 6.9); and esp. Isa. 5.1–7.

13. Redactional observations offer intriguing support for this suggestion. Cf. the discussion to follow in ch. 6, pp. 145–6.

14. Similarly Davies and Allison, *Matthew*, II:776.

15. So also G. Barth, 'Matthew's Understanding of the Law', in Günther Bornkamm, Gerhard Barth and Heinz Joachim Held, *Tradition and Interpretation in Matthew* (trans. Percy Scott, Philadelphia: Westminster, 1963), 60.

16. Dodd, *Parables*, 16; emphasis added.

17. Fuchs, *Historical Jesus*, 221–2.

18. Funk, *Language*, 133; cf. also Bultmann, *History*, 198; Thiselton, 'Reader-Response Hermeneutics', 79–126.

19. J. Gibson, 'Hoi Telonai kai hai Pornai,' *JTS* 32 (1981), 430, argues that prostitutes and tax collectors were linked together because they both collaborated with Rome's occupying forces. Perhaps; more probably, their notorious impiety secured the link.

20. So McNeile, *Matthew*, 306, for whom Jesus' declaration means only that the tax gatherers and prostitutes are nearer the kingdom than the religious authorities.

21. So also, e.g., A. Schlatter, 'Jesu Gleichnis von den beiden Söhnen', *Jahrbuch der Theologischen Schule Bethel* 2 (1931), 42; D. E. Garland, *The Intention of Matthew 23* (Leiden: Brill, 1979), 84; cf. BDF section 245a.

22. J. Marcus, 'Entering into the Kingly Power of God', *JBL* 107 (1988), 663–75, contends that references to 'entering the kingdom' are not about the human action necessary to enter God's future realm but rather participation in 'the already inaugurated explosion of God's power into the world; they are not so much declarations of the conditions for future salvation as summonses to join now in God's apocalyptic battle' (674). This conclusion, however, does justice neither to the wider narrative generally nor to this text in particular. Since it is linked both verbally and conceptually to 7.21–23 and to 25.11–13, it is difficult to exclude the notion of future judgement from 21.31.

23. D. A. Hagner, 'Righteousness in Matthew's Theology', in *Worship, Theology and Ministry in the Early Church: Essays in Honor of Ralph P. Martin* (ed. M. J. Wilkins and T. Paige, 101–20, Sheffield: JSOT, 1992), 108. See Hagner for a list of representatives both of this developing 'trend' and of the position he defends, namely, that in some instances the Matthean use of δικαιοσύνη refers to gift and in others to demand.

24. Ibid., 110.

25. Ibid., 112.

26. Ibid., 115–17.

27. Ibid., 118.

28. Ibid., 117.

29. Ibid., 117.

30. On the use of (ה)צדק at Qumran and in the Tannaitic literature, see B. Przy-bylski, *Righteousness in Matthew and His World of Thought* (Cambridge University Press, 1980), 13–76.

31. Cf., e.g., Isa. 46.13; 51.5; 62.1–2; 63.1.

32. Cf., e.g., Gen. 20.5; Ps. 7.8 (LXX 7.9); 15.2 (14.2); 18.20, 24 (17.21, 25); 38.20 (37.21); Prov. 2.9, 20; 8.20; 12.28; 15.9; 17.23; Isa. 5.7; 11.5; 16.5; 26.9–10; 57.12; 60.17; 61.8; 64.5.

33. If, as I suggest in the following chapter, already in this parable the evangelist thinks of Isaiah's vineyard, perhaps it is also significant that there Yahweh laments the failure of his people to *practise* righteousness (Isa. 5.7).

34. So 2 Pet. 2.21, cf. Prov. 8.20; 12.28; 16.31; 17.23; 21.16; Job 2.13; Tob. 1.3; 1QS 4.2; *Jub.* 23.21, 26; 25.15; *1 Enoch* 82.4; 91.18–19; 94.1, *Barn.* 1.4; 5.4; *Apoc. Pet.* E 7; *Apoc. Pet.* A 22, 28.

35. See above p. 100.

36. Two lines of evidence make this conclusion clear. First, in the Lucan parallel, Jesus says: 'Why do you call me "Lord, Lord" and not *do what I tell you* (6.46)?' Second, Matt. 7.24, introduced as it is by the inferential particle οὖν, draws its conclusion from 7.21–23: '*Therefore, everyone who hears these words of mine and does them* will be like a wise man who built his house upon a rock.' The one who obeys Jesus secures his future.

37. Hagner, *Matthew 1–13*, 360.

38. That the will of the Father here is obedience to God himself rather than to Jesus' teaching, as in 7.21, is probably to be attributed to the fact that at issue now is the Jewish leaders' response to the Baptist.

39. See 1QS 8.12–16 (cf. 9.19–20) for the application of Isa. 40.3 to the community that retreats to the wilderness to 'prepare the way of the Lord' by the study of the Law.

40. Cf. Josephus, *Ant.* 18.114–17.

41. On the relationship of 21.23–27 and 3.7–10, see esp. B. Charette, *The Theme of Recompense in Matthew's Gospel* (JSNTSup 79; Sheffield: JSOT, 1992), 135.

42. As Luz, *Matthew 1–7*, 237, observes: 'Δικαιοσύνη can be understood in all Matthean passages as human behavior, in some it *must* be so understood.' Perhaps exegetes most often find reference to gift rather than demand in the uses of δικαιοσύνη at 5.6 and 6.33. Even there, however, in the context of the Sermon in which δικαιοσύνη occurs three other times at pivotal points (5.10, 20; 6.1) and each time clearly refers to the practice of righteousness, I find an ethical sense more compelling. On the use of δικαιοσύνη at 3.15, cf. David Hill, *Greek Words and Hebrew Meanings: Studies in the Semantics of Soteriological Terms* (Cambridge University Press, 1967), 126–7: 'δικαιοσύνη does not simply refer to the righteous character of that baptism as something which conforms to the divine will and which must therefore be accepted: rather it refers to the righteousness of life which was the demand laid on those who accepted that baptism (cf. Matt. 21:32) . . . This interpretation is consonant with Matthew's special use of the term.'

43. But Hagner, 'Righteousness', 111 n. 2, following J. Reumann, *Righteousness in the New Testament: 'Justification' in the United States Lutheran–Roman Catholic Dialogue* (Philadelphia: Fortress, 1982), 129, thinks that both gift and demand are present.

44. Similarly Lambrecht, *Treasure*, 101; cf. also Luz, 'Disciples', 107.
45. ἦλθεν . . . ἐν ὁδῷ δικαιοσύνης raises at least one further question: is the reader to think of John's conduct or his message? Michaelis, 'ὁδός', *TDNT* V:86–7, suggests the former. While the parallel construction at 11.18 may offer support for Michaelis's interpretation, in this context the accent seems to fall on John's message. As we have noted, Jesus' question at 21.25 brings John into his dispute with the Pharisees. There, however, unlike 11.18, the subject is not John's lifestyle but the authority of his baptism. Moreover, the fact that the religious authorities are charged with their failure to believe the Baptist implies a message to be rejected. Similarly, e.g., J. Jeremias, *New Testament Theology* (trans. John Bowden, London: SCM, 1971), 46; J. A. Ziesler, *The Meaning of Righteousness in Paul* (Cambridge University Press, 1972), 131–2; Hill, *Matthew*, 298. Perhaps, however, it is not necessary to distinguish sharply between John's teaching and his conduct. Davies and Allison, *Matthew*, III:170 n. 45, are representative of those scholars who find reference here both to John's behaviour and to his message. See also, e.g., Strecker, *Der Weg*, 187; A. Kretzer, *Die Herrschaft der Himmel und die Söhne des Reiches* (Würzburg: Echter, 1971), 158; Przybylski, *Righteousness*, 96.
46. Anderson, *Narrative Web*, 75.
47. Elsewhere Jesus heals another Gentile (15.21–28), those possessed (12.32–34), blind (15.29–31; 20.29–34; 21.12–17) and maimed (12.9–14; 15.29–31; 21.12–17).
48. Cf. Hos. 6.6, cited twice in Matthew: 9.13 (Matt. diff Mark) and 12.7 (Matt. [+] Mark).
49. On 'this generation' in Matthew, see above the discussion at pp. 53–4.
50. προσκυνέω is ambiguous, and can mean either 'to prostrate oneself before someone as an act of reverence, fear, or supplication', or 'to prostrate oneself in worship' (J. P. Louw and E. A. Nida (eds.), *Greek–English Lexicon of the New Testament Based on Semantic Domains* (2 vols., New York: United Bible Societies, 1988, 1989), I:218, 540), but of a series of observations suggests that the evangelist intends to move his readers to genuine worship. First, in this narrative the object of προσκυνέω must be either Jesus or God (2.2, 8, 11; 4.9, 10; 8.2; 9.18; 14.33; 15.25; 18.26; 20.20; 28.9, 17). Second, Matthew's redaction of the relevant Marcan texts suggests that Matthew reserves προσκυνέω for contexts in which genuine worship is appropriate. On five separate instances, Matthew inserts προσκυνέω into traditional Marcan material. Four times the subjects of προσκυνέω are supplicants who approach Jesus (cf. 8.2; 9.18; 15.25; 20.20). In the final case the disciples in the boat (14.33, cf. 14.22) are the subject of προσκυνέω and προσεκύνησαν αὐτῷ is modified by λέγοντες· ἀληθῶς θεοῦ υἱὸς εἶ. Matthew has radically rewritten the ending of this pericope. In Mark's version the hard hearts of the disciples prevent them from understanding (cf. Mark 6.51–52). This modification is consistent with the ameliorated portrait of the disciples that we find elsewhere in Matthew's narrative. But I suspect that Matthew's redaction here is not designed solely to soften Mark's harsh portrait of the twelve. Is it not likely that Matthew, with one eye fixed squarely on his readers, seeks to lead them toward the only appropriate response to one who walks on water and calms his followers' terror with the words, θαρσεῖτε, ἐγώ εἰμι (14.27)? Certainly later Christian readers of Matthew's Gospel would naturally find in the use

of προσκυνέω here, in conjunction with a confession of Jesus' Sonship, reference to genuine worship. And if the redactional insertion of προσκυνέω here seems designed to evoke a response of worship from the reader, may this not also be the case in the other insertions? Nor is it only Matthew's redactional insertions that are noteworthy. Matthew eliminates both Marcan uses of προσκυνέω (Mark 5.6; 15.19). In neither instance is the *'worship'* offered to Jesus exemplary.

Third, the use of προσκυνέω in the parable of The Unforgiving Servant (18.23–35) offers an instructive parallel to the evangelist's redaction of Mark. In Matthew's parable, vv. 26 and 29 respectively record the pleas for mercy found on the lips of the first servant as he addresses the king, and of the second servant as he cries out to the first. The evangelist has crafted this part of his narrative so that the approaches of the two debtors and their appeals are almost identical:

26 πεσὼν οὖν ὁ δοῦλος   προσεκύνει αὐτῷ λέγων·
   μακροθύμησον ἐπ᾽ ἐμοί, καὶ πάντα ἀποδώσω σοι.
29 πεσὼν οὖν ὁ σύνδουλος αὐτοῦ παρεκάλει αὐτὸν λέγων·
   μακροθύμησον ἐπ᾽ ἐμοί, καὶ   ἀποδώσω σοὶ

In v. 29, however, παρακαλέω replaces προσκυνέω. This is significant because the king, whom the first servant beseeches (18.26), points metaphorically to God (cf. 18.34–35). The second servant beseeches only his fellow servant (18.29). Even in this tightly structured unit within the parable, the evangelist employs προσκυνέω only when its object is God (cf. H. J. Held, 'Matthew as Interpreter of the Miracle Stories', in Günther Bornkamm, Gerhard Barth and Heinz Joachim Held, *Tradition and Interpretation in Matthew* (trans. Percy Scott, Philadelphia: Westminster, 1963), 229–30 n. 3, who reaches similar conclusions).

Fourth, the story of Jesus' testing by the devil (4.1–11) has prepared the reader to find in προσκυνέω reference to something more than the homage one might pay even the most exalted human figure: worship must be reserved exclusively for God (4.10).

Fifth, that προσκυνέω can appear in this narrative together with προσέρχομαι (so 8.2; 9.18 (v.l.); 14.33 (v.l.); 20.20; 28.9) or κύριος (so 8.2; 15.25; 18.26 (v.l.)) further encourages the reader to embrace Jesus as one worthy of full-orbed worship; cf. J. R. Edwards, 'The Use of Προσέρχεσθαι in the Gospel of Matthew', *JBL* 106 (1987), 65–74.

Finally, in two texts unique to his Gospel, Matthew reports that the response of Jesus' followers when he appeared to them after his resurrection was worship (28.9, 17). The cumulative force of the evidence suggests that the evangelist sought to lead his readers toward this same post-Easter vantage point.

Does this suggest that historical considerations fall by the wayside as the evangelist paints the characters in his story with a post-Easter brush? Perhaps not. Perhaps the ambiguity that surrounds terms like προσκυνέω and κύριος enables the evangelist faithfully to report the events of his narrative even while summoning his reader to responses that surpassed the characters in the story. For the leper of 8.2, kneeling before Jesus could hardly mean all that it would mean for the post-Easter reader who followed in his steps. Equally, for the post-Easter reader who identifies with this leper, kneeling before Jesus could hardly mean *only* what it meant for the leper (cf. J. D. Kingsbury, 'The Miracle of the Cleansing of the Leper as an Approach to the Theology of Matthew', *CurTM* 14 (1977): 345–6).

51. Held, 'Miracle Stories', 284–91.

52. This conclusion naturally influences our understanding of the address, κύριε, that is scattered through these stories. Commentators continue to discuss the exact nuance that κύριε might have expressed on the lips of the leper, the centurion and other supplicants at the story level (cf., e.g., Hagner, *Matthew 1–13*, 203–4), but what the evangelist wishes to communicate at the discourse level is at least of equal import. Here, if our prior conclusions about the role of the miracle stories in eliciting praying faith are correct, there can be little doubt that the evangelist invites his readers to address Jesus as Lord of the Church.

53. See also 9.20–22, 27–31; 15.21–28; 20.29–34.

54. This is only reinforced by the repeated echoes of the Baptist's preaching in Jesus' proclamation (3.2, cf. 4.17; 3.7, cf. 12.34; 3.7, cf. 23.33; 3.10, cf. 7.19; 3.12, cf. 13.30; 3.7–10, cf. 8.5–13).

55. *Pace* Gundry, *Matthew*, 424, who thinks that this second chance probably refers to the ministry of Jesus. Lambrecht, *Treasure*, 103, thinks that the 'you' of v. 32 is transparent, that the evangelist not only thought of the second opportunity for repentance that the Jewish authorities refused, but also of the persistent Jewish unbelief in his own day.

56. Not surprisingly, Jesus' story nearly mirrors John's. Like the Baptist, Jesus finds acceptance for his message that issues in repentance among the marginalised in Israel (cf., e.g., 8.5–13; 9.9–13; 15.22–28). Like the Baptist, Jesus comes 'in the way of righteousness' (cf. 3.15; 5.6, 10, 20; 6.1, 33) and speaks with the authority of the God of Israel (cf., e.g., 17.5). And, like the Baptist, Jesus meets with consistent disbelief and rejection from the Jewish leadership (cf., e.g., 9.1–13, 32–34; 11.16–19; 12.1–14, 22–45).

57. See Snodgrass, 'Recent Research', for a survey of recent studies of this parable.

58. Cf. the discussion in ch. 2, pp. 42–3, above.

59. Cf. also the use of ἀκούω in 17.5.

60. See Stanton, *New People*, 73–6; Scott and Dean, 'Sound Map', 311–78.

61. On the socio-economic standing of the γεωργοί in late antiquity, see C. A. Evans, 'Jesus' Parable of the Tenant Farmers in Light of Lease Agreements in Antiquity', *JSP* 14 (1996), 65–83.

62. Cf. A. Milavec, 'The Identity of "the Son" and "the Others": Mark's Parable of the Wicked Husbandmen Reconsidered', *BTB* 20 (1990), 34: 'By borrowing and noticeably modifying the familiar opening, an artful storyteller evokes the mood and theme of a familiar story at the same time that he signals that a *new* version of this old parable is about to be presented.' See also Jean-Pierre Duplantier, 'Les vignerons meurtriers: Le travail d'une parabole', in *Les paraboles évangéliques: Perspectives nouvelles* (ed. Jean Delorme, 259–70, Paris: Les Editions du Cerf, 1989), 260–3.

63. In language that finds echoes elsewhere in Matthew (most notably at 7.15–20), God declares: καὶ ἔμεινα τοῦ ποιῆσαι σταφυλήν, ἐποίησεν δὲ ἀκάνθας (Isa. 5.2; cf. 5.4). Once again, in 5.7, when the metaphor is dropped and

the fruit for which God waited is described, we meet themes that would later become especially important in this Gospel, expressed in vocabulary familiar to readers of Matthew's narrative: ἔμεινα τοῦ ποιῆσαι κρίσιν, ἐποίησεν δὲ ἀνομίαν καὶ οὐ δικαιοσύνην ἀλλὰ κραυγήν. On lawlessness in Matthew, see Stanton, *New People*, 47–9.

64. Most commentators simply pass over these references without comment, presumably because they judge them insignificant; cf., e.g., Gnilka, *Das Matthäusevangelium*, II:227; Bonnard, *Matthieu*, 315; Garland, *Reading Matthew*, 218; Gundry, *Matthew*, 423; Hagner, *Matthew 14–28*, 620; but note also Luz, *Matthäus*, III:222; Davies and Allison, *Matthew*, III:176 n. 8.

65. B. Chilton, *The Isaiah Targum: Introduction, Translation, Apparatus and Notes* (Edinburgh: T. & T. Clark, 1987), 10–11; emphasis original, marking departures from the Hebrew text.

66. Cf. *t. Sukkah* 3.15; *t. Me'il.* 1.16.

67. *1 Enoch* 89.56, 66b–67, cf. 89.3; *Barn.* 16.1–2, 4, 5.

68. C. A. Evans, 'On the Vineyard Parables of Isaiah 5 and Mark 12', *BZ* 28 (1984), 82–4; cf. B. Chilton, *A Galilean Rabbi and His Bible: Jesus' Own Interpretation of Isaiah* (London: SPCK, 1984), 111–14.

69. C. A. Evans, 'God's Vineyard and Its Caretakers', in *Jesus and His Contemporaries* (Leiden: Brill, 1995), 401; similarly G. J. Brooke, '4Q500 1 and the Use of Scripture in the Parable of the Vineyard', *DSD* 2 (1995), 279–85; W. J. C. Weren, 'The Use of Isaiah 5, 1–7 in the Parable of the Tenants (Mark 12, 1–12; Matthew 21, 33–46)', *Bib* 79 (1998), 15–17.

70. M. Trimaille, 'La parabole des vignerons homicides', in *Les paraboles évangéliques: Perspectives nouvelles* (ed. Jean Delorme, 247–58, Paris: Les Editions du Cerf, 1989), 255–6, thinks that Matthew focuses upon the city rather than the temple. I am not certain, however, that the two can be neatly separated (cf. 23.37–38).

71. Cf. 11.25; 12.1; 14.1; 24.45. On the other hand, at 8.29 καιρός seems to refer to an appointed time, still future, about which the demons knew – the time of their torment. At 13.30 καιρός, qualified by τοῦ θερισμοῦ, points metaphorically to the judgement at the end of the age. At 26.18 ὁ καιρός μου, much like the Johannine ὥρα, signals the appointed time of Jesus' passion. The remaining two occurrences of καιρός are found in this parable, here and at 21.41.

72. Cf. the following discussion of 21.41.

73. καρπός stands as the direct object of a verb in Matthew 14 times. In 11 instances the verb is ποιέω (3.8, 3.10, 7.17 (2×), 7.18 (2×), 7.19, 12.33 (2×), 13.26, 21.43). Elsewhere the verb is: δίδωμι (13.8); λαμβάνω (21.34); ἀποδίδωμι (21.41).

74. Both δοῦλος and δοῦλοι are found in the LXX in descriptions of the prophets. But the phrase οἱ δοῦλοι (or παῖδες) αὐτοῦ οἱ προφῆται becomes especially common in describing the collective ministry of the prophets. Cf. 1 Kgs. 14.18; 15.29; 2 Kgs. 9.7, 36; 10.10; 14.25; 17.13, 23; 21.10; 24.2; Ezra 9.11; Isa. 20.3; 44.26; 50.10; Jer. 7.25; 25.4; 33(26).5; 29.19; 42(35).15; 51(44).4; Ezek. 38.17; Dan. 9.6, 10; Amos 3.7; Zech. 1.6; see also Rev. 10.7; 11.18. Already Irenaeus, *Against Heresies*, 4.36.2 (*ANF* 1:515) found in Matthew's twofold sending of the servants reference to the pre- and post-exilic prophets. This reading remains common; cf., e.g., Jeremias, *Parables*, 72; J. D. Crossan,

'The Parable of the Wicked Husbandmen', *JBL* 90 (1971), 453; J. D. Hester, 'Socio-Rhetorical Criticism and the Parable of the Tenants', *JSNT* 45 (1992), 31; R. Feldmeier, 'Heil im Unheil. Das Bild Gottes nach der Parabel von den bösen Winzern (Mk. 12, 1–12 par)', *TBei* 25 (1994), 14 n. 29 ('vielleicht'). Snodgrass, *Wicked Tenants*, 57, is sceptical: 'Matthew would not have limited the number in the first group of servants to three if he were trying to depict accurately a group of the prophets.'

75. On the significance of stoning in the Hebrew Scriptures and for the Rabbis, see Van Tilborg, *Jewish Leaders*, 56.
76. See, e.g., 2 Kgs. 9.7; 17.13–14; 2 Chron. 24.19–22; Ezra 9.10–11; Neh. 9.26; Jer. 7.25–26; 25.4–7; 26.5; 29.19; 35.15; 44.4–5; Dan. 9.6, 10; Amos 2.11–12; 3.7.
77. τῶν πρώτων links the parable verbally to the preceding story, where πρῶτος appears at least once (21.28, cf. 21.31).
78. Cf. 5.11–12 and 23.29–37.
79. With ὕστερος (21.37, cf. 21.29, 31 (v.l.), 32) and ἰδόντες (21.38, cf. 21.32), two more links are forged between The Two Sons and The Tenants.
80. As several scholars have noted, the vineyard is called אחסנא in the Isaiah Targum. Cf. Jones, *Matthean Parables*, 384 n. 161; Evans, 'God's Vineyard', 401. On the question of whether or not the parable presents a 'realistic' portrait of the laws of inheritance, see E. Bammel, 'Das Gleichnis von den bösen Winzern (Mk.12,1–9) und das jüdische Erbrecht', *RIDA* 3rd series, 6 (1959), 11–17, but also S. R. Llewelyn, 'Self-Help and Legal Redress: The Parable of the Wicked Tenants', *NewDocs* 6 (1992), 86–105.
81. Cf. Hagner, *Matthew 14–28*, 621.
82. Cf. the discussion of this reading in ch. 6, pp. 154, 239 n. 95.
83. For the first time in the narrative, Jesus' opponents confront his claim, even if still veiled, to be the son of God. Cf. Kingsbury, 'Wicked Husbandmen'.
84. Cf. Stanton, *New People*, 77–84.
85. Cf. Isa. 5.4: τί ποιήσω ἔτι τῷ ἀμπελῶνί μου . . .
86. Not a few scholars find an allusion to the destruction of Jerusalem here; cf., e.g., Van Tilborg, *Jewish Leaders*, 49, and Lambrecht, *Treasure*, 119.
87. If we were correct earlier in finding an allusion to the temple in Jesus' reference to the tower that was built in the vineyard (as in *Tg. Isa.* 5.2), it is perhaps also significant that the Targum refers to the destruction of the temple at 5.5.
88. Cf. 15.14; subsequently 23.16, 17, 19, 24, 26.
89. The word also appears twice in the parables of ch. 13. At 13.8 the seed that fell on good soil produced fruit (ἐδίδου καρπόν); again the production of fruit distinguishes the genuine from the spurious. At 13.26, in the parable of The Tares when the plants (i.e., the sons of the kingdom; cf. 13.37) came up and bore fruit, then the weeds also appeared.
90. Jer. 17.7–10 is especially noteworthy, both because of its parallels to Ps. 1 and to Matthean thought.
91. So already Jülicher, *Die Gleichnisreden*, II:395; similarly, e.g., Klostermann, *Das Matthäusevangelium*, 172; Trilling, *Das Wahre Israel*, 57; M. Hubaut, *La parabole des vignerons homicides* (Paris: Gabalda, 1976), 59; Gundry, *Matthew*, 428–9.
92. The plural form is found at 16.3, but the text is probably secondary.

93. Similarly, Van Tilborg, *Jewish Leaders*, 57; Charette, *Recompense*, 140.
94. Cf. Acts 4.11; 1 Pet. 2.4, 7.
95. Cf. E. Lohmeyer, 'Das Gleichnis von de bösen Weingärtnern', *ZST* 18 (1941), 242–59.
96. Similarly C. A. Evans, 'On the Vineyard Parables of Isaiah 5 and Mark 12', *BZ* 28 (1984), 85. For Evans this implicit threat to the temple establishment displaces the vindication of the rejected stone as the main point of the saying; cf. Evans, 'God's Vineyard', 404 n. 49. He also argues, following M. Black, 'The Christological Use of the Old Testament in the New Testament', *NTS* 18 (1971–2), 12–14, and Snodgrass, *Wicked Tenants*, 63–4; 113–18, that the link between the stone saying and the parable is tightened by the אבן-בן word play that is reflected in the Targums, but not preserved in the LXX. Tg. Ps. 118.22 reads: 'The boy which the builders abandoned was among the sons of Jesse and he is worthy to be appointed king and ruler' (Evans, 'God's Vineyard', 403). Like Evans, Brooke argues that the stone saying forms an integral part of the original parable but suggests that the link between Isa. 5 (perhaps in another form) and Ps. 118 is probably made by means of a catchword rather than a word play. In this case the common motif of building may supply the catchword association. Once more he finds 4Q500 significant since in line 3 the winepress is built with stones (בנוי באבנין) ('4Q500', 287–89; 293).
97. Hagner, *Matthew 14–28*, 623, thinks that 'διὰ τοῦτο ... refers back not to the immediately preceding quotation but to the parable itself'. Cf. Trilling, *Das Wahre Israel*, 60. Probably, however, one need not choose between the two. Introduced by διὰ τοῦτο, 21.43 looks back both to 21.42 and to the preceding parable.
98. Did the Jewish leaders, then, forfeit something that was already theirs? This would seem to be the most natural understanding of the language; but see Snodgrass, *Wicked Tenants*, 90 n. 74.
99. So, too, Gundry, *Matthew*, 430.
100. Like ἀρθήσεται, the passive δοθήσεται points to divine action.
101. See here esp. Stanton, *New People*, 378–80. *Pace* G. Bornkamm, 'End-Expectation and the Church in Matthew', in Bornkamm, Günther, Barth, Gerhard and Held, Heinz Joachim, *Tradition and Interpretation in Matthew* (trans. Percy Scott, Philadelphia: Westminster, 1963), 43; L. Schottroff, 'Das Gleichnis vom grossen Gastmahl in der Logienquelle', *EvT* 47 (1987), 207, and W. Weren, 'The Use of Isaiah 5,1–7', 22, 24, the future tenses of 21.43 simply adopt the temporal perspective of the speaker, and do not point to a judgement reserved for the eschatological future.
102. Not long ago most scholars dismissed Matthew 21.44 as an early interpolation from Luke 20.18. B. Lindars, *New Testament Apologetic: The Doctrinal Significance of the Old Testament Quotations* (London: SCM, 1961), 174 n. 2; Trilling, *Das Wahre Israel*, 57 n. 15; Bornkamm, 'λικμάω', *TDNT* IV:281 n. 7; and Metzger, *Textual Commentary*, 47, are representative. But the tide of scholarly opinion seems to have shifted; cf. the careful defence of this position that Snodgrass, *Wicked Tenants*, 66–71, offers. See also Swaeles, 'L'Arrière-fond scripturaire', 310–13; K. and B. Aland, *The Text of the New Testament* (trans. Erroll F. Rhodes, Grand Rapids: Eerdmans, 1987), 232–3; W. L. Kynes, *A Christology of Solidarity: Jesus as the*

Representative of his People in Matthew (Lanham, MD: University Press of America, 1991), 141–2; Lambrecht, *Treasure*, 108–9; Gundry, *Matthew*, 430–1; Jones, *Matthean Parables*, 387–8; Luz, *Matthäus*, III:217.

The main lines of this defence may be summarised as follows. (1) The placement of the verse in Matthew does not follow the Lucan sequence as one would expect if the verse were an interpolation from Luke. (2) The slight differences between the Matthean and Lucan stone saying likewise argue that its presence in Matthew is not the result of an interpolation. (3) The Matthean sequence, which at least initially seems illogical, may have led to the exclusion of the verse. (4) The external evidence stands squarely in favour of the inclusion of v. 44 (cf. Luz, *Matthäus*, III:217 n. 11; K. and B. Aland, *Text*, 232).

At each point, however, this argument can be challenged. (1) The presence of Matt. 21.43 introduces a factor not present in Luke with the result that, if it were inserted into Matthew under the influence of the Lucan saying, it could not both immediately follow the first stone saying and immediately precede the response of the Jewish leaders. As it now stands in Matthew, it does follow Luke's sequence in immediately preceding the response of the Jewish leaders to Jesus' parable. (2) It is true that the saying is preserved in slightly different wording in Matthew, but the variation is indeed slight (the Matthean version of the saying includes καί and replaces ἐκεῖνον with τοῦτον) and hardly is substantial enough to call the (potential) influence of the Lucan saying into question. (3) It may equally be countered that Matthew would never have located the verse here to begin with (cf. Allen, *Matthew*, 233; Trilling, *Das Wahre Israel*, 57 n. 15). Allen notes that 21.43 looks very much like the conclusion of the pericope. Certainly, elsewhere Matthew exhibits a demonstrable redactional tendency to explain enigmatic or parabolic traditional material. And elsewhere these explanations and applications often stand in final, emphatic, position (cf., e.g., 5.16 (Matt. [+] Mark, Luke); 12.45 (Matt. [+] Luke); 15.20 (Matt. diff Mark); 16.11–12 (Matt. [+] Mark); 17.13 (Matt. [+] Mark); 18.14 (Matt. diff Luke), 35 (No par); 20.16 (No par); 24.42 (Matt. diff Luke), 44 (Matt. par Luke), 51 (Matt. diff Luke); 25.13 (No par)). This seems to be precisely the function granted to 21.43, and suggests that Matthean style favours the omission of 21.44. On the other hand, if 21.44 is authentic, we must explain why it would be eliminated. In my view it is more likely that later copyists included 21.44 under the influence of Luke 20.18 than that the puzzling sequence in the Matthean text prompted them to exclude 21.44. If this is true, then both intrinsic and transcriptional probabilities favour the omission of 21.44. (4) The weight of the external evidence has indeed clearly favoured the authenticity of 21.44. But the recent publication of P[104] from Oxyrhynchus may shed new light on the problem. J. D. Thomas dates the fragment 'to the second half of the second century', making it 'one of the earliest surviving texts of Matthew' ('Matthew xxi.34–37; 43 and 45 (?)', in *The Oxyrhynchus Papyri, vol. LXIV* (ed. E. W. Handley, U. Wartenberg, R. A. Coles, N. Gonis, N. W. Haslam and J. D. Thomas, 7–9, London: Egypt Exploration Society, 1997), 8; cf. the preface to M. W. Haslam et al., (eds.), *The Oxyrhynchus Papyri, vol. LXV* (London: Egypt Exploration Society, 1998), where the number assigned to this fragment is announced).

Matt. 21.34–37 and perhaps 43, 45 appear on this fragment, none of which appear elsewhere in extant papyri. The difficulty in establishing a certain text must make any reading tentative. The text of Matt. 21.34–37 appears on one side of the fragment and is clearly identifiable. Unfortunately, only 'indecisive traces' remain on the other side. For Thomas, only one letter is beyond all doubt; two others are almost certain. Nevertheless, he continues: 'No text from the preceding verses in Matthew fits well with the slight traces remaining. But in the following verses there does seem to be one place which could fit without too much difficulty, namely xxi 43 and 45. This involves the assumption that the papyrus omitted verse 44, since the traces before and after the epsilon in line 16 do not permit the reading of the start of verse 44' ('Matthew XXI', 9). If this reconstruction were accepted, then one of the earliest extant texts of the Gospel would omit 21.44. However, even if we reject this new evidence as too tenuous, we must at least ask whether the external evidence here can overturn the force of the internal evidence. Here text-critical methodological assumptions will largely determine the outcome. For my part, I am hesitant to overturn the strong internal evidence arising from the convergence of intrinsic and transcriptional probabilities on the basis of external evidence. See further E. J. Epp and G. D. Fee, *Studies in the Theory and Method of New Testament Textual Criticism* (Grand Rapids: Eerdmans, 1993), 124–40; J. K. Elliott, 'Thoroughgoing Eclecticism in New Testament Textual Criticism', in *The Text of the New Testament in Contemporary Research: Essays on the Status Quaestionis* (ed. Bart D. Ehrman and Michael W. Holmes, 321–35, Grand Rapids: Eerdmans, 1995); M. W. Holmes, 'Reasoned Eclecticism in New Testament Textual Criticism', in *The Text of the New Testament in Contemporary Research: Essays on the Status Quaestionis* (ed. Bart D. Ehrman and Michael W. Holmes, 336–60, Grand Rapids: Eerdmans, 1995).

103. Kingsbury, 'Wicked Husbandmen', thinks that they also recognise that Jesus claims a relationship to God that is distinct from the prophets.

104. So Luz, *Theology*, 118.

105. Similarly Senior, *Passion*, 26.

106. Contrast the use of τέκνον in the first parable (21.28 (2×)) with υἱός in the second (21.37 (2×), 21.38).

107. Contra Linnemann, *Parables*, 166 n. 18; E. Lemcio, 'The Parables of the Great Supper and the Wedding Feast: History, Redaction and Canon', *HBT* 8 (1986), 14.

108. Cf. 9.15; 25.1–13; and John 3.29. On the use of the wedding feast as an image for the eschatological kingdom, cf. Isa. 62.1–5 and especially Rev. 19.6–9. For the more general portrait of feasting in the final kingdom, cf. Isa. 25.6–8; *2 Bar.* 29.4–8; *1 Enoch* 62.14; Matt. 8.11–12.

109. δεῦτε provides one more verbal link to The Tenants (cf. 21.38).

110. J. D. M. Derrett, 'The Parable of the Wicked Vinedressers', in *Law in the New Testament* (London: Darton, Longman & Todd, 1970), 153; cf. R. Bauckham, 'The Parable of the Royal Wedding Feast (Matthew 22:1–14) and the Parable of the Lame Man and the Blind Man (Apocryphon of Ezekiel)', *JBL* 115 (1996), 484: 'It is only because interpreters so regularly fail to register the political significance of the wedding feast of the king's son that they equally regularly find v. 7 explicable only as an allegorical reference to the destruction of Jerusalem which has been inserted

incongruously into the story.' Both Bauckham, 'Wedding Feast', 484 n. 46, and Derrett, 'Parable', 134–5, cite the parable in *Exod. Rab.* 18.10: 'God was like a king who made festivities in honour of his son and slew his enemies. The king then announced: "He who rejoices with me may come to the festivity of my son, but he who hates me shall be slain with my enemies." '

111. Lambrecht, *Treasure*, 132. For a critique of this way of reading the parable, see Bauckham, 'Wedding Feast'.

112. R. Bauckham argues that the Matthean parable has a narrative integrity and must be read on its own terms. Bauckham easily exposes the weaknesses of earlier readings of the parable that imported Lucan features into the Matthean story. He presses further, arguing that lack of verisimilitude cannot be used as a reliable indication of the presence of allegory ('Wedding Feast', 483). These are important correctives, provided that we underline the qualifications that allegory often does lack narrative integrity and that a lack of verisimilitude may well stand as its signal. My point here is that the parable needs to be read against the backdrop of the wider *Gospel narrative*. There is an integrity here, too, that should not be overlooked. Set in the context of this trilogy and of the developing Matthean story, the reader naturally finds allegorical import in the details of this story. As I proceed to argue, the narrative itself demands it.

113. κρατέω 22.6, cf. 21.46; more importantly, τοὺς δούλους αὐτοῦ . . . ἀπέκτειναν; 22.6, cf. 21.35.

114. ἀπόλλυμι; 22.7, cf. 21.41; ἐκεῖνος; 22.7, cf. 21.40.

115. So, e.g., Wellhausen, *Das Evangelium Matthaei*, 111; B. W. Bacon, 'Two Parables of Lost Opportunity', *HibJ* 21 (1922–3), 345; G. D. Kilpatrick, *The Origins of the Gospel According to St. Matthew* (Oxford: Clarendon, 1964), 30; E. P. Blair, *Jesus in the Gospel of Matthew* (Nashville: Abingdon, 1960), 43 n. 71, 60, 89, 161; Strecker, *Der Weg*, 35; 112–13; C. W. F. Smith, 'The Mixed State of the Church in Matthew's Gospel', *JBL* 82 (1963), 156; Trilling, *Das Wahre Israel*, 85; Walker, *Heilsgeschichte*, 56–7; Steck, *Israel*, 304; L. Gaston, *No Stone on Another* (Leiden: Brill, 1970), 484 n. 1; H. Frankemölle, *Jahwebund und Kirche Christi* (Münster: Aschendorff, 1974), 250–9; Garland, *Matthew 23*, 203 n. 127; J. P. Meier, *Matthew* (Dublin: Veritas, 1980), 247; G. W. H. Lampe, 'A.D. 70 in Christian reflection', in *Jesus and the Politics of His Day* (ed. Ernst Bammel and C. F. D. Moule, Cambridge University Press, 1984), 165–6; Davies and Allison, *Matthew*, I:132; Howell, *Matthew's Inclusive Story*, 219, 240–1; Carter and Heil, *Matthew's Parables*, 174.

116. B. Reicke, 'Synoptic Prophecies on the Destruction of Jerusalem', in *Studies in the New Testament and Early Christian Literature* (ed. D. E. Aune, 121–34, Leiden: Brill, 1972), 121; similarly Allen, *Matthew*, 326 (but cf. also p. 234); K. H. Rengstorf, 'Die Stadt der Mörder (Matt. 22:7)', in *Judentum, Urchristentum, Kirche* (ed. W. Eltester, 106–29, Berlin: Töpelmann, 1960), 106–29; J. A. T. Robinson, *Redating the New Testament* (London: SCM, 1976), 20; E. Ellis, Dating the New Testament, *NTS* 26 (1980), 488 n. 4; Lemcio, 'Great Supper', 14; Donahue, *Gospel in Parable*, 94; Blomberg, *Interpreting the Parables*, 120; Gundry, *Matthew*, 436–7; cautiously Hagner, *Matthew 14–28*, 628–30; with similar caution Jones, *Matthean Parables*, 403–4.

117. Briefly, the main lines of the argument that denies the presence of an *ex eventu* prophecy here may be summarised as follows. (1) The reference to the burning of the city in 22.7 does not point conclusively to the events of AD 70; on the contrary it was an established *topos*, common in Near Eastern literature as well as the Hebrew Scriptures, Josephus, and rabbinic literature. (2) While, unlike other *ex eventu* visions, there is nothing in this prophecy that specifically reveals knowledge of the events of AD 70, some of the details positively contradict what we know to have taken place. (3) If we find reference to the destruction of Jerusalem here, we must conclude that, for the evangelist, the Gentile mission only commences after AD 70, but this stands in clear contradiction to 28.18–20. These arguments, however, do not seem to have convinced the majority of contemporary scholars who continue to find an *ex eventu* prophecy here most probable. A typical response to the problems raised above runs something like this. (1) Even if we grant that Matthew employs an established *topos* here, this still does not answer the more important question, namely, what prompted Matthew to insert this *topos* into *this* parable? Most probably, it was reflection on the events of the Jewish war. (2) We should not expect from an allusion inserted into a traditional parable the same sort of *ex eventu* creativity that is sometimes apparent. (3) The conclusion that Matthew refers here to AD 70 need not lead to the conclusion that, for him, the Gentile mission commences after the destruction of Jerusalem. To insist upon this is to require from an allusion the consistency of a carefully developed argument.

118. Most scholars have concluded that if Matthew here thinks of the destruction of Jerusalem, then there is clear evidence of an *ex eventu* origin. But the matter is probably not so simple. After concluding that v. 7 need *not* point to the destruction of Jerusalem, D. Hagner, *Matthew 14–28*, 628–9, maintains that, even if it does, one still need not conclude that it is *ex eventu*. Hagner is right – there are *two* separate questions here.

119. So Garland, *Matthew 23*, 167–8, who refers to the following texts: Gen. 15.16; Dan. 4.34 (LXX); 8.23 (LXX); *1 Enoch* 50.2; *2 Macc.* 6.12–14; Wis. 11.20; *4 Ezra* 4.36–37; cf. Dan. 5.25–27; 1 Thess. 2.15–16; Rom. 2.5; 4Q185 2.9–10; *Tg. Neof.* Gen. 14.19; *Barn.* 5.11; *Gos. Pet.* 17.

120. The exact force of διὰ τοῦτο is disputed. Garland, *Matthew 23*, 174, thinks that the relationship of the 'therefore' to the reason for the commission of the prophets has been altered by the insertion of vv. 32–33. But διὰ τοῦτο probably looks back to vv. 29–31 as well as vv. 32–33. It is true that the reference to final judgement is now explicit in Matt. (v. 33) and, in this sense, διὰ τοῦτο takes on 'a more fateful connotation', but it is difficult to avoid the conclusion that this is already implicit in the Q saying (cf. Luke 11.50). In any case, for both Matthew and Luke, the reason for the commission is the murderous nature of the Jewish leaders. The commission gives them opportunity to confirm their guilt and so evoke judgement.

121. See also our earlier discussion of these texts at pp. 53–4; cf. 12.39; 16.4; 17.17.

122. Cf. 23.33: ὄφεις, γεννήματα ἐχιδνῶν, πῶς φύγητε ἀπὸ τῆς κρίσεως τῆς γεέννης;

123. See Allison, 'Matt. 23:39', 75–84; and Stanton, *New People*, 249–51.

124. At 22.3 and 23.37, the similarity is verbal as well as conceptual: καὶ οὐκ ἤθελον ἐλθεῖν (22.3); καὶ οὐκ ἠθελήσατε (23.37).

125. Compare 22.6 (ἀπέκτειναν (τοὺς δούλους αὐτοῦ)) with 23.37 (ἡ ἀποκτεί-νουσα τοὺς προφήτας). Note also that φονεῖς, which occurs only at 22.7 in the Synoptic tradition, finds an echo in τῶν φονευσάντων (23.31) and ἐφονεύσατε (23.35).

126. But cf. also Schottroff, 'Das Gleichnis', 207, who finds here a more general allusion to the judgement of all those who rebel against God.

127. Perhaps we should add with Hagner, *Matthew 14–28*, 629–30, that the twice-repeated announcement that 'everything is ready' (22.4) fits especially well with the notion of the dawning kingdom.

128. Hare, *Jewish Persecution*, 121.

129. Similarly Hilary, *Comm. in Matth.* 22.4 (PL 9.1043); Chrysostom, *Homilies on the Gospel of Saint Matthew* 69.1 (*NPNF*[1] 10:421–2); Wellhausen, *Das Evangelium Matthaei*, 110; F. Hahn, *Mission in the New Testament* (trans. Frank Clarke, London: SCM, 1965), 79–80 (for whom the pre- and post-paschal missions are in view); J. D. Kingsbury, *Matthew: Structure, Christology, Kingdom* (Philadelphia: Fortress, 1975), 72; L. Sabourin, *The Gospel According to Matthew* (Bombay: St. Paul Publications, 1982), 775–6; Lambrecht, *Treasure*, 136–7; M. Knowles, *Jeremiah in Matthew's Gospel* (JSNTSup 68; Sheffield: JSOT, 1993), 115–16; Luz, *Matthäus*, III:240–1. Zahn (*Matthäus*, 628–30) and Walker (*Heilsgeschichte*, 91–3) defend a variant of this interpretation, identifying the first servants (22.3) as John and Jesus, the second (22.4) as the apostles.

In any case, the more important point for our understanding of the parable is the identification of the second group. Perhaps most scholars find reference, respectively, to the prophets of the old era and apostles of the new era in vv. 3–4. So, e.g., Jerome, *Comm. in Matth.* 22.3; Calvin, *Harmony*, II:107; Jülicher, *Die Gleichnisreden*, II:421; Klostermann, *Das Matthäusevangelium*, 174 ('Propheten, Apostel?'); Jeremias, *Parables*, 54; Hasler, 'Die Hochzeit', 31; Funk, *Language*, 171–2; Hummel, *Die Auseinandersetzung*, 85; Linnemann, *Parables*, 95; A. Weiser, *Die Knechtsgleichnisse der synoptischen Evangelien* (München: Kösel, 1971), 66–7; R. Batey, *New Testament Nuptial Imagery* (Leiden: Brill, 1971), 43; Schweizer, *Matthew*, 417–18; Meier, *Matthew*, 247; Howell, *Matthew's Inclusive Story*, 151; Kynes, *Solidarity*, 135; Stanton, *New People*, 153, 158–9; Hagner, *Matthew 14–28*, 629. In a variation of this view, Weiss, *Matthäus*, 373–4, finds reference to the prophets at 22.3 and to John and Jesus at 22.4.

On a third reading, the OT prophets are in view in both 22.3 and 22.4. So, e.g., Irenaeus, *Against Heresies*, 4.36.5 (*ANF* 1:516–17); Irenaeus is less than clear here, however; he certainly thinks of the prophets of the old era at 22.3, but he *may* think of the apostles at 22.4; A. Harnack, *The Sayings of Jesus: The Second Source of St. Matthew and St. Luke* (trans. J. R. Wilkinson, London: Williams and Norgate, 1908), 120 n. 1; D. W. Michaelis, *Die Gleichnisse Jesu* (Hamburg: Furche-Verlag, 1956), 151; Trilling, 'Zur Überlieferungsgeschichte', 264; *Das Wahre Israel*, 84; E. Haenchen, 'Das Gleichnis vom grossen Mahl', in *Die Bibel und Wir* (Tübingen: Mohr, 1968), 139; W. Bindemann, 'Das Mahl des Königs: Gründe und Hintergründe der Redaktion von Mt. 22,1–14', *Theologische Versuche* 15 (1985), 22; M.

Davies, *Matthew* (Sheffield: JSOT, 1993), 150–1; Gundry, *Matthew*, 434, 437; Davies and Allison, *Matthew*, III:197 n. 21; Carter and Heil, *Matthew's Parables*, 172. Plummer, *Matthew*, 301–2, Schottroff, 'Das Gleichnis', 206, and Jones, *Matthean Parables*, 409, deny that any precise correspondence is to be found between the servants of 22.3, 4 and any *historical* servants of God.

Finally, Van Tilborg, *Jewish Leaders*, 48–9, seems to suggest that the two missions envisioned in The Wedding Feast are identical to those in The Tenants: 'In both parables servants are sent twice. Remarkably, however, Mt 21,33–46 elaborates at large upon the first mission while Mt 22,1–14 does so upon the second.'

130. If the parable's polemic here seems understated after the dramatic events of vv. 6–7, the use of ἄξιος elsewhere in the narrative is at least noteworthy. Of the nine times that the word appears in this Gospel, only here and at 3.8 does it stand outside of the Mission Discourse (ch. 10). At 10.10 it appears in a saying that defends the right of itinerants to expect support. Three times it describes those who welcome or reject the apostles in their mission (10.11, 13 (2×)), and three times, preceded by a negative particle, those who fail to yield first allegiance to Jesus (10.37 (2×), 38). The similarity between these mission texts and our parable is striking. As there, so here, *worthiness* is measured by one's response to the mission and message of the apostles. Cf. Acts 13.46! Rev. 3.4 is interesting in light of 22.11–13; there we read: 'Yet you still have a few names in Sardis, people who have not soiled their garments; and they shall walk with me in white, for they are worthy.'

131. Cf. the similar use of πορεύομαι in commissions given to the apostles at 10.6–7 (to 'the lost sheep of the house of Israel') and, especially, at 28.19 (to 'all nations').

132. Even so, Hare, *Jewish Persecution*, 148, oversteps the evidence: 'The invitation to the messianic banquet, offered so persistently and as persistently refused, will be offered no more (22.8f.). In the future converts from Israel will not be refused, but their conversion will not be sought. Henceforth the mission is not to Israel and the Gentiles but only to the Gentiles.' Isolated from its context, the reader might arrive at this conclusion. But the first parable in the trilogy depicts the inclusion of the unlikely *Israelite*, while the second defines the nation to whom the kingdom is transferred along ethical and not ethnic lines. It is not so much that judgement of the Israelite as of Israel that is pronounced. By her persistent rebellion, she has forfeited her position of favour.

133. See the extended discussion in ch. 4 above.

134. So also, e.g., Jeremias, *Parables*, 54; Bindemann, 'Das Mahl', 22; Stanton, *New People*, 153; U. Luz, 'Matthew's Anti-Judaism: Its Origin and Contemporary Significance', *CurTM* 19 (1992), 405–15. Cf. once more Acts 13.46; Rom. 11.11–32.

135. συνήγαγον πάντας οὓς εὗρον (22.10) answers ὅσους ἐὰν εὕρητε καλέσατε (22.9).

136. Bornkamm, 'End-Expectation', 20–1.

137. So, e.g., Hasler, 'Die Hochzeit', 29; Smith, 'Mixed State', 149; Goulder, *Midrash*, 59, 168; Bindemann, 'Das Mahl', 23; Charette, *Recompense*, 149; Gundry, *Matthew*, 438; Jones, *Matthean Parables*, 406. Lemcio, 'Great

Supper', 14–15, and P. Luomanen, 'Corpus Mixtum – An Appropriate Description of Matthew's Community?', *JBL* 117 (1998), 469–80, are two notable exceptions. In my view, Luomanen's recent essay rightly challenges the appropriateness of this designation (*corpus mixtum*) for the Matthean community (if indeed we can legitimately speak of such a community), but wrongly argues that 22.8–14 describes 'not the formation of the Christian congregation but the preparation for the last judgment' (475). 22.8–10 does refer to the universal mission in his view, a necessary prerequisite of the end (24.14), but no positive response is described. Of the several weaknesses that confront this interpretation, we note three. First, this reading ignores the obvious fact that the feast to which these replacement guests are invited is the same one as that to which the earlier guests were invited (22.8–10, cf. 22.3–4). But the former invitations were hardly invitations to judgement! Second, surely reclining at this feast implies acceptance of the invitation (22.10). Third, *pace* Luomanen, this narrative never forbids inviting sinners to the kingdom; it only establishes repentance as a condition. Not the healthy, but the sick need a physician (9.9–13).

138. See A. Vaccari, 'La Parabole du Festin de Noces (Matthieu, XXII, 1–14)', *RSR* 39 (1951), 142–5, for the suggestion that the king's inspection reflects an oriental custom.

139. Bauckham, 'Wedding Feast', 486.

140. Ibid., 485.

141. Ibid.

142. For Bauckham, however, reading the story at another level does not entail merely decoding the symbolic wedding garment. Instead, its role in the story needs to be appreciated. In private correspondence, he writes: 'Not bothering to put on a wedding garment is behaving as though the banquet were not the extraordinarily special occasion it is. Not taking the obligations of the Gospel seriously is failing to see or disregarding what a supremely important matter the kingdom of God is.' The parable then 'makes a coherent religious point: Those who are unworthy of entering the kingdom of God are not only those who spurn the Gospel invitation but also those who ostensibly accept it while rejecting what it really represents' ('Wedding Feast', 488).

143. Irenaeus, *Against Heresies*, 4.36.6 (*ANF* 1:517); but his exposition also sounds a clear ethical note.

144. Augustine, *Sermon* 40.4–6; *Sermon* 45.4–7 (*NPNF*[1] 6:393–5; 407–8).

145. J. Schniewind, *Das Evangelium nach Matthäus* (Göttingen: Vandenhoeck & Ruprecht, 1956), 221–2.

146. H. Schlier, 'The Call of God', in *The Relevance of the New Testament* (New York: Herder and Herder, 1968), 254.

147. Michaelis, *Gleichnisse*, 162; Kynes, *Solidarity*, 138, prefers to speak of 'fruit worthy of repentance'.

148. So, e.g., Hasler, 'Die Hochzeit', 30 ('bessere Gerechtigkeit'); Goulder, *Midrash*, 108; similarly, Lambrecht, *Treasure*, 134. Jones, *Matthean Parables*, 406, prefers righteousness to good works on the grounds of the common association in Matthew of 'King', 'Kingdom' and 'righteousness'.

149. Trilling, 'Zur Überlieferungsgeschichte', 259–60; similarly Blair, *Jesus*, 92, 108. Chrysostom, *Homilies on the Gospel of Saint Matthew* 69.2 (*NPNF*[1] 10:423), describes the wedding garment as 'life and practice'. For a sketch

of the pre-modern interpretation of the wedding garment, and the wider parable, see F. W. Beare, 'The Parable of the Guests at the Banquet', in *The Joy of Study* (ed. Sherman E. Johnson, 1–14, New York: Macmillan, 1951).

150. In a recent article D. Sim rejects the 'consensus view' – that Matthew is not thinking of an actual garment, but is rather referring symbolically to the ethical requirements for entrance to the consummated kingdom: 'The problem with this interpretation is that it confuses cause (fulfilling the conditions of entry) with effect (receiving the eschatological robe). By ignoring this distinction between the requirements for wearing the robe and the garment itself, the common view fails to interpret Matthew in terms of the rich apocalyptic world-view of his time, and risks losing sight of his debt to it' ('Matthew 22.13a and *1 Enoch* 10.4a: A Case of Literary Dependence?', *JSNT* 47 (1992), 17–18). It is not uncommon, as Sim rightly notes, to read of a special eschatological garb, especially white clothing, in apocalyptic texts (cf., e.g., Rev. 3.4–5; 6.11; 7.9, 13–14; 19.8; 22.14; 2 Cor. 5.1–4; *1 Enoch* 62.15–16; *4 Ezra* 2.39–41, 44). But, against Sim, the function of this garment motif is not at all uniform and is certainly not to be taken literally in every case (cf. 'Literary Dependence?', 17). Typically, the garment does portray some sort of eschatological blessing (the effect). But apocalyptic visionaries do not appear to be as concerned with the distinction Sim draws as he is. It seems clear that these eschatological garments can portray either the blessing of the new era, or the cause of that blessing, or both. Rev. 19.8 provides an instructive example. There, in describing the marriage supper of the Lamb, John writes: 'it was granted her to be clothed with fine linen, bright and pure – for the fine linen is the righteous deeds of the saints.' Here John removes the metaphor and points to the *cause* of eschatological blessing (cf. Rev. 3.4–5; 22.14–15; *4 Ezra* 2.39–41).

Even if, with Sim, the reader should think of the wedding garment as the effect (eschatological blessing), then surely 22.11–13 warns the reader to address the issue of cause (what secures eschatological blessing) on this side of the judgement.

151. The servants addressed by the king are now διάκονοι rather than δοῦλοι, perhaps because they refer to angelic rather than human ministers (cf. 13.27, 30, 41, 49). Jones, *Matthean Parables*, 409, suggests that the διάκονοι 'are . . . so designated because they serve at table'.

152. Τὸ σκότος τὸ ἐξώτερον occurs three times in Matthew (cf. 8.12; 25.30), but nowhere else in the NT. On the striking parallels between Matt. 22.13a and *1 Enoch* 10.4a, see esp. Sim, 'Literary Dependence?', 3–19.

153. Ἐκεῖ ἔσται ὁ κλαυθμὸς καὶ ὁ βρυγμὸς τῶν ὀδόντων occurs 7 times in the NT – once at Luke 13.28 (par Matt. 8.12), and elsewhere only in Matthew (13.42, 50; 22.13; 24.51; 25.30). Gundry, *The Use Of The Old Testament In St. Matthew's Gospel* (Leiden: Brill, 1967), 77, proposes an allusion to Ps. 112 (111).10.

154. *Contra* Sim, 'The Man without the Wedding Garment [Matthew 22.11–13]' *HeyJ* 31 (1990), 173, who concludes that the rejection of the Jewish leaders from the eschatological feast is the primary theme of 22.11–13.

155. B. Meyer, 'Many (= All) are Called, but Few (= Not All) are Chosen', *NTS* 36 (1990), 89–97; cf. E. Boissard, 'Note sur l'interprétation du texte "Multi sunt vocati, pauci vero electi" ', *RThom* 52 (1952), 569–85.

156. Meyer, 'Many are Called', 90, points to Matt. 13.8, 32b; 22.10; Mark 4.8, 32; Luke 13.19; 14.23b; 18.8; to this list we might add Matt. 8.11–12 (par Luke 13.28–29).
157. Cf. Num. 26.52–56.
158. Cf. Num. 13.18; Deut. 28.38; 1 Sam. 14.6; 2 Chron. 14.11 (LXX 14.10); Jer. 42.2 (49.2); Hag. 1.6, 9; 1 Macc. 3.18.
159. In addition to 7.13–14 and 22.14, cf. 9.37; 25.21, 23; elsewhere ὀλίγος appears only at 15.34. Meyer, however, thinks that both at 7.13–14 and at 25.21, 23, we have further examples of the semitising idiom ('Many are Called', 95 n. 14).
160. Ibid., 91.
161. Ibid., 96. Cf., e.g., F. Manns, 'Une tradition rabbinique réinterprétée dans l'évangile de Mt 22,1–10 et en Rm 11,30–32', *Anton* 63 (1988), 424.
162. Lambrecht, *Treasure*, 135.
163. See the summary of his argument at pp. 26–8 above; Kretzer, *Herrschaft*, 150, also finds a neat progression in the trilogy and also stresses the role Israel plays as an example, warning the church. Not surprisingly, the strengths and weaknesses of his reading nearly parallel Schweizer's.

6 The trilogy in redaction-critical perspective

1. Jülicher, *Die Gleichnisreden*, 385: 'das echte Wort des echten Jesus ist . . .' So also, e.g., Kilpatrick, *Origins*, 30; N. Perrin, *Rediscovering the Teaching of Jesus* (London: SCM, 1967), 118–19; Bultmann, *History*, 177; H. Weder, *Die Gleichnisse Jesu als Mataphern* (Göttingen: Vandenhoeck & Ruprecht, 1978), 230–3; Luz, *Matthäus*, III:207–08.
2. Jeremias, *Parables*, 63.
3. Van Tilborg, *Jewish Leaders*, 47–63; see our earlier discussion in ch. 2, pp. 26, 39–46.
4. H. Merkel, 'Das Gleichnis von den "ungleichen Söhnen" [Matth. xxi.28–32]', *NTS* 20 (1974), 254–61; Gundry, *Matthew*, 422–4; so also Goulder, *Midrash*, 322 n. 27; 414–15; For Davies and Allison, *Matthew*, III:165, '[a] redactional origin is possible'.
5. Of the many scholars who conclude that a Q saying stands behind Matt. 21.32 and Luke 7.29–30, see, e.g.: Strecker, *Der Weg*, 153 n. 1; Van Tilborg, *Jewish Leaders*, 52–3; C. Tuckett, *The Revival of the Griesbach Hypothesis* (Cambridge University Press, 1983), 148–50; *Q and History*, 116 n. 33; Lambrecht, *Treasure*, 95–7; D. Catchpole, *The Quest for Q* (Edinburgh: T. & T. Clark, 1993), 66 n. 28.

    Others, however, remain sceptical: cf., e.g., Harnack, *Sayings*, 118; T. W. Manson, *The Sayings of Jesus* (London: SCM, 1937; reprint, 1949), 70; P. Hoffmann, *Studien Zur Theologie der Logienquelle* (Münster: Aschendorff, 1972), 194–5; Weder, *Gleichnisse*, 231 n. 106; J. D. Crossan, *In Fragments: The Aphorisms of Jesus* (New York: Harper and Row, 1983), 330–45; J. Fitzmyer, *Luke I–IX* (AB 28; New York: Doubleday, 1981), 671; M. Sato, *Q und Prophetie: Studien zur Gattungs-und Traditionsgeschichte der Quelle Q* (Tübingen: Mohr, 1988), 20; D. Bock, *Luke*, vol. I, *1:1–9:50* (Grand Rapids: Baker, 1994), 659.

6. As critical appraisals of studies in Matthean vocabulary point out, statistical analyses may easily become servants of favoured hypotheses. See P. Luomanen, *Entering the Kingdom of Heaven: A Study on the Structure of Matthew's View of Salvation* (Tübingen: Mohr, 1998), 63–6, and especially I. Jones, *Matthean Parables*, 7–31, for important critiques of earlier studies in Matthean vocabulary.

7. See the discussion above, at p. 40.

8. Similarly, e.g., Hill, *Matthew*, 297; Schweizer, *Matthew*, 410.

9. 3×: Matt. [+] Mark; 1× Matt. [+] Luke; 31× Matt. diff Mark; 3–6× Matt. diff Luke; 2× Matt. < Mark; 0× Matt. < Luke.

10. Nevertheless Jones, *Matthean Parables*, 294–6 n. 48, 391, classifies προσ-ελθών as traditional, perhaps because of the syntactical patterns he discusses – here participle, dative noun or pronoun, verb: 19.16 (diff Mark); 21.28, 30 (No par); 26.49 (par Mark 14.45); 27.58 (diff Mark; par Luke 23.52). The pattern is not especially common, but of the seven Synoptic occurrences of this construction, five stand in Matthew and only one (26.49) is demonstrably traditional. At Matt. 19.16 and 27.58, the entire construction is absent from the Marcan parallel, and at 26.49 Mark's λέγει becomes εἶπεν in accord with the typical Matthean pattern – a pattern which appears twice in our parable (21.28, 30). Part of our disagreement seems to be terminological. Jones envisions an historical situation in which the circulation of oral traditions left clear marks upon the Synoptic tradition as evidenced by the common patterns that may be detected there (*Matthean Parables*, 7–16; cf. L. Hartman, *Testimonium Linguae: Participial Constructions in the Synoptic Gospels* (ConBNT 19; Lund: Gleerup, 1963), 28–56). On his view, discussions of redactional insertions or alterations need to take the history of the pre-Synoptic tradition seriously. An evangelist may merely prefer one variant of the tradition over another. Thus, Matthean departures from Mark, e.g., could be *traditional* (i.e., not *redactional*) departures. The issues here are complex. I do not want to deny either the influence of the oral tradition on the Synoptics in general or Matthew's use of other traditions (oral or written) in his final redaction of the Gospel. Nevertheless, I am happy to refer to Matthean modifications of Mark as redactional, even if that happens under the influence of other *traditions* (which are extremely difficult to isolate), since those editorial modifications presumably reflect the *preference* of the evangelist.

11.

Construction	Matt.	Mark	Luke	Total
1: ἀποκριθεὶς δὲ ὁ Ἰησοῦς εἶπεν	7	—	3	10
1a: καὶ ἀποκριθεὶς ὁ Ἰησοῦς εἶπεν	3	2	6	11
1b: ἀποκριθεὶς ὁ Ἰησοῦς εἶπεν	1	—	—	1
1c: τότε ἀποκριθεὶς ὁ Ἰησοῦς εἶπεν	1	—	—	1
2: ὁ δὲ ἀποκριθεὶς εἶπεν	19	2	6	27
2a: καὶ ἀποκριθεὶς εἶπεν	1	1	4	6
2b: ἀποκριθεὶς εἶπεν	—	—	1	1
3: ἀποκριθεὶς δὲ . . . εἶπεν (with subject specified + not ὁ Ἰησοῦς)	9	—	6	15
3a: καὶ ἀποκριθεὶς . . . εἶπεν (with subject specified + not ὁ Ἰησοῦς)	2	—	4	6

(*cont.*)

Construction	Matt.	Mark	Luke	Total
3b: τότε ἀποκριθεὶς . . . εἶπεν (with subject specified + not ὁ Ἰησοῦς)	1	—	—	1
3c: ἀποκριθεὶς . . . εἶπεν (with subject specified + not ὁ Ἰησοῦς)	—	—	1	1
4: ὁ δὲ ἀποκριθείς + present/imperfect/future of λέγω subject either specified or unspecified	1	11	6	18
5: ἀποκρίνομαι in a finite form	9	14	9	32
6: ἀποκρίνομαι in infinitive form	1	—	—	1
TOTAL	55	30	46	131

12. Matt. 19× = 1×: Matt. par Mark; 5–6×: No par; 1×: Matt. [+] Mark; 10×: Matt. diff Mark; 1–2×: Matt. diff Luke; 1×: Matt. < Mark.
13. θέλημα (Matt. 6×; Mark 1×; Luke 4×); πατρός (Matt. 64×; Mark 18×; Luke 56×). On the other hand, Matthew's use of πατήρ for God is distinctive: Matt. 46×; Mark 4×; Luke 17× + 3×; John 118× (W. Schenk, *Die Sprache des Matthäus* (Göttingen: Vandenhoeck & Ruprecht, 1987), 288).
14. 1×: No par (21.31)
    1×: Matt. diff Mark (12.50)
    2×: Matt. diff Luke (7.21; 18.14).
    Elsewhere in the NT, we meet the phrase only at John 6.40 (though Gal. 1.4 is similar).
15. 6.10 = Matt. diff Luke; 26.42 = Matt. diff Mark.
16. Asyndetic use of λέγει/ουσιν in the historical present

    Matt.: 28×
    6×: No par (13.51; 17.25; 20.7 (2×); 21.31 (2×))
    3×: Matt. [+] Mark (19.10, 18; 26.25)
    18×: Matt. diff Mark (9.29; 16.15; 19.7, 8, 20; 20.21, 22, 23, 33; 21.41, 42; 22.21, 42, 43; 26.35, 64; 27.22 (2×))
    1×: Matt. diff Luke (18.22)
    1×: Matt. < Mark
    0–1×: Matt. < Luke

    Mark: 1×
    1×: Mark [+] Matt. (9.19)

    Luke: 2×
    1–2×: No par (16.7; 19.22(?))
    0–1×: Luke diff Matt. (19.22(?))

17. λέγει αὐτῷ/οῖς ὁ Ἰησοῦς: Matt. 12×; Mark 2×; Luke 0×. Ἰησοῦς itself occurs 150× in Matt., as compared to 80× in Mark, and 88× in Luke.
18. δικαιοσύνη – NT: 92×

    Matt. 7×:
    1–2×: No par (6.1; 21.32(?))

1×: Matt. [+] Mark (3.15)
2×: Matt. [+] Luke (5.10, 20)
2–3×: Matt. diff Luke (5.6; 6.33; 21.32(?))

Mark: 0×

Luke: 1×

1×: No par (1.75).

19. On the use of δικαιοσύνη in Matthew's narrative, see above pp. 102–5.
20. For Jones, *Matthean Parables*, 392, ὁδὸς δικαιοσύνης is traditional.
21. δύο occurs more frequently in Matthew than in either Mark or Luke (40×; Mark 17×; Luke 26–29× (text?)) and in some instances its presence seems more than incidental. But not only is the word relatively common in both Mark and Luke; if the story of The *Two* Sons is traditional, then probably so too is δύο (cf. Luke 15.11).
22. The asterisk here (and throughout) signals the fact that a *variant* form of the same word or construction appears in the parallel text.
23. This motif was already present in the Marcan account of The Tenants (12.2–8) but is not pronounced in the Lucan parable of The Great Supper, although there too the invited guests are given advance notice prior to their invitation on the day of the feast (14.16–17).
24. See above ch. 2, pp. 40–1.
25. Interestingly, as a title for John, Ἰωάννης ὁ βαπτιστής is most common in Matt. (7×; Mark 2×; Luke 3×).
26. Held, 'Miracle Stories', 236; cf. Matt. 18.1–5; 19.3–9, 16–22, 27–30; 22.42–46; and their Marcan parallels.
27. We have further evidence, then, that the echoes noted above – namely, λέγουσιν, λέγει αὐτοῖς ὁ Ἰησοῦς, λέγω ὑμῖν ὅτι – betray the hand of the evangelist. On ἡ βασιλεία τοῦ θεοῦ, which many (e.g., Schweizer, *Matthew*, 410; Luz, *Matthäus*, III:211) ascribe to pre-Matthean tradition, see our discussion of 21.43 (p. 148).
28. We have seen evidence of Matthew's hand at several points in Matt. 21.32. On the distinctively Lucan features, see, e.g., Hoffmann, *Studien*, 194–5; Tuckett, *Revival*, 148–50.
29. Matt. 11.2–6, cf. Luke 7.18–23; Matt. 11.7–11, cf. Luke 7.24–28; Matt. 11.12–15, cf. Luke 16.16; Matt. 21.31b–32, cf. Luke 7.29–30 (?); Matt. 11.16–19, cf. Luke 7.31–35.
30. Tuckett, *Revival*, 150, suggests that αἱ πόρναι may also stem from the Q saying, the Lucan 'all the people' being redactional; similarly Gundry, *Matthew*, 423.
31. Similarly Jones, *Matthean Parables*, 393–6.
32. Snodgrass, *Wicked Tenants*; cf. X. Léon-Dufour, 'La parabole des vignerons homicides', in *Études d'évangile* (Paris: Seuil, 1965), 303–44; J. A. T. Robinson, 'The Parable of the Wicked Husbandmen: a Test of Synoptic Relationships', *NTS* 21 (1975), 443–61; J. B. Orchard, 'J. A. T. Robinson and The Synoptic Problem', *NTS* 22 (1976), 346–52.
33. Similarly, e.g., W. Radl, 'Zur Struktur der eschatologischen Gleichnisse Jesu', *TTZ* 91 (1983), 123; but see also Linnemann, *Parables*, 166–7; Sato, *Q und Prophetie*, 22.

34. So, e.g., Kilpatrick, *Origins*, 30; Trilling, 'Zur Überlieferungsgeschichte', 263; R. Swaeles, 'L'orientation ecclésiastique de la parabole du festin nuptial en Mt 22, 1–14', *ETL* 36 (1960), 663–71; S. Pedersen, 'Zum Problem der vaticinia ex eventu. (Eine Analyse von Mt. 21,33–46 par.; 22,1–10 par.)', *ST* 19 (1965), 169; S. Schulz, *Die Spruchquelle der Evangelisten* (Zürich: Theologischer, 1972), 398; J. Fitzmyer, *Luke X–XXIV* (AB28A; New York: Doubleday, 1985), 1050–2; J. Kloppenborg, *The Formation of Q* (Philadephia: Fortress, 1987), 229–30.
35. Harnack, *Sayings*, 120.
36. So, e.g., Zahn, *Matthäus*, 626; A. Plummer, *A Critical and Exegetical Commentary on the Gospel According to S. Luke* (4th edn, Edinburgh: T. & T. Clark, 1901; reprint, 1905), 359–60; J. Hawkins 'Probabilities as to the So-Called Double Tradition of St. Matthew and St. Luke', in *Oxford Studies in the Synoptic Problem* (ed. W. Sanday, 96–138. Oxford: Clarendon, 1911), 127; H. Palmer, 'Just Married, Cannot Come', *NovT* 18 (1976), 241–57; C. Blomberg, 'When is a Parallel Really a Parallel? A Test Case: The Lucan Parables', *WTJ* 46 (1984), 78–103.
37. So, e.g., B. H. Streeter, *The Four Gospels* (London: Macmillan, 1936), 243–4; Dodd, *Parables*, 12; E. Linnemann, 'Überlegungen zur Parabel vom großen Abendmahl, Lc 14.15–24 / Mt 22.1–14', *ZNW* 51 (1960), 253–4; Luz, *Matthäus*, III:232–3; Davies and Allison, *Matthew*, III:194 ('tentatively').
38. Blomberg, 'Lucan Parables', 78–103.
39. Cf., e.g, Matt. 24.29–31 par Luke 21.25–28.
40. So, e.g., tentatively Derrett, 'Parable', 126–7; Blomberg, 'Lucan Parables', 90.
41. So, e.g., Allen, *Matthew*, 235; Dodd, *Parables*, 122; J. D. Crossan, 'Parable and Example in the Teaching of Jesus', *NTS* 18 (1972), 302 n. 3; Schweizer, 'Auf W Trillings Spuren', 147.
42. So, e.g., Bacon, 'Two Parables', 345; Barth, 'Law', 59 n. 9; Luz, *Matthäus*, III:234–5; Davies and Allison, *Matthew*, III:194–5.
43. The following statistics are taken from Schenk, *Sprache*: ἐκεῖ: Matt. 28×; Mark 11×; Luke 16×; ἀνάκειμαι: Matt. 5×; Mark 3×; Luke 1×; ἔνδυμα: Matt. 7x; Mark 0×; Luke 1× (nowhere else in the NT); ἑταῖρε: Matt. 3× (nowhere else in the NT); τότε: Matt. 90×; Mark 6×; Luke 4×; σκότος: Matt. 7×; Mark 1×; Luke 4×; ἐκβάλλ(ω) εἰς τὸ σκότος τὸ ἐξώτερον: Matt. 3×; Mark 0×; Luke 0×; ἐκεῖ ἔσται ὁ κλαυθμὸς καὶ ὁ βρυγμὸς τῶν ὀδόντων: Matt. 6×; Mark 0×; Luke 1×.
44. See Matt. 8.12; 24.51; 25.30.
45. For many the tension that exists in a story in which a king who gathers from the streets all who will come to his feast, good or bad, and then evicts the one who fails to come properly attired, can be most easily accounted for if the evangelist has joined two separate parables; so, e.g., Hagner, *Matthew 14–28*, 631.
46. Trilling, 'Zur Überlieferungsgeschichte', 254–8.
47. R. Dillon, 'Towards a Tradition-history of the Parables of the True Israel (Matthew 21:33–22:14)', *Bib* 47 (1966), 40. Hasler, 'Die Hochzeit', 25–35, also stressed the unevenness of the parable, and found evidence of a threefold stratification: ecclesiological, salvation–historical and polemical.

48. See p. 100 above.
49. Perhaps we should also note that what the vineyard of God's people did produce was ἀνομία (Isa. 5.7). The question of 21.31a recalls 7.21–23. There we find two groups of people – those who do the will of the Father and so enter the kingdom and those who do ἀνομία and so are excluded! Cf. Kretzer, *Herrschaft*, 157.
50. But cf. 21.15.
51. Matt. 21.23 (diff Mark); 26.3 (diff Mark); 26.47 (diff Mark); 27.1 (diff Mark). But note also Luke 22.66: τὸ πρεσβυτέριον τοῦ λαοῦ.
52. See, e.g., Stanton, *New People*, 331–2; Gundry, *Matthew*, 425.
53. So, e.g., McNeile, *Matthew*, 302.
54. See esp. W. Telford, *The Barren Temple and the Withered Tree* (JSNTSup 1; Sheffield: JSOT, 1980).
55. So Gnilka, *Das Matthäusevangelium*, II:212–13; Hagner, *Matthew 14–28*, 605–7; Telford, *Barren Temple*, 69–94, concludes that, having removed nearly all the markers that suggest the story is to be understood symbolically, Matthew turns the pericope into a normal miracle story that functions now as a paradigm for Christian faith and prayer. But the Matthean pericope seems symbolic in its own right, pointing forward to this parable where, by the end, the symbolism is lifted. See further Charette, *Recompense*, 133–4.
56. So Gundry, *Matthew*, 426.
57. Snodgrass, *Wicked Tenants*, 61, finds evidence of Matthean priority here: not only is the parable more effective if the hearers pronounce their own judgement – a parable ending with a rhetorical question answered by the person who asked it is a singular phenomenon; but 'effective rhetoric' is scarcely an index of priority, and we have already noted Matthew's penchant for forming or enlarging conversations (cf. Held, 'Miracle Stories', 236).
58. Cf. 15.14; 23.16, 17, 19, 24, 26.
59. Cf. the discussion of Matt. 21.41 at pp. 113–16.
60.

	Matt.	Mark	Luke
ὅστις	29×	4–5×	21×
ἀποδίδωμι	18×	1×	8×
καρπός	19×	5×	12×
καιρός	10×	5×	13×

61. See the more complete discussion at pp. 115–16.
62. λέγει αὐτοῖς ὁ Ἰησοῦς echoes 21.31 where, as here, it follows the (self-) indictment pronounced by the Jewish leaders. The polemical question that Jesus asks his adversaries in Mark follows in only slightly modified fashion in Matthew. The emphatic οὐδέποτε (cf. 21.16) replaces Mark's οὐδέ, and Mark's τὴν γραφὴν ταύτην gives way to Matthew's ἐν ταῖς γραφαῖς.
63. Against Allen, *Matthew*, 231–2, and M. Pamment, 'The Kingdom of Heaven in the First Gospel', *NTS* 27 (1981), 211–32, no sharp distinction should be drawn between *kingdom of heaven* and *kingdom of God* in Matthew generally, nor here in 21.43; see Davies and Allison, *Matthew*, I:390–1.

64. So, e.g., Jeremias, *Parables*, 60 n. 53; Snodgrass, *Wicked Tenants*, 66; Jones, *Matthean Parables*, 388. Sabourin, *Matthew*, 772, finds the work of a later redactor here.
65. See esp. Trilling, *Das Wahre Israel*, 58.
66. Apart from 21.43 and the textually uncertain 6.33 (diff Luke) and 19.24 (par Mark), ἡ βασιλεία τοῦ θεοῦ appears in Matthew only at 12.28 (par Luke) and 21.31 (No par).
67. Trilling, *Das Wahre Israel*, 59; cf. 4.23 (diff Mark); 8.12 (diff Luke); 9.35 (diff Luke); 12.28 (par Luke); 13.19 (diff Mark); 13.38 (No par); 13.43 (No par); 21.31 (No par); 21.43 ([+] Mark); 24.14 (diff Mark); 25.34 (No par); 26.29 (diff Mark).
68. So, e.g., Lambrecht, *Treasure*, 119–20; Gundry, *Matthew*, 429–30. On balance, however, I think it more likely that 21.43 influenced 21.31.
69. The aorist participle of ἀκούω commonly links narrative in each of the three Synoptic Gospels, but especially in Matthew where it functions this way in 21 instances, only five of which have parallels in Mark (4×) or Luke (1×).
70. Cf. our earlier discussion at p. 118.
71. Cf., e.g., τοὺς δούλους αὐτοῦ . . . ἀπέκτειναν (22.6, cf. 21.34); ἀπόλλυμι (22.7, cf. 21.41); ἐκεῖνος (22.7, cf. 21.40).
72. On the possible allusion to Deut. 20.5–7 and 24.5 in Luke, see Derrett, 'Parable', 126–55; P. Ballard, 'Reasons for Refusing the Great Supper', *JTS* 23 (1972), 341–50; and, for a more cautious judgement, Palmer, 'Just Married'. In *Gos. Thom.* 64, the excuses appear in expanded form and with a notable commercial bent, and the concluding pronouncement follows suit: 'Businessmen and merchants will not enter the Places of My Father.'
73. Gundry, *Matthew*, 435.
74. Similarly Hagner, *Matthew 14–28*, 627. Again the evangelist supplies links, both verbal and syntactical, to the earlier parables in the triad: ἀπέρχομαι: 22.5, cf. 21.29, 30; μέν . . . δέ . . . δέ: 22.5, cf. 21.35. Both the verb and the construction are common in Matthew – ἀπέρχομαι: Matt. 35×; Mark 22×; Luke 19× + 6×; John 21×; μέν . . . δέ: Matt. 19×; Mark 3×; Luke 8× (Schenk, *Sprache*, 165, 254).
75. Van Tilborg, *Jewish Leaders*, 61, insists that the insertion of vv. 6–7 must come from the hand of a particularly clumsy interpolator, a different hand than is responsible for the redaction of vv. 3–5. But what he regards as clumsy interpolation might equally well be judged a carefully calculated insertion from the hand of an evangelist more concerned with the theological point to be scored than with maintaining the boundaries of a realistic narrative.
76. Note the inferential οὖν at 22.9; the word is common in Matthew: Matt. 57×; Mark 5×; Luke 31× + 62×; John 194× (Schenk, *Sprache*, 381).
77. The verse is transitional and, at several points, the vocabulary is typically Matthean: συνάγω: Matt. 24×; Mark 5×; Luke 6× + 11×; John 7; πονηρός: Matt. 26×; Mark 2×; Luke 13× + 8×; John 3×; πονηρός vs. ἀγαθός: Matt. 10×; Mark 0×; Luke 4×; ἀνακείμαι: Matt. 5×; Mark 2×; Luke 2× + 0×; John 4× (Schenk, *Sprache*, 55; 161; 179).
78. Elsewhere in Matthew, ἄνθρωπος is followed by a noun that stands in apposition to it at 9.32 (Matt. diff Luke); 11.19 (Matt. par Luke); 13.28 (No par; but the word order is switched: ἐχθρὸς ἄνθρωπος); 13.45 (No par); 13.52 (ἀνθρώπῳ οἰκοδεσπότῃ; No par); 18.23 (No par); 20.1 (ἀνθρώπῳ

οἰκοδεσπότῃ; No par); 22.2 (Matt. diff Luke; or No par). By contrast, this construction never appears in Mark and in Luke only at 7.34 (par Matt. 11.19).

Seven of the 12 NT occurrences of οἰκοδεσπότης are found in Matthew: 10.25; 13.27, 52; 20.1, 11; 21.33; 24.43. Five times the word appears in parables, four times in parables that are unique to this Gospel (13.27, 52; 20.1, 11). In three of these parables (four uses of the word: 13.27; 20.1, 11; 21.33), the householder in the metaphor represents God. See also Robinson, 'Wicked Husbandmen', 445; Lambrecht, *Treasure*, 118; and, for a different evaluation, Snodgrass, *Wicked Tenants*, 46 n. 8.

ὅστις too is common in Matthew (29×; Mark 4/5×; Luke 21×). Only once does Matthew's use of ὅστις demonstrably stem from either the Marcan or the Q tradition (16.28, cf. Mark 9.1). Cf. the similar Matthean introductions to the parables at 13.52; 20.1; 22.2; 25.1.

79. Cf. pp. 218–19 n. 74.
80. Similarly Gundry, *Matthew*, 425.
81. Gundry, *Matthew*, 426, thinks the Matthean redaction implies that the entire harvest belongs to the householder.
82. Matthew changes Mark's ἔσχατον to ὕστερον.
83. Snodgrass, *Wicked Tenants*, 59. Earlier Robinson, 'Wicked Husbandmen', 447, concluded: 'Of all the versions Mark here appears to be the *most* allegorical and Matthew the least!' Robinson accepted the general priority of Mark's version of the parable, but this lack of Christological development in Matthew prompted him to argue for a *Grundschrift* or Ur-Gospel that lies behind them all. More recently Milavec, 'Identity', 33, springing off Robinson's observations, finds in *Matthew's* redaction evidence that *Mark* never intended to 'allegorize Jesus as The Son'. Jones, *Matthean Parables*, 382, reaches still another conclusion – the omission of ἀγαπητός 'is pre-Matthean, perhaps as the sentence was re-ordered when *The Tenants* and *The Two Sons* were linked.'
84. For several reasons Matthew's replacement of ἔσχατος seems less significant. First, the argument that ὕστερος is more primitive assumes that Mark intends the reader to find eschatological overtones in his use of ἔσχατος. These overtones seem natural to later readers but the word is found seventeen times in the Synoptic tradition and, elsewhere, always *without* obvious eschatological overtones. At 22.27 (cf. Mark 12.22), Matthew will once again replace Mark's ἔσχατος with ὕστερος. There Mark's ἔσχατος, like Matthew's ὕστερος, simply indicates that the woman, having outlived the seven brothers whom the Sadducees envision, was the last to die.

Nor, if one does conclude that Mark's ἔσχατος was intended to offer a Christological hint, does it necessarily follow that Matthew's account is prior. Of the twelve occurrences of ὕστερος in the NT, nine are found in the Synoptics, seven in Matthew. Its comparative prominence in Matthew and the fact that elsewhere Matthew imports the word into Marcan contexts (22.7; 26.60; cf. 4.2 where, in a Q context, only Matthew uses ὕστερος) suggests that Matthew's redaction here may simply reflect his verbal preference. It may also be influenced by 21.29, 32, where the word also appears, thus forming another of the verbal echoes designed to tie the parables together (similarly Gundry, *Matthew*, 427; Jones, *Matthean Parables*, 382–3). Finally, one should note that, like Mark, Luke describes the son as ἀγαπητός, but his version is so structured that one reads neither that the son was sent ἔσχατος or ὕστερος. Is his version also prior to Mark's? Probably the significance of Matthew's replacement of ἔσχατος has been overstated.

85. See Matt. 3.17; 12.18; 17.5; Mark 1.11; 9.7; 12.6; Luke 3.22; 20.13.

86. The question of the son's identity in the Jesuanic parable is highly disputed. W. Kümmel, 'Das Gleichnis von den bösen Weingärtnern', in *Heilsgeschehen und Geschichte* (Marburg: Elwert, 1965), 215–17, is representative of those who find in the allegorical reference to the son evidence that the early church composed the parable; similarly U. Mell, *Die 'anderen' Winzer: Eine exegetische Studie zur Vollmacht Jesu Christi nach Markus 11,27–12,34* (Tübingen: Mohr, 1994), 114–15. By contrast J. Blank, 'Die Sendung des Sohnes: Zur christologischen Bedeutung des Gleichnisses von den bösen Winzern Mk 12,1–12', in *Neues Testament und Kirche* (ed. J. Gnilka, 11–41, Freiburg: Herder, 1974), who also attributes the parable to the post-Easter community, thinks that the 'Son-designation' may well go back to Jesus. A. Gray, 'The Parable of the Wicked Husbandmen', *HibJ* 19 (1920–1), 42–52, argued that the Baptist was the son in the parable Jesus told; for more recent defences of this position, see M. Lowe, 'From Parable of the Vineyard to Pre-Synoptic Source', *NTS* 28 (1982), 257–63, and D. Stern, 'Jesus' Parables from the Perspective of Rabbinic Literature: The Example of the Wicked Husbandmen', in *Parable and Story in Judaism and Christianity* (ed. C. Thoma and M. Wyschogrod, 42–80, Mahwah: Paulist, 1989), 58–68. J. C. O'Neill, 'The Source of the Parables of the Bridegroom and the Wicked Husbandmen', *JTS* 39 (1988), 485–9, suggests the opposite – that the son in the story was indeed Jesus, but that it was the Baptist who told the story. His intent was to warn the Jewish leaders not to follow through with their plan to kill Jesus. R. Aus, *The Wicked Tenants and Gethsemane. Isaiah in the Wicked Tenants' Vineyard, and Moses and the High Priest in Gethsemane: Judaic Traditions in Mark 12: 1–9 and 14: 32–42* (Atlanta: Scholars Press, 1996), 57, thinks that Jesus intended an allusion to Isaiah ('LXX Isa 5:1 has ἠγαπημένος twice'), but Jesus *may* have sensed parallels between the prophet's conflict with Israel's leaders and his own. For Hengel, 'Das Gleichnis von den Weingärtnern Mc. 12, 1–12 im Lichte der Zenon Papyri und der rabbinischen Gleichnisse', *ZNW* 59 (1968), 30–1, 37–8, as for Dodd, *Parables*, 129–31, the son is not a component of an elaborate theological allegory; his appearance is instead required by the inner logic of the story. Nevertheless, there is a correspondence between the son in the parable and Jesus. Even as the tenants' murder of the vineyard owner's son elicited the owner's retaliation, so the Jewish leaders' contemplated murder of Jesus would evoke divine judgement. B. Van Iersel, 'Das Gleichnis von den bösen Winzern', in *'Der Sohn' in der synoptischen Jesusworten* (Leiden: Brill, 1968), 144, thinks that, although the story focuses upon the tenants, the son is granted a secondary role, and that Jesus' reference to the son does function as a self-designation – 'wenn auch indirekt und äusserst diskret'. Charlesworth, 'Jesus as "Son" and the Righteous Teacher as "Gardener"', in *Jesus and the Dead Sea Scrolls* (ed. J. H. Charlesworth, 140–75, New York: Doubleday, 1992) is representative of those who maintain that the parable is authentic and testifies to Jesus' own self-understanding – he was God's son (cf. Ps. 2). Gundry, *Matthew*, 427, is bolder: the parable bears witness to

'Jesus' consciousness of unique divine sonship'. J. and R. Newell, 'The Parable of the Wicked Tenants', *NovT* 14 (1972), 236, posit a *Sitz im Leben* in which Jesus' parable challenges the violence encouraged by the Zealots in their attempt to regain Israel's land. On this reading, the son is simply 'the foreign son of a foreign landowner'. For more recent developments of the suggestion that the parable focuses upon the tenants' legitimate claims to the land, see Hester, 'Socio-Rhetorical Criticism'; Herzog, *Subversive Speech*, 98–113; E. Horne, 'The Parable of the Tenants as Indictment', *JSNT* 71 (1998), 111–16. Both T. Schramm, *Der Markus-Stoff bei Lukas* (SNTSMS 14; Cambridge University Press, 1971), 168 n. 2, and A. Milavec (discussing the Marcan version of the parable), 'A Fresh Analysis of the Parable of the Wicked Husbandmen in the Light of Jewish–Christian Dialogue', in *Parables and Story in Judaism and Christianity* (ed. Clemens Thoma and Michael Wyschogrod, 81–117, New York: Paulist, 1989), 99–105; 'Identity', 32–3, have argued that the son in the parable had no specific metaphorical reference.

87. Cf. Gundry, *Matthew*, 427: 'Then he replaces "beloved" with "his" for a parallel with the distinctive phrase "his slaves" in vv 34 and 35.'

88. Similarly Trilling, *Das Wahre Israel*, 56–7.

89. ὁ υἱὸς αὐτοῦ finds an echo at 22.2. It is at least possible that this has also influenced Matthew's redaction here. That the evangelist intended to create another link between the parables by introducing the son into the second story seems likely. That he preferred not to describe this son as ἀγαπητός in both instances seems reasonable.

90. Many in the church's history have read this parable as if this were its *primary* intent. So, e.g., Chrysostom, *Homilies on the Gospel of Saint Matthew* 67.2 (*NPNF*[1] 10:411); Jerome, *Comm. in Matth.* 21.28 (PL 26.155–6); among modern exegetes, see J. Meier, *The Vision of Matthew: Christ, Church, and Morality in the First Gospel* (New York: Paulist, 1979), 149–50; K. Clark, 'The Gentile Bias in Matthew', in *The Gentile Bias and Other Essays* (Leiden: Brill, 1980), 2; J. Drury, *The Parables in the Gospels: History and Allegory* (London: SPCK, 1985), 96; cf. also Hummel, *Die Auseinandersetzung*, 25.

91. Similar observations could be made about vocabulary: where Mark has ὑπολήνιον, and Isaiah προλήνιον, Matthew substitutes ληνόν. ληνός (winepress) is found only five times in the NT – here and four times in John's Apocalypse (14.19, 20 (2×); 19.15). Mark's ὑπολήνιον (wine-trough) occurs only here. See further Weren, 'The Use of Isaiah 5,1–7', 18–21.

92. Cf. our earlier discussion at pp. 110–11 above.

93. Snodgrass suggests that the complexity of Mark 12.5b is more easily explained if Mark found the two Matthean triads (the first three servants sent; the two groups of servants followed by the son) too bulky and so modified them, and adds: 'The assumption of Markan priority leaves unexplained the complexity of Mark 12,5b, which is obviously cumbersome and an uncommon mode of progression' (*Wicked Tenants*, 58). If, however, Mark intended to remove the 'bulk' from this part of the (Matthean) narrative, then he failed! On the other hand, if the Marcan story is prior, and if Mark 12.5b is as awkward as Snodgrass concludes, then it will surprise no one that Matthew (and Luke) has improved upon the Marcan style here.

94. The two variant readings are both harmonisations. Θ reproduces Mark's ἀπέκτειναν αὐτὸν καὶ ἐξέβαλον ἔξω τοῦ ἀμπελῶνος; D, it, et al., reproduce

the variant reading in Mark that, notably, is also read by D: αὐτὸν ἀπέκτειναν καὶ ἐξέβαλον ἔξω τοῦ ἀμπελῶνος.

95. Snodgrass, *Wicked Tenants*, 60, objects to this conclusion because, unlike John (19.17, 20) and the author of Hebrews (13.12f.), neither Matthew nor Luke shows interest in, or even awareness of, Jesus' death outside of the city and because this interpretation requires the reader to identify the vineyard as Jerusalem in spite of the fact that there are no other hints of such an allusion and, by 21.43, the vineyard is explicitly identified as the kingdom (similarly Milavec, 'Identity', 33). Instead, he suggests that Mark's redaction may be designed to underline the contempt with which the tenants treated the son by highlighting the desecration of the corpse.

I think it more likely, however, that Matthew knew that Jesus was crucified outside Jerusalem. Mark 15.20b reads: 'And they led him out (ἐξάγουσιν) to crucify him.' There is some ambiguity here since Mark may only intend to describe their departure from the praetorium (cf. 15.16). But v. 21 helps remove this ambiguity: 'They compelled a passer-by, *who was coming in from the country* (ἐρχόμενον ἀπ' ἀγροῦ) to carry his cross; it was Simon of Cyrene.' Surely this description of Simon is more natural if the soldiers were leading Jesus out of the city and not merely from the praetorium. The same ambiguity exists in Matthew. Matthew replaces Mark's ἐξάγουσιν with ἀπήγαγον – they led him away (27.31, cf. Mark 15.20). He then, however, inserts Ἐξερχόμενοι δὲ εὗρον ἄνθρωπον . . . If Matthew is following the Marcan text here, most probably he too thinks of the procession's exit from Jerusalem. Furthermore, all four evangelists agree that Jesus was crucified at the place called Golgotha (Matt. 27.33; Mark 15.22; Luke 23.33; John 19.17), which was located outside of the city walls. Hebrews and John confirm that, at least in some early Christian circles, the knowledge of Jesus' death outside of the city was passed on and granted significance. All of this suggests that the evangelists would all have been aware of the fact that Jesus was crucified outside of the city.

With regard to Snodgrass's second objection, one need not *identify* the vineyard as Jerusalem in order to see allusion to Jesus' crucifixion outside of the city here in v. 39. The degree of continuity between symbol and referent, as well as consistency in the manner in which a symbol is used, will vary from parable to parable and within a single parable (cf. Jones, *Matthean Parables*, 374, who speaks of an 'explanatory web of allusions'). Few would want to argue that throughout the parable the vineyard represents the kingdom of God, but by vv. 41 and 43, this is precisely what it represents. A recognition of the fluid nature of metaphorical language removes the sting from this second objection.

96. G. Stanton, *New People*, 152, has argued that Matthew's distinctive salvation–historical concerns are also evident in 21.42, suggesting that in Matthew the stone that the builders rejected points no longer allegorically to Jesus but instead to the ἔθνος of 21.43. In support of this exegesis, Stanton first notes the two significant alterations that Matthew makes at v. 45. There Matthew introduces the Pharisees and they recognise that the parable is *about* them (περὶ αὐτῶν) and the chief priests – not merely against them (πρὸς αὐτούς) (i.e., the chief priests and scribes and elders [see 11.27]) as in Mark (12.12). Second, Stanton points to the following parable where, he suggests,

the second group of servants are the equivalent of 'the stone the builders rejected,' Christian prophets and ministers. Upon their rejection, the king acts swiftly and decisively, bringing judgement on Israel (22.6–7, cf. 23.34), and inviting the Gentiles to the wedding feast (22.8–10).

This interpretation is provocative, but in the end fails to convince. Stanton's reading is capable of explaining the close (διὰ τοῦτο) relationship between vv. 42 and 43 well, but not more so than a Christological reading. On both readings the inferential conclusion of v. 43 is based on the assertion of v. 42. Much the same could be said of Stanton's second observation. The redactional changes in v. 45 accord nicely with his interpretation but do not seem less suitable for a Christological reading where the parable is *about* the Pharisees and chief priests because they are the tenants who reject the Son.

More interesting is the support that Stanton finds for this exegesis in the parable that follows. However, adopting his interpretation of the second group of servants (22.4–6) does not necessarily support his understanding of the earlier parable. One might find here progression rather than repetition, so rounding out Israel's guilt. Having earlier rejected the prophets (21.28–32) and Jesus (21.33–46), they 'fill up the measure of their fathers' by their violent rejection of Jesus' followers – the prophets of the new era (22.1–10) (so also Howell, *Matthew's Inclusive Story*, 151 n. 1).

Too many obstacles remain to abandon a Christological reading of v. 42. The parable itself has prepared the reader for a Christological interpretation. The rebellion of the tenants reaches its climax in the murder of the son and *this* rebellion elicits the condemnation that v. 41 pronounces and v. 43 echoes and interprets. And if the parable itself has prepared the reader to think, in v. 42, of the rejection of the son, then so, too, has the wider narrative of the First Gospel. The escalating controversy between Jesus and the Jewish leaders that has, since the earliest stages, been part of Matthew's story, dominates the landscape in chs. 21–2 and, from there, moves quickly towards its resolution. Their rejection of Jesus dominates this part of the Gospel and prepares the reader for a Christological reading of 21.42 – he is the stone that they, the builders, rejected.

97. See the discussion at p. 148 above.
98. Cf. above ch. 4, pp. 91–5.
99. Cf. also Matt. 7.24, 26; 25.1, where the future passive form of ὁμοιόω replaces the aorist passive. D. A. Carson, 'The ὅμοιος Word-Group as Introduction to some Matthean Parables', *NTS* 31 (1985), 277–82, argues that Matthew prefers the aorist tense when emphasis falls upon what the kingdom has already become, while reserving the future tense for texts that focus on the consummation. Schenk, *Sprache*, 94; 372, offers the following statistics: ὁμοιόω: Matt. 8×; Mark 1×; Luke 3× + 1×; John 0×; passive: Matt. 7×; Mark 0×; Luke 0×; ἡ βασιλεία τῶν οὐρανῶν: Matt. 32×; nowhere else in the NT.
100. Cf. 21.33 and the notes there on both of these as markers of Matthean style.
101. εἰς τοὺς γάμους occurs 4× in the Synoptic tradition, all in Matt., and three times within this parable (elsewhere, 25.10). Cf. Schenk, *Sprache*, 114.
102. Curiously, Bultmann, *History*, 175, concludes that Matthew is responsible for this multiplication 'since it would seem to be more appropriate that a king should have more than one δοῦλος'.

103. The first guests 'were not willing to come' (καὶ οὐκ ἤθελον ἐλθεῖν); Matthew is fond of θέλω: Matt. 42×; Mark 24×; Luke 28× + 14×; John 23× (Schenk, *Sprache*, 282).

104. δεῦτε (which provides another link to The Tenants (cf. 21.38)): Matt. 6×; Mark 3×; Luke 0× + 0×; John 1× (Schenk, *Sprache*, 175).

105. The word itself occurs more frequently in Mark than Matthew: Matt. 17×; Mark 28×; Luke 3× + 5×; John 43× (Schenk, *Sprache*, 397–9). But, as Schenk notes, the use of πάλιν at the beginning of a sentence typifies Matthean style, being found 11× in this position in the Matthew, but only once each in Mark (14.61) and Luke (23.20).

106. See ch. 5, pp. 122–3 above.

107. Cf. 21.34 (par Mark 12.2), 36 (par Mark 12.4); 22.3 (cf. Luke 14.17), 4, 6, 8 (cf. Luke 14.21). Whereas in Luke the same (industrious?) servant is in view throughout, in Matthew we have here a new group of servants, the former ones having been murdered.

108. See pp. 102–5 above.

109. Cf. Kretzer, *Herrschaft*, 163, whose reflection on the similarities between Matt. 13.18 and 21.33 lead him to a similar conclusion.

110. See also I. H. Marshall, *The Gospel of Luke* (Exeter: Paternoster, 1978), 431; Davies and Allison, *Matthew*, II:394.

111. Here I am referring only to his use of ἀκούω in this pericope (Mark 4.10–12) and in the interpretation of the parable that follows (Mark 4.13–20). Mark 4.9 departs from this pattern and may indeed have influenced Matthew.

112. Of the several uses of συνίημι in this context (13.13, 14, 15 (2×), 19, 23), only 13.13 comes from traditional Marcan material.

113. Gundry, *Matthew*, 424, commenting on the Matthean redaction here, says: 'This replacement . . . stresses the necessity of hearing Jesus' teaching.'

114. The only other occurrence of the word in the Gospel. The word occurs only 4× in the Synoptic tradition, all in this parable: Mark 12.1 par Matt. 21.33, Luke. 20.9; and Matt. 21.41.

115. Similarly Kretzer, *Herrschaft*, 161.

116. See ch. 5, pp. 115–16 above.

117. Cf. F. Mussner, 'Die bösen Winzer nach Mt 21, 33–46', in *Antijudaismus im Neuen Testament?* (ed. W. P. Eckert, N. P. Levinson, and M. Stöhr, 129–34, Munich: Kaiser, 1967), 129–34, who also stresses the paraenetic function of 21.43.

7 Conclusions

1. As I have repeatedly stated, however, even such a radical reconstitution of God's people as these parables envision hardly entails the crass replacement of Israel by *Gentile* Christianity.

Appendix   The text of the parable of The Two Sons

1. The list of witnesses supplied in Table 6 follows the summary offered in NA[27]; see further Swanson, *Matthew*, 208. No extant papyrus includes 21.28–32.

2. Michaels, 'Regretful Son', 15–26; see Schulz, *Die Mitte der Schrift* (Stuttgart: Kreuz, 1976), 169, for a more recent, but also a more typical defence of reading 3.

3. Michaels 'Regretful Son', 22 (in the last clause, Michaels follows the old Latin MSS c and e: 'quod non credidistis ei.'). Cf. already Irenaeus, *Against Heresies*, 4.36.8 (*ANF* 1:518): 'The parable of the two sons also: those who are sent into the vineyard, of whom one indeed opposed his father, but afterwards repented, when repentance profited him nothing.'

4. Michaels is not the first to resort to conjecture here. Westcott and Hort, *The New Testament in the Original Greek*; reprint, vol. I, London: Macmillan, 1909, 584, suspected that the Jewish leaders' answer (λέγουσιν· ὁ ὕστερος) may have been an early interpolation. This text is one of three in this Gospel (and one of 62 in the NT) that Westcott and Hort believed probably contains some primitive error (*New Testament*, 1:584–8). Even so, this conjecture is fundamentally different in nature from Michaels's, which posits an *understanding* of the parable that is not witnessed in any extant MS.

5. Wellhausen, *Das Evangelium Matthaei*, 106–8. So also A. Merx, *Die vier kanonischen Evangelien nach ihrem ältesten bekannten Texte* (vol. II, Berlin: Reimer, 1902), 291–7; E. Hirsch, *Frühgeschichte des Evangeliums* (2nd edn, Tübingen: Mohr, 1951), 317.

6. In fact as early as Jerome, *Comm. in Matth.* 21.32 (*PL* 26, 156), we meet the suggestion that the Jews intentionally answered incorrectly to spoil the point of the parable. Nevertheless Jerome also added that in true copies of the original text, we find the answer 'first' rather than 'last'; see B. Metzger, 'St Jerome's explicit references to variant readings in manuscripts of the New Testament', in *Text and Interpretation: Studies in the New Testament presented to Matthew Black* (ed. E. Best and R. McL. Wilson, 179–90, Cambridge University Press, 1979), 181.

7. So, e.g., Westcott and Hort, *New Testament*, 2:16; J. Schmid, 'Das textgeschichtliche Problem der Parabel von den zwei Söhnen', in *Vom Wort des Lebens* (ed. N. Adler, 68–84, Münster: Aschendorff, 1951), 69–72; K. and B. Aland, *Text*, 310; Metzger, *Textual Commentary*, 45; Luz, *Matthäus*, III:204. Several decades ago, however, H. A. Guy, 'The Parable of the Two Sons (Matt. xxi. 28–31)', *ExpTim* 51 (1939–40), 204–5, suggested that reading 3 may only be the most difficult reading for *Westerners*. Earlier, W. Macgregor, 'The Parable of the Two Sons', *ExpTim* 38 (1926–7), 498–501, had made a similar suggestion. In a recent article, W. E. Langley, 'The Parable of the Two Sons (Matthew 21:28–32) against Its Semitic and Rabbinic Backdrop', *CBQ* 58 (1996), 232, echoes this sentiment but, in the end, argues that the sense of the parable is not materially affected by the variant readings: 'Jesus, in Matthew's portrayal, can contentedly wait on his opponents' answer because he is prepared to use the rabbinic hermeneutical principle of *qal wahômer* on whatever answer they come up with' (Ibid., 238). Later he explains: 'If you say that son A, even though he was subsequently obedient, failed to do his father's will, because he was initially disobedient, or that son B, even though he was initially obedient, failed to do his father's will, because he was subsequently disobedient, then how much more disobedient must the son be who is both initially and subsequently disobedient?' (Ibid., 240). This argument, however, fails to do justice to the Matthean shaping of

parable. Whatever the origin of the parable, in its Matthean context there can be only one answer to the question Jesus poses. Moreover, *pace* Langley, the application reveals that the answer to the question in fact matters a great deal since the parable is about not only exclusion from, but also entrance to, the kingdom (21.31b).

8. Similarly Weder, *Gleichnisse*, 233 n. 120; Davies and Allison, *Matthew*, III:167 n. 18.

9. K. and B. Aland, *Text*, 310, suggest that this third reading 'does not accord with the style and narrative methods of the gospel of Matthew' but do not elaborate.

10. So, e.g., Metzger, *Textual Commentary*, 45; Davies and Allison, *Matthew*, III:167 n. 18.

11. The negative is omitted in D (c) e ff[1]* sy[s]; D it sy[s,(c)] witness the earlier reading we designated 3 above.

12. Cf. Schmid, 'Das textgeschichtliche Problem', 70–8.

13. For some, however, two considerations tilt the balance in favour of the first reading. First, Metzger, *Textual Commentary*, 45–6, suggests that reading 1 receives support from slightly better mss. Second, K. and B. Aland, *Text*, 310, find reading 2 weakened by the variations found in Θ *f*[13] and 700 which 'have very much the appearance of a later form developing in a variety of ways' (similarly Jülicher, *Die Gleichnisreden*, 377; Metzger, *Textual Commentary*, 45–6).

14. Allen, *Matthew*, 229.

15. So also Metzger, *Textual Commentary*, 46.

16. Similarly, e.g., Zahn, *Matthäus*, 618; Lohmeyer, *Matthäus*, 310; Metzger, *Textual Commentary*, 46; Davies and Allison, *Matthew*, III:167 n. 18; Luz, *Matthäus*, III:205.

17. Moreover, as Schmid, 'Das textgeschichtliche Problem', 81, rightly notes, arguments like these typically assume that either 1 is a correction of 2 or vice versa, when in fact 3 may provide the middle factor. See the discussion below.

18. Wellhausen, *Das Evangelium Matthaei*, 106; similarly Jülicher, *Die Gleichnisreden*, 376; K. and B. Aland, *Text*, 310; Davies and Allison, *Matthew*, III:167 n. 18.

19. As Macgregor, 'Two Sons', 499, long ago pointed out; similarly Carson, 'Matthew', 449.

20. A point that Luz, *Matthäus*, III:205, correctly recognises.

21. Cf. 238 n. 90.

22. Plummer, *Matthew*, 294, is representative of those who have found intrinsic support for reading 1 in the conclusion that οὐ θέλω must precede ἐγώ, κύριε, which seems to be an emphatic response to the earlier dismissal of the father's command; but Schmid, 'Das textgeschichtliche Problem', 84, rightly counters that ἐγώ, κύριε makes fine sense as the first son's response, setting up the contrast between *his own* words and actions.

23. Westcott and Hort, *New Testament*, II:17. As we have seen, both the fact that salvation–historical concerns could also have been important to later copyists, and that the evangelist explicitly applies the parable to the *Jewish* marginal and elite – not Israel and the Gentiles – effectively nullify the force of this suggestion as an aid towards establishing the original text.

24. Macgregor, 'Two Sons', 499. Macgregor cites as examples the parables of The Lost Sons (Luke 15.22–32), The Tenants, and The Great Supper; it is not obvious to me how the first of these fits this pattern.
25. J. Derrett, 'The Parable of the Two Sons', in *Studies in the New Testament* (vol. I, Leiden: Brill, 1977), 78. Earlier in the same article, Derrett argues that the portrait of a son who is initially and instinctively rebellious but in the end obedient is more typical of a younger son (τῷ ἑτέρῳ/τῷ δευτέρῳ) than the older sibling (τῷ πρώτῳ). Whether or not such a psychological reading could shed light here, this parable never distinguishes between the two on the basis of age (unlike Luke's story of two sons; cf. Luke 15.12, 25).
26. See now, however, P. Foster, 'A Tale of Two Sons: But Which One Did the Far, Far Better Thing? A Study of Matt 21.28–32', *NTS* 47 (2001), 26–37. Foster perhaps overestimates his ability to isolate the 'pre-Matthean' form of the parable but he does see the significance of the Matthean context for this textual question.
27. See pp. 135–8 above.
28. See further p. 149 above.
29. Nor, as we argued in ch. 6, pp. 135–8, is this the only point in the *application* at which Matthew links The Two Sons to The Tenants or The Wedding Feast.
30. See the chart on p. 27.
31. However, it is at least noteworthy, as Schmid, 'Das textgeschichtliche Problem', 82 and n. 23, points out, that the salvation–historical reading could be adapted to both readings 1 and 2 in the early church.
32. Metzger, *Textual Commentary*, 45.
33. Schmid, 'Das textgeschichtliche Problem'; this, of course, could be the case if either reading 1 or 2 was original. So already Westcott and Hort, *New Testament*, II:16, who also preferred reading 2.
34. Cf. W. Richards, 'Another Look at the Parable of the Two Sons', *BR* 23 (1978), 8–9.
35. Schmid, 'Das textgeschichtliche Problem', 72–6.
36. There may, of course, have been other factors involved that are no longer possible to recover. It may even be (as both Michaels, 'Regretful Son', and Jones, *Matthean Parables*, 396, have suggested) that the continuing oral circulation of the traditional parable has left its mark on the MS tradition here. Weder, *Gleichnisse*, 234, attributes the rise of reading 1 to the application of the parable to the Christian community. On this reading, the repentance of the tax gatherers and prostitutes (the 'no-sayer') would have stood first, since the 'yes-saying' son would correspond to subsequent members of the community whose declared allegiance to God was not matched by faithful obedience.
37. Schmid, 'Das textgeschichtliche Problem', 83.

BIBLIOGRAPHY

Abbreviations for journal titles and book series follow Patrick H. Alexander, John F. Kutsko, James D. Ernest, et al. (eds.), *The SBL Handbook of Style*, Peabody, MA: Hendrickson, 1999.

Aland, Kurt and Aland, Barbara, *The Text of the New Testament*, trans. Erroll F. Rhodes, Grand Rapids: Eerdmans, 1987.

Albright, W. F. and Mann, C. S., *Matthew*, AB 26; Garden City: Doubleday, 1971.

Allen, Willoughby C., *A Critical and Exegetical Commentary on the Gospel According to Matthew*, 3rd edn, ICC; Edinburgh: T. & T. Clark, 1912; reprint, 1922.

Allison, Dale C., *The New Moses: A Matthean Typology*, Edinburgh: T. & T. Clark, 1993.

   'Matt. 23:39 = Luke 13:35b as a Conditional Prophecy', *JSNT* 18 (1983), 75–84.

   'The Structure of the Sermon on the Mount', *JBL* 106 (1987), 423–45.

   'Who will come from East and West? Observations on Matt. 8.11–12/Luke 13.28–29', *IBS* 11 (1989), 158–70.

Anderson, Janice Capel, *Matthew's Narrative Web: Over, and Over, and Over Again*, JSNTSup 91; Sheffield: JSOT, 1994.

   'Double and Triple Stories, The Implied Reader, and Redundancy in Matthew', *Semeia* 31 (1985), 71–89.

Aus, Roger David, *The Wicked Tenants and Gethsemane. Isaiah in the Wicked Tenants' Vineyard, and Moses and the High Priest in Gethsemane: Judaic Traditions in Mark 12:1–9 and 14:32–42*, Atlanta: Scholars Press, 1996.

Austin, J. L., *How to Do Things With Words*, Oxford: Clarendon, 1962.

Bacon, B. W. , 'Two Parables of Lost Opportunity', *HibJ* 21 (1922–3), 337–52.

Ballard, Paul H., 'Reasons for Refusing the Great Supper', *JTS* 23 (1972), 341–50.

Bammel, Ernst , 'Das Gleichnis von den bösen Winzern (Mk.12,1–9) und das jüdische Erbrecht', *RIDA* 3rd series, 6 (1959), 11–17.

Barth, Gerhard, 'Matthew's Understanding of the Law', in Bornkamm, Günther, Barth, Gerhard and Held, Heinz Joachim, *Tradition and Interpretation in Matthew*, trans. Percy Scott, Philadelphia: Westminster, 1963.

Bartlett, John R., *The First and Second Books of the Maccabees*, Cambridge University Press, 1973.

Barton, Stephen C., *Discipleship and Family Ties in Mark and Matthew*, SNTSMS 80; Cambridge University Press, 1994.

Batey, Richard A., *New Testament Nuptial Imagery*, Leiden: Brill, 1971.

Bauckham, Richard, *The Climax of Prophecy: Studies on the Book of Revelation*, Edinburgh: T. & T. Clark, 1993.

'Tamar's Ancestry and Rahab's Marriage: Two Problems in the Matthean Genealogy', *NovT* 37 (1995), 313–29.

'The Parable of the Royal Wedding Feast (Matthew 22:1–14) and the Parable of the Lame Man and the Blind Man (Apocryphon of Ezekiel)', *JBL* 115 (1996), 471–88.

Bauckham, Richard (ed.), *The Gospels for All Christians*, Grand Rapids: Eerdmans, 1998.

Bauer, David R., *The Structure of Matthew's Gospel: A Study in Literary Design*, Sheffield: Almond, 1988; reprint, 1989.

Beare, Francis W., *The Gospel According to Matthew*, Oxford: Blackwell, 1981.

'The Parable of the Guests at the Banquet', in *The Joy of Study*, ed. Sherman E. Johnson, 1–14, New York: Macmillan, 1951.

Beasley-Murray, George R., *Jesus and the Kingdom of God*, Grand Rapids: Eerdmans, 1986.

Benoit, P., *L'Évangile Saint Matthieu*, 4th edn, Paris: Les Éditions du Cerf, 1972.

Bindemann, W. , 'Das Mahl des Königs: Gründe und Hintergründe der Redaktion von Mt. 22,1–14', *Theologische Versuche* 15 (1985), 21–9.

Birdsall, J. Neville, 'A Note on the Textual Evidence for the Omission of Matthew 9.34', in *Jews and Christians*, ed. James D. G. Dunn, 117–22, Tübingen: Mohr, 1992.

Black, Matthew , 'The Parables as Allegory', *BJRL* 42 (1960), 273–87.

'The Christological Use of the Old Testament in the New Testament', *NTS* 18 (1971–2), 1–14.

Blair, Edward P., *Jesus in the Gospel of Matthew*, Nashville: Abingdon, 1960.

Blank, Josef, 'Die Sendung des Sohnes: Zur christologischen Bedeutung des Gleichnisses von den bösen Winzern Mk 12,1–12', in *Neues Testament und Kirche*, ed. J. Gnilka, 11–41, Freiburg: Herder, 1974.

Blass, F., Debrunner, A. and Funk, R. W., *A Greek Grammar of the New Testament and Other Early Christian Literature*, University of Chicago Press, 1961.

Blomberg, Craig L., *Interpreting the Parables*, Leicester: Apollos, 1990.

'When is a Parallel Really a Parallel? A Test Case: The Lucan Parables', *WTJ* 46 (1984), 78–103.

'The Parables of Jesus: Current Trends and Needs in Research', in *Studying the Historical Jesus: Evaluations of the State of Current Research*, ed. Bruce Chilton and Craig A. Evans, 231–54, Leiden: Brill, 1994.

Bock, Darrell L., *Luke*, vol. I, *1:1–9:50*, Grand Rapids: Baker, 1994.

Boissard, Edmond , 'Note sur l'interprétation du texte "Multi sunt vocati, pauci vero electi" ', *RThom* 52 (1952), 569–85.

Bonnard, Pierre, *L'Évangile Selon Saint Matthieu*, 3rd edn, Geneva: Labor et Fides, 1992.

Booth, Wayne C., *The Rhetoric of Fiction*, 2nd edn, University of Chicago Press, 1983.

Bornkamm, Günther, 'End-Expectation and the Church in Matthew', in Bornkamm, Günther, Barth, Gerhard and Held, Heinz Joachim, *Tradition and Interpretation in Matthew*, trans. Percy Scott, Philadelphia: Westminster, 1963.

Boucher, Madeleine, *The Mysterious Parable*, Washington: The Catholic Biblical Association of America, 1977.

Brooke, George J. , '4Q500 1 and the Use of Scripture in the Parable of the Vineyard', *DSD* 2 (1995), 268–94.

Brower, K. E., '"Let the Reader Understand": Temple and Eschatology in Mark', in *The Reader Must Understand*, ed. K. E. Brower and M. W. Elliot, 119–43, Leicester: InterVarsity, 1997.

Brown, Raymond E., *The Birth of the Messiah*, 2nd edn, New York: Doubleday, 1993.

   The Death of the Messiah: From Gethsemane to the Grave, New York: Doubleday, 1994.

   'Parable and Allegory Reconsidered', *NovT* 5 (1962), 36–45.

Brown, S. , 'The Matthean Apocalypse', *JSNT* 4 (1979), 2–27.

   'The Matthean Community and the Gentile Mission', *NovT* 22 (1980), 193–221.

Bruce, F. F., *The Time is Fulfilled*, Exeter: Paternoster, 1978.

Bultmann, Rudolf, *The History of the Synoptic Tradition*, trans. John Marsh, Oxford: Blackwell, 1963; reprint, 1972.

Caird, G. B., *New Testament Theology*, ed. L. Hurst, Oxford: Clarendon, 1994.

Calvin, J., *A Harmony of the Gospels Matthew, Mark and Luke,* 3 vols., ed. David W. Torrance and Thomas F. Torrance, Carlisle: Paternoster, 1972.

Cargal, Timothy B. , '"His Blood be upon us and upon our Children": A Matthean Double Entendre?', *NTS* 37 (1991), 101–12.

Carlston, Charles E., *The Parables of the Triple Tradition*, Philadelphia: Fortress, 1975.

Carson, D. A. , 'The Jewish Leaders in Matthew's Gospel: A Reappraisal', *JETS* 25 (1982), 161–74.

   'Matthew', in *The Expositor's Bible Commentary*, ed. F. Gaebelein, VIII: 3–599, Grand Rapids: Zondervan, 1984.

   'The ὅμοιος Word-Group as Introduction to some Matthean Parables', *NTS* 31 (1985), 277–82.

Carter, W., *Matthew: Storyteller, Interpreter, Evangelist*, Peabody, MA: Hendrickson, 1996.

Carter, W. and Heil, J. P., *Matthew's Parables: Audience-Oriented Perspectives*, Washington: The Catholic Biblical Association of America, 1998.

Casey, M., *Son of Man: The Interpretation and Influence of Daniel 7*, London: SPCK, 1979.

Catchpole, D., *The Quest for Q*, Edinburgh: T. & T. Clark, 1993.

Charette, Blaine, *The Theme of Recompense in Matthew's Gospel*, JSNTSup 79; Sheffield: JSOT, 1992.

Charles, R. H., *The Testaments of the Twelve Patriarchs*, London: Black, 1908.

   The Greek Versions of the Testaments of the Twelve Patriarchs, Oxford: Clarendon, 1908.

Charlesworth, J. H., 'Jesus as "Son" and the Righteous Teacher as "Gardener"', in *Jesus and the Dead Sea Scrolls*, ed. J. H. Charlesworth, 140–75, New York: Doubleday, 1992.

Chatman, Seymour, *Story and Discourse: Narrative Structure in Fiction and Film*, London: Cornell University Press, 1978.

Chilton, Bruce, *A Galilean Rabbi and His Bible: Jesus' Own Interpretation of Isaiah*, London: SPCK, 1984.

   The Isaiah Targum: Introduction, Translation, Apparatus and Notes, Edinburgh: T. & T. Clark, 1987.

Clark, K., 'The Gentile Bias in Matthew', in *The Gentile Bias and Other Essays*, Leiden: Brill, 1980.

Cope, O. Lamar, *Matthew: A Scribe Trained for the Kingdom of Heaven*, Washington: The Catholic Biblical Association of America, 1976.

Crossan, John Dominic, *In Parables: The Challenge of the Historical Jesus*, New York: Harper and Row, 1973.

In Fragments: The Aphorisms of Jesus, New York: Harper and Row, 1983.

'The Parable of the Wicked Husbandmen', *JBL* 90 (1971), 451–65.

'Parable and Example in the Teaching of Jesus', *NTS* 18 (1972), 285–307.

Culler, Jonathan, *On Deconstruction: Theory and Criticism After Structuralism*, Ithaca: Cornell University Press, 1982.

Darr, John A., *On Character Building: The Reader and the Rhetoric of Characterization in Luke-Acts*, Louisville: Westminster/John Knox, 1992.

Davies, Margaret, *Matthew*, Sheffield: JSOT, 1993.

Davies, W. D. and Allison, Dale C., Jr., *A Critical and Exegetical Commentary on the Gospel According to Saint Matthew*, ICC; 3 vols., Edinburgh: T. & T. Clark, 1988–97.

De Jonge, M., 'Christian Influence in The Testaments of the Twelve Patriarachs', in *Studies on the Testaments of the Twelve Patriarchs*, ed. M. De Jonge, 193–246, Leiden: Brill, 1975.

Derrett, J. D. M., 'The Parable of the Wicked Vinedressers', in *Law in the New Testament*, London: Darton, Longman & Todd, 1970.

'Allegory and the Wicked Vinedressers', *JTS* 25 (1974), 426–32.

'The Parable of the Two Sons', in *Studies in the New Testament*, vol. I, Leiden: Brill, 1977.

Deutsch, C., *Hidden Wisdom and the Easy Yoke: Wisdom, Torah and Discipleship in Matthew 11.25–30*, JSNTSup 18; Sheffield: JSOT, 1987.

Dillon, R. J. , 'Towards a Tradition-history of the Parables of the True Israel (Matthew 21:33–22:14)', *Bib* 47 (1966), 1–42.

Dodd, C. H., *The Parables of the Kingdom*, London: Nisbet & Co. Ltd., 1935; reprint, 1941.

Donahue, John R., *The Gospel in Parable: Metaphor, Narrative and Theology in the Synoptic Gospels*, Philadelphia: Fortress, 1988.

Donaldson, Terence L., *Jesus on the Mountain: A Study in Matthean Theology*, JSNTSup 8; Sheffield: JSOT, 1985.

Dozeman, T. , '*Sperma Abraam* in John 8 and Related Literature', *CBQ* 42 (1980), 342–58.

Drury, John, *The Parables in the Gospels: History and Allegory*, London: SPCK, 1985.

'The Sower, the Vineyard, and the Place of Allegory in the Interpretation of Mark's Parables', *JTS* 24 (1973), 367–79.

Dschulnigg, Peter , 'Positionen des Gleichnisverständnisses im 20. Jahrhundert', *TZ* 45 (1989), 335–51.

Duplantier, Jean-Pierre, 'Les vignerons meurtriers: Le travail d'une parabole', in *Les paraboles évangéliques: Perspectives nouvelles*, ed. Jean Delorme, 259–70, Paris: Les Éditions du Cerf, 1989.

Edwards, J. R. , 'The Use of Προσέρχεσθαι in the Gospel of Matthew', *JBL* 106 (1987), 65–74.

Edwards, Richard A., *Matthew's Story of Jesus*, Philadelphia: Fortress, 1985.

Elliott, J. Keith, 'Thoroughgoing Eclecticism in New Testament Textual Criticism', in *The Text of the New Testament in Contemporary Research: Essays on the Status Quaestionis*, ed. Bart D. Ehrman and Michael W. Holmes, 321–35, Grand Rapids: Eerdmans, 1995.

Ellis, E. Earle, 'Dating the New Testament', *NTS* 26 (1980), 487–502.

Emerton, J. A. , 'An Examination of Recent Structuralist Interpretation of Genesis XXXVIII', *VT* 26 (1976), 79–98.

'Judah and Tamar', *VT* 29 (1979), 403–15.

Epp, Eldon Jay and Fee, Gordon D., *Studies in the Theory and Method of New Testament Textual Criticism*, Grand Rapids: Eerdmans, 1993.

Evans, Craig A. , 'On the Vineyard Parables of Isaiah 5 and Mark 12', *BZ* 28 (1984), 82–6.

'God's Vineyard and Its Caretakers', in *Jesus and His Contemporaries*, Leiden: Brill, 1995.

'Jesus' Parable of the Tenant Farmers in Light of Lease Agreements in Antiquity', *JSP* 14 (1996), 65–83.

Feldmeier, R. , 'Heil im Unheil. Das Bild Gottes nach der Parabel von den bösen Winzern (Mk. 12,1–12 par)', *TBei* 25 (1994), 5–22.

Fiebig, Paul, *Altjüdische Gleichnisse und die Gleichnisse Jesu*, Tübingen: Mohr, 1904.

Die Gleichnisreden Jesu im Lichte der rabbinischen Gleichnisse des neutestamentlichen Zeitalters. Ein Beitrag zum Streit um die 'Christusmythe' und eine Widerlegung der Gleichnistheorie Jülichers, Tübingen: Mohr, 1912.

Filson, Floyd V., *A Commentary on the Gospel According to St. Matthew*, London: Black, 1960.

Fitzmyer, Joseph A., *Luke I–IX*, AB 28; New York: Doubleday, 1981.

Luke X–XXIV, AB 28A; New York: Doubleday, 1985.

Fletcher-Louis, C. H. T., 'The Destruction of the Temple and the Relativization of the Old Covenant: Mark 13:31 and Matthew 5:18', in *The Reader Must Understand*, ed. K. E. Brower and M. W. Elliot, 145–69, Leicester: InterVarsity, 1997.

Fortna, Robert Tomson, *The Fourth Gospel and Its Predecessor*, Edinburgh: T. & T. Clark, 1988.

Foster, Paul , 'A Tale of Two Sons: But Which One Did the Far, Far Better Thing? A Study of Matt 21.28–32', *NTS* 47 (2001), 26–37.

Fowler, Robert M., *Let the Reader Understand: Reader-Response Criticism and the Gospel of Mark*, Minneapolis: Fortress, 1991.

'Who is "the Reader" in Reader Response Criticism?', *Semeia* 31 (1985), 5–23.

'Reader-Response Criticism: Figuring Mark's Reader', in *Mark and Method: New Approaches in Biblical Studies*, ed. Janice Capel Anderson and Stephen D. Moore, 50–83, Minneapolis: Fortress, 1992.

France, R. T., *Jesus and the Old Testament*, London: Tyndale Press, 1971.

Matthew, TNTC; Grand Rapids: Eerdmans, 1985.

Matthew: Evangelist and Teacher, Grand Rapids: Academie, 1989.

'Exegesis in Practice: Two Samples', in *New Testament Interpretation*, ed. I. H. Marshall, 253–81, Grand Rapids: Eerdmans, 1977.

Fuchs, Ernst, *Studies of the Historical Jesus*, trans. Andrew Scobie, London: SCM, 1964.

Funk, Robert W., *Language, Hermeneutic, and the Word of God*, New York: Harper and Row, 1966.

Gaechter, Paul, *Das Matthäus-Evangelium*, Innsbruck: Tyrolia, 1963.

Garland, David E., *The Intention of Matthew 23*, Leiden: Brill, 1979.

Gaston, Lloyd, *No Stone on Another*, Leiden: Brill, 1970.

'The Messiah of Israel as Teacher of the Gentiles: The Setting of Matthew's Christology', *Int* 29 (1975), 24–40.

Gerhardsson, Birger , 'If We Do Not Cut the Parables Out of Their Frames', *NTS* 37 (1991), 321–35.

Gibbs, James M. , 'Purpose and Pattern in Matthew's Use of the Title "Son of David"', *NTS* 10 (1964), 446–64.

Gibson, J. , 'Hoi Telonai kai hai Pornai', *JTS* 32 (1981), 429–33.

Gnilka, Joachim, *Das Matthäusevangelium*, HTKNT 1; 2 vols., Freiburg: Herder, 1986, 1992.

Goldstein, Jonathan A., *1 Maccabees*, AB 41; Garden City: Doubleday, 1976.

Goulder, Michael D., *Midrash and Lection in Matthew*, London: SPCK, 1974.

Gray, A., 'The Parable of the Wicked Husbandmen', *HibJ* 19 (1920–21), 42–52.

Green, H. Benedict, *The Gospel According to Matthew*, Oxford University Press, 1975.

Grundmann, Walter, *Das Evangelium nach Matthäus*, Berlin: Evangelische Verlagsanstalt, 1968.

Gundry, Robert H., *The Use Of The Old Testament In St. Matthew's Gospel*, Leiden: Brill, 1967.

Matthew: A Commentary on His Handbook for a Mixed Church under Persecution, 2nd edn, Grand Rapids: Eerdmans, 1994.

Guy, H. A. , 'The Parable of the Two Sons (Matt. xxi. 28–31)', *ExpTim* 51 (1939–40), 204–5.

Haenchen, Ernst, 'Das Gleichnis vom grossen Mahl', in *Die Bibel und Wir*, Tübingen: Mohr, 1968.

Hagner, Donald A., *Matthew 1–13*, WBC 33A; Dallas: Word, 1993.

Matthew 14–28, WBC 33B; Dallas: Word, 1995.

'Righteousness in Matthew's Theology', in *Worship, Theology and Ministry in the Early Church: Essays in Honor of Ralph P. Martin,* ed. M. J. Wilkins and T. Paige, 101–20, Sheffield: JSOT, 1992.

Hahn, F., *Mission in the New Testament*, trans. Frank Clarke, London: SCM, 1965.

Hare, D. R. A., *The Theme of Jewish Persecution of Christians in the Gospel According to St. Matthew*, Cambridge University Press, 1967.

Matthew, Louisville: John Knox, 1993.

Hare, D. R. A. and Harrington, D. J. , '"Make Disciples of all the Gentiles" (Mt 28:19)', *CBQ* 37 (1975), 359–69.

Harnack, Adolf, *The Sayings of Jesus: The Second Source of St. Matthew and St. Luke*, trans. J. R. Wilkinson, London: Williams and Norgate, 1908.

Harrington, Daniel J., *The Gospel of Matthew*, Collegeville, MN: The Liturgical Press, 1991.

Hartman, Lars, *Testimonium Linguae: Participial Constructions in the Synoptic Gospels*, ConBNT 19; Lund: Gleerup, 1963.

Haslam, M. W., Jones, A. and Maltomini, F. et al. (eds.), *The Oxyrhynchus Papyri, vol. LXV*, London: Egypt Exploration Society, 1998.

Hasler, V. , 'Die königliche Hochzeit, Matth 22, 1–14', *TZ* 18 (1962), 25–35.

Hawkins, J. C., 'Probabilities as to the So-Called Double Tradition of St. Matthew and St. Luke', in *Oxford Studies in the Synoptic Problem*, ed. W. Sanday, 96–138. Oxford: Clarendon, 1911.

Hedrick, Charles W., *Parables as Poetic Fictions: The Creative Voice of Jesus*, Peabody, MA: Hendrickson, 1994.

Heil, John Paul, *The Death and Resurrection of Jesus: A Narrative–Critical Reading of Matthew 26–28*, Minneapolis: Fortress, 1991.

Held, Heinz Joachim, 'Matthew as Interpreter of the Miracle Stories', in Bornkamm, Günther, Barth, Gerhard and Held, Heinz Joachim, *Tradition and Interpretation in Matthew*, trans. Percy Scott, Philadelphia: Westminster, 1963.

Hengel, M. , 'Das Gleichnis von den Weingärtnern Mc. 12, 1–12 im Lichte der Zenon Papyri und der rabbinischen Gleichnisse', *ZNW* 59 (1968), 1–39.

Herzog, W. R. II., *Parables as Subversive Speech: Jesus as the Pedagogue of the Oppressed*, Louisville: Westminster/John Knox, 1994.

Hester, James D. , 'Socio-Rhetorical Criticism and the Parable of the Tenants', *JSNT* 45 (1992), 27–57.

Hill, David, *Greek Words and Hebrew Meanings: Studies in the Semantics of Soteriological Terms*, Cambridge University Press, 1967.

  The Gospel of Matthew, London: Marshall, Morgan and Scott, 1972.

Hirsch, Emanuel, *Frühgeschichte des Evangeliums*, 2nd edn, Tübingen: Mohr, 1951.

Hoffmann, Paul, *Studien Zur Theologie der Logienquelle*, Münster: Aschendorff, 1972.

Hollander, H. W. and De Jonge, M., *The Testament of the Twelve Patriarchs: A Commentary*, Leiden: Brill, 1985.

Holmes, Michael W., 'Reasoned Eclecticism in New Testament Textual Criticism', in *The Text of the New Testament in Contemporary Research: Essays on the Status Quaestionis*, ed. Bart D. Ehrman and Michael W. Holmes, 336–60, Grand Rapids: Eerdmans, 1995.

Holtzmann, Heinrich Julius, *Die Synoptischen Evangelien*, Leipzig: Engelmann, 1863.

Hooker, Morna , 'Uncomfortable Words: X. The Prohibition of Foreign Missions (Mt 10.5–6)', *ExpTim* 82 (1971), 361–5.

  'In his own Image?' in *What About the New Testament? Essays in Honour of Christopher Evans*, ed. M. Hooker and C. Hickling, 28–44, London: SCM, 1975.

Horne, Edward H. , 'The Parable of the Tenants as Indictment', *JSNT* 71 (1998), 111–16.

Howell, David B., *Matthew's Inclusive Story: A Study in the Narrative Rhetoric of the First Gospel*, JSNTSup 42; Sheffield: JSOT, 1990.

Hubaut, Michel, *La parabole des vignerons homicides*, Paris: Gabalda, 1976.

Hummel, Reinhart, *Die Auseinandersetzung zwischen Kirche und Judentum in Matthäusevangelium*, Munich: Kaiser, 1966.

Iser, W., *The Implied Reader: Patterns of Communication in Prose Fiction from Bunyan to Beckett*, Baltimore: Johns Hopkins University Press, 1974.

  The Act of Reading: A Theory of Aesthetic Response, London: Routledge & Kegan Paul, 1978.

'The Reading Process: A Phenomenological Approach', in *Reader-Response Criticism: From Formalism to Post Structuralism*, ed. Jane P. Tompkins, 50–69, Baltimore: Johns Hopkins University Press, 1980.

Jeremias, Joachim, *The Parables of Jesus*, 3rd edn, trans. S. H. Hooke, London: SCM, 1954; reprint, 1955.

   The Eucharistic Words of Jesus, trans. Norman Perrin, London: SCM, 1966.

   New Testament Theology, trans. John Bowden, London: SCM, 1971.

Johnson, Luke Timothy, *The Gospel of Luke*, Collegeville, MN: The Liturgical Press, 1991.

   'On Finding the Lucan Community: A Cautious Cautionary Essay', *SBLSP* 16 (1979), 87–100.

Jones, Geraint V., *The Art and Truth of the Parables: A Study in their Literary Form and Modern Interpretation*, London: SPCK, 1964.

Jones, Ivor H., *The Matthean Parables: A Literary and Historical Commentary*, Leiden: Brill, 1995.

Jülicher, D. Adolf, *Die Gleichnisreden Jesu*, 2nd edn, Tübingen: J. C. B. Mohr, 1910.

Jüngel, Eberhard, *Paulus und Jesus*, Tübingen: Mohr, 1962.

Kee, H. C., 'Testaments of the Twelve Patriarchs: A New Translation and Introduction', in *The Old Testament Pseudepigrapha*, vol. I, *Apocalyptic Literature and Testaments*, ed. James H. Charlesworth , 775–828, New York: Doubleday, 1983.

Kilpatrick, G. D., *The Origins of the Gospel According to St. Matthew*, Oxford: Clarendon, 1964.

Kingsbury, J. D., *The Parables of Jesus in Matthew 13: A Study in Redaction-Criticism*, London: SPCK, 1969.

   Matthew: Structure, Christology, Kingdom, Philadelphia: Fortress, 1975.

   Matthew as Story, 2nd edn, Philadelphia: Fortress, 1988.

   'The Miracle of the Cleansing of the Leper as an Approach to the Theology of Matthew', *CurTM* 14 (1977): 342–9.

   'The Parable of the Wicked Husbandmen and the Secret of Jesus' Divine Sonship in Matthew: Some Literary-Critical Observations', *JBL* 105 (1986), 643–55.

   'Reflections on "The Reader" of Matthew's Gospel', *NTS* 34 (1988), 442–60.

   'The Plot of Matthew's Story', *Int* 46 (1992), 347–56.

   'Review of *A Gospel for a New People*, by Graham N. Stanton', *JTS* 44 (1993), 647–52.

Kissinger, Warren S., *The Parables of Jesus: A History of Interpretation and Bibliography*, London: Scarecrow, 1979.

Kittel, G. and Friedrich, G. (eds.), *Theological Dictionary of the New Testament*, trans. Geoffrey W. Bromiley, 10 vols., Grand Rapids: Eerdmans, 1964–76.

Klauck, H. J., *Allegorie und Allegorese in Synoptischen Gleichnistexten*, Münster: Aschendorff, 1978.

Kloppenborg, John S., *The Formation of Q*, Philadelphia: Fortress, 1987.

Klostermann, Erich, *Das Matthäusevangelium*, 2nd edn, Tübingen: Mohr, 1927.

Knowles, Michael, *Jeremiah in Matthew's Gospel*, JSNTSup 68; Sheffield: JSOT, 1993.

Kosmala, H. , 'His Blood on Us and on Our Children (The Background of Matt. 27, 24–25)', *ASTI* 7 (1970), 94–126.

Kretzer, Armin, *Die Herrschaft der Himmel und die Söhne des Reiches*, Würzburg: Echter, 1971.

Kümmel, W. G., 'Das Gleichnis von den bösen Weingärtnern', in *Heilsgeschehen und Geschichte*, Marburg: Elwert, 1965.

Kupp, David D., *Matthew's Emmanuel: Divine Presence and God's People in the First Gospel*, SNTSMS 90; Cambridge University Press, 1996.

Kynes, W. L., *A Christology of Solidarity: Jesus as the Representative of his People in Matthew*, Lanham, MD: University Press of America, 1991.

Lachmann, C., *Novum Testamentum Graece et Latine*, Berlin, 1842.

Lagrange, M.-J., *Évangile selon Saint Matthieu*, 7th edn, Paris: Gabalda, 1948.

Lambrecht, Jan, *Out of the Treasure: The Parables in the Gospel of Matthew*, Louvain: Peeters, 1992.

Lampe, G. W. H., 'A.D. 70 in Christian reflection', in *Jesus and the Politics of His Day*, ed. Ernst Bammel and C. F. D. Moule, Cambridge University Press, 1984.

Lampe, Peter and Luz, Ulrich, 'Diskussionsüberblick', in *Das Evangelium und die Evangelien*, ed. Peter Stuhlmacher, 413–31, Tübingen: Mohr, 1983; ET 'Overview of the Discussion', in *The Gospel and the Gospels*, ed. Peter Stuhlmacher, 387–404, Grand Rapids: Eerdmans, 1991.

Langley, Wendell E. , 'The Parable of the Two Sons (Matthew 21:28–32) against Its Semitic and Rabbinic Backdrop', *CBQ* 58 (1996), 228–43.

Lanser, S. S., *The Narrative Act: Point of View in Prose Fiction*, Princeton University Press, 1981.

Lategan, B. C., 'Some Unresolved Methodological Issues', in *Text and Reality: Aspects of Reference in Biblical Texts*, by B. C. Lategan and W. S. Vorster, 3–25, Atlanta: Scholars Press, 1985.

Lemcio, Eugene E., *The Past of Jesus in the Gospels*, Cambridge University Press, 1991.

'The Parables of the Great Supper and the Wedding Feast: History, Redaction and Canon', *HBT* 8 (1986), 1–26.

Léon-Dufour, X., 'La parabole des vignerons homicides', in *Études d'évangile*, Paris: Seuil, 1965.

Levine, Amy-Jill, *The Social and Ethnic Dimensions of Matthean Social History: 'Go nowhere among the Gentiles . . .' (Matt. 10:5b)*, Lewiston, NY: Mellen, 1988.

Lindars, Barnabas, *New Testament Apologetic: The Doctrinal Significance of the Old Testament Quotations*, London: SCM, 1961.

Linnemann, Eta, *Parables of Jesus*, trans. John Sturdy, London: SPCK, 1966.

'Überlegungen zur Parabel vom großen Abendmahl, Lc 14.15–24 / Mt 22.1–14', *ZNW* 51 (1960), 246–55.

Llewelyn, S. R. , 'Self-Help and Legal Redress: The Parable of the Wicked Tenants', *NewDocs* 6 (1992), 86–105.

Loader, W. R. G. , 'Son of David, Blindness, Possession, and Duality in Matthew', *CBQ* 44 (1982), 570–85.

Lohmeyer, Ernst, *Das Evangelium Matthäus*, ed. Werner Schmauch, Göttingen: Vandenhoeck and Ruprecht, 1956.

'Das Gleichnis von de bösen Weingärtnern', *ZST* 18 (1941), 242–59.

Long, V. Philips, *The Art of Biblical History*, Grand Rapids: Zondervan, 1994.

Longman, T., *Literary Approaches to Biblical Interpretation*, Grand Rapids: Academie, 1987.

Louw, Johannes P. and Nida, Eugene A. (eds.), *Greek–English Lexicon of the New Testament Based on Semantic Domains*, 2 vols., New York: United Bible Societies, 1988, 1989.

Lövestam, Evald, *Jesus and 'this Generation': A New Testament Study*, Stockholm: Almqvist & Wiksell, 1995.

Lowe, M., 'From Parable of the Vineyard to Pre-Synoptic Source', *NTS* 28 (1982), 257–63.

Lührmann, D., *Die Redaktion der Logienquelle*, Neukirchen-Vluyn: Neukirchener, 1969.

Luomanen, Petri, *Entering the Kingdom of Heaven: A Study on the Structure of Matthew's View of Salvation*, Tübingen: Mohr, 1998.

'Corpus Mixtum – An Appropriate Description of Matthew's Community?', *JBL* 117 (1998), 469–80.

Luther, Martin, *Luther's Works*, ed. Jaroslav Pelikan, vol. VII, *Lectures on Genesis Chapters 38–44*, St. Louis: Concordia, 1965.

Luz, Ulrich, *Das Evangelium nach Matthäus*, EKKNT; 3 vols., incomplete, Zürich: Benzinger, 1985–97. ET, vol. I: *Matthew 1–7: A Continental Commentary*, trans. Wilhelm C. Linss, Minneapolis: Fortress, 1989.

The Theology of the Gospel of Matthew, trans. J. Bradford Robinson, Cambridge University Press, 1995.

'The Disciples in the Gospel according to Matthew', in *The Interpretation of Matthew*, ed. Graham Stanton, 98–128, Philadelphia: Fortress, 1983.

'Matthew's Anti-Judaism: Its Origin and Contemporary Significance', *CurTM* 19 (1992), 405–15.

Macgregor, W. M., 'The Parable of the Two Sons', *ExpTim* 38 (1926–7), 498–501.

McKnight, Scot, *A Light Among the Nations: Jewish Missionary Activity in the Second Temple Period*, Minneapolis: Fortress, 1991.

'Gentiles', in *Dictionary of Jesus and the Gospels*, ed. J. Green and S. McKnight, 259–65, Downers Grove: InterVarsity, 1992.

'A Loyal Critic: Matthew's Polemic with Judaism in Theological Perspective', in *Anti-Semitism and Early Christianity: Issues of Polemic and Faith*, ed. Craig A. Evans and Donald A. Hagner, 55–79, Minneapolis: Fortress, 1993.

McNeile, A. H., *The Gospel According to Matthew*, London: Macmillan, 1915.

Maier, Gerhard, *Matthäus-Evangelium*, vol. II, Neuhausen-Stuttgart: Hänssler, 1980.

Manns, F., 'Une tradition rabbinique réinterprétée dans l'évangile de Mt 22,1–10 et en Rm 11,30–32', *Anton* 63 (1988), 416–26.

Manson, T. W., *The Sayings of Jesus*, London: SCM, 1937; reprint, 1949.

The Teachings of Jesus, Cambridge University Press, 1951.

Marcus, Joel, 'Entering into the Kingly Power of God', *JBL* 107 (1988), 663–75.

'The intertextual polemic of the Markan vineyard parable', in *Tolerance and Intolerance in Early Judaism and Christianity*, ed. Graham N. Stanton and Guy G. Stroumsa, 211–27, Cambridge University Press, 1998.

Marguerat, Daniel, *Le Jugement dans l'Évangile de Matthieu*, Geneva: Labor et Fides, 1981.

Marshall, I. Howard, *The Gospel of Luke*, Exeter: Paternoster, 1978.

Matera, F. J., 'The Plot of Matthew's Gospel', *CBQ* 49 (1987), 233–53.

Mays, J. L., *Psalms*, IBC; Louisville: John Knox, 1994.

Meier, John P., *The Vision of Matthew: Christ, Church, and Morality in the First Gospel*, New York: Paulist, 1979.

Matthew, Dublin: Veritas, 1980.

'Nations or Gentiles in Matthew 28:19?', *CBQ* 39 (1977), 94–102.

'Two Disputed Questions in Matt. 28.16–20', *JBL* 96 (1977), 407–24.

Mell, Ulrich, *Die 'anderen' Winzer: Eine exegetische Studie zur Vollmacht Jesu Christi nach Markus 11,27–12,34*, Tübingen: Mohr, 1994.

Merenlahti, Petri and Hakola, Raimo, 'Reconceiving Narrative Criticism', in *Characterization in the Gospels: Reconceiving Narrative Criticism*, ed. David Rhoads and Kari Syreeni, 13–48, JSNTSup 184; Sheffield Academic Press, 1999.

Merkel, Helmut , 'Das Gleichnis von den "ungleichen Söhnen" [Matth. xxi.28–32]', *NTS* 20 (1974), 254–61.

Merx, Adalbert, *Die vier kanonischen Evangelien nach ihrem ältesten bekannten Texte*, vol. II, Berlin: Reimer, 1902.

Metzger, Bruce M., *A Textual Commentary on the Greek New Testament*, 2nd edn, Stuttgart: German Bible Society, 1994.

'St Jerome's explicit references to variant readings in manuscripts of the New Testament', in *Text and Interpretation: Studies in the New Testament presented to Matthew Black*, ed. E. Best and R. McL. Wilson, 179–90, Cambridge University Press, 1979.

Meyer, B. F., *The Aims of Jesus*, London: SCM, 1979.

'Many (= All) are Called, but Few (= Not All) are Chosen', *NTS* 36 (1990), 89–97.

'The Challenges of Text and Reader to the Historical–Critical Method', *Concilium* 1 (1991), 3–12.

Michaelis, D. Wilhelm, *Die Gleichnisse Jesu*, Hamburg: Furche-Verlag, 1956.

Michaels, J. R. , 'The Parable of the Regretful Son', *HTR* 61 (1968), 15–26.

Milavec, Aaron A., 'A Fresh Analysis of the Parable of the Wicked Husbandmen in the Light of Jewish–Christian Dialogue', in *Parables and Story in Judaism and Christianity*, ed. Clemens Thoma and Michael Wyschogrod, 81–117, New York: Paulist, 1989.

'The Identity of "the Son" and "the Others": Mark's Parable of the Wicked Husbandmen Reconsidered', *BTB* 20 (1990), 30–7.

Mills, R. G., 'Redaction Criticism in Matthean Studies: A Literary Critical Defence', Ph.D. thesis, University of Otago, 1997.

Minear, P., 'The Disciples and the Crowds in the Gospel of Matthew', *AThR Supplementary Series* 3 (1974), 28–44.

Mitton, C. L. , 'Threefoldness in the Teaching of Jesus', *ExpTim* 75 (1964), 228–30.

Moffat, James, *An Introduction to the Literature of the New Testament*, 3rd edn, Edinburgh: T. & T. Clark, 1918.

Moore, Stephen D., *Literary Criticism and the Gospels*, London: Yale, 1989.

Poststructuralism and the New Testament: Derrida and Foucault at the Foot of the Cross, Minneapolis: Fortress, 1994.

'Deconstructive Criticism: The Gospel of the Mark', in *Mark and Method: New Approaches in Biblical Studies*, ed. Janice Capel Anderson and Stephen D. Moore, 84–102, Minneapolis: Fortress, 1992.

Morgan, R., with Barton, J., *Biblical Interpretation*, Oxford University Press, 1988.

Moule, C. F. D., 'Jesus in New Testament Kerygma', in *Essays in New Testament Interpretation*, Cambridge University Press, 1982.

Mussner, Franz, 'Die bösen Winzer nach Mt 21, 33–46', in *Antijudaismus im Neuen Testament?*, ed. W. P. Eckert, N. P. Levinson and M. Stöhr, 129–34, Munich: Kaiser, 1967.

Neusner, Jacob, *Torah from the Sages. Pirke Avot: A New American Translation and Explanation*. Chappaqua, NY: Rosell, 1984.

Newell, Jane E. and Raymond R. , 'The Parable of the Wicked Tenants', *NovT* 14 (1972), 226–37.

O'Brien, Peter , 'The Great Commission of Matthew 28:18–20: A Missionary Mandate or Not?', *RTR* 35 (1976), 66–78.

Ogawa, Akira, *L'histoire de Jésus chez Matthieu: La signification de l'histoire pour la théologie matthéenne*, Frankfurt: Peter Lang, 1979.

'Paraboles de l'Israël véritable? Reconsidération critique de Mt. xxi 28–xxii 14', *NovT* 21 (1979), 121–49.

Olmstead, Wesley G., 'Review of David C. Sim, *The Gospel of Matthew and Christian Judaism*', *JRH* 25 (2001), 88–90.

O'Neill, J. C. , 'The Source of the Parables of the Bridegroom and the Wicked Husbandmen', *JTS* 39 (1988), 485–9.

Orchard, J. B. , 'J. A. T. Robinson and The Synoptic Problem', *NTS* 22 (1976), 346–52.

Overman, J. Andrew, *Church and Community in Crisis: The Gospel According to Matthew*, Valley Forge, PA: Trinity Press, 1996.

'Matthew's Parables and Roman Politics: The Imperial Setting of Matthew's Narrative with Special Reference to His Parables', *SBLSP* 34 (1995), 425–39.

Palmer, H. , 'Just Married, Cannot Come', *NovT* 18 (1976), 241–57.

Pamment, Margaret , 'The Kingdom of Heaven in the First Gospel', *NTS* 27 (1981), 211–32.

Patte, Daniel, *The Gospel According to Matthew: A Structural Commentary on Matthew's Faith*, Philadelphia: Fortress, 1987.

Pedersen, Sigfred , 'Zum Problem der vaticinia ex eventu. (Eine Analyse von Mt. 21,33–46 par.; 22,1–10 par.)', *ST* 19 (1965), 167–88.

Perrin, Norman, *Rediscovering the Teaching of Jesus*, London: SCM, 1967.

Jesus and the Language of the Kingdom, London: SCM, 1976.

Petersen, Norman R., *Literary Criticism for New Testament Critics*, Philadelphia: Fortress, 1978.

Plummer, Alfred, *A Critical and Exegetical Commentary on the Gospel According to S. Luke*, 4th edn, Edinburgh: T. & T. Clark, 1901; reprint, 1905.

An Exegetical Commentary on the Gospel According to S. Matthew, London: Robert Scott, 1909; reprint, 1915.

Powell, Mark Allan, *What is Narrative Criticism?* Minneapolis: Fortress, 1990.

'The Plot and Subplots of Matthew's Gospel', *NTS* 38 (1992), 187–204.

'Narrative Criticism', in *Hearing the New Testament: Strategies for Interpretation*, ed. Joel B. Green, 239–55, Grand Rapids: Eerdmans, 1995.

'Characterization on the Phraseological Plane in the Gospel of Matthew', in *Treasures New and Old: Recent Contributions to Matthean Studies*, ed.

David R. Bauer and Mark Allan Powell, 161–77, Atlanta: Scholars Press, 1996.

'Toward a Narrative–Critical Understanding of Matthew', in *Gospel Interpretation: Narrative-Critical and Social-Scientific Approaches*, ed. J. D. Kingsbury, 9–15, Harrisburg: Trinity Press, 1997.

Prince, Gerald, 'Introduction to the Study of the Narratee', in *Reader-Response Criticism: From Formalism to Post-Structuralism*, ed. Jane. P. Tompkins, 7–25, London: Johns Hopkins University Press, 1980.

Przybylski, Benno, *Righteousness in Matthew and His World of Thought*, Cambridge University Press, 1980.

Rabinowitz, P. J., *Before Reading: Narrative Conventions and the Politics of Interpretation*, Ithaca: Cornell University Press, 1987.

Radl, Walter , 'Zur Struktur der eschatologischen Gleichnisse Jesu', *TTZ* 91 (1983), 122–33.

Reicke, B., 'Synoptic Prophecies on the Destruction of Jerusalem', in *Studies in the New Testament and Early Christian Literature*, ed. D. E. Aune, 121–34, Leiden: Brill, 1972.

Rengstorf, K. H., 'Die Stadt der Mörder (Matt. 22:7)', in *Judentum, Urchristentum, Kirche,* ed. W. Eltester, 106–29, Berlin: Töpelmann, 1960.

Reumann, John, *Righteousness in the New Testament: 'Justification' in the United States Lutheran–Roman Catholic Dialogue*, Philadelphia: Fortress, 1982.

Rhoads, David and Michie, Donald, *Mark as Story: An Introduction to the Narrative of a Gospel*, Philadelphia: Fortress, 1982.

Richards, W. L. , 'Another Look at the Parable of the Two Sons', *BR* 23 (1978), 5–14.

Ricoeur, Paul , 'Narrative Time', *Critical Inquiry* 7 (1980), 169–90.

Riggenbach, E., 'Zur Exegese und Textkritik zweier Gleichnisse Jesu', in *Aus Schrift und Geschichte*, Stuttgart: Calwer, 1922.

Rimmon-Kenan, S., *Narrative Fiction: Contemporary Poetics*, London: Methuen, 1983.

Robinson, J. A. T., *Redating the New Testament*, London: SCM, 1976.

'The Parable of the Wicked Husbandmen: a Test of Synoptic Relationships', *NTS* 21 (1975), 443–61.

Ross, J. M. , 'Floating Words', *NTS* 38 (1992), 153–6.

Sabourin, L., *The Gospel According to Matthew*, Bombay: St. Paul Publications, 1982.

Saldarini, A., *Matthew's Christian–Jewish Community*, University of Chicago Press, 1994.

Sanders, E. P., *Jesus and Judaism*, London: SCM, 1985.

Sato, Migaku, *Q und Prophetie: Studien zur Gattungs-und Traditionsgeschichte der Quelle Q*, Tübingen: Mohr, 1988.

Schenk, Wolfgang, *Die Sprache des Matthäus*, Göttingen: Vandenhoeck & Ruprecht, 1987.

Schlatter, A. , 'Jesu Gleichnis von den beiden Söhnen', *Jahrbuch der Theologischen Schule Bethel* 2 (1931), 35–63.

Schlier, H., 'The Call of God', in *The Relevance of the New Testament*, New York: Herder and Herder, 1968.

Schmid, Josef, *Das Evangelium nach Matthäus*, Regensburg: Pustet, 1959.

'Das textgeschichtliche Problem der Parabel von den zwei Söhnen', in *Vom Wort des Lebens*, ed. N. Adler, 68–84, Münster: Aschendorff, 1951.

Schniewind, Julius, *Das Evangelium nach Matthäus*, Göttingen: Vandenhoeck & Ruprecht, 1956.

Schottroff, Luise , 'Das Gleichnis vom grossen Gastmahl in der Logienquelle', *EvT* 47 (1987), 192–211.

Schramm, T., *Der Markus-Stoff bei Lukas*, SNTSMS 14; Cambridge University Press, 1971.

Schulz, Siegfried, *Die Spruchquelle der Evangelisten*, Zürich: Theologischer, 1972.

Die Mitte der Schrift, Stuttgart: Kreuz, 1976.

Schweizer, Eduard, *Matthäus und seine Gemeinde*, Stuttgart: KBL Verlag, 1974.

The Good News According to Matthew, trans. David E. Green, Atlanta: John Knox, 1975.

'Matthäus 21–25', in *Orientierung an Jesus: Zur Theologie der Synoptiker*, ed. Paul Hoffmann, 364–71, Freiburg: Herder, 1973.

'Auf W Trillings Spuren zu Mt 22,1–14', in *Christus bezeugen*, ed. Karl Kertelge, Traugott Holtz, and Claus-Peter März, 146–9, Leipzig: St. Benno, 1989.

Scott, Bernard Brandon, *Hear Then The Parable: A Commentary on the Parables of Jesus*, Minneapolis: Fortress, 1989.

Scott, Bernard Brandon and Dean, Margaret E., 'A Sound Map of the Sermon on the Mount', in *Treasures New and Old: Recent Contributions to Matthean Studies*, ed. David R. Bauer and Mark Allan Powell, 311–78, Atlanta: Scholars Press, 1996.

Selbie, W. B. , 'The Parable of the Marriage Feast', *ExpTim* 37 (1926), 266–9.

Senior, Donald, *The Passion of Jesus in the Gospel of Matthew*, Wilmington, DE: Michael Glazier, 1985.

The Gospel of Matthew, Nashville: Abingdon, 1997.

Sider, John W. , 'Rediscovering the Parables: The Logic of the Jeremias Tradition', *JBL* 102 (1983), 61–83.

Sim, David C., *The Gospel of Matthew and Christian Judaism: The History and Social Setting of the Matthean Community*, Edinburgh: T. & T. Clark, 1998.

'The Man without the Wedding Garment (Matthew 22:11–13)', *HeyJ* 31 (1990), 165–78.

'Matthew 22.13a and *1 Enoch* 10.4a: A Case of Literary Dependence?', *JSNT* 47 (1992), 3–19.

'The "Confession" of the Soldiers in Matthew 27.54', *HeyJ* 34 (1993), 401–24.

'The Gospel of Matthew and the Gentiles', *JSNT* 57 (1995), 19–48.

Smith, C. W. F. , 'The Mixed State of the Church in Matthew's Gospel', *JBL* 82 (1963), 149–63.

Smith, Robert Harry , 'Matthew 28:16–20, Anticlimax or Key to the Gospel', *SBLSP* 32 (1993), 589–603.

Snodgrass, Klyne R., *The Parable of the Wicked Tenants*, Tübingen: Mohr, 1983.

'Recent Research on the Parable of the Wicked Tenants: An Assessment', *BBR* 8 (1998), 187–216.

'From Allegorizing to Allegorizing: A History of the Interpretation of the Parables of Jesus', in *The Challenge of Jesus' Parables*, ed. Richard N. Longenecker, 3–29, Grand Rapids: Eerdmans, 2000.

Stanton, Graham N., *Jesus of Nazareth in New Testament Preaching*, Cambridge University Press, 1974.
The Gospels and Jesus, Oxford University Press, 1989.
A Gospel for A New People: Studies in Matthew, Edinburgh: T. & T. Clark, 1992.
Steck, Odil Hannes, *Israel und das gewaltsame Geschick der Propheten: Untersuchungen zur Überlieferung des deuteronomistischen Geschichtbildes im Alten Testament, Spätjudentum und Urchristentum*, Neukirchen-Vluyn: Neukirchener, 1967.
Stern, David, 'Jesus' parables from the Perspective of Rabbinic Literature: The Example of the Wicked Husbandmen', in *Parable and Story in Judaism and Christianity*, ed. C. Thoma and M. Wyschogrod, 42–80, Mahwah: Paulist, 1989.
Sternberg, Meir, *The Poetics of Biblical Narrative: Ideological Literature and the Drama of Reading*, Indiana University Press, 1985.
Strecker, Georg, *Der Weg der Gerechtigkeit*, Göttingen: Vandenhoeck & Ruprecht, 1962.
Strack, Hermann L. and Billerbeck, Paul, *Kommentar zum Neuen Testament aus Talmud und Midrash*, 6 vols., Munich: C. H. Beck, 1922–1961.
Streeter, B. H., *The Four Gospels*, London: Macmillan, 1936.
Struthers-Malbon, Elizabeth, 'Narrative Criticism: How Does the Story Mean?', in *Mark and Method: New Approaches in Biblical Studies*, ed. Janice Capel Anderson and Stephen D. Moore, 23–49, Minneapolis: Fortress, 1992.
Swaeles, Romain , 'L'Arrière-fond scripturaire de Matt. xxi.43 et son lien avec Matt. xxi. 44', *NTS* 6 (1960), 310–13.
'L'orientation ecclésiastique de la parabole du festin nuptial en Mt 22, 1–14', *ETL* 36 (1960), 655–84.
Swanson, Reuben J., *New Testament Manuscripts: Matthew*, Sheffield Academic Press, 1995.
Tagawa, K. , 'People and Community in the Gospel of Matthew', *NTS* 16 (1970), 149–62.
Tasker, R. V. G., *The Gospel According to St. Matthew*, Leicester: InterVarsity, 1961.
Telford, W., *The Barren Temple and the Withered Tree*, JSNTSup 1; Sheffield: JSOT, 1980.
Thiselton, Anthony C., *New Horizons in Hermeneutics*, London: HarperCollins, 1992.
'The Parables as Language-Event: Some Comments on Fuch's Hermeneutics in the Light of Linguistic Philosophy', *SJT* 23 (1970), 437–68.
'Reader-Response Hermeneutics, Action Models, and the Parables of Jesus', in *The Responsibility of Hermeneutics*, ed. Roger Lundin, Anthony C. Thiselton and Clarence Walhout, 79–126, Grand Rapids: Eerdmans, 1985.
Thomas, J. David, 'Matthew xxi.34–37; 43 and 45 (?)', in *The Oxyrhynchus Papyri, vol. LXIV*, ed. E. W. Handley, U. Wartenberg, R. A. Coles, N. Gonis, M. W. Haslam and J. D. Thomas, 7–9, London: Egypt Exploration Society, 1997.
Tompkins, Jane P. (ed.), *Reader-Response Criticism: From Formalism to Post Structuralism*, Baltimore: Johns Hopkins University Press, 1980.

Trilling, Wolfgang, *Das Wahre Israel: Studien zur Theologie des Matthäus-Evangeliums*, 3rd edn, Munich: Kösel, 1964.

'Die Täufertradition bei Matthäus', *BZ* 2 (1959), 271–89.

'Zur Überlieferungsgeschichte des Gleichnisses vom Hochzeitsmahl Mt 22, 1–14', *BZ* 4 (1960), 251–65.

Trimaille, Michel, 'La parabole des vignerons homicides', in *Les paraboles évangéliques: Perspectives nouvelles*, ed. Jean Delorme, 247–58, Paris: Les Éditions du Cerf, 1989.

Tuckett, Christopher, *The Revival of the Griesbach Hypothesis*, Cambridge University Press, 1983.

'Thomas and the Synoptics', *NovT* 30 (1988), 132–57.

Q and the History of Early Christianity, Edinburgh: T. & T. Clark, 1996.

Uspensky, B., *A Poetics of Composition*, trans. V. Zavarin and S. Wittig, Berkeley: University of California Press, 1973.

Vaccari, Alberto , 'La Parabole du Festin de Noces (Matthieu, XXII, 1–14)', *RSR* 39 (1951), 138–45.

Vanhoozer, Kevin J., *Is There a Meaning in this Text? The Bible, the Reader and the Morality of Literary Knowledge*, Leicester: Apollos, 1998.

Van Iersel, B. M. F., 'Das Gleichnis von den bösen Winzern', in *'Der Sohn' in der synoptischen Jesusworten*, Leiden: Brill, 1968.

Van Tilborg, Sjef, *The Jewish Leaders in Matthew*, Leiden: Brill, 1972.

Via, Dan O., *The Parables: Their Literary and Existential Dimension*, Philadelphia: Fortress, 1967.

Vorster, W. S., 'Meaning and Reference: The Parables of Jesus in Mark 4', in *Text and Reality: Aspects of Reference in Biblical Texts*, by B. C. Lategan and W. S. Vorster, 27–65. Atlanta: Scholars Press, 1985.

Walker, P. W. L., *Jesus and the Holy City: New Testament Perspectives on Jerusalem*, Grand Rapids: Eerdmans, 1996.

Walker, Rolf, *Die Heilsgeschichte im ersten Evangelium*, Göttingen: Vandenhoeck & Ruprecht, 1967.

Watson, Francis, *Text and Truth*, Grand Rapids: Eerdmans, 1997.

'Toward a Literal Reading of the Gospels', in *The Gospels for All Christians*, ed. Richard Bauckham, 195–217, Grand Rapids: Eerdmans, 1998.

Weaver, Dorothy Jean, *Matthew's Missionary Discourse: A Literary Critical Analysis*, JSNTSup 38; Sheffield: JSOT, 1990.

Weder, Hans, *Die Gleichnisse Jesu als Mataphern*, Göttingen: Vandenhoeck & Ruprecht, 1978.

Weiser, Alfons, *Die Knechtsgleichnisse der synoptischen Evangelien*, München: Kösel, 1971.

Weiss, Bernhard, *Das Matthäus-Evangelium*, 7th edn, Göttingen: Vandenhoeck & Ruprecht, 1898.

Wellhausen, J., *Das Evangelium Matthaei: Übersetzt und Erklärt*, Berlin: Reimer, 1904.

Weren, W. J. C. , 'The Use of Isaiah 5,1–7 in the Parable of the Tenants (Mark 12,1–12; Matthew 21,33–46)', *Bib* 79 (1998), 1–26.

Westcott, Brooke Foss and Hort, Fenton John Anthony, *The New Testament in the Original Greek*, 2nd edn, vol. II, *Introduction*; *Appendix*, London: Macmillan, 1896.

The New Testament in the Original Greek; reprint, vol. I, London: Macmillan, 1909.

Wilcox, M. 'The Promise of the "Seed" in the New Testament and the Targumim', *JSNT* 5 (1979), 2–20.

'Text Form', in *It is Written: Scripture Citing Scripture*, ed. D. A. Carson and H. G. M. Williamson, 193–204, Cambridge University Press, 1988.

Wilder, Amos N., *Early Christian Rhetoric: The Language of the Gospel*, London: SCM, 1964.

Wright, N. T., *The New Testament and the People of God*, London: SPCK, 1992.

Jesus and the Victory of God, Minneapolis: Fortress, 1996.

Young, Brad H., *Jesus and His Jewish Parables: Rediscovering the Roots of Jesus' Teaching*, New York: Paulist, 1989.

Zahn, D. Theodor, *Das Evangelium des Matthäus*, Leipzig: Deichert, 1903.

Ziesler, J. A., *The Meaning of Righteousness in Paul*, Cambridge University Press, 1972.

INDEX OF PASSAGES

INDEX OF SELECTED TOPICS AND MODERN AUTHORS